THIS IS NO LONGER THE PROPERTY
OF THE SEATTLE PUBLIC LIBRARY

D0573650

Prosecutor
Defender
Counselor

—m—

THE MEMOIRS OF

ROBERT B. FISKE JR.

Smith/Kerr Associates LLC
www.smithkeer.com

Copyright © 2014 by Robert B. Fiske Jr.
All rights are reserved.

No part of this book may be reproduced or transmitted in any form by any
means, electronic or mechanical, including photocopying and recording, or by
any information storage or retrieval system, without written permission from

Smith/Kerr Associates LLC
One Government Street, Suite1, Kittery, ME 03904
www.smithkerr.com

Cover and interior designs by Kim Arney
Composition by Kim Arney

Printed in the U.S.A.
First Edition

ISBN 13: 978-0983062219
ISBN 10: 0-983062218

—⚹—

To Janet
My love, who was such an
important part of everything in this book,
and so much more

—⚹—

CONTENTS

Foreword by The Honorable Robert A. Katzmann . . . . *ix*
Preface . . . . *xi*
Acknowledgments . . . . *xv*

SECTION I	**A FAMILY OF LAWYERS**	**1**
SECTION II	**THE BEGINNINGS**	**10**
CHAPTER 1	Law School, 1952–1955	10
CHAPTER 2	U.S. Attorney's Office, Summer 1954	15
CHAPTER 3	Davis Polk Wardwell Sunderland & Kiendl, 1955–1957	18
SECTION III	**ASSISTANT UNITED STATES ATTORNEY, 1957–1961** . . .	**27**
CHAPTER 4	Henry "the Dutchman" Grunewald	30
CHAPTER 5	Hazard Gillespie Becomes United States Attorney	32
CHAPTER 6	Customs Inspectors on the Take	34
CHAPTER 7	John Dioguardi ("Johnny Dio")	36
CHAPTER 8	Fortune and Anthony Pope	40
SECTION IV	**DAVIS POLK, 1961–1976**	**44**
CHAPTER 9	Price-Fixing, Multi-District Litigation, and "You're Off the Payroll and Onto the Lease"	46
CHAPTER 10	Return to Darien (and Ice Hockey)	51
CHAPTER 11	Texas Gulf Sulphur	56
CHAPTER 12	Thalidomide	60
CHAPTER 13	Other Cases and Personalities	65
SECTION V	**UNITED STATES ATTORNEY FOR THE SOUTHERN DISTRICT OF NEW YORK, 1976–1980**	**69**
CHAPTER 14	The Office and the Team	72
CHAPTER 15	The Postmaster General, A Bullet-Proof Vest, My DEA Beetle, How I Took Up Running, and My Tennis Game from *Guys and Dolls*	76

CHAPTER 16   Hands-On, Open-Minded, Tested by Washington. 80

CHAPTER 17   Three More Years! Senator Moynihan and My Full Term 84

CHAPTER 18   Trials and Appeals 86

CHAPTER 19   The Trial of Nicky Barnes 89

CHAPTER 20   The Trial of Anthony Scotto and Anthony Anastasio 99

CHAPTER 21   Socialist Workers Party v. Attorney General
               of the United States. 107

CHAPTER 22   A Case That Didn't Happen. 115

CHAPTER 23   Assessments 117

SECTION VI   NEW CHALLENGES AT DAVIS POLK, 1980–1989 123

CHAPTER 24   Three Mile Island 124

CHAPTER 25   USFL v. NFL 138

SECTION VII   PROFESSIONAL SERVICE, POLITICAL PERIL 146

CHAPTER 26   The American College of Trial Lawyers 146

CHAPTER 27   The Federal Bar Council. 150

CHAPTER 28   The ABA Committee on Federal Judiciary
               and Judge Robert Bork 152

CHAPTER 29   Deputy Attorney General and the Bork Fallout 161

SECTION VIII   DAVIS POLK, 1989–1994 168

CHAPTER 30   The America's Cup 169

CHAPTER 31   In Praise of the Outdoors: New Zealand,
               Fly Fishing, and Vermont 181

CHAPTER 32   Building a White Collar Crime Practice 184

CHAPTER 33   E.F. Hutton and George Ball 188

CHAPTER 34   Paul Thayer. 191

CHAPTER 35   United States v. David Brown. 198

CHAPTER 36   Clark Clifford 210

SECTION IX   WHITEWATER INDEPENDENT COUNSEL, 1994 220

CHAPTER 37   How It Came About 221

CHAPTER 38   The Independent Counsel Team. 227

CHAPTER 39   An Early Breakthrough 230

CHAPTER 40   White House Subpoenas 233

CHAPTER 41   Taking the Fiske 236

CHAPTER 42   The Investigation Continues 238

CHAPTER 43　The Death of Vincent Foster 240
CHAPTER 44　I Question the Clintons. 246
CHAPTER 45　The Results 248
CHAPTER 46　Outcry 249
CHAPTER 47　The Independent Counsel Court. 253
CHAPTER 48　Calming Troubled Waters. 255
CHAPTER 49　An Assessment. 256

SECTION X　DAVIS POLK, 1994–2010 . . . . **259**
CHAPTER 50　Judge John H. McBryde 259
CHAPTER 51　Public Service While in Private Practice 269
CHAPTER 52　The Suzuki Samurai: Kathryn Rodriguez v. Suzuki 273
CHAPTER 53　The Suzuki Samurai: Suzuki v. Consumers Union 280
CHAPTER 54　Pete Nicholas and Boston Scientific 286
CHAPTER 55　Burlington Resources 289
CHAPTER 56　Bicycling 294
CHAPTER 57　Alfred Taubman. 297
CHAPTER 58　Michigan Law School Fellowships .305
CHAPTER 59　Fred Wilpon, Saul Katz and the New York Mets 308
CHAPTER 60　The Mets and Bernie Madoff. 313

A Last Word *322*
Author's Note *324*
Appendix *325*
Notes *326*
Credits *343*
Index *345*

FOREWORD

NO LAWYER COMMANDS greater respect than Robert B. Fiske Jr., whose five decades of service to the legal profession stand as a model of unsurpassed excellence. In the engaging pages that follow, Mr. Fiske describes his life in the law as a prosecutor, defender and counselor. The expanse and depth of his career are breathtaking, and to any lawyer, humbling in the range of its accomplishments. Indeed, if he had only been a prosecutor, or only been a defense lawyer, the corpus of Robert Fiske's professional activity would have been notable in and of itself. To have excelled in every facet of a lawyer's life only reinforces the magnitude of the Fiske career.

As the U.S. Attorney for the Southern District of New York from 1976-1980, Robert Fiske, among his many successes, personally secured the conviction of drug kingpin Leroy "Nicky" Barnes and the labor racketeering convictions of Anthony Scotto and Albert Anastasio. He served famously as Independent Counsel in the Whitewater Investigation from January to October 1994. As a defense lawyer at Davis Polk & Wardwell, he was the man to see for Clark Clifford and Robert Altman in the BCCI case; he successfully represented David Brown, former chair of the board of General Development Corporation; he prevailed in a multi-billion dollar suit stemming from the Three Mile Island accident; he represented Alfred Taubman and Fred Wilpon in their high profile cases; he was co-counsel in the winning defense of the National Football League in the antitrust suit brought by the U.S. Football League. The list goes on and on. And, apart from his litigation activities, Fiske has contributed to public service in a variety of ways—for instance, as a member of the New York State Judicial Compensation Commission; as Chairman of the Judicial Commission on Drugs and the Courts appointed by New York State Chief Judge Judith S. Kaye; and as a member of the Webster Commission reviewing FBI Security programs.

Because of Robert Fiske's unquestioned integrity and abilities, not only has the legal system been well-served, but so has the ideal of good government. It was because of Fiske's qualities that Senator Daniel P. Moynihan could demonstrate his commitment to the nonpolitical administration of justice by allowing Fiske, a Republican and an appointee of a Republican President, to complete his term as U.S. Attorney. And it was because of Fiske's unquestioned integrity and abilities that Attorney General Janet Reno would call on him to investigate Whitewater.

It is not simply Robert Fiske's professionalism that is widely celebrated. It is his commitment to serving the greater good, to serving as a mentor and role model. As Dean William Treanor, then of Fordham Law School, eloquently said, upon Mr. Fiske's award of the prestigious Stein Prize: "Bob Fiske's is truly an example of a model life in the law—a life marked not just by excellence and success, but by dedication to the public service, to professionalism, to mentoring, and ethics." Fred Hafetz, Fiske's Chief of the Criminal Division recounted: "When Bob Fiske first came in as United States Attorney, a young prosecutor had a large and complex fraud investigation against a high-visibility person. Fiske made the call not to go with the case because he did not think it could be proved. It showed real guts that he had the judgment to say no, particularly because investigations often develop a momentum of their own. And it was a call for which he earned the wide respect of the office." Summing up a widely shared sentiment, Judge Jed S. Rakoff, who served as an Assistant United States Attorney under Robert Fiske, put it this way: "As a lawyer, a public servant, a purveyor of justice and judgment, and a man of heart and dignity, Bob Fiske is the living ideal to which the rest of us can only aspire. I cannot imagine a greater antidote to cynicism, or a greater source of pride, than to have been one of his 'team.'"

In an age too often punctuated by glitz, celebrity, and self-promotion, Robert Fiske's life reminds us of the virtues of character and competence. *Prosecutor Defender Counselor* is must reading for any lawyer who strives to serve the legal profession and the public.

—Robert A. Katzmann
Chief Judge
United States Court of Appeals for the Second Circuit

PREFACE

"President William J. Clinton, having been called for examination by the Independent Counsel, and having been first duly sworn by the notary, was examined and testified as follows:

Examination by the Independent Counsel
By Mr. Fiske:
Q: You are the President of the United States?
A: Yes."

—⚏—

WHEN I ENTERED Hutchins Hall for my first class at the University of Michigan Law School in the fall of 1952, I could not have imagined that forty-two years later I would find myself in the Treaty Room at the White House conducting a criminal investigation of the President of the United States.

Attorney General Janet Reno had appointed me to investigate President Clinton's conduct with respect to Whitewater in the same way Attorney General Elliot Richardson selected Archibald Cox to conduct the Watergate investigation of President Nixon. It was one result of what has been an extremely gratifying career, combining forty-six years in private practice at the same law firm with three separate periods of government service totaling nine years.

At the urging of family and friends, I decided to write a book about my life in the law. I hope that my experiences as a federal prosecutor and as a lawyer in private practice will not only make interesting reading, but might also be of some educational value to younger lawyers or persons considering the law as a career.

The law is not just any career. Its finest practitioners have understood they have a responsibility. One such practitioner was Judge Simon H. Rifkind, whose name lives on in the form of an award made annually by the Jewish Theological Seminary. It is for distinguished public service, reflecting Judge Rifkind's own career and ideals. I am proud to say I received the Simon H. Rifkind Award in 2000, and the plaque that I received is inscribed with his essential credo: "The practice of law is a power in trust: not for the personal benefit of the individual lawyer, but for the benefit of the members of the community."

I have done my best to model my career on that principle.

Both aspects of my life in the law have been rewarding. As a government lawyer I have represented the United States in investigating and prosecuting criminal cases. As a lawyer in private practice, I have represented individuals and companies who came to me in times of trouble and who looked to me to make things better for them. I found over the years that there was a powerful synergy in combining private practice with periods of public service which makes lawyers who divide their careers this way better at both. Lawyers in government who have experience in private practice have a better understanding of the workings of the business and financial communities they are investigating. They also have a broader, more balanced experience upon which to make crucial judgments as to the right way to proceed.

Conversely, lawyers with experience in government service—with the vastly increased responsibilities those positions bring—can be much more effective in private practice. And having held a high-profile government position certainly helps attract clients. A day after the owner of the Three Mile Island nuclear plant in Pennsylvania sued the maker of the reactor over the near-meltdown that threatened disaster for millions the maker selected me to defend the case. Its general counsel later told the *American Lawyer,* "He seemed to have had a pretty good track record as United States Attorney."

Mentors shape future generations of law practitioners. My career was highly influenced by three principal mentors to whom I will be forever grateful: J. Edward Lumbard, S. Hazard Gillespie Jr. and Lawrence E. Walsh. It is no coincidence that all three combined highly successful careers in private practice with equally successful periods of government service. Lumbard, one of the name partners in the law firm that became Donovan, Leisure, Lumbard, Newton & Irvine, served as an Assistant United States Attorney, and years later returned to public service for the rest of his career as United States Attorney, United States Circuit Judge, and later Chief Judge of the Court of Appeals for the Second Circuit. Walsh served as an Assistant District Attorney, counsel to New York Governor Thomas Dewey, U.S. District Judge and Deputy Attorney General of the United States before joining Davis Polk & Wardwell where, starting in 1960, he became a highly successful partner and leader of the bar—President of the American and

New York State Bar Associations—over a twenty-year period in private practice. And Gillespie, after also serving as New York State Bar Association President, served as U.S. Attorney for the Southern District of New York before returning to Davis Polk and rising to even higher prominence in the private sector.

From Judge Lumbard I learned, as he put it, "never assume a God damn thing." I also learned from him the importance of public service. The summer I spent in his office as a student assistant during his tenure as U.S. Attorney became the motivational springboard for everything I did later in public service. He remained my role model—and mentor to the extent he could be—from the Second Circuit. When I became U.S. Attorney I tried to run the office as he did.

From Hazard Gillespie I learned the skills of advocacy. Working under him I learned how to write a persuasive brief. He was a great believer in the statement of facts: "Write that persuasively," he said, "and you are 90 percent there." On oral argument he stressed what he learned from his mentor, John W. Davis: "Go for the jugular." I learned from him how to be an aggressive and effective advocate while still being courteous and civil to your adversary.

From Judge Walsh, whose first job was working for Judge Lumbard, I learned to think about the case the way the decision maker will—don't get enmeshed in your own partisan view. Also, be candid with the court; if there are bad facts bring them out yourself and try to deal with them. He taught us to never be satisfied with *good enough*. "Always," he said, "push yourself until you have done the very best you can." He was an out-of-the-box thinker long before anyone coined that phrase. He urged us to never be satisfied with a by-the-book approach until we—himself included—had tested our imaginations to see if there were a better way to solve the problem.

Finally, though I never worked under him, I learned a lot from Whitney North Seymour about personal relationships and thoughtfulness. I was in my first year at Davis Polk and at the bottom of a large team working on a big case that involved several defendants, each represented by a separate law firm. One of those firms was Simpson Thacher & Bartlett, and leading its team was Seymour—one of the giants of the bar. At a meeting of the firms, with twenty or twenty-five lawyers in the room, I introduced myself to Mr. Seymour as Bob Fiske. He said, "I will call you Bob if you will call me Whit." Three weeks later, at another large meeting, I walked in and he said, "Hi, Bob." I found it extraordinary that he would go out of his way to remember the name of each of the most junior associates in the other firms. Fifty-nine years later the impression that made still resonates.

Having benefited from the lessons and examples of these extraordinary mentors, it was important to me, both at Davis Polk and in government service, to be the same kind of mentor to the younger lawyers with whom I was working. In June 2010, I spoke at the tenth anniversary of the Inn of Court in New York and expressed my views on the importance of mentoring:

"It is the professional obligation of every lawyer to help in the development of younger lawyers. It is something we owe to the individual lawyers—it is also something we owe to the profession. Improving the quality of lawyering by younger lawyers improves the quality of lawyering as a profession."

As I said in that speech mentoring means helping with the development of professional skills—passing on to younger lawyers what I learned from my mentors. It means teaching by specific instruction. It means teaching by example, when the younger lawyer can learn by watching—in court, at meetings with clients and in more general interactions. It means teaching by giving the younger lawyer the maximum amount of responsibility to learn by doing—on his or her own—followed by constructive suggestions. Equally important, mentoring means not just helping with the development of professional skills. It means instilling the right values at an early, impressionable stage in a young lawyer's career: integrity, the highest ethical standards; fairness and—as Hazard Gillespie showed me—civility and courtesy.

Looking back at my career, right up there with the courtroom victories and professional successes I have had stands the gratification that has come from watching the professional development of those young lawyers. I've seen them grow to become a United States senator, federal and state judges, high government officials in the Justice Department, law school deans, general counsels of major corporations and universities, bar association presidents, and leaders of the bar.

So, with my mentors and those with whom I have worked in mind, I launch my story with a quote from John W. Davis, the West Virginian whose name leads Davis Polk even to this day. He graduated from law school at Washington and Lee in 1895 and was elected class orator. "The lawyer," Davis said in his speech, "has always been the sentinel of the watchtower of liberty."

That's the ideal, not always reachable, but always worth striving for.

ACKNOWLEDGMENTS

JUST AS THIS BOOK IS, at least in part, an acknowledgment of the many people to whom I owe so much in my career and in my life in general, this page is an acknowledgment of those who inspired it and helped bring it to fruition. And like the book itself, I have no doubt that the minute it comes off the press I will remember a large number of people I've failed to thank or mention. Nevertheless, I'm going to try with advance apologies for any oversights.

I will start by thanking the many people at Davis Polk who have helped make this book possible. First and foremost is my long-time assistant Michele Corelli who, going back to March 1976, lived through many of the events described. Her assistance in the preparation of the manuscript, providing substantive suggestions, as well as attention to detail, was invaluable. I am also grateful to 2013 summer associates Stephanie Goldfarb and Daniel Magy as well as legal assistants Ethan Anderson and Chad Lilly, all of whom did important factual research together with fact and citation checking of the manuscript. Finally, thanks are owed to Dan Hanson, Audrey Evans and Mark Zaleck in the DPW library for their help with factual research; to David Alumbaugh, Vivian Chen and Anthony Ferrara in the DPW graphics department for their help with the artwork; to Alexis Clark in the records center for her assistance in researching and locating old files; and to Rebecca Gonzalez for her assistance in the finalization of the manuscript.

Numerous people, whose names are in the book, made valuable comments on sections or chapters describing events or cases in which they participated. Beyond that, I am especially grateful to Elkan and Susan Abramowitz, Jim Benkard, Evan Caminker, Fred and Myra Hafetz, Roby Harrington and Cindy O'Hagan who reviewed a series of drafts of the entire book and made valuable suggestions that contributed immeasurably to its success.

And I am especially grateful to John Rousmaniere—a gifted writer, sailor, nautical historian—*and* my hiking companion in the mountains of Vermont and New Hampshire—who not only read and made meaningful comments on the book but put me in touch with my editor, Nick Taylor—whose editing improved the book immeasurably—and my publishers Spencer Smith and Jean Kerr, who brought the book to life.

Finally, I am grateful for the encouragement received from the members of my family—pictured below at Janet's and my mutual 80th birthday celebration on Block Island in July 2011.

Front row: (with Janet and Me) George and Sam Fiske
Back row: Roby, Calvin and Ryan Williams, Susan and Rusty Williams, Linda and Bob Fiske

Jonathan Parker Bishop Fiske family, 1912

—⁓—

A FAMILY OF LAWYERS

I HAVE LAWYERS ON both sides of my family.

My father, Robert Bishop Fiske, worked in private practice as a corporate general counsel, and devoted some of his career to public service—a wide-ranging career that shared some aspects with my own. His private practice was with Root, Clark, Buckner & Howland, the firm that later became Dewey, Ballantine, Bushby, Palmer & Wood and—still later—Dewey & LeBoeuf before it dissolved. He served as general counsel, Vice President and director of the American Cyanamid Company, at the time a major force in the pharmaceutical industry and a leader in developing antibiotics. His public service occurred decades apart, first with the depression-era Reconstruction Finance Corporation in the early 1930's and then, from 1959 into 1960, as an assistant secretary general of the North Atlantic Treaty Organization (NATO).

On my father's side the Fiske family prospects had not always been tied to the law. Dad grew up in Auburndale, Massachusetts, a town a few miles west of Boston that was part of Newton where he went to high school. His father, Jonathan Parker Bishop Fiske, was a brilliant inventor with little business sense. While working for his father in the Fiske Brick Company, he produced revolutionary brick-making equipment that became standard in the industry. The Fiske Brick Company, however, was crippled during World War I by freight embargoes brought on by war production and transportation crises. When that happened my grandfather moved to Martin Lockheed, an arms maker. After the war he was hired by William D. Durant, the President of General Motors, to develop the business that later became Delco. GM at the time was interested in creating an electric refrigerator, an embryonic idea the ice companies were laughing at. My grandfather got involved. He successfully developed the first electric refrigerator, which he named Frigidaire and formed the Frigidaire Corporation.

The prosperity that resulted was short-lived. In the early 1920's DuPont obtained working control of General Motors and replaced all of GM's top people, including Durant. My grandfather left, taking with him the patent for the Frigidaire. He then made two bad business judgments. Believing that the new management of General Motors would fall on its face, he sold all his GM stock. He also sold the Frigidaire patent to the Kelvinator Company for $75,000 in its stock. Since then GM has split over 200 times, while Kelvinator merged with Nash Motors before quietly fading away in the face of competition from the likes of GM and GE.

I don't know if those vicissitudes steered my father to the law. I do know that they introduced him to experiences that revealed a special talent. Dad enjoyed and was comfortable with people from all walks of life. It's a trait I admire and have tried to emulate. I attribute it to his seafaring days.

After graduating from Newton High School in 1918, near the end of World War I, he was accepted by Yale in the class of 1922 and enrolled in the Naval Reserve Officers Training Corps. He spent the summer working in a Massachusetts shipyard, and then started in ROTC as an apprentice seaman doing military drills on the New Haven Green with a mixed course of naval and academic study. When the war ended on November 11, Yale's navy training unit disbanded. Confusion reigned in the completely civilian routine that replaced it, so he decided to wait until the fall of 1919 to start at Yale. In the meantime he joined the Merchant Marine.

During the next year he served as an ordinary seaman on the S.S. *Erny*, carrying supplies to some of the remaining Expeditionary Forces in France and bringing some of the troops home, and on the S.S. *Lake Agomac* carrying cargo to and from Trinidad and Cuba. It was an experience from which, as he put it, "I learned a lot about human nature and companionship in a common endeavor, which transcends race, religion, education and social background and brings forth, in varying proportions, the basic good and bad in all of us."

That observation came from an autobiography he wrote in 1973, in which he described some feats of derring-do at sea, the first of which resulted from an argument that led to a bet.[1] He was strong for his size, and another sailor refused to believe he could climb the ship's wire ratline to the crosstrees on the cargo mast that rose above the deck—hand-over-hand—some forty feet straight up without using his feet.

"I did, and won my bet," he wrote. "But it wasn't worthwhile. Utterly exhausted from the climb, I hadn't enough strength left to descend slowly. I slid the last twenty feet, burning my hands badly. Then the loser showed that 'basic bad' by refusing to pay up—and I never did collect."

I learned later, when my brothers and I learned to sail at our father's hand, just how terrifying it can be to climb the mast in a rolling sea to solve some problem that can't be solved any other way. He had encountered such a problem on the trip back from France on the S.S. *Erny*. A signal flag got stuck at the tip of a yardarm forty feet above the deck. He was sent to clear it and the ship was rolling.

"As the whole ship's company craned their necks I climbed the shrouds, through the crosstrees and out onto the yardarm, the ship's roll taking me out over the west abyss, away to starboard and then away to port. No footrope or rigging to hang onto, as in an old square-rigger. Only a polished arm, with its tip fifteen tantalizing feet away, a steel deck forty, and a lively ocean sixty!

With my heart pounding, I embraced the arm like a tenderfoot when his feet come out of the stirrups of his first horse—and shinnied my belly-flop way, inch-by-inch, those agonizing miles to the end of the arm. Thank God the flag had been pulled up all the way. I could reach the pulley, clear it and back up. I have never before or since been as close to fainting as when I landed back on deck."[2]

Frightening moments aside, he had a real love for the sea and went back to it during the next two summers while he was in college at Yale. In the summer of 1920 he sailed to Bermuda as a common seaman on the M.S. *Edith Nute* and to Egypt as a quartermaster on the S.S. *Kentuckian*. A year later he sailed to Germany as a quartermaster on the S.S. *Ipswich*. When he returned from that voyage, in the late summer of 1921, his father had lost his job at General Motors and the family could no longer afford to send him to Yale. He had to go to work. Through his uncle, Silas Howland, he got a job on the docks in Philadelphia as a freight checker with the American-Hawaiian Steamship Company, which operated a fleet of coastal freight ships between New York and San Francisco. He worked there a year and saved enough money so, with some help from my grandmother's savings, he could return to Yale.

Watching my father over the years, it became apparent to me that his many months in the Merchant Marine and on the Philadelphia docks gave him a deep understanding of, and an affinity for, people from all stations of life. He was comfortable with blue collar and with white collar people, and he recognized the value of their work. He acted on his values, convincing American Cyanamid to create a pension fund for the shoe shine man who polished management's shoes every day. The company's CEO liked him enormously, but no more than the shoe shine man. He set a great example for me and my two brothers.

Mom & Dad

My mother, born Lenore Seymour, was a midwestern girl from Minnesota who attended Smith College in Northampton, Massachusetts. She starred academically and—at five-two—as the center of the basketball team. She met my father at a dinner party in St. Paul in 1924 and married him in Paris five years later, after he was sent there to help open an office for his law firm. They returned to New York in 1930—living in Brooklyn Heights where I joined them on December 28.

In the summer of 1933 Dad left the Reconstruction Finance Corporation and returned to Root Clark. He and Mom bought a house in Darien, Connecticut. My brothers McNeil Seymour and John Adams were born in January 1934 and September 1935, respectively, and the three of us grew up there. Dad, meanwhile, was lured away from Root Clark by an offer from American Cyanamid to work in its legal department, where he started on January 1, 1934.

My early days were filled with memories of music. Mom was an extremely accomplished pianist, who could play a complicated classical score without having seen it before. We had a Knabe grand piano in our home, which she would play whenever the pressure to do so became intense enough. She also enjoyed playing "four hands"—two pianos—with other accomplished pianists in the area. She struggled to teach the piano to me and my two brothers when we were old enough, but only Mac—who inherited the Knabe—was any good at it.

She was an excellent cook with a true chef's imagination. During the Depression and then World War II, we maintained a fairly frugal lifestyle. War rationing limited staples, but Mom added produce from the "Victory Garden" where we—and many other wartime families—grew vegetables. We had a chicken coop, so we had eggs, and Dad would kill a chicken for our mid-day Sunday dinners. We never took family vacation trips, but starting in the early 1940's Dad joined a fishing club in the Catskills, called the Balsam Lake Club, that had fishing rights on the Beaverkill River. We would go up together over a weekend, fish the stream, and at night we would sit around the fire in the old wooden clubhouse amid conversation with the other members. Dad was at his most eloquent when he described the joys of fishing in his book:

"Standing in one of the seven 'beats' on our six miles of stream . . . brings a blessed detachment from the complexities and dilemmas of the contemporary world. And when the line tightens and jerks and runs, the absorption and suppressed excitement drives everything out of mind and for a moment or for a few minutes washes clean the brain so filled with the worries and disenchantments of the other world which take up most of our lives."

Family at Balsam Lake Club

After the war our financial pressures eased considerably. Mom applied her cooking skills to the many dinner parties she and my father held at our home while we were growing up.

In 1957 they moved from Darien to a house on Hamburg Cove in Lyme, Connecticut, where they expanded an already wide circle of friends. Dad's blue-collar affinities remained intact. After the FBI spoke to the butcher at the Cove Landing Store during Dad's vetting for the NATO job, the butcher joked that he'd told the agents, "I don't know him very well, but I understand he has a very powerful radio and antenna in his attic."

The NATO job took my parents to Paris. Soon after their return in 1960 they built a guesthouse on the property where my brothers and I and our families descended in an annual "stampede." Mom loved her grandchildren and they loved her. Perhaps to make up for having all boys, she lavished special attention on her granddaughters, who would scamper over to the main house early in the morning when she would read to them from *Charlotte's Web, The Jungle Book, Stuart Little,* and *Winnie the Pooh*. She even helped them build an Eeyore House in the woods on the property.

My mother's brother McNeil V. Seymour, after whom my brother Mac was named, was also a lawyer. He practiced in St. Paul, Minnesota, with the firm of O'Brien, Horn, Stringer, Seymour & O'Connor. His career wasn't as varied as Dad's, but his life as a lawyer featured some very high stakes cases. One involved the field notes of Captain William Clark, chronicling the first two years of the Lewis and Clark expedition. They lay undiscovered for years until they were found in 1952 in the attic of a St. Paul home. The government claimed ownership, but Uncle Mac represented the owners of the house and argued successfully that they were their personal papers. The victorious owners donated the papers to the Minnesota Historical Society. The chronicles eventually reached the Beinecke Library at Yale.

He devoted time and intellect to the profession. He served for a time as the President of the Board of Bar Examiners for the State of Minnesota and taught at St. Paul College of Law—now known as William Mitchell. Two of his colleagues on the faculty were Warren Burger and Harry Blackmun both of whom became U.S. Supreme Court justices.

One of his sons, McNeil V. Seymour Jr.—my first cousin—also became a lawyer. He rose to prominence with the St. Paul firm of Briggs and Morgan, where he served for four years on the board and for several years as a vice-president, specializing in probate law, estate planning and real estate.

The younger of my two brothers, John, became a lawyer as well. His professional interests evolved into an alternative to the tooth-and-claw legal battles that can result when couples decide to divorce.

John started at Winthrop Stimson Putnam & Roberts in New York. After two years he and his wife, Martie, decided they would rather live in Boston. After four years at the Boston firm of Choate Hall & Stewart, he joined the Boston Corporation Counsel's Office, where he became the first Assistant Corporation Counsel as well as legal advisor to the Boston Police Department. He helped negotiate peaceful demonstrations against the Vietnam War, and when 100,000 people gathered on the Boston Common to hear Senator George McGovern there were only four arrests. He also persuaded the Boston Police to stop arresting street musicians by pointing out that leaving an empty guitar case open is not "soliciting."

In 1974 he was asked by the Supreme Judicial Court to become their Executive Secretary—then the only administrative position for the Massachusetts judicial system. He worked with Chief Justice Edward Hennessey and a governor's judicial commission headed by Professor Archibald Cox to develop a comprehensive plan of court reform and reconstruction. He left that role in the spring of 1978, and spent a year bicycling through Europe and backpacking in Asia with Martie and their three children. When they returned, after helping our parents celebrate their fiftieth wedding anniversary in Paris and—as he put it—"honing mediation skills in a four person tent," they decided John should open a divorce mediation practice for couples who didn't want to duke it out, but wanted a friendly divorce without the expense of two attorneys.

The idea was new at the time. The Boston Bar Association had just finished writing the first ethical opinion in the United States that it is permissible for a lawyer to act as divorce mediator as long as (s)he does not represent either spouse and tells them they each have a right to their own lawyer. With the support of many and the opposition of some, the practice took off and grew. In 1988 he and two colleagues founded Divorce Mediation Training Associates. He has spent much of his time since then training other lawyers in divorce mediation, while continuing to mediate his own cases. John estimates he has mediated more than 2,500 divorces and separations since 1979 and counseled couples who used the mediation process to stay married. He was a pioneer and innovator in developing what has become such an important part of family law today.

Mac, our middle brother, was a contrarian—that is, not a lawyer. While John had followed in my footsteps—attending Pomfret School for high school, then Yale and Michigan Law School—Mac went to Loomis and Williams College, then joined the

Air Force. Later he became a banker and a businessman. It's probably natural to want to be different from your older brother, and Mac went his own way to an interesting and successful career.

As a second lieutenant in the Air Force, Mac served for three years as a navigator on a KC-97 that refueled Air Force bombers in mid-flight. He was stationed at a series of bases, the last being Hunter Air Force Base near Savannah, Georgia where he met Tiena Von Puffelen, a minister's daughter. They were married in January 1959, decided to head west, and settled in Denver where Mac took a job in the training program at the First National Bank and became a loan officer.

He left the bank in 1975 to start his own consulting business, working with a number of various small business enterprises in which he became part owner. Later he founded and co-owned MacCourt Products, a leading maker of lawn and patio ponds and other home products.

After Mac left the bank, he became associated with a group of Denver businessmen who purchased the Steamboat Springs ski area. It is a recreational paradise. He and Tiena bought a triplex overlooking one of the ski trails that, after renovations, accommodates up to twenty people. They named it "Over the Edge." In 1996 we began a tradition of family ski weekends over the Martin Luther King Jr. holiday in January. At first it was the three brothers and a few friends, but it quickly grew into a multi-generational, all-male weekend—with grandsons qualifying when they reached age nine. In 2007 Mac's daughter, Julia, bought a condo down the mountain from "Over the Edge," which she named "Over the Top" and our family holiday went coed.

Three brothers at Steamboat

Well, so we are not exclusively a family of lawyers. But I like to think that we—me and my brothers, our wives, and the generations that have followed[3]—are a family *shaped* by the lawyers in our lives.

What we wanted to do when we grew up wasn't something my brothers and I talked about when we were young. I vividly remember sailing, playing softball in elementary school and pickup baseball games after school when the boy with the ball was always the captain. I spent every deep winter afternoon playing ice hockey on an outdoor pond, and my only thought about the future was to play more hockey. On weekend afternoons we parted with a dime apiece to get into the local movie house to watch cartoons and black-and-white features and the Movietone news with accounts of the latest battles in the war, but the future was as far away as the war.

It was only later, in college, that the law came into play. When it did appear as my vision of the future, a large part of the stimulus came from reading a book.

SECTION II

—⁓—

THE BEGINNINGS

CHAPTER 1

Law School, 1952–1955

IN THE SUMMER OF 1950—before my junior year at Yale—our family went to Bermuda for a vacation. We went by ship, the *Queen of Bermuda*, from New York to Hamilton, which took a couple of days. There was plenty of idle time, and someone had recommended I read a book entitled *Courtroom* by Quentin Reynolds. It was about the career of a prominent criminal defense lawyer, Samuel Liebowitz.

I finished the book before we got to Bermuda. I was fascinated by the stories of his trials—the people he defended, and the tactics he used to defend them. That, together with a growing sense—gained from history and political science courses—of the important role lawyers play in shaping the course and direction of society, motivated me to go to law school. I was also inspired by my father's career.

Dad had been the Editor-in-Chief of the *Yale Law Journal* in 1925–26, and was a good friend of the Dean of the Yale Law School, Wesley Sturges. He arranged for me to meet with Dean Sturges to discuss a potential legal career and the best choice of law schools. I started by saying I thought four years in New Haven was enough, and I didn't think I would apply to the Yale Law School. He quickly replied, "I have looked at your college transcript and I think that is a wise choice."

With that out of the way, we proceeded to have a very productive talk. He recommended Harvard and Michigan. Looking back, I realized that I had been in the East all my life. I had grown up in Darien, Connecticut, gone to public school there for eight years, then to private schools in New England before going to Yale. I had spent all of my summers in New England and with the exception of trips to visit my grandmother in St. Paul, Minnesota, I couldn't recall having been any place significantly west of the

Law quadrangle, University of Michigan

Hudson River. So, I thought it would be an interesting and different experience—one that would broaden my horizons—to go to Michigan: Midwest, Big Ten, Co-Ed. This was one of the best decisions I ever made.

I still remember my first class in law school. It offered a sharp contrast to the learning process I experienced in college. At Yale you learned through memorizing books and lectures. In law school I was exposed to the Socratic method of teaching.

The class was Property and the professor was Allan Smith. He began by telling us we had better get used to hypotheticals, because that was the cornerstone of law school teaching. And so it started: "*A* has a brand new 1952 Chevrolet. He drives it to work every day, and it's his pride and joy. One morning he comes out and it is gone—stolen. He is devastated. He calls the police, and starts riding the bus to work. The second day, as the bus is stopped at a light, he looks out the window and sees his car sitting in *B*'s driveway. He jumps off the bus, knocks on *B*'s door and tells him, 'You have my car.' 'What do you mean?' says *B*, 'It is my car. I just bought it from *C*.'"

Professor Smith asked the class: "Okay, so who gets the car?" One student put up his hand and replied: "I think it should be *A*."

"Why?"

"Because it was his car and it was stolen."

"But what about *B*? He bought it in good faith from *C*."

Professor Smith put several more questions to the student that made his position sound indefensible. At that point another student volunteered that he thought *B* was entitled to the car. Professor Smith then reversed his position: "What about *A*? It was his car and it's not his fault it was stolen." He followed with a series of questions sympathetic to A's position that made the support of B look indefensible.

At that point the bell rang—class was over. I had no idea whether the car belonged to A or to B, but I knew I had been exposed to a process of analytical thinking I had never experienced before.

Later, Professor Smith became dean of the law school. This was in the early 1960's, a time when large New York law firms were noted for hiring only from the top 10 percent of the class. At an alumni luncheon in the city, Dean Smith told us—to puzzlement and then laughter—that he was helping New York firms by having a higher percentage of each class finish in the top 10 percent.

All through law school, the most important criteria for a good grade on an exam was finding the issue. We were taught that once we knew what the problem was the answer was available through research. I think that critical thinking and analysis, which was so much a part of my law school training, is why lawyers play such prominent roles in all aspects of society—government and business—as well as in the legal profession itself.

Today, with my average college grades and only slightly better LSAT score, I would never have been admitted to Michigan, or any other first-tier law school. As I went into my law school experience, I was conscious that most of my former college classmates were out starting their careers. They were getting a three-year head start, so I determined to work as hard as I possibly could—something I had not done at prep school or college—to try to do as well as possible.

The key, I found early on, was staying ahead, or at least not falling behind. In addition to thoroughly preparing for each class, I kept a running outline that I added to every three days or so. That way, at exam time I had a huge head start because I simply needed to review something I had already prepared. The preparation paid off. Course grades came in one-by-one by postcard in the early summer of 1953 to our mailbox at 71 Five Mile River Road in Darien. I ended with a GPA of 3.97—third in the class.

The next two years were easier. My GPA went down a little, ending at 3.75, but I kept my No. 3 ranking and made the Law Review, ending up as one of four associate editors. And, the 3.75 was good enough for Order of the Coif—the law school equivalent of Phi Beta Kappa. So, Michigan Law School was a big academic success.

My other reasons for deciding on Michigan also paid off.

The experience of being in a large Big Ten University was broadening. I watched Michigan football along with 100,000 other fans, and helped cheer the Michigan hockey team to the NCAA championship—they won five of six between 1951 and

1956. Parties at Phi Delta Phi, the fraternity I joined in my second year, were another diversion from the daily grind. Then there were evenings at the Pretzel Bell.

The Pretzel Bell was a bar. It had a fairly high ceiling, and groups would order a pitcher of beer with a bowl of hard-boiled eggs. The challenge was to toss an egg with just the right amount of force to crack the shell against the ceiling. Falling short was bad, and hitting the ceiling with such force that the eggshell shattered was considered even worse. The challenge intensified as the evening went on and more pitchers of beer were consumed.

Today, the Pretzel Bell is gone, but our favorite Ann Arbor restaurant triggers other memories. It's the Gandy Dancer, which occupies the former railroad station (Gandy Dancer was the name for a railroad worker). After vacations at home, I rode the train back to Ann Arbor. A Penn Central train, appropriately called "The Wolverine," went from New York to Chicago. I would board at Penn Station at 6:00 p.m. Sunday night, have dinner in the dining car as the train progressed north along the Hudson River, and then go to the Pullman car where I had a berth. The porter would wake me when the train arrived in Detroit—invariably on time at 7:00 a.m. The next stop was Ann Arbor at 7:45 a.m., in time for me to walk up the hill to the law school for an 8:00 a.m. Monday morning class.

During Christmas vacation, in my junior year, I became engaged to Janet Tinsley, who was going to Skidmore. She grew up in Darien where we met when we were both 14. We went together on and off—mainly on—through high school and college. Going back to school we rode the train together to Albany where she got the bus to Saratoga Springs while I continued on to Ann Arbor.

We were married the next summer, on August 21, 1954, and so my third year of law school was also our first year of marriage. She got a job as a receptionist/telephone operator/bookkeeper at Vokar Corporation, a small company in nearby Dexter, where she got a crash course in Michigan geography. On her second day the head of the company asked her to put through a call to Charlie Stevens in Birmingham, twenty miles away. She called Alabama.

August 21, 1954

We lived in a small apartment in a house at 702 Oakland, across the street from the law school. The house was later demolished in favor of a parking lot—"They paved paradise and put up a parking lot"[4]—but today, fittingly, the parking lot has given way to a new law school building—South Hall.

We couldn't have had a better first year of marriage. Third year in law school is not as grueling as the first two, and we had plenty of time to enjoy Ann Arbor, develop close and lasting friendships, and generally get a great marriage—sixty years as of the publication of this book—off to a good start.

CHAPTER 2

U.S. Attorney's Office, Summer 1954

IN THE SPRING OF 1953, newly-elected President Dwight D. Eisenhower appointed Herbert Brownell, a prominent New York lawyer with extensive political experience, to be his Attorney General. On Brownell's recommendation, the President selected J. Edward Lumbard to be the United States Attorney for the Southern District of New York. Lumbard was just what the office needed.

By 1952, at the end of the Truman administration and twenty years of Democratic administrations, the U.S. Attorney's Office for the Southern District had lost its former luster. Most of its lawyers were hired on the basis of political or other connections with little or no regard for merit. Assistant United States Attorneys (AUSAs) were permitted to engage in the private practice of law. Many were intent only on decorating their resumes. The last two documents entered in many of their office files, even old ones, were an indictment and a press release.

Lumbard came from a different tradition. He had been an Assistant United States Attorney in the halcyon days of the early 1930's, when the office was led by Emory Buckner and included such budding luminaries as Thomas E. Dewey, later Governor of New York and the Republican candidate for president against Truman in 1948; John M. Harlan, later a United States Supreme Court Justice; Edmund Palmieri and William Herlands, who would become U.S. district judges; and George Leisure, a co-founder of the Donovan Leisure law firm. It was an office totally dedicated to professionalism over politics.

Lumbard had been a judge. Governor Dewey had appointed him to fill the remainder of a vacant term as a justice of the New York State Supreme Court—which in New York is the name given the trial courts—for New York and Bronx counties, a seat he lost during the next election in heavily Democratic New York City. Upon becoming United States Attorney, Lumbard made the office a full-time job. He fired all the unqualified AUSAs and replaced them with able young men and women—not many women in those days but even a few was an improvement—without regard to their political or personal ties. He kept the most talented and experienced of the AUSAs to train the new recruits, a job he joined by giving afternoon lectures, staging mock trials over which he presided, and setting up sessions with outstanding former AUSAs including two U.S. Supreme Court justices, several Southern District judges, and other distinguished public servants. When they'd had enough training, he gave the new blood enormous responsibilities that they would never have gotten so soon in private practice. They justified his faith and training.

Judge Lumbard was a very good friend of my father's and, in the fall of 1953 in my second year at law school, he and his wife came to have Thanksgiving dinner at our home in Darien. He told me he was planning a new program in the United States Attorney's Office that would bring in second year law students in the summer to work one-on-one with a designated Assistant United States Attorney. "We can't pay you anything, but it should be a really good experience," he said.

He was right. Living at home, I could afford to work for nothing, and it was a tremendous experience. Indeed, it turned out to be the motivational springboard for everything I did later in public service.

I was one of about forty second year students. The group included Herbert Wachtell, who—with Marty Lipton—later built the prominent mergers and acquisitions law firm Wachtell, Lipton, Rosen & Katz; Gerard Goettel, later a federal judge; Fiovorante Perotta, who would become New York State Insurance Commissioner; and Tom Debevoise, who became Attorney General of Vermont before he was thirty. I also induced two of my Michigan Law School classmates to come along with me.

I was extremely fortunate to be assigned to work with Fred Nathan. No one could have started his professional career under better tutelage. The highlight of the summer was a two-week trial before Judge Palmieri of a major drug dealer named Tony DeAngelo and two of his associates. I wrote briefs on the admissibility of evidence, helped write requests to charge, participated in witness interviews and strategy planning sessions for the trial, and sat next to Fred at the counsel table during the trial.

The key witness, nicknamed "Shorty," had pled guilty to a narcotics violation and had been cooperating with the Bureau of Narcotics in the hope of reducing his sentence. He was brought from protective custody in a New York City jail for trial preparation in Fred's office. Shorty's stunning but heroin-addicted girlfriend—she may have been his fiancée—could not visit him in jail because they were not married and she was not officially "family." So, Tom Dugan, the narcotics agent in charge of the case and later the U.S. Marshal for the Southern District, brought her to Fred's office several times so she could talk to Shorty before or after one of his prep sessions. But shortly before trial, we were all stunned to get word that she had died of an overdose. We were sure she'd been murdered.

DeAngelo could not be prosecuted on a murder charge in the federal courts, but he was indicted for obstruction of justice in her death. In the original drug case, Shorty testified, and all the defendants were convicted. DeAngelo got a fifteen-year sentence. This was heady stuff for a second year law student.

At the end of the summer Fred wrote a thoughtful and generous memorandum to Judge Lumbard about my work. He would go on to a highly successful career as a partner at Kelley Drye & Warren; first Assistant Corporation Counsel in the City of New York; and President of the Federal Bar Council.

The summer ended with my marriage to Janet. Judge Lumbard attended the wedding. On my last day in the office I went in to thank him for the magnificent experience. I said I really wanted to come back as an Assistant United States Attorney when I graduated. He said he hoped I would, but counseled against doing it right after graduation. He recommended that I first spend some time at a large firm where I could receive some valuable training.

Later, in 1955, President Eisenhower would name Judge Lumbard to the Second Circuit Court of Appeals, where he became Chief Judge. In the meantime, I took his advice.

CHAPTER 3

Davis Polk Wardwell Sunderland & Kiendl, 1955–1957

IN THOSE DAYS all the hiring by large private firms was done over the holiday break in December of a student's third and final year. There were no summer programs to speak of. I'd been lucky to work in the U.S. Attorney's Office, but most second year students wanted to spend their last summer—before plunging into law practice—doing something completely different like traveling through Europe or canning salmon in Alaska.

I spent three days in December 1954 visiting five firms: Davis Polk Wardwell Sunderland & Kiendl; Milbank, Tweed Hope, Hadley & McCloy; Root, Clark, Buckner, Howland & Ballantine; Sullivan & Cromwell; and Donovan Leisure Newton & Irvine. It was a seamless blur. They all seemed the same. Every one had a corporate department, a litigation department, a tax department and a trusts and estates department, and each said they were the best at everything.

The firms were virtually indistinguishable, except that I really liked the people I met at Davis Polk. I came home after the last day and said to Janet, "I can't choose between these firms based on the work they do, but I want to be at a firm that has people like Nelson Adams."

Nelson had been the Editor-in-Chief of the *Harvard Law Review* and clerked for Judge Learned Hand on the Second Circuit Court of Appeals. He headed Davis Polk's tax department and also the firm's hiring committee. I liked him instantly, an opinion confirmed over the years as I learned that his door was always open to discuss an issue or a problem. He was straightforward and down-to-earth, and his advice was thoughtful and valuable. I was far from the only young lawyer who came to Davis Polk because of him.

The firm had about ninety lawyers at the time. It hired four or five new associates each year. They were invariably male, white and graduates of the Harvard, Yale or Columbia law schools, with an occasional outlier from Virginia slipping in. The mold broke, or at least cracked a bit, in 1955 when they hired Sam Pryor from Pennsylvannia and me from Michigan. Years would pass, however, before the major firms brought in women or minorities.

I started in June 1955. John W. Davis had died only two months earlier. He wasn't a founder; the history of the firm dates to 1849. But every one of the twenty-three partners had his picture on his wall, a graphic demonstration of what he meant to the firm. He had been a congressman from West Virginia, Solicitor General of the United States, Ambassador to the Court of St. James's, and the Democratic nominee for president of the United States in 1924—a race he lost to Calvin Coolidge. As Solicitor General, and at Davis Polk, he argued more cases before the United States Supreme Court than anyone else in the twentieth century. He was, hands down, the leader of the New York Bar, and probably the most prominent lawyer in the country.

I made a starting salary of $4,200, which after taxes amounted to less than $300 a month. Janet and I spent $90 of that to rent a furnished third-floor walk-up at 332 West 89th Street between Riverside Drive and West End Avenue. It was only two rooms, and the kitchen was so small that when Janet washed the dishes I stood in the living room to dry them and handed them back to her to put away.

We both worked in those early days, although Janet had not yet started her job in the program information department of CBS-TV, answering questions from callers who wanted information about shows like Arthur Godfrey and "The $64,000 Question." On my first day on the job, we got a rude welcome to life in New York City. Janet called me at the office. She was frantic. We enjoyed listening to music on a record player that plugged into a socket in the back of a radio. That morning, when she plugged the radio into a wall socket, it had erupted in noisy crackling and a cloud of smoke. Frightened that the apartment might go up in flames, she threw the whole apparatus into the bathtub and turned on the water. I was angry at the loss of the radio and the trauma it had inflicted on my wife, and I called the landlord for an explanation. He said, "You must have an ac radio. This is dc current."

Outraged, I said, "You never told us."

He replied, "You never asked."

How were we to know New York still had vestiges of Thomas Edison's old dc distribution system that were phasing out in favor of ac? Still, I should have known from law school: "*Caveat emptor!*"

On my third day of work I found out that everyone wore hats. That morning I received a call from senior partner F.A.O. Schwarz's office. "Bob, this is Fritz Schwarz," he said. "Get your hat and meet me at the elevator. We are going over to J.P. Morgan."

Fresh from Ann Arbor I didn't have a hat, but needless to say I bought one that day at lunchtime. The dress code called for gray fedoras from Labor Day to Memorial Day.

In the summer it was straw hats—boaters, like the ones worn in Vaudeville tap dance routines. They were sporty, with a cloth band with colored stripes. You could buy the bands separately, and replace a blue and yellow one with red and green—and so on—whenever the spirit moved you.

This went on until John F. Kennedy was elected President. He never wore a hat. All of a sudden hats on men went out of style and never came back.

The Davis Polk office was downtown at 15 Broad Street, a building that housed the law firms Cravath, Swaine & Moore and Milbank Tweed as well. We all labored under primitive working conditions.

There were no photocopiers or word processors of any kind. Everything was typed by hand. Word processing computers were a futurist's pipe dream. Even Thermofax, and later Xerox, were several years away. The only way to create multiple copies of a document was by typing with sheets of carbon paper inserted between the requisite number of copies. Seven was the practical limit. If the secretary made a mistake, the only solution was to take all the paper out of the typewriter, erase the mistake separately on each copy, and then put everything back in and start again. The more copies there were, the harder the last copy was to read. We used to sit around in multiple-party litigation and decide which other lawyer we liked the least—that lawyer would get the last carbon copy.

Fifteen Broad Street had no air conditioning. You would open the window on a warm day and hope a breeze wouldn't send your papers flying, not to mention dirt blowing off the windowsill. The firm had a rule: if the temperature went above ninety degrees, everyone could go home. But the only way to spread the word was to type up a memorandum and manually distribute it around the office. By that time it was time to go home anyway—which was just as well. Since we all wore white shirts, sweat and carbon paper had by now combined to make us unpresentable with grungy cuffs.

The steno pool frowned on handwritten submissions, so we lawyers had to dictate whatever it was we were composing. Ralph Carson was the most brilliant partner in the firm. An Oxford graduate, he used to exchange memoranda in Latin with another senior partner, Porter Chandler. Carson had an extraordinarily skilled secretary whose name was Ann Craib. Legend had it that one night before a brief was due, he sat down with a pile of books from the library and dictated, from beginning to end, an entire brief—facts and argument. At the conclusion, he got up and left, saying to Miss Craib, "Type that up and send it off to the printer." He—and she—were that good!

Miss Craib stayed after Carson left at the end of the day and worked in the steno pool to earn overtime. New associates, who worked late and needed a secretary, encountered their worst nightmare when they called the steno pool and heard the words, "Miss Craib will be right up." None of us had any experience in dictating, so it was not an easy process under the best of circumstances. Having her sit across the desk, pencil and pad in hand, looking expectant—and mentally tapping her foot with obvious comparisons to Carson going through her head—was intimidating. It was not uncommon for her to say, from time to time, "Are you sure you wouldn't rather say it this way?" It was a suggestion I was always grateful to accept, and after the usual false starts we would somehow muddle through.

I liked Miss Craib. She was never as crusty as her exterior suggested. Over the years we became good friends, and when she retired I gave the main speech honoring her at the firm party.

—⚏—

The senior partner in the litigation department was Theodore Kiendl, the last of the names on our firm letterhead and undoubtedly the leading trial lawyer of his era. He had a formidable personality and piercing steel blue eyes. Everything for him was black or white—there was no gray. He could be very intimidating—he was to all of us except for one associate, Ed Jacobs, who worked on a lengthy case with him. They discovered a mutual interest in chess, so Kiendl set up a chessboard in his office. He would make a move during the day when time allowed and in the evening—Ed was always there in the evening—Ed would go into his office, study the board and make his move. The next day Mr. Kiendl would make his move, and so on. Chess has been criticized for being a slow game, but this was the ultimate. Mr. Kiendl almost always won.

MY FIRST TRIAL

I had played hockey at Yale with a friend named Bill Donaldson. Bill would go on to found Donaldson, Lufkin & Jenrette and chair both the New York Stock Exchange and the Securities and Exchange Commission. But in the fall of 1955 a chauffer's license was vital to his income in his role as special assistant to G. Herbert Walker, the CEO of the investment banking firm of G.H. Walker & Company—and the grandfather of George Herbert Walker Bush. Bill called me one day that fall to say he had just received a ticket for going 70 in a 55 mile-an-hour zone on the Hutchinson River Parkway.

This was a high-stakes case, as he would lose his chauffeur's license if he were convicted.

The first step, of course, was to try to develop the facts and to see if there were witnesses who could be called on his behalf. His wife, Evan, said she thought she could help establish that he could not have been speeding. I asked her why. She said, "Well, a few minutes earlier he had been going 75, and I told him to slow down." Even as a brand new lawyer, I knew I had to look elsewhere for helpful evidence.

We went to trial in the Bronx Traffic Court. Bill's defense was that he had only momentarily accelerated to pass a slower moving car. The problem was that the "slower moving car" was going about 65. I cross examined the trooper and got him to acknowledge that he generally would allow drivers to go 10 miles over the speed limit without stopping them for speeding, and that he generally would allow a driver to exceed the speed limit to pass another car that was driving at the limit. But, he would not agree that you could apply those defenses one on top of the other. The judge declined my request for a dismissal.

With no alternative I put my client on the stand. He started by informing the judge of his role with Mr. Walker of the Wall Street investment banking firm G.H. Walker & Company. I thought the case was surely over at that point. Much to my surprise, and I believe to Bill's as well, the judge concluded by saying, "Donaldson, I think you're guilty, but I am going to acquit you anyway because I don't think a fine would mean anything to someone of your obvious wealth."

On the basis of that dubious reasoning, I won my first trial and Bill kept his chauffeur's license.

About two weeks later I received a call summoning me to the office of George Brownell, the decidedly austere, somewhat distant, and extremely formidable, managing partner of the firm. I had never met Mr. Brownell, and I walked down the hall wondering what I could possibly have done wrong in such a short period of time. When I was ushered into his office he handed me a letter, on the letterhead of G.H. Walker & Company, advising him of what a rising young star the firm had in its litigation department. The letter, which had obviously made a great impression on him, was signed by William H. Donaldson, Special Assistant to G. Herbert Walker.

I have had a number of significant trials and some significant victories in the years since then. But it all started with Bill Donaldson in the Bronx Traffic Court.

BIG RESPONSIBILITIES

All the new Davis Polk associates started out in the unassigned pool. The idea was to spend a year exposed to different kinds of work before deciding which department to join. Virtually all of my work was in litigation—I knew from the previous summer that is what I wanted to do—but I had one significant corporate assignment. It showed how Davis Polk gave associates substantial responsibilities at a very young age. That is still true today.

One Friday afternoon during my first year, I received a call asking me to come and see Leighton Coleman. He was one of the senior partners, and the lawyer for the firm's largest and most important client, J.P. Morgan.

Mr. Coleman said that Roosevelt Raceway, a Long Island harness racing track, was doing a major $100 million expansion. The New York State legislature had just passed a bill giving the raceway major tax relief, which was the only way it could pay back the money it planned to borrow for the project. J.P. Morgan was the lender. However, they worried that the tax relief bill wasn't constitutional.

After he explained all this to me, Mr. Coleman said the bank needed to know by Monday morning. He asked me to have an opinion letter on his desk first thing. He then said, "By the way, you should know that New York Attorney General Jacob Javits has just written an opinion saying the bill is unconstitutional."

So, I worked all weekend. I analyzed the statute, the relevant cases, the Javits opinion, and late Sunday night finished an opinion letter. The last paragraph said, "While not free from doubt, we think the better view is that the statute is constitutional." I left it on his desk and went home.

I came in early Monday morning and waited for a call from Mr. Coleman. When it came at 9 a.m. I went to his office carrying the books with the relevant cases, expecting a probing discussion. Mr. Coleman was sitting behind his desk with the opinion letter in front of him. He looked up and said, "So, Bob, you think the statute is constitutional?"

I said, "Well, it is a close call but yes, I do."

He said, "okay," signed the letter for the firm and said to his secretary, "Send it over to the bank." Apparently, if I thought it was constitutional, that was good enough for him.

The bank made the loan, the raceway expanded and the statute was challenged. It was upheld in the trial court and on appeal, by the Appellate Division and the New York Court of Appeals—but by a divided vote in both courts.

It had obviously been a very close question—we were taking on the Attorney General—but Mr. Coleman was content to rest entirely on my analysis and judgment. I like to use this case as an example of why young lawyers at Davis Polk can expect an uncommon level of responsibility early in their careers.

CHARTING MY OWN COURSE

Not all of my cases put the same weight on my shoulders. Between June 1955 and August 1957 I worked on a variety of cases for several partners, principally Hazard Gillespie and, his even more exacting litigation partner, Taggart Whipple. Mr. Gillespie's were commercial cases in the New York State courts and in the Southern District. Mr. Whipple's was a massive civil antitrust case.

The Department of Justice had sued all the major oil companies alleging a world-wide price-fixing conspiracy. We represented Exxon's predecessor company, Esso, jointly with Sullivan & Cromwell. This came about because Esso wanted to be represented by the person it felt was the number one lawyer in New York. That had been John W. Davis and, until he died, Davis Polk had been Esso's sole counsel—with Ralph Carson and Taggart Whipple doing most of the work. After he died Arthur Dean of Sullivan & Cromwell took his mantle and Esso went to him. So, we were doing it together.

The government had served a sweeping document request, calling for papers from all over the world. Esso had gathered a massive volume of material and stored it in a set of floor-to-ceiling filing cabinets that occupied an entire floor of a building at Rockefeller Center. Two teams of associates, three from each firm, were assigned to review the documents. We were checking for responsiveness to the subpoena, instances of attorney-client privilege, and an elusive thing called "sensitivity." We could decide which documents were responsive, but when issues of attorney-client privilege and sensitivity arose—if a paper contained a derogatory comment about a Saudi sheik, for example—we set those aside for further review by our superiors.

This was a time-consuming, extremely tedious process. The Davis Polk team included two Bostonians, Faneuil Adams and Quincy Adams Shaw McKean. They and the Sullivan & Cromwell associates had already been at it for several months when I started, in the spring of 1957, and were projecting several more months before we would be through.

It was gruesome work, and productivity was low. The six of us would arrive around 9 a.m. and start reading. Before the first hour had elapsed someone would come up with an aside, "Say, did anyone see the play Peewee Reese made last night?" Whether or not anyone had seen the Dodger game, we'd start talking and the document review stopped in its tracks. That would go on intermittently throughout the day—it didn't take much to distract us from the documents—until it was time to go home.

I had been doing this for about three weeks when one day Judge Lumbard called. He asked, "Don't you think it's about time you applied to the U.S. Attorney's Office?"

He had told me after my summer there that I needed some professional training. Now that I had it, he was suggesting I do what I had wanted to do.

I went to Hazard Gillespie and told him I wanted to apply to the U.S. Attorney's Office. He reacted very negatively. He said no one from Davis Polk had ever done that; it would be a huge mistake; and, I should not assume that if I did it the firm would take me back. Even if I were allowed to come back, he said, I would have been away and out of contact with the partners, thereby falling behind my classmates who would be working with them every day. The other litigation partners I had been working with agreed with him.

I called Judge Lumbard and told him the partners were giving me a lot of flak. He asked, "Have any of them done it?" He was saying they had no real knowledge of what the experience was like. Lawyers moving from private firms to work as AUSAs was a brand new phenomenon. That would change in later years, but at the time very few of the major firms sent associates to the U.S. Attorney's Office. I went back to Mr. Gillespie and told him I still thought I wanted to do it. He reiterated how strongly he felt; that this would be a big mistake; and, again urged me not to do it.

A few days later he called me in and showed me a Second Circuit opinion in a case he had been assigned by the court to argue. This, he said, is the kind of extra-curricular experience I could get if I stayed at the firm. He also told me he thought I should get some advice from a person outside of Davis Polk. He recommended I talk to Bruce Bromley, the senior partner at Cravath, Swaine & Moore and one of the most respected members of the New York Bar. Mr. Gillespie said Judge Bromley, having served on the New York Court of Appeals, could give me some valuable advice on public service.

Judge Bromley supported everything the Davis Polk partners had been saying. "You are with a wonderful firm. You have the opportunity to learn from giants of the bar like Ralph Carson and Hazard Gillespie. You will throw that all away if you leave and go to the U.S. Attorney's Office where the experience isn't that valuable anyway."

This really made it hard. The Davis Polk partners, led by Mr. Gillespie, were telling me in no uncertain terms not to do this. They very well might not allow me to come back, and even if I did my career at the firm would be seriously damaged. If I went I—a second year associate—would not only be rejecting their advice, I would be rejecting what they considered the outside, objective view of one of the most respected members of the New York Bar, who had himself been in public service. On the other hand, I had been there. I had experienced the DeAngelo trial with Fred Nathan and thought it *was* valuable. I felt the appeal of public service strongly.

One night in May Janet and I went for a walk in Riverside Park near our apartment. We walked around for a couple of hours, discussing the pros and cons. I remember saying at the end, "I understand all the arguments for and against. I know there is a big risk, but I just have a feeling deep down that this is what I want to do. When I am eighty years old, looking back at my career, I do not want to have spent it all in private practice. I want this to be part of it."

Janet encouraged me to go for it.

So, the next morning I went in and told Mr. Gillespie. He was very gracious, saying that he knew I had given it very careful consideration, and he wished me all the best.

SECTION III

—m—

ASSISTANT UNITED STATES ATTORNEY, 1957–1961

JUDGE LUMBARD, SINCE HE gave me his strong recruiting push, had been appointed to the Second Circuit Court of Appeals, so he was not on hand for my arrival. The new U.S. Attorney was Paul Williams, and he swore me in as an Assistant United States Attorney for the Southern District of New York in August 1957. Arthur Savage, a young associate from Lord, Day and Lord, was sworn in at the same time. He went to the Civil Division and I went to the Criminal Division.

The U.S. Attorney's Office was located in the federal courthouse at Foley Square in downtown Manhattan. There were approximately fifty assistants—thirty in the Criminal Division and twenty in the Civil Division versus the one hundred fifty criminal and seventy civil AUSAs today. The Criminal Division was on the fourth floor and the Civil Division was on the floor below. The floor itself was essentially a square, with offices on each side of three legs of the square. It was a very collegial, open-door setting. If you wanted to consult a colleague for advice, you only had to walk across or down the hall. The layout had another advantage, one the architect probably hadn't considered.

Our daughter Linda, our first child, was born in September 1956, almost a year before I went to the U.S. Attorney's Office. One result was that Janet and I moved from our two-room West Side walkup to a garden apartment in suburban Tarrytown. During the week I rode the train to work, but I also worked a lot of weekends—particularly when on trial. When Linda was old enough I brought her to town with me in our station wagon with her tricycle, which I'd unload and bring upstairs. She could ride the complete fourth floor loop and, being very gregarious, would stop along the way to chat with the other assistants. It could take her as long as an hour to make it all the way around. That, together with playing with a primitive dictating machine and her coloring book, could keep her occupied until it was time to go home.

I started out in the Short Trials Unit, today called General Crimes. There were seven of us under the leadership of Ed Cuniffe. If, as former New York Chief Judge Sol

Wachler is supposed to have said, "a grand jury would indict a ham sandwich," I got a demonstration in one of my first cases.

It was a simple agent-buy narcotics case, the kind traditionally given to brand new AUSAs. I previewed the evidence by telling the grand jury they would hear Agent Doherty testify that, posing as a drug purchaser, he bought a one-quarter ounce of heroin from the defendant. I then left the grand jury room to get Agent Doherty, who was waiting outside. I was talking with him when the bell rang summoning me back into the grand jury.

When I re-entered the room the foreman said, "We have voted the indictment." I replied something to the effect, "I have only been here a few days, but I think it might be better if you hear the evidence before you vote."

I had my first trial within a month. The defendant had stolen a Social Security check from the payee's mailbox, forged his name and cashed the check. In his statement he denied stealing the check, but admitted signing the payee's name and cashing it, claiming he had been given the check by someone—who said he was the payee—and had told him to sign his name and cash it.

The judge was Edward Weinfeld. He had been appointed by President Truman in 1950 and was already a legend by the time I came to the office in 1957. He was brilliantly incisive, had total command of every case—no matter how complicated—and had a reputation for being extremely demanding in what he expected from the lawyers who appeared before him. He insisted on punctuality. A lawyer who was late for trial would enter the courtroom to find the jury waiting in the jury box where Judge Weinfeld had installed them, and he made sure they knew whom to blame. Someone once said he was like the Old Testament God, which described not only his physical appearance but the apprehension he inspired in young lawyers. He arrived at the courthouse before dawn every morning. When the rest of us arrived we'd see his name invariably topping the sign-in sheet next to the time, usually around 4:45 a.m. We debated whether it would be a good thing or a bad thing for one of us to come in at 4:00 a.m. some morning and take the top spot, but nobody ever had the nerve to try it.

In anticipation of the trial, I left no stone unturned. I visited the grocery store where the check was cashed and had the post office inspectors take pictures of the inside of the store. Even though the defendant had admitted signing the payee's name, I obtained writing samples from him and had a handwriting expert verify the writing on the check was his.

Bob Bjork joined me at the counsel table for the trial. It was the practice to have a senior AUSA join a new assistant to provide guidance and general reassurance until he got his feet wet. Bob had had several trials before Judge Weinfeld. I called the post office inspector who had taken the defendant's statement. Then I called the grocery store clerk, showed him the pictures from inside the store and asked, "Was this the way the store looked the day the defendant came in and presented the check?" Not noticing the judge was becoming impatient, I plowed ahead and called the handwriting expert. I was only a few questions into my examination when Judge Weinfeld interrupted and asked all counsel to approach the bench. When we got there the judge ignored me and spoke to Bob. "Mr. Bjork," he said, "don't you think the government is over-trying this case?"

I won—without the handwriting expert—and won my next case, too. It was another stolen check/forgery case before Judge Weinfeld. A few days after the second trial I went down to Davis Polk to have lunch with my friend Louis Stanton—with whom I had shared an office—who would go on to become a judge in the Southern District. As I walked down the hall I passed Mr. Kiendl's office. He was then in his early seventies but still active. As I went by he waved for me to come in. He asked how it was going

"It's going great," I said. "I have had two trials and won them both. The only problem," I added, "is when I get up to give my opening statement, I have this really queasy feeling in the pit of my stomach."

Mr. Kiendl looked at me and said, "Let me tell you something. If the time ever comes in your career when you get up to make an opening statement and you *don't* have that feeling in your stomach, it's time to quit."

CHAPTER 4

Henry "the Dutchman" Grunewald

I WON MY NEXT TWO TRIALS: an assault on a ship on the high seas, and a theft from the docks. Then the powers that be decided I was ready for the big time, at least in the second chair. The case was *United States v. Grunewald*, one of the major scandals arising from the last years of the Truman administration.

It was a tax-fixing case. The defendants were Daniel Bolich, an assistant commissioner of the Internal Revenue Service; Max Halperin, a New York lawyer; and Henry "the Dutchman" Grunewald, a Washington influence peddler/fixer. It was said of Grunewald, to demonstrate his influence, that he could walk into any senator's office without taking his hat off. Bolich lived in a suite in the Washington Hotel maintained by Grunewald.

The roots of the case went back ten years.

In 1947 and 1948 two New York business firms, Pattullo Modes and Gotham Beef Co., were under investigation by the IRS for suspected tax evasion. Pattullo Modes, a New York dress manufacturer that would later to change its name to Loehman's, had concealed $300,000 in unreported income; Gotham Beef had failed to report income of $100,000. Both companies retained the New York law firm of Schopick and Davis, which shared space with Halperin. After the firm tried unsuccessfully to obtain no-prosecution rulings from the New York office of the IRS, Schopick and Davis told Halperin they needed some "real help." Halperin steered them to Grunewald, an old friend of his, and—more important—a close friend of Bolich. Pattullo Modes produced $100,000 in cash, and Gotham Beef $60,000, to be delivered to "the man in Washington." Bolich interceded with the New York office of the IRS, resulting in no-prosecution decisions in both cases, and the cash was delivered.

The three defendants tried to conceal what had happened. Bolich attempted to have the IRS report on the Pattullo case "doctored," and steps were taken to cover up the traces of the cash paid to Grunewald. A congressional investigation that started in 1951 triggered more concealment. Bolich caused the disappearance of certain records linking him to Grunewald, and the tax dodging firms were warned to keep quiet. In 1952 the two firms and the defendants were called before a federal grand jury in Brooklyn, renewing the more recent cover-up attempts. These attempts at concealment, however, were in vain. The taxpayers and some of Halperin's associates revealed the entire scheme.

The defendants were indicted in 1954, and all three were convicted. They appealed, claiming the statute of limitations. The Second Circuit affirmed the convictions two-to-one, but in a landmark decision negating acts of concealment as sufficient to extend the statute of limitations a unanimous Supreme Court reversed them. In May 1957 the case came back to the Southern District for retrial.

By then all five members of the original prosecution team had left the office, so the case was assigned to one of the most experienced AUSAs, Robert Kirtland. I tried the case with him. He did most of it: the opening statement, summation, direct examination of most of the key witnesses, and the cross examination of Halperin. I examined the government witnesses in the Gotham Beef case, wrote the requests to charge and various evidentiary memoranda, and provided general support and assistance.

After a seven-week, hotly contested trial, the jury deadlocked—a hung jury resulting in a mistrial. Then two things happened: Bob Kirtland left the office and Grunewald died. The lawyers for Bolich and Halperin appealed to us to drop the case. I argued for a third trial, even without Grunewald. Arthur H. Christy, the acting U.S. Attorney—Paul Williams had resigned to seek the Republican nomination for governor—backed me up. We tried the case again, for another seven weeks, before Judge Edward Dimock. This time I took the lead role and did the opening and summation, direct examination of the key witnesses, and the cross examination of Halperin. Charlie Shaffer backed me up.

After two days of deliberation the jury came back with a verdict—both defendants were acquitted. I was devastated. One of the most important cases the government had brought in the post-Truman era had ended in an acquittal—with me as the lead prosecutor.

I don't think I slept at all that night. The next morning Judge Dimock invited me to drop by his chambers. He told me he thought I had done a great job. Indeed, he said I won his office pool three votes to one, even though I obviously lost twelve to none before the jury. I still remember his gracious gesture. He knew how bad I felt, and he did his best to make me feel better.

CHAPTER 5

Hazard Gillespie Becomes
United States Attorney

PAUL WILLIAMS LOST the Republican gubernatorial nomination to Nelson Rockefeller and returned to private practice at Cahill Gordon & Reindel. Arthur Christy, formerly Williams' Chief Assistant, was filling the role pending the next presidential appointment. He was the bettors' choice amid much speculation about who would head the office, but the person selected was a total surprise to all of us.

On January 3, 1959, I was riding in on the train from Tarrytown when I unfolded *The New York Times* and saw the front page news: "S. Hazard Gillespie Jr. selected as the next United States Attorney for the Southern District of New York." I spent the rest of the ride trying to comprehend the significance—indeed, the irony—of this development since he had tried so hard to keep me from leaving for the office two years earlier.

Gillespie sworn in by Chief Judge Ryan

I barely reached my office when the phone rang. It was him. "Well, you were right," he said. "Can I come and see you so you can tell me all about the U.S. Attorney's Office?"

I went to see him instead, and it was a great day. He was extremely magnanimous, and complimented me for having made the decision to go to the office over his objections. I gathered some political horse-trading was involved in his appointment. He was only forty-eight, and had rejected the idea of a federal judgeship a year earlier. Then when the Southern District slot came open there was some back-and-forth between New York's two senators, Jacob Javits and Ken Keating, before he was approved. Javits had asked him to commit to a later run for governor, which he refused. Hazard asked me to stay on as Assistant Chief of the Criminal Division and I readily accepted. During the next two years he emphasized the irony, telling audiences, "Bob Fiske went to the U.S. Attorney's Office over my dead body." He was a great leader, a great teacher, and a great mentor.

GILLESPIE FILLS STAFF

U. S. Attorney Here Promotes Five Assistants

The New York Times,
June 25, 1959

ROBERT B. FISKE JR.

R.B. Fiske Promoted By US Attorney

Assistant Chief of Criminal Division. Tarrytown News,
June 25, 1959

CHAPTER 6

Customs Inspectors on the Take

MY NEXT MAJOR TRIAL was in the fall of 1959. It involved two Italian haberdashers and six U.S. Customs inspectors. Giuseppe Battaglia and Domenico Guarna sold upscale men's clothing at stores in Milan, Italy and on Park Avenue. Battaglia was also the American sales representative for the Italian clothing lines sold in his retail stores.

In January 1954 Battaglia arrived in New York by ship with a collection of samples. Customs Inspector Benjamin Danis inspected his luggage. Afterward, because Danis had been "very nice and very fast," Battaglia invited Danis to his office to receive some neckties. There, Danis issued Battaglia an invitation to smuggle in whatever he wanted because Danis and his fellow Customs Inspector William Lev "were in a position to let pass everything."

In the two years that followed Battaglia and Guarna—between them—made eleven trips to the United States, carrying merchandise in large commercial trunks for delivery to their customers. Lev and Danis—told in advance which ship they were coming in on—were able to be assigned to baggage examination on every day when a smuggling operation was scheduled.

The deal between Battaglia and the inspectors was that they would split the amount of duty saved. The problem for the inspectors was that—since they were not opening the trunks—they had to take Battaglia's word for what the value of the clothing was and how much duty was saved. There was no honor among thieves on Pier 84; $135,000 worth of men's haberdashery was smuggled in, saving $35,000 in duty. Battaglia and Guarna paid the inspectors $3,500. In 2014 dollars the figures would be ten times higher.

On Guarna's last trip in 1957 two other customs inspectors saw Lev ignoring procedure by allowing some trunks to stay closed. They found Guarna waiting outside with his cleared baggage and asked him to open the trunks. When he did they arrested him for smuggling. Guarna cooperated and so did Battaglia after Guarna gave him up. We went to trial against Lev, Danis and four other customs inspectors.

We demonstrated how the merchandise-filled trunks would have looked if they'd been opened. Danis and Lev each took the stand. The jury found their testimony unbelievable and convicted them and three of the other four inspectors.

After the trial a juror sent me a fan letter that went a long way to lessen the impact of the Bolich/Halperin acquittals. He wrote, in part, "As the tale unfolded . . . it became apparent that the fundamental integrity of the U.S. Customs Service was involved and that the government's case was in very capable hands. After your devastating argument I couldn't imagine there being a more able man for the job."

I had a conversation with Battaglia just before his sentence. He pressed me to tell him he wouldn't go to jail, and I told him all I could do was bring his cooperation to the attention of the court. Finally, the day before his sentencing, he told me he was going to open a store in Beverly Hills, and he had looked at a new Chrysler station wagon that he was planning to drive out to California. He said, "Mr. Fiske, I know you can't tell me whether I will go to jail. Just tell me, should I buy the station wagon?"

I still couldn't tell him anything. But he didn't go to jail, and he did buy the station wagon.

Some time later, the U.S. Customs Service expressed its gratitude for the convictions. In the spring of 1960 my father and mother were returning by ship from Paris where my father had completed his service as assistant secretary general of NATO. I had not seen them for almost two years. I told the supervising customs agent in New York about this, and he arranged for me to go out with the pilot who got on at Ambrose Light to bring the ship through New York Harbor to the pier. I boarded the ship and surprised my parents by knocking on the door of their stateroom at 7 a.m. and saying, "Welcome Home!" We shared a glorious ride through New York Harbor with bands playing and flags flying, past the Statue of Liberty, to the dock.

CHAPTER 7

John Dioguardi ("Johnny Dio")

JOHN DIOGUARDI, BETTER KNOWN AS "Johnny Dio," was one of the most notorious labor racketeers of the 1950's.

He was born on the lower East Side of New York, and became involved in labor racketeering at the age of fifteen through his uncle, who was working for Lucky Luciano. In his early years he established and ran a protection racket in New York City's garment district. In 1937 he was convicted of extortion and spent three years in Sing Sing. After prison he lived briefly in Allentown, Pennsylvania where he established a dress business, which he sold and then returned to New York.

As time went on he became infamous for the creation of "paper" local unions in the garment industry. They extorted money from non-union employers—who wanted to avoid unionization—and from unionized employers—who wanted to avoid strikes. And by getting his locals admitted to the Joint Council of the Teamsters Union, Dio was able to swing the election that resulted in the ousting of Teamsters President Dave Beck in favor of Jimmy Hoffa.

In 1955 the Permanent Subcommittee on Investigations of the U.S. Senate Committee on Government Operations began holding hearings on labor racketeering. Senator John L. McClellan from Arkansas chaired the committee and Robert F. Kennedy was its Chief Counsel. Early on, they focused on Dio's role in Hoffa's election. Dio refused to answer any questions—invoking the Fifth Amendment 140 times.

The hearings drew blanket media coverage. Labor columnist Victor Riesel was writing a series of columns for the *New York Mirror* and also providing information to the U.S. Attorney's Office on racketeering in the trucking and garment industries. On April 5, 1956, Riesel had dinner at Lindy's Restaurant at 51st Street and Broadway. As he emerged a slender, black-haired man in a blue and white lumber jacket stepped out of the doorway and hurled a bottle of sulfuric acid in his face. Riesel ended up totally blind.

A few months later, on July 28, 1956, the twenty-eight-year-old acid thrower, Abraham Telvi, was found dead on Mulberry Street in Little Italy with a bullet in his head. Two thugs with connections to Telvi were arrested in his death. After one of them, Gandolfo "Sheiky" Miranti, talked to the FBI, Paul Williams announced the arrest of Johnny

Dio punches photographer outside Senate hearing room

Dio as the "master-mind" of the crime. Dio, Charles Tuso, Charles Carlino, Nick Bando and Theodore Rij were all charged with arranging the acid blinding to prevent Riesel from testifying before the grand jury investigating labor racketeering.

In September seven defendants—including Telvi's brother Leo—were indicted, pled not guilty, and a November trial date was set. Carlino changed his plea in October and began cooperating with the government. The trial of Bando, Leo Telvi and Miranti was severed from the others and went forward. They were all convicted after a three-week trial and received five-year sentences.

The trial of Dio, Tuso and Rij was set down for May 21, 1957, with Miranti and Bando expected to be the key witnesses against Dio. However, on the day the trial was supposed to begin, Williams told Judge William Herlands the government could not proceed because "certain witnesses" had been threatened and refused to testify. After Judge Herlands adjourned the trial to allow the grand jury to investigate, Miranti and Bando both refused to testify before the grand jury. They invoked the Fifth Amendment even after Judge Herlands directed them to testify. Furious, the judge sentenced them to an additional five years for contempt. His statement made banner headlines in the *Daily News* and *Daily Mirror:* "This is not a case of constitutional silence; this is a case of underworld lockjaw."

The government had no choice but to drop the case from the calendar, which it did on May 28, 1957, with a statement by Williams:

"The majesty of the law itself is on trial where the underworld intimidation of witnesses causes the collapse of the government's case.

The Department of Justice, however, is not powerless. While this is a tragedy, I assure the court that this does not close the book. It is just the beginning of the fight."

Two years later Dio was convicted in New York State Court of extortion and sentenced to fifteen to thirty years. Also, he and his bodyguard, Theodore Ray—the Theodore Rij indicted for the acid blinding—faced federal tax evasion charges. With Dio in state prison there was no pressure to try the tax case. However, in 1959 the Appellate Division reversed the extortion conviction and dismissed the indictment. With that the Dio tax case took on new urgency.

Around the same time, Hazard Gillespie asked me to become Chief of the Organized Crime and Racketeering Section. The first thing I did when I accepted the position was to take over—and try—the Dio case.

Judge Weinfeld scheduled the trial for April 1960. Dio was represented by one of the best defense lawyers of that era, William "Colonel" Kleinman. He was very able and also very straightforward and ethical. Judge Weinfeld liked and respected him. Shortly before the trial Kleinman told Judge Weinfeld he wanted to waive a jury and have the case tried by the judge. He said, "There is no juror in the City of New York who can give Johnny Dio a fair trial."

Both defendants were charged with felony tax evasion. Dio was charged with failing to report $65,000 in income, thereby evading $20,000 in taxes. Ray was charged with evading $273 in taxes. They also faced a conspiracy charge on Dio's tax evasion. Dio had failed to file any tax return for 1951 and 1952, and Ray had failed to file in 1950. Failure to file was only a misdemeanor, but coupled with "affirmative acts of concealment" it became a felony.

The government's proof came principally from two witnesses: Leon Bregman and Jack Ulrich. Bregman operated a non-union ladies' garment company called Haughty Frocks. In the spring of 1950 he began to encounter trouble with union organizers. He testified he was introduced to Dio, who he was told could be helpful. He agreed to pay Dio $15,000 a year in order to stay non-union. He made the payments for three years and then told Dio he could no longer afford them. Bregman also testified that Ray had been on the payroll of Haughty Frocks—under the fictitious name of Samuel Aaronson—for more than a year with a weekly wage of $50. Then he increased Ray's weekly wage to $150—still paying Ray $50 but using the other $100 to pay Dio.

Jack Ulrich was president of the Women's Shoulder Pad Association, a group of employers. He testified that his members were having difficulties with the International Ladies' Garment Workers' Union, as well as in trying to enforce industry rules and regulations. He met Dio through a former employee, and sought his help "to stabilize the industry." Ulrich testified that he paid Dio $5,000 in two cash payments at the end of April 1951. In May Dio came back. He said he would need an additional $150 to $200 a week for his services; and it should be carried on the association payroll in the name of Teddy Ray. The total paid to Dio in this fashion was $1,822. Ray reported this amount on his 1951 tax return—with $252 withheld for taxes—but dodged additional tax by overstating his exemptions.

Kleinman and Ray's lawyer, Daniel Greenberg, attacked the credibility of both witnesses, suggesting that they had pocketed some of the money in the payoff scheme.

I defended their credibility on grounds that their testimony was corroborated by other witnesses and they had no motive to lie. They were not testifying in order to get immunity or a reduced sentence. They had no reason to come into court and, under oath with the penalty of perjury, tell a story implicating Johnny Dio unless it was true. This was before the Witness Protection Program. I told them how much I admired their courage.

Judge Weinfeld apparently agreed. When he delivered his opinion he said, "I find no rational basis upon which to conclude that their testimony was animated by any consideration other than a purpose to tell the truth and to relate the facts as they occurred. Accordingly, each defendant is found guilty as charged."

With my parents in Paris at the time during Dad's stint with NATO—Janet and I used their house on Hamburg Cove in Lyme from time to time for weekends or vacations. The day after the verdict we went up there—after dispatching a telegram to Paris: "Johnny Dio convicted. Prosecutor resting at Hamburg Cove."

Dio was sentenced to four years, and Ray to fifteen months, in prison.

New York Mirror, *April 8, 1960*

CHAPTER 8

Fortune and Anthony Pope

IN 1906, GENEROSO POPE left his birthplace in Benevento, Italy to come to the United States. At age sixteen, with four dollars in his pocket, he started working for Colonial Sand and Gravel in New York City, the world's largest supplier of construction materials. He rose until, in 1928, he owned the company. With his acquired wealth he purchased *Il Progresso Italo-Americano*, the largest and most influential Italian newspaper in the United States, other Italian newspapers in New York and Philadelphia and two radio stations. By then he was a powerful force in New York City Democratic politics.

When he died in 1950 majority ownership of Colonial Sand & Stone—as it was then named—passed to the first two of his three sons, Fortunato, called "Fortune," and Anthony. Their younger brother Generoso Jr., known as Gene, owned one-third, but was not active in the company's management. By the mid-50's Fortune Pope, the older of the two, was widely regarded as one of the most influential Italian-Americans in the United States.

In 1960 New York City and the New York State Investigation Commission began to probe allegations that the New York City Sanitation Department had been billed by Colonial Sand & Stone for rock salt it never received. It came to light that while Colonial Sand & Stone held the contract and the work was done using its facilities, personnel and equipment, the Pope brothers had Colonial Sand & Stone "sub-contract" the work to companies wholly-owned by them and that received over $865,000 in revenues without doing the work.

Hazard Gillespie took a major interest in the case and I worked on it with him. Together with Irving Pollack, the head of the Enforcement Division of the Securities and Exchange Commission, we drafted an indictment charging the Popes with criminal violations of the securities laws. Colonial Sand & Stone was listed on the American Stock Exchange. It had gone public in 1958, and we alleged that the Popes had made false and misleading statements in the registration statement for the initial public offering and in proxy statements for the years 1959 and 1960 when they were being elected to the board of directors.

The statements listed several companies wholly-owned by the Popes and stated that "each of these enterprises deals with the Company on terms at least as advantageous to the Company as those which would be available to it on the open market." The companies actually were used as intermediaries and conduits to divert and conceal the diversion of business and profits from Colonial Sand & Stone for the personal benefit of the Popes. Mr. Gillespie and I presented the case to the grand jury, which voted the indictment on July 19, 1960.

The Popes arrived for the arraignment with an entourage from Cahill Gordon, including three former United States Attorneys: John Cahill, who successfully prosecuted Second Circuit Judge Martin Manton for bribery; Matthew Correa, who had been Cahill's Chief Assistant during the Manton trial and had then succeeded him as U.S. Attorney; and my former boss Paul Williams. The team also included two other partners, one a former FBI agent, and three associates. The Popes pleaded not guilty and Cahill proclaimed their innocence, dismissing the indictment as a "poorly pled civil diversion of corporate opportunity claim."

A month later we were back in court defending against motions to dismiss. Mr. Gillespie argued two of the motions and I argued the others. When I stood up to argue there was a dramatic validation of my decision to come to the United States Attorney's Office. Cahill was arguing for the Popes. One of my law school classmates from Michigan was part of the defense team. He was the last man on their team and I was arguing for the government against John Cahill.

We won the motions and began to prepare for trial before Judge Weinfeld, who kept the case for trial because he had heard the motions.

We were anxious to get the case tried. John F. Kennedy had been elected President; the Democrats were coming into power; and we were concerned about what might happen with the Popes being such powerful figures in the Democratic Party. We pressed for a December trial date in a conference with Judge Weinfeld. John Cahill protested, telling the judge that he was getting married and would be on his honeymoon. Judge Weinfeld sided with Cahill, granted the adjournment until January, and for years loved to tell the story of how Hazard Gillespie tried to deny Cahill his honeymoon.

Kennedy was inaugurated on January 20, 1961. The day before was no less active in our world than it was in Washington. Anticipating a return to Davis Polk once the new administration was in place, and now with two kids and a third on the way— Bob was born in June 1958 and Janet was five months pregnant with Sue—we had

2 POPE BROTHERS INDICTED BY U. S.

Both Accused of Diverting Funds From Concern in Rock-Salt Operation

The New York Times,
July 20, 1960

INDICTED: Anthony Pope, president of Colonial Sand and Stone Company. He and his brother, Fortune Pope, were indicted for violating the securities laws.

bought a house in Darien, Connecticut. We chose the 19th to move from our Tarrytown apartment. I thought I could join the moving party, but it was also the day a photographer came in to take the office picture. I wanted to be there to be in the picture, but it kept getting postponed. Then it started to snow—heavily—18 inches! It took me nine hours to get home, the last few miles driving our twelve-year-old Chevrolet—with chains on the tires—behind a snow plow at fifteen miles an hour. But Janet, Linda and Bob were so glad to see me when I finally arrived that they ignored my absence on moving-in day and gave me a hero's welcome.

Shortly after the Democrats took over, Hazard Gillespie resigned and went back to Davis Polk. He told me he felt the Pope case was in good hands. The Popes appealed to Bobby Kennedy, the new Attorney General, and were rebuffed. Kennedy told Bill Hundley, Chief of the Organized Crime and Racketeering Section in Washington, "I hope they go to jail." That precipitated plea negotiations, and in March the Popes pled guilty to four counts of the indictment and *nolo contendere* to the other four.

United States Attorney's Office, January 19, 1961

I had returned to Davis Polk when they came up for sentencing in April, but I came back to handle it. Judge Weinfeld called the Pope brothers "stupid." Since they owned two-thirds of Colonial Sand & Stone, they didn't need to solicit proxies in the first place. He chided them for ignoring their "definitive responsibility to public stockholders." In the end he gave them a fine, but no jail sentence.

—W—

DAVIS POLK, 1961–1976

MY RETURN TO DAVIS POLK in March 1961 had not been a given. One of my good friends at Yale had been John Hincks, who had grown up in Hartford, Connecticut and gone on to Yale Law School and from there to one of Hartford's leading firms, Robinson, Robinson & Cole. We had stayed in touch, and sometime in 1960, as I was beginning to reflect on life after the United States Attorney's Office, he encouraged me to consider Hartford.

The big selling point was a more relaxed professional schedule. He said almost all Hartford lawyers were home by six or seven every night and rarely worked weekends. This opened other opportunities, including politics. John said, "Anyone who devotes himself to it has a fifty-fifty chance of becoming his party's candidate for governor."

So in the fall of 1960, while preparing for the Pope trial, I took a few days off and went up to Hartford for a series of interviews at different firms. In the end, however, I didn't see enough variety in the cases they handled. And I knew that if I were not happy at work, I would not be happy at home. So I decided to go back to Davis Polk.

I returned as an associate, but with enhanced credentials. While I had been gone for three-and-a-half years without working with Davis Polk partners, I had worked as closely as anyone could with Hazard Gillespie, who was rejoining the firm with greater stature after serving as the United States Attorney. In addition, Lawrence E. Walsh, who had been at Davis Polk briefly in the 1930's, and had gone on to be counsel to Governor Dewey, Chairman of the New York Waterfront Commission, a Southern District federal judge and, most recently, Deputy Attorney General of the United States, was also coming back to the firm. I knew he would appreciate my experience as an AUSA.[5]

But it wasn't all peaches and cream.

I had the sense that the litigation partners—other than Gillespie and Walsh—wanted to let me know—some more obviously than others—that four years as an AUSA complete with headlines in the *Daily News* and front page stories in the *Times* on the Dio and Pope cases, did not make me an automatic lock for partner. This was especially true given that the four lawyers who had started when I did had stayed at the firm doing what associates do, which wasn't getting headlines, but rather helping out those very partners.

Early on Taggart Whipple, a very intimidating, strong-willed and demanding partner, asked me to work on a case for Texas Instruments. It involved an antitrust investigation into one of Texas Instrument's subsidiaries in Attleboro, Massachusetts. Don Fox, one of the four who'd stayed behind, was the principal associate working on the case. Whipple called me into his office and told me we had to respond to a document subpoena from the antitrust division. He said he wanted me to help Don with the document production.

We went off to Attleboro the next day. The documents were all stored in cardboard boxes in an old warehouse. No one had been in there for quite a while and when I pulled the first box off the shelf it came down with a huge cloud of dust. There were over a hundred boxes we had to go through, and after the first day I traded my suit and white shirt for blue jeans and a T-shirt.

Standing there coughing as the dust swirled down, I thought, one year ago I was putting Johnny Dio in jail. What am I doing here in this dusty warehouse, doing a document review for Don Fox? But I decided to just tough it out. This was clearly the right course of action; in retrospect, it seems clear this was a test by Whipple. If I had complained, I am sure it would have backfired: "Who does he think he is?" I did the document production, passed the test, and got along fine with him after that—although almost all of my work from then on was for Gillespie and Walsh on two major matters.

CHAPTER 9

Price-Fixing, Multi-District Litigation, and "You're Off the Payroll and Onto the Lease"

GILLESPIE WAS REPRESENTING Allis-Chalmers Manufacturing Company in the massive civil litigation that followed the 1960 price-fixing conviction of twenty manufacturers of electrical equipment. There were 1,800 separate cases brought by utilities that had purchased the equipment at inflated prices, far and away the greatest volume of litigation arising out of a single fact pattern that had ever occurred. There has never been a case, or series of cases, that involved so many of the most prominent lawyers all across the country on both sides. And the way the judiciary handled it led to the establishment of the Judicial Panel on Multi-District Litigation.

It started in 1959 when the Justice Department's Anti-Trust Division investigated complaints by the Tennessee Valley Authority (TVA) that it had repeatedly received identical bids from competing manufacturers even though the bids were submitted in sealed envelopes.

Four separate grand juries were convened, and 196 witnesses were subpoenaed. Some of them eventually revealed the details of a mammoth, nationwide price-fixing scheme. The scheme covered twenty-nine products ranging from turbine generators, power switchgear, transformers and condensers to porcelain insulators, lightning arresters and meters. The annual sales of the affected products totaled more than $270,000,000. Westinghouse and General Electric were involved in all or most of the product areas. Our client, Allis-Chalmers, was a distant third.

One prong of the conspiracies was simple price fixing: competitors would meet and agree to raise prices for the product in question, typically 10 percent. The other prong was more complex, involving division of the market. Participating companies basically kept the share of the market they previously had. If Company A, for instance, had under competitive conditions secured 20 percent of the available business, then it would be given the opportunity to submit the lowest bid on 20 percent of the new contracts. The remainder of the companies would bid at slightly higher levels.

But sometimes, because of factors including company reputation or available servicing arrangements, the final contract went to a firm that wasn't the low bidder. Thus

46

the conspirators often argued among themselves about the proper division of spoils. Sometimes they would draw lots to determine who would submit the lowest bid. At other times they fell back on a rotating system referred to as the "phase of the moon."

The conspirators hid behind a camouflage of fictitious names and elaborate codes. The attendance roster for the meetings was known as the "Christmas card list" and the gatherings as "choir practice." The offenders used public telephones for much of their communication, and they met either at trade association conventions—where their relationships would appear reasonable—or at sites selected for their anonymity.

Group members communicated by way of codes and symbols. They mailed one another letters to home—not office—addresses, and left off return addresses and other identifying information. Written communications were destroyed promptly after receipt. Or, they were supposed to be. One of the conspirators had stored up a cachet of documents. When he grew disaffected he became a cooperating witness and his material a main source of ammunition for the government.

The Department of Justice filed twenty indictments against the participating companies. Of the forty-five individuals indicted, twenty-six were officers or managers with Westinghouse or GE. All of the corporate and most of the individual defendants entered pleas of guilty or *nolo contendere*. Chief Judge James Cullen Ganey, the judge to whom the cases were assigned in the Eastern District of Pennsylvania, imposed fines totaling $1,721,000 on the corporate defendants and $136,000 on the individuals. The fines were unprecedented for an antitrust violation, and the thirty-day jail terms handed to seven of the individuals were also firsts for an antitrust case. (The terms would be far higher today under current sentencing guidelines.)

The 1,800 treble damage suits that followed in the aftermath of the convictions threatened to overwhelm the federal judicial system. Many of the plaintiffs were private utilities such as Consolidated Edison, Consumers Power, and Appalachian Power Company. Others were municipally-owned utilities, or Rural Electrification Administration Cooperatives. If each case proceeded as an independent lawsuit, the total number would clog calendars and disrupt the normal business of the courts. Duplication was another problem. Much of the evidence to be discovered in any given case would also be the object of discovery in many others. There was enormous potential for confusion and conflict, with hundreds of parties all over the country seeking to depose the same witnesses or get hold of the same documents.

To try to manage the situation, the Judicial Conference of the United States established the Coordinating Committee for Multiple Litigation of the United States District

Courts. There were nine judges on the Committee from around the country. They developed uniform pre-trial procedures to avoid repetitious and overlapping discovery, including a national depository for documents, a uniform set of interrogatories, a schedule for hearing motions that would provide for early and uniform rulings on important questions of law, and a national deposition program in which each witness would be deposed once, in front of one of the judges on the Committee.

The deposition was binding in every case, and every lawyer who had a case involving that witness was free to come and ask questions. Early on, the plaintiffs' leading lawyers established a committee, and one of those lawyers would initiate the questioning, with follow-ups by other lawyers. As a result the depositions could—and usually did in the case of the major witnesses—last several days.

Allis-Chalmers Vice President John McMullen was one of the witnesses whose deposition was taken in this fashion. His responsibilities covered five separate product lines: turbine generators, power transformers, power switchgear, meters and circuit breakers. His deposition applied to the largest number of cases of any witness. It was scheduled for Hollywood, Florida in December. For both those reasons it attracted the largest number of lawyers of any deposition taken in the program.

Hazard Gillespie and I went to West Allis, a suburb of Milwaukee, to prepare McMullen for his testimony. It took almost a week. We stayed at the Milwaukee Athletic Club, which had a bar called the Elephant Room that featured elephant heads and tusks on the walls. We knew from earlier depositions that one of the most significant price-fixing meetings had occurred in that room, when McMullen's counterparts at GE and Westinghouse had come to Milwaukee and agreed with him on a 10 percent price increase for turbine generators. Gillespie and I would spend the day at Allis-Chalmers preparing him to testify and then revisit the scene of the crime that evening at the price-fixing table in the Elephant Room.

The deposition, when it came, lasted a week. It was a bonanza for the south Florida economy. All of the lawyers showed up the first day to note their appearances on the record. Then, while Gillespie and I sat through testimony chronicling one antitrust violation after another, most of the rest of them left for the golf courses, the beaches, the jai alai games or the dog tracks. After five days of this they reappeared visibly suntanned on the last day to ask one or two questions about whether McMullen's activities had affected electrical equipment purchases for, say, the City of Omaha.

The conspirators operated on two levels: the executives met to agree on the broad parameters of the conspiracy, while "the working group" of lower-level employees met to implement the broad instructions. The law firms in the litigation mirrored the same structure in our periodic meetings with Judge Sylvester J. Ryan of the Court Coordinating Committee. The firm heavyweights argued for pre-trial orders and directives, while associates drafted the orders. The latter quickly became known as "the working group."

Judge Ryan kept his sense of humor during the long process. Once when Howard Aibel, GE's in-house counsel for the litigation, tried to downplay GE's role by sitting in the back row of the courtroom, Ryan waved him to come down front saying, "In my church, Mr. Aibel, the sustaining member of the congregation sits in the front pew."

Testimony in the depositions made denying the price-fixing conspiracy impossible. Nonetheless, in the first case to go to trial, involving only GE and Westinghouse, their lawyers felt they had valid defenses. Their theory held that the price increases resulted from economic factors unrelated to the agreements and that the prices were fair.

Harold Kohn represented the plaintiff, the Philadelphia Electric Company. Kohn was flamboyant, but highly effective and his adversaries underestimated him. After all the evidence of price-fixing had been introduced, the proof turned to causation and damages. GE and Westinghouse each called an economic expert who told the jury the price increases could be explained by factors such as plant capacity and production costs. Kohn's cross examination dripped with sarcasm. He asked the witnesses if they thought the executives were just wasting their time by traveling across the country to clandestine meetings to reach price-fixing agreements.

He called no damage expert of his own—introducing instead a chart of power transformer prices. The line on the chart increased steadily through the conspiracy period to a high the day before the indictments were returned. After the indictments the line dropped precipitously back to its pre-conspiracy starting point.

The jury was out only a few hours before coming back with a verdict that after trebling reached $29 million—one of the highest ever up to that time.[6] This result—and one or two other trials where the plaintiffs prevailed—convinced the defendants to settle and draw five years of litigation to a close. GE paid out over $200 million, Westinghouse over $100 million, and Allis-Chalmers just under $50 million.[7]

In the aftermath Congress, in 1968, established the Judicial Panel on Multi-District Litigation. It consists of seven judges appointed by the Chief Justice who can transfer cases pending in two or more districts that involve common questions of fact to a single judge in a selected district for coordination of discovery and to prevent inconsistent rulings. Through the end of 2012 the panel had transferred more than 400,000 lawsuits—in more than 2,400 multi-district litigations—in cases involving securities fraud, product liability, price-fixing, intellectual property infringement, airplane crashes and employment practices.

Another milestone was my own. I achieved partnership at Davis Polk in 1964, with no repercussions from my absence as an AUSA. Hazard Gillespie told me, "You're off the payroll and onto the lease." The electric equipment price-fixing cases, which ended the next year, were among the most memorable in the country's history and it was exciting to be part of it.

CHAPTER 10

Return to Darien (and Ice Hockey)

BACK IN DARIEN, since our snowy moving day in January 1961, I found that the return to my teenage stomping ground reconnected me with the sport that had been a big part of my life when I was growing up. I played ice hockey almost from the time I could walk. The house my family lived in from 1939 to 1946 was a quarter-of-a-mile from Tison's Pond, a small pond that froze over in early December and stayed frozen through February. (Note to climate change skeptics: now it freezes for only a day or two each year.) I was part of a group of neighborhood boys who played hockey there every afternoon after school and on weekends. There were no indoor rinks; throughout New England hockey was played outside on frozen ponds.

This created some interesting dynamics. There were no boards, obviously, so an errant pass could go a long way before a skater tracked it down. The goals were usually a pair of galoshes at each end, and no one ever took hard shots for the same reason. Sometimes we played on Five Mile River, and that meant an extra hazard. Eel fishermen would cut holes in the ice and prod the river bottom with their eel spears. They liked peace and quiet, and boys playing hockey provided neither. When a pass went toward an eel hole no amount of shouting could persuade them to block the puck; it could disappear into the hole for all they cared, and sometimes we thought they helped it on its way.

From playing so often in the winter, I became a good skater and a good stick handler. But the lack of boards meant I never developed a good shot. At Pomfret—the prep schools also played outdoors, either on a frozen pond or rinks they built and flooded—I played on the second line in my junior year and was center on the first line in my senior year. That was the year, as it turned out, that we had so much snow that the ice collapsed into the pond and our season was cancelled after just three games.

I went out for hockey when I entered Yale in the fall of 1948, but that year's freshman class had to be the best group of hockey players ever to come into Yale in a single class. They came from prep schools all over New England and I had less experience than any of them. I made the team, but as a center on the fourth line that didn't see much action. Our freshman team went undefeated with only one slightly close game—a 9-7 win over Brown.

Tying on our skates

Eight members of our class made the varsity the next year and Yale hockey was a powerhouse for the rest of my time there. It won the Ivy League, beat the likes of Boston College and Boston University, and in my senior year went to the NCAA final four where it lost to Colorado College 4-3. Such a team had no use for a freshman fourth line center, but I played for three years on an informal junior varsity team called the Yale Cougars. We had a good team and played a good schedule including games against smaller colleges. Four Cougars moved up to the varsity when my class of hockey stars graduated.

Hockey remained a part of my life at Michigan Law School. I started a team we called the Legal Eagles, and we played similar teams from other graduate schools. Then, after a post-graduation hiatus while I was getting my feet wet as a lawyer, the move to Darien immersed me in hockey once again.

The Darien Hornets, a team formed by a number of my college hockey friends, played in the Commuter League. It had two divisions; we were in the North along with Bedford, New Canaan, Bronxville, and Greenwich, while the South included Beaver

Dam on the north shore of Long Island and three teams in northern New Jersey. We held a playoff at the end of the year. Most of the players had played in college, so it was good, highly competitive hockey, and it had a social component that was as enjoyable as the competition. We played on Sunday afternoons. The visitors would bring their wives and young children, and the home team provided post-game beer and sandwiches.[8]

As time went on, the league became popular with graduating hockey players. Every year we had an infusion of young, highly-skilled talent[9] and finally, as an act of self-protection, we drafted a rule that only five players on a team could be under thirty. I played in the Commuter League until I was fifty.

My work with Davis Polk was all-encompassing, but in most cases weekends were my own and allowed me to start coaching boys' hockey teams. In 1970 our family joined the New Canaan Winter Club, which had an outside skating rink. The Winter Club had a boys' hockey program and its teams, of various age groups, played schedules of twelve or so games against other nearby youth hockey teams.

Hockey is a great sport to coach because it combines individual and team skills. A good coach works with each player to develop his skating, stick handling, passing and shooting, and to meld these individual talents into a team game with playmaking, covering in the defensive zone, power plays, short-handed drills and so forth. I also enjoyed it because it was a wonderful opportunity to instill the right values in young players—teamwork, 100 percent effort 100 percent of the time, and sportsmanship. Hockey made teaching teamwork easy; I stressed that an assist counts as much as a goal. I learned very early on that athletic coaches influence the values of the players they coach. There is nothing better than a coach with the right values and nothing worse than a coach with the wrong ones—a win-at-all-costs attitude without regard to what is best for the players.

Bob was twelve then, and I had a rule against coaching my own children. It was a difficult situation; if your son was an outstanding player and you kept him in the game, the other parents would inevitably complain that you were playing favorites and their kids weren't playing enough. But, if you kept your child on the bench that would cause disappointment that would be hard to explain at home. Bob was playing on a Pee Wee team in the Winter Club, so I took on coaching duties for the Squirts, who were nine and ten-year-olds. They had a lot of ability and enthusiasm and were fun to coach.

One win came over a team from Long Island that had come up to play on the outdoor ice at the Crystal Rink in Norwalk. Leo Skidd owned and ran the Crystal Rink, and many of us knew and liked him from playing Darien Hornets games there.[10]

The Long Island team was banging its sticks on the wall before the game and otherwise making noise when Leo went in and asked them to quiet down. One kid retorted with the f-word, and Leo said, "That kid is not playing on my ice." Rather than joining Leo in the reprimand, his coach said if the boy couldn't play the team wouldn't play either. He asked me to help change Leo's mind "so we can have a game." But I told him I agreed with Leo; the kid had been way out of line. "If you want to take your team back to Long Island, go ahead," I said. He backed down and benched the kid; we played the game, and beat them.

My stint coaching the Squirts lasted just two years because in 1973 Darien built an indoor rink and we started a boys' hockey program there. The New Canaan boys I had coached went on, as Pee Wees, to make the Connecticut state tournament. Their coach also coached the next age group, the Bantams, and they made the playoffs, too. With the games overlapping, the Bantams' coach asked me if I would come back and coach my old group; I agreed enthusiastically.

Our first game was against Hamden and I came to appreciate what 2008 Republican vice presidential candidate Sarah Palin meant when she said, "The only difference between a pit bull and a hockey mom is lipstick": throughout the game, a group of Hamden hockey moms stood behind our eleven-year-old goalie ringing cow bells and taunting him with cries of, "sieve, sieve," and worse. We beat Hamden in overtime despite the cow bells, won the next three games and ended up in the finals against West Haven. Nobody expected this, given a mediocre regular season that had included losses to three of the teams in the playoffs, and so a crisis loomed. Most of the players' families had planned winter vacations for the week following the playoffs. But if we beat West Haven we would be Connecticut state champs and, instead of sunning in the Caribbean or skiing in Vermont or Colorado, they would go on to the New England tournament the next weekend. West Haven solved the dilemma, however, by beating our team two-to-one in overtime.

Our Darien youth hockey program evolved quickly. We had enough players for four Pee Wee teams. They would be sponsored by local businesses and play one another in an intramural league. I signed on as one of the coaches and we developed a system to get all the players on the ice. It involved dividing the players by talent; the best five would wear blue tape in their helmets, the second five red tape, and the third five green tape. The five Blues from each team would face off against each other, play for two minutes, then—even in the middle of play—the whistle would blow and the Reds would take the ice, and so on. All the boys got equal time that way, and the coaches weren't tempted to spend all their time with the best players.

My team won the intramural league in each of the first two years, by which time we had developed enough skilled players to field a travel team—we had a good team and won most of our games. I coached the traveling Pee Wees in 1975 and 1976, but the demands I faced as U.S. Attorney for the Southern District of New York made it too difficult to continue after that.

Coaching those boys in New Canaan and Darien during those years was both stimulating and rewarding. The hockey sticks inscribed with "Thank you, Mr. Fiske" and the teams' signatures are among my most prized memorabilia.

CHAPTER 11

Texas Gulf Sulphur

IN THE SPRING OF 1964 the mining company Texas Gulf Sulphur discovered a huge copper vein at one of its mines in Timmons, Ontario. By April 12 Wall Street was alive with rumors and articles appeared in *The New York Times* and the *New York Herald Tribune*. Texas Gulf decided to put out a press release to quell the rumors, which it did late that day, stating that "the work done to date has not been sufficient to reach definite conclusions and any statement as to size and grade of ore would be premature and possibly misleading."

The press release information appeared the morning of April 13. On April 16, three days later, after further drilling reports had been received, the company convened a press conference where it announced "a major discovery"—a copper ore strike of at least 25 million tons. Texas Gulf's stock rose almost seven points to $30⅛ and reached a high of $58 by the end of the month.

A year later in April 1965, the Securities and Exchange Commission (SEC) sent shock waves through the corporate world by bringing its first-ever major insider trading case against Texas Gulf Sulphur and a number of its officers and directors.

The SEC charged that Texas Gulf had misled investors in the April 12 press release by understating the significance of the drilling results up to that point. The complaint charged a number of Texas Gulf officers, who had made purchases of stock and calls in the days immediately preceding the April 16 press conference, with insider trading. And it charged two outside directors with insider trading based on purchases made while the 10 a.m. press conference was still going on.

Thomas S. Lamont, a director of Morgan Guaranty Trust Company, was one of the outside directors. The charges took him by surprise. Today the SEC gives a potential defendant a "Wells Notice" saying it is considering charges and inviting a response. No warning preceded the charges in 1965, and Lamont, who had no reason to think he had done anything wrong, reeled with shock at the wave of adverse publicity resulting from the fraud charge against him. Hazard Gillespie and I handled his defense.

The case against Lamont came down to timing. As a Morgan Guaranty director, he also served on its Trust and Investment Committee. The chair of the Committee, Longstreet

Hinton, had been giving Lamont a friendly hard time about how poorly Texas Gulf stock had been doing. Lamont was on hand at the April 16 press conference and, after he heard the announcement of the major copper strike, he decided to call Hinton. He waited as reporters rushed out of the room to telephone in the news. The press conference continued and at 10:40 a.m., forty minutes after it convened, he went outside and called Hinton, somewhat gleefully.

S.E.C. Insider Suit Names Texas Gulf Sulphur Aides

13 Charged With Buying Shares While Delaying Report on Ore—Lamont of Morgan Bank Is a Defendant

The New York Times, *April 20, 1965*

"Street, this is Tom," he said, according to testimony. "Take a look at the broad tape. There is some news on Texas Gulf."

"Is it good?" Hinton asked.

"Yes."

Hinton did not wait to look at the broad tape. He checked with the trading desk, learned the stock was up three points and immediately placed two orders for a total of 13,000 shares. As it turned out the news did not appear on the broad tape until fourteen minutes later, at 10:54 a.m., and the SEC charged Lamont with "tipping" Hinton with inside information.

Before trial we tried to show that the news was actually public at the time of Hinton's purchases notwithstanding the delay in the Dow Jones broad tape. *The Northern Miner*, a Canadian trade paper, had carried a full report of the ore discovery in its April 16 edition, which had hit the newsstands early that morning.[11] But too few newsstands had it. And too few people had heard of the Ontario Minister of Mines' announcement of the strike to the Canadian press at 9:40 that morning. Accordingly, we based our defense of Lamont on demonstrating his lack of *scienter* (intent to defraud) and his good faith.

We deposed Jerry Bishop, the reporter from the Dow Jones Instant News Service who had been at the press conference. He testified that he had phoned in the news to Dow Jones at around 10:10 a.m. and would have expected the news to appear on the broad tape "within ten minutes." We argued to Judge Dudley Bonsal, the Southern District Judge trying the case, that Lamont, who acted reasonably, should not be the victim of the fact that the Dow Jones Instant News Service failed to live up to its name.

The other outside director charged with insider trading was Francis G. Coates, a partner in a Houston, Texas law firm who had purchased stock right after the announcement was made. Albert Connolly of Cravath was defending him, and he taught me a valuable lesson. I wanted to depose the person at Dow Jones who had taken Bishop's call. In my ex-prosecutor mode, I wanted to work him over to highlight his long delay in getting out the news. Connolly dissuaded me. He said, "I am afraid he will say, to protect himself, 'I don't remember when I got the call from Bishop. All I know is I got the news on the tape a few minutes after he called.' Then we will have a real mess. Leave it as it is, undisputed that the call was made at 10:10 a.m. and the news should have been on the tape instantly after that."

That advice has stayed with me ever since: when you have an advantage, recognize it and leave it at that.

The SEC tried to switch its definition of "inside information" a week before the trial. Earlier it had taken the position that news ceases to be inside information when it is carried on the broad tape. Then the agency argued that news retains its "inside" character for some unidentified additional time until the investing public has had an adequate opportunity to evaluate the news. We had a field day with that. One analyst's letter quoted Texas Gulf itself as saying it might take six months to evaluate the discovery. And when Judge Bonsal asked at what point Lamont should have been able to purchase the stock, the SEC's lawyer conceded that "it is nearly impossible to formulate a rigid set of rules."

We argued in our post-trial brief that the agency had in effect turned its rule-making authority over to the court, and was seeking to have the rule applied retroactively to cover a period when it was unknown to those who had to be shown to have acted knowingly to constitute a violation.

Judge Bonsal dismissed the case against both Lamont and Coates. He held that trading should be permitted once the announcement was made and told the SEC, if it wanted an evaluation period when trading was off limits, it should use its rule-making powers to impose one. He held the "gloomy" April 12 press release was nevertheless not "misleading or deceptive on the basis of the facts then known." He found insider trading violations by two officers who had purchased shares on April 15 and April 16 before the press conference, but exonerated the officers who had purchased stock, or calls to buy stock, between November 1963 and April 9, 1964.[12]

After Judge Bonsal's decision, and while the case was on appeal, Lamont died. Many who knew him believed that the trauma from being charged with fraud by the SEC was a factor contributing to his early death.

The Second Circuit took a very different view of the case. In a landmark opinion rendered *en banc* by a divided court, it reversed almost every part of Judge Bonsal's decision that favored the defendants.[13]

It sent the case back to Bonsal to take a new look at whether the April 12 press release was misleading to a reasonable investor, and—if so—whether it was issued without due diligence. It said he should have recognized that the buyers who made stock or call purchases before April 16 at least thought they were acting on material information. As for Coates the appeals court said it was not a defense that he bought stock after the announcement had been made but "... at the minimum, Coates should have waited until the news could reasonably have expected to appear over the media of widest circulation, the Dow Jones broad tape ..."[14]

That was what Lamont had done, and although beyond the court's reach now, he was implicitly exonerated by them.

In retrospect the case against Lamont never should have been brought. He was a person acting in good faith, his integrity had been maligned, his career stained and perhaps his life shortened by an agency that many felt at that time was more interested in headlines than fairness. His case helped stimulate the Wells Notice procedure. Had it been in effect then, and had we been able to make all the arguments to the SEC we made in court, it might have prevented this injustice from occurring.

CHAPTER 12

Thalidomide

ON OCTOBER 1, 1957, a German company named Chemie Grunenthal introduced a new drug called thalidomide. It was marketed as a breakthrough sleeping pill called Contergan that had been proven, through both animal and clinical testing, to be completely safe even in amounts that would typically cause overdose and death. That distinguished it from every other known sedative. The company cited a man who had taken 144 capsules; he slept for several days and woke up with no after-effects except a slight headache and some hunger pangs.

The drug immediately became wildly popular in Germany. Contergan was inexpensive and didn't require a prescription. By the end of the first year it sold at a rate of 90,000 packets a month. Chemie Grunenthal then began negotiating license agreements with a number of foreign companies. One of these was American, Richardson-Merrell, Inc. (RMI), and after taking a license RMI filed a new drug application for thalidomide on September 12, 1960. It planned to market it as Kevadon.

RMI's sales of Kevadon hinged on approval by the U.S. Food and Drug Administration (FDA) which required a finding that it was both effective and safe. The company expected quick approval. Effectiveness was not an issue, and Contergan had been sold in Germany for over three years with no reports of any significant side effects. The application went to Dr. Frances O. Kelsey, who had arrived at the FDA from a medical practice in Vermillion, South Dakota just one month earlier. Thalidomide had landed on her desk apparently because her superiors considered it a straightforward application.

FDA rules said that if the agency did not contact the manufacturer within sixty days the application automatically became effective. Dr. Kelsey did not want that to happen. She was troubled by a feeling that, as she put it, "the claims were just too glowing—too good to be true" and that the clinical reports were "really more testimonials than scientific studies." So, in November, before the sixty-day deadline, she sent the company a letter with a number of questions about the animal and clinical studies. RMI was still answering them when, in February 1961, she discovered a letter in the December 1960 issue of the *British Medical Journal* suggesting that prolonged use of thalidomide resulted in peripheral neuritis—a loss of sensation of the nerves in the hands and the feet. Angered by the fact that RMI had not disclosed this article, she requested further animal studies and clinical information.

At the same time, unbeknownst to either RMI or Dr. Kelsey, information was beginning to circulate in Germany about a rash of birth deformities. They were called phocomelia, a congenital malformation of development where the upper appendage of the arm or leg is absent, so that the hands or feet are attached to the body like stumps. In June 1961 a lawyer in Hamburg, Germany contacted Professor Widukind Lenz at the Children's Hospital at Hamburg University. He said that both his wife and sister had given birth to babies with shrunken arms and theorized that something in his town was responsible for the defects. Lenz investigated and quickly learned of other reported cases of similar defects. He interviewed the mothers and by November found a common thread. In almost twenty cases the mothers had taken Contergan.

Lenz reported the results to Chemie Grunenthal, which withdrew Contergan from the market. RMI reported this news to Dr. Kelsey and withdrew the new drug application. From criticizing Kelsey for "foot-dragging," the company now had cause to thank her for keeping from the market a drug that had caused over 3,000 deformities in Germany. But that was not the end of the story.

RMI had continued to conduct clinical investigations while the application was still pending. As part of the process the company had given thalidomide to over 800 doctors in teaching hospitals throughout the country. It claimed this was legitimate research aimed at evaluating the drug's safety and effectiveness in hospital conditions.

The FDA argued that it was an illegal pre-marketing program. RMI's detail men—the force that introduced new drugs to hospitals and pharmacists—had been told to "contact teaching hospitals . . . for the purpose of selling them on Kevadon." "Detailing and selling Kevadon to the doctor" topped the list as a minimum goal for the studies.

The FDA pressed hard for a criminal prosecution. The Justice Department declined, citing insufficient evidence to bring a criminal case. But the company faced a number of civil suits from mothers who had given birth to deformed children and said they'd received the drug as part of a hospital program. RMI retained Davis Polk and Judge Walsh and I handled the defense. I was in charge of defending the company's witnesses in their depositions and locating and preparing expert witnesses.

Initially everyone felt that the suits would be very defensible. Prior to thalidomide there had never been a drug that was completely safe for the mother, but crossed the placental barrier and injured the fetus. In all known cases situations that could harm the fetus, as in the case of German measles, also harmed the mother. That caused the assumption that if the drug were safe for women, as it clearly was, it would be safe for the fetus as well. This assumption was so strong that it had never been part of the testing protocols to test a new drug in pregnant animals.

Doctors and druggists, therefore, tended to give the company a pass. The tenth annual International Congress of Pediatrics that met in Lisbon, Portugal—soon after the discovery of the birth defects—included leading doctors in teratology, the field of malformations; they issued a statement concluding that "the tragedy of thalidomide, the drug responsible for the births of thousands of malformed children, could not have been avoided." Leading pharmacologists reported, after a conference in 1963, that they "could not see how, in the light of present knowledge, [the thalidomide] tragedy could have been predicted." Earlier, a leading pharmacologist wrote in *Obstetrics and Gynecology* that given "careful testing by the manufacturers" and a lack of tipoffs in the drug's structure, "It was totally unexpected that thalidomide might produce such monstrously malformed infants."

While it believed it had a sound defense, RMI decided it would try to settle any case in which it believed that women who were part of a clinical testing program in the United States had taken thalidomide during the key ten-day period in the first trimester, when limb formation was occurring, and the child had the basic symptoms of phocomelia. There were very few of those, as it turned out. There were others who clearly did not meet that standard: the injuries were not typical thalidomide injuries and the company did not believe the women had been given the drug. It decided to take those cases to trial.

The first case changed their minds.

During a state court trial in Los Angeles, handled by local trial counsel selected by RMI's insurers, Shirley McCarrick claimed to have received the drug on October 10, 1961, from Dr. Thomas Sullivan, a staff doctor at a UCLA hospital. Dr. Sullivan categorically denied ever giving her the drug. He was not a clinical investigator; he testified that he had never had any thalidomide in his possession and was not even aware of the existence of the drug in October 1961.

Mrs. McCarrick could not describe the tablet she said Dr. Sullivan had given her when she was deposed less than a year later. However, at the trial in 1971 she had recovered her memory. She testified that Dr. Sullivan must have wanted her to have a boy because he had given her a blue pill with a concentric circle around it and the letter M. By then there had been numerous public descriptions of the pill used in the hospital program. Indeed, President Kennedy had described the pill on national television and urged viewers to look in their medicine cabinets and destroy pills matching that description.

Her baby's injuries were not phocomelia. She had a shortened left leg, resulting from a missing fibula. Several experts, including Dr. Lenz, testified that this was congenital, and could not have been caused by thalidomide ingestion. And the date McCarrick said she took the pill was several weeks past the time when limb development in the fetus had been completed; anything she took on or after that day could not have affected her baby's leg.

The evidence was clear, but the first sign of trouble came when the jury had been out only a few minutes. It asked in a note, "What is the net worth of the defendant?"

The jury eventually brought in a verdict of $2 million—$1 million in compensatory damages and $1 million in punitive damages. Two jurors said later they did not believe the mother took thalidomide, but voted for the verdict anyway. The case was settled for a lesser amount while on appeal, but the message was clear: if Richardson-Merrell could not win a case where the mother clearly had not taken the drug, they had better settle the rest—and they did.

More thalidomide cases emerged from Canada. The drug had been approved there and was marketed by an RMI subsidiary for several months. A total of 122 thalidomide defective births resulted. In 1973 a group of twenty-six mothers from Quebec, who had taken the drug and had phocomelia children, sued RMI in federal court in New Jersey. They brought the suit there because Quebec had a one-year statute of limitations that was not tolled for minors, whereas New Jersey had a two-year statute of limitations that was tolled for minors until they were twenty-four.

Defending RMI in this case meant advocating for the statute of limitations in Quebec. I represented the company, together with a New Jersey lawyer named Pete Perretti from Riker Danzig. We moved to dismiss on the grounds that the Quebec statute barred the cases. The district judge denied the motion, holding that the New Jersey statute applied.[15] The Third Circuit reversed on appeal, holding that New Jersey did not have a sufficient interest in the cases. It held that the Quebec statute applied and dismissed the New Jersey cases.[16]

The company then authorized us to settle the cases. We retained Quebec counsel and worked with the mothers and their representatives. They were led by Maurice "Rocket" Richard, the legendary former star of the Montreal Canadians hockey

Denver Stable owner
Mark Loewe trainer
June 20, 1989
Mellow Wisdom 2nd

Purse $6,500
STARLIGHT EXP
The Meadowlands

William Fahy driver
Pace 1 mile
Time 1:56:1
Snowhawk 3rd

Trophy Presented By Janet Fiske

team and an idol in Quebec. As a life-long hockey player, working with Richard was a great thrill. Over the next year we negotiated settlements that were fair to both the mothers and the company.

Pete Perretti and I became close friends and worked together on several other cases after that. In 1989 he was appointed Attorney General of New Jersey by Governor Kean to fill a vacancy caused by the resignation of the incumbent. One of the perks of his office was the use of a state box at the Meadowlands, and in June of that year he invited us to the trotting races. The highlight of the evening was his arranging for Janet to present the trophy to the winner of the third race—Starlight Express.

In retrospect RMI did the right thing in a bad situation. The horrible birth defects caused by thalidomide are a cautionary tale about drug testing, and Dr. Kelsey was a genuine hero to American mothers of that era for slowing down its application for approval.

CHAPTER 13

Other Cases and Personalities

JOHN JENRETTE

What I've always liked about being a lawyer, and especially a litigator, is the job's capacity to bring me into contact with the unexpected. You meet rogues and pillars of the bar and both may wind up your friends in the long run. You meet future headline makers whose headlines, when they make them, cause your jaw to drop. And, of course, each case has its own components—a combination of ingredients requiring you to become an expert on the run and learn things you never dreamed of learning—which is why practicing law keeps being fun.

My fifteen years at Davis Polk after returning from the U.S. Attorney's Office featured several other cases that are worth remembering for both their contacts and challenges.

In 1974 a plaintiff's lawyer in South Carolina named John Jenrette brought a class action suit on behalf of six tobacco farmers against eleven tobacco companies—charging them with fixing prices at tobacco auctions. He announced his campaign for Congress on the courthouse steps at the same time he announced the suit.

I represented R.J. Reynolds and, together with Murray Bring of Arnold & Porter who represented Philip Morris, served as co-lead counsel for the entire group. Each company had a large New York or Washington firm as its regular counsel and brought in a South Carolina firm as local counsel. We decided to attack the class action status of the suit. This took Murray and me throughout South Carolina to take depositions from the warehousemen who stored the tobacco and the auctioneers they employed at eleven different auction sites. Judge Robert Chapman, who was assigned to the case, presided over those depositions.

Days of depositions often ended with dinner and drinks with our South Carolina counterparts, and they were good companions. We learned a lot about South Carolina law practice and one caveat; many lawyers aspired to a federal court appointment such as Judge Chapman's for, among other reasons, the fact that at that time judges made more money.

We learned a lot about tobacco auctions, too. The depositions showed that the prices at the auctions varied from area to area, from day to day and from grade to grade, increasing as the season progressed and the quality of tobacco leaves improved. The tobacco companies bought a wide range of grades. Some did not bid at all on certain grades or withdrew after purchasing a specific quantity.[17]

In June of 1975 we argued the class action motion in Florence, South Carolina. I divided the argument with Murray, and it lasted all morning. The lawyers then moved on to Myrtle Beach for an afternoon at the beach followed by a long and memorable party with our South Carolina friends.

Judge Chapman ruled for the defense. He said that because of the predominance of the individual issues on injury and damages over the common issue of violation, the case was unmanageable as a class action.[18] Jenrette appealed to the Fourth Circuit, where Judge Chapman's decision was reversed in a two-to-one opinion written by Judge Charles Wyzanski, a visiting judge from Massachusetts.[19] Later, the Fourth Circuit judges agreed that important Fourth Circuit law should not be made by a judge from Massachusetts. They heard the case *en banc* and reinstated Judge Chapman's decision.[20] That, for all practical purposes, ended the case with a victory for the companies.

Jenrette, meanwhile, was one of those future headline makers who make your jaw drop. He was elected to Congress as the case proceeded and was reelected twice. In his third term, in 1980, he was convicted of bribe-taking in the Abscam scandal and served thirteen months in prison. His wife Rita, from whom he was divorced in 1981, appeared nude in *Playboy* the same year and revealed that they had made love behind a column on the steps of the Capitol during a break in an all-night legislative session. Appropriately, this escapade gave rise to the comedy group that called itself Capitol Steps.

CHOLESTEROL DRUG CASES

Earlier, at the same time it was dealing with thalidomide, Richardson-Merrell faced a much bigger problem in connection with its drug MER/29. This was a cholesterol-reducing drug the company touted as "the first safe agent to inhibit body-producing cholesterol," but later withdrew from the market after acknowledging it caused side effects including cataracts.

In April 1963 a grand jury in Washington, D.C. indicted RMI and three of its executives for having falsified scientific data in its 1959 new drug application. Judge Walsh persuaded the district judge to accept pleas of *nolo contendere*, which precluded use of the criminal plea in what had grown by then to be hundreds of civil suits around the country. The suits were based on the undisclosed side effects.

The *nolo* pleas brought the company a light $80,000 fine and probation for the three executives. Dick Nolan and I worked extensively with Judge Walsh on the civil cases, interviewing witnesses, taking and defending depositions and lining up expert witnesses. Virtually all of the cases were settled. A few went to trial, conducted by Walsh and Nolan, resulting in plaintiffs' verdicts but not significant damages.

GASTON SHUMATE

Fast forward back to the 1970's, when I handled a case that in some ways forecast the complex and frenetic Wall Street trading atmosphere that emerged decades later.

In 1973 Gaston Shumate, a Texas stockbroker, brought suit in Dallas against the New York Stock Exchange (NYSE), the American Stock Exchange, and the National Association of Securities Dealers (NASD). Shumate was a member of the NASD, but not of the New York or American Exchanges, and did his buying and selling in the over-the-counter market. Stocks that were not listed on either exchange accounted for most of the trading in the over-the-counter market. One segment of the market, however, consisted of trades outside of the exchanges of stocks that were listed on one of them. This was called "the third market." In 1967 to facilitate trading in the over-the-counter market, the NASD constructed a system called the National Association of Securities Dealers Automated Quotation System, or NASDAQ. Both the NYSE and the American Exchange objected to including listed stocks, and NASDAQ opened operations without them. Several months later, however, they were added.

Shumate's suit alleged that the defendants had violated the Sherman Act by engaging in two separate conspiracies: to exclude securities listed on the two exchanges from the NASDAQ at its inception, and to ignore such securities after they were included.

Bill Jackson of Milbank Tweed represented the NYSE. He was the son of Robert Jackson, FDR's Attorney General, Supreme Court justice and Nuremberg prosecutor. Bob Bicks of Breed Abbott and Morgan represented the NASD. He had headed the Justice Department's Antitrust Division and brought the electrical equipment price-fixing indictments. I represented the American Stock Exchange. We each retained local counsel in Dallas.

In the fall of 1973 the cases went to trial before Judge Robert M. Hill and a Texas jury. Shumate rested his case after five days and we moved for a directed verdict.

The Texas lawyers had handled everything before the jury, but Bill, Bob and I argued the motions to dismiss. On a Monday morning following the arguments on Friday, with the jury waiting in the jury room, Judge Hill granted the motion and dismissed the case. He ruled that Shumate had proved the first conspiracy but not the second, and—in any case—had failed to show he was injured by either one. The Fifth Circuit affirmed his decision.[21]

MORRIS HARRELL

I got to know Morris Harrell during this case. He was a giant of the Texas bar who had been retained by the NYSE and was lead counsel at the trial. Over the course of his career he was President of the Texas bar, President of the American Bar Association and President of the American College of Trial Lawyers, the last an organization in which I was active. Judges and lawyers all around the country both respected and liked him—not always a given—and he was clearly the lawyer of choice for any out-of-state lawyer who needed someone in Dallas. He had the great lawyer's gift for metaphor; once I asked him what he thought about another Texas lawyer and he said, "Let's just say there's more feathers than chicken there." I attended a College of Trial Lawyers' meeting during his presidency that he ended by announcing the next day's golf and tennis schedule. Morris—heavy and unathletic—then added, "As for me and Rusty (his wife), we're going to do nothing, and we're not even going to start doing that until 10 o'clock."

In the early 1970's I had two cases in which I represented companies that had hired a star salesman away from a competitor. In each case, the salesman had a no-compete clause in his contract, and his former employer sued to enjoin him from working for my client. Both cases alleged a violation of the no-compete clause and misappropriation of trade secrets in the form of customer lists.

Southern District Judge Harold R. Tyler Jr. heard both cases, which were not connected. I argued against motions for preliminary injunctions in both and in each case, after an evidentiary hearing, he denied them, ruling that the restrictions of the non-compete clause were unenforceable, and that the names of customers were not a trade secret.

In the process, I did more than just win two cases. Neither Judge Tyler nor I knew it at the time, but my appearances before him laid the groundwork for much bigger things to come.

SECTION V

—⁓—

UNITED STATES ATTORNEY FOR THE SOUTHERN DISTRICT OF NEW YORK, 1976–1980

IN EARLY 1975, in the aftermath of Watergate, the Department of Justice was in disarray. John Mitchell, Richard Nixon's first Attorney General, had been convicted of obstruction of justice and perjury in connection with the Watergate break-ins. Richard Kleindienst, who had followed him before the scandal broke, also became embroiled in Watergate and resigned after less than a year in office; he later pleaded guilty to perjury for testimony given during his confirmation hearings. His successor, Elliot Richardson, had served for only a year when he refused Nixon's order to fire Archibald Cox, the Watergate Special Prosecutor, who had enraged Nixon by subpoenaing the White House tapes. Nixon fired Richardson in the infamous "Saturday Night Massacre" and, after a period of time during which Robert Bork served as acting Attorney General, named William Saxbe, a senator from Ohio, as the third attorney general in three years and the fourth of his imperiled administration.

In the wake of Nixon's resignation, President Ford in February 1975 made a bold move to restore credibility to the Justice Department. Saxbe resigned to become Ambassador to India and Ford appointed Edward H. Levi, President of the University of Chicago and former Dean of the Chicago Law School, as Attorney General. It was a superb choice; Levi had a widespread reputation for integrity, non-partisanship and scholarship.

Levi made an equally compelling move. He had spent almost all of his forty-year career at the University of Chicago and had little experience in law enforcement or civil litigation. Recognizing this, he persuaded Judge Tyler, who had been an AUSA under Judge Lumbard and later the first head of the Civil Rights Division, to resign from the federal bench and become Deputy Attorney General—to essentially run the day-to-day operations of the Justice Department.

Judge Tyler called me soon after his appointment was announced in March. He hadn't been sworn in and I went to see him in his chambers. He said he was looking to fill several positions at the DOJ. He complimented my performances when I'd appeared before him and said he knew my history in the U.S. Attorney's Office. He also said he had received good reviews from people with whom he had checked.

He asked if I would be interested in becoming the Assistant Attorney General in charge of the Criminal Division. It was a thrilling offer. I was forty-four and the pull of public service was strong. There were four assistant attorneys general; the other divisions were Civil, Civil Rights, and Lands. All were presidential appointees and would report to him.

I told him I was very interested. But after several meetings in Washington with him and with Attorney General Levi, Tyler told me that Levi had his eye on Dick Thornburgh, the U.S. Attorney in Pittsburgh, and while I was Tyler's choice the outcome wasn't certain.

Other factors entered the equation. Linda was in her first year at the University of North Carolina at Greensboro. Bob was sixteen and attending Darien High School and Sue, fourteen, was at Middlesex Junior High in Darien. It would not have affected Linda that much, but it would have been very difficult for the two young ones to move to a new setting in Washington. After much thought I decided to take myself out of the running. This turned out to be for the best.

In September when *The New York Times* reported that Paul Curran, the U.S. Attorney for the Southern District of New York announced his resignation I immediately called Judge Tyler in Washington. "Everything I told you about why I took myself out of the running for the head of the Criminal Division has no application to this job," I said. "I really would be interested in it."

He said, "Don't worry, I have already given your name to the FBI for the background check."

For the next two weeks friends kept calling to say the FBI was asking questions about me. Then, suddenly, the inquiries stopped. Curran and I were friends—we had been fellow AUSAs together under Hazard Gillespie—and I called to ask if he knew what was going on. He said that Jacob Javits, New York's senior Senator and a Republican, was furious that Tyler had launched the FBI checks without consulting him. "You don't pick U.S. attorneys; I do," he told Tyler. What was worse, Javits had his own candidate, a good lawyer and effective prosecutor who had been an AUSA under Paul Williams. So, everything was up in the air. Javits and the selection committee for New York's other senator, Republican James Buckley, both interviewed me. Ironically, I got an important boost from Judge Bruce Bromley, who twenty years earlier had advised me not to go from Davis Polk to the U.S. Attorney's Office. Judge Bromley was influential in New York City Republican circles, and he took me to see Vincent Albano, the New York County Republican leader where, through a lot of cigar smoke, he vouched for my credentials. Then I waited.

As I waited I reflected on the role politics would play in the selection process. I was a registered Republican, but had never been active in party politics. I had never contributed to either Javits or Buckley and, in fact, living in Connecticut, had never voted for them. Fortunately it turned out that Judge Tyler's advocacy prevailed over any political considerations.

In late November I heard that things were moving towards a final resolution. Then on December 9 I was in Cincinnati in a meeting at the William S. Merrell Company, a subsidiary of Richardson-Merrell, when the general counsel's secretary came in and handed me a note.

"Please call your secretary immediately," it said. "You have an important phone call to make."

I called her. She said I should call Senator Javits. I called him and he said, "Bob, I have decided that you will be the next United States Attorney."

It was late February before President Ford nominated me. After a perfunctory fifteen-minute appearance before the Senate Judiciary Committee and a short wait for Senate confirmation, I was sworn in by Chief Judge David Edelstein on March 1, 1976.

CHAPTER 14

The Office and the Team

THE SOUTHERN DISTRICT of New York has always had a special place in the hearts of the U.S. Attorneys who served there. Henry L. Stimson had been U.S. Secretary of War under Presidents Taft and both Roosevelts and Secretary of State under Hoover, but the U.S. Attorney for the Southern District, where he served from 1906 to 1909, topped his list of public service jobs. It "has always been my first love," he said in 1933, according to Elting Morison's 2003 biography. "I felt then, and I still feel that there is no other public office . . . which makes such a direct and inspiring call upon the conscience and professional zeal of a high-minded lawyer as that office, or in which courageous effort and steady poise bring such a sense of satisfaction of the occupant."

Now I was the occupant, and I hoped to emulate Stimson's formula of courage and poise.

Before I was sworn in I had been meeting with the executive staff, reviewing applications for AUSA positions. My interim predecessor, Tom Cahill, had left vacancies open for me to fill. Among other things I wanted to increase the number of women on the staff, since of the approximately ninety lawyers in the office only eight—less than 10 percent—were women. My initial reaction was that I would initiate a targeted program to increase the number of women. However, as I started reviewing the pending applications, it became very clear that no such program would be needed; all we had to do was make hiring decisions on the merits and the imbalances would take care of themselves.

Once I was official my own executive staff was a top priority. Outside of the people who worked directly with me as chief, executive and administrative assistants, the big jobs were chiefs of the Criminal and Civil Divisions.

The Southern District covered ten counties—Manhattan and the Bronx in New York City and Westchester, Sullivan, Rockland, Orange, Putnam, Dutchess, Columbia and Greene counties in what is loosely referred to as "upstate." The Criminal Division investigated and prosecuted all federal crimes in the district and was organized into General Crimes (where the new AUSAs started), Major Crimes, Official Corruption, Narcotics and Business Frauds. Each had its own chief. The Civil Division represented the government in tax cases and in the defense of government agencies in cases that ranged from mail truck accidents to misconduct of federal officials to challenges to important federal programs. It also conducted affirmative litigation in the areas of civil rights and environmental compliance, each of which had its own unit and its own chief.

The United States Attorney's Office for the Southern District of New York since the Lumbard days has been a seamless institution in two important respects. Because the AUSA hiring is entirely non-political and done totally on the merits, each new U.S. Attorney inherits and retains a cadre of highly qualified AUSAs, needing only to make his or her own appointments to the key executive positions. And in doing that it is common—indeed customary—for a new U.S. Attorney to reach back to the alumni of one or more predecessor U.S. Attorneys, regardless of their political persuasion. In my case Taggart Adams was doing a fine job as Chief of the Civil Division and he agreed to stay on.[22] Elkan Abramowitz, a highly respected white collar criminal defense lawyer with superb judgment and equally superb personal skills, was an easy choice to head the Criminal Division. For Chief Assistant I selected Dan Murdock, a partner at Donovan Leisure. He, like Abramowitz, had been an AUSA under Bob Morgenthau. Joe Jaffe switched from Criminal Division Assistant to become Administrative Assistant. When he left in 1977 to become district attorney of Sullivan County, he was replaced by John Kenney, another experienced Criminal Division assistant who, while in that position, successfully prosecuted the international financier Michele Sindona and several bank officials for causing the collapse of the Franklin National Bank.

John's responsibilities included dealing with the media. The AUSAs understood that any media inquiry was to be referred to him. It was important to me that there be no "off the record" leaks of information relating to our investigations and the system worked well.

They were all great choices. They each did a superb job and the Office was extremely fortunate to have them. During my term Elkan was succeeded by Fred Hafetz and John Doyle (another Morgenthau AUSA). Tag was succeeded by Frank Wohl and Naomi Reice Buchwald, who was the first woman to be appointed chief of either division.[23] And they all hit the ground running; we never skipped a beat.

But the appointment that had the most long-term impact was that of executive assistant: I was able to persuade Bill Tendy to leave his position as head of the New York State Attorney General's Task Force on Organized Crime and come back to the office where he had served before. He was an extraordinary person who became a legend in the United States Attorney's Office and throughout law enforcement.

BILL TENDY

Bill was born in Brooklyn in 1915. His father died three years later and his mother took him to Ireland. She could not support them both, so she left him in the care of relatives and returned to the United States. They, too, were poor and when authorities found him wandering and living in the streets he was placed in St. Michael's Orphanage where he was educated by nuns and remained for four years before returning to this country.

Seven years later he left high school to help support his family as a messenger for Consolidated Edison. He took night classes to complete high school at the age of twenty-seven and a year later, in 1943, he entered the army and became an infantry lieutenant. Discharged in 1946 he returned to Consolidated Edison and studied law at Fordham, earning his degree in 1949. He practiced law in East Harlem until his appointment in 1957 at age 42 as an AUSA in the Southern District.[24]

He started two weeks after I did, and we worked closely together when he headed the Narcotics Unit and I headed the Organized Crime Unit. After I returned to Davis Polk in 1961, he stayed on for another ten years under Bob Morgenthau and successfully prosecuted a number of major narcotics violators and organized crime figures. He received the Attorney General's Award for Meritorious Service in 1970 and the AUSAs who worked with him considered him a friend and mentor. To Congressman Claude Pepper, then chair of the House Select Committee on Crime, he was "the ablest, the best informed, most effective narcotics prosecutor in the United States."

Returning to the U.S. Attorney's Office, Bill had a wealth of "street smarts" and rapport with the Drug Enforcement Administrtation (DEA) agents and other law enforcement agencies, including the New York City Police. He talked their language; he thought like they did; and they loved working with him. The former law firm associates and federal judge law clerks who worked with him as AUSAs took a little time to embrace his style, but when they did they were all in. One of them, Richard Mescon, who came to the Office from a clerkship with Judge Edelstein, recalled an interrogation in which Tendy demonstrated his unique talents.

Joey DiPalermo, an aging don and a fixture in the drug trade, was the defendant. The issue was who had said what during a recorded conversation in an Elizabeth Street social club about attempts to bribe a federal official. Surveillance agents placed DiPalermo in the building, but it was difficult to identify the voices of the people speaking on the tape and, therefore, to prove that the defendant had participated in the conversation. One portion of the tape, however, was clear as a bell—an exchange about two federal judges: Milton Pollack, who was referred to as "Polly," and Edward Weinfeld. After some back and forth about which of the two had been seen in the neighborhood, a commanding voice interrupted saying, "It wasn't Polly, it was Weinfeld. I used to see him walk his dog every day." When another voice suggested the first might be mistaken, the first again intruded, "I know Weinfeld. I was the foist guy he sentenced when he became a judge."

Court records showed that the DiPalermo wasn't the first defendant Weinfeld had sentenced, but if he had said that he was implicated in the bribe investigation.

Tendy sat down to talk with DiPalermo after his arrest. There were police detectives and federal agents and AUSAs in the room, but the conversation was entirely between these two seasoned veterans of the criminal justice system. Tendy started by talking about a 1917 "flop" the defendant had taken for gambling and the two shared a laugh. He continued to go over the rap sheet, touching on the high points, until he got to a 1950 drug conviction.

"Who was the judge in that case?" Tendy asked.

"Judge Weinfeld," said the defendant.

"No way. He couldn't have been on the bench that long."

"It was too Weinfeld," said the defendant, raising his voice. "You know, I was the foist guy he sentenced when he became a judge."

A motion to suppress was denied. The tape and the statement were admitted, Di-Palermo was tied to yet another in a long list of crimes, and Bill Tendy's considerable legend continued to grow. Bill became Chief Assistant after Dan Murdock left[25] and stayed in the Office for another ten years, serving under John Martin and Rudy Giuliani until his death in 1986.[26]

With Bill Tendy

The Postmaster General, A Bullet-Proof Vest, My DEA Beetle, How I Took Up Running, and My Tennis Game from *Guys and Dolls*

DESPITE MY GOOD fortune in assembling a first-class staff, I knew when I went to the United States Attorney's Office there would be moments of high stress. I was ready for that, but believed that at least I would no longer have to deal with unhappy clients. I quickly learned otherwise.

In my second week an article appeared on the front page of the *New York Law Journal* about a case our Civil Division had successfully defended. The plaintiff was a businessman who had sued the U.S. Postal Service, claiming that the Post Office had lost documents he had sent to a prospective customer and that, as a result, he had lost a business transaction worth hundreds of millions of dollars. The district judge had dismissed the complaint, accepting the government's affirmative defense that consequential damages were not available on this type of claim. The court went on to say, the article reported, that it was therefore unnecessary to reach the government's other affirmative defense—that anyone who entrusted a valuable document to the U.S. Postal Service was guilty of contributory negligence.

My phone rang about 2:00 p.m. the afternoon the article appeared. The Postmaster General—my client—was on the line, and he was angry. He wanted to know—his exact words—"What the hell is going on up there?" I disclaimed responsibility, explaining that I had only been there for two weeks.

Also, in my second week, I passed a newsstand on my way to work and the front page of the *Daily News* jumped out at me: "Contract Out on Special Prosecutor." I bought the paper and read that the mob had offered $300,000 to anyone who would kill the New York City Special Narcotics Prosecutor, Sterling Johnson. As it happened, I was having lunch with him that day.

The U.S. Attorney's Office was at 1 St. Andrew's Plaza, and when I met Sterling in the courtyard to walk to the restaurant I noticed he looked different. Muscular and heavy-set, he appeared even larger than usual. I commented, and he told me he was wearing a bullet-proof vest.

That was unnerving enough, but then we reached the restaurant he had picked. It was long and narrow. He walked all the way to the back and took the seat closest to the wall facing the door, leaving me sitting with my back to the door. It was an uneasy hour—we did not linger over coffee—and another sharp reminder of how different life was going to be at 1 St. Andrew's Plaza.

Not long after that, I received a call from John Fallon, Regional Administrator of the DEA in New York. "Bob," he said, "we have just forfeited and taken ownership of two brand new cars that were seized in a drug raid. One is a Mercedes-Benz 450 SEL 6.9, and the other is a Volkswagen Beetle. One is for me, and one is for you. Guess which one you are getting?"[27]

And so I started a four-year span of driving to and from the office in a souped-up, royal blue, Volkswagen Beetle. It was a great deal—I had free parking in the U.S. Court-house garage. I would leave home ahead of the traffic a little after 6:00 a.m. and be in the office by 7:15 a.m. At night, unless I was staying in the apartment I rented in the city—which I did once or twice a week—I would leave at 7:00 p.m. when the traffic had thinned and get home around 8:30 p.m.

Soon after I started doing this, I arrived at the office one morning feeling sick and decided to return home. I was on the Hutchinson River Parkway when a state trooper pulled me over for speeding. He asked for my license and registration. I handed them over, but the registration was not in my name. It said something like, "Peter Franklin, Bronx, NY." I apologized for speeding and explained that I felt sick and wanted to get home as quickly as possible. I also explained that the registration was not in my name because it was a DEA undercover car, and the DEA had given it to me to drive because I was the United States Attorney for the Southern District of New York.

The trooper wasn't buying this. I could hear him as he called the information including the name on the registration and my name into his headquarters: "Hey Pete, I got this guy here I stopped for speeding. He says he was speeding because he is sick and wants to get home and get this . . ."—he was laughing at this point—". . . he says it is a DEA undercover car and get this . . ."—laughing even harder—". . . he says he is the U.S. Attorney for the Southern District of New York."

There was a two or three minute pause while headquarters checked the information. Then I heard the trooper say with a tone of incredulity, "He is?" When he came back to the car he said, "Sorry, sir. Have a good day and I hope you feel better soon."

The city apartment was downtown near New York University. I rented it before I was sworn in because I felt the U.S. Attorney for the Southern District needed a residence in New York, and I knew there would be long nights at the office when I couldn't conveniently drive home. At first it was just a place to sleep. But as time went on it became part of a new regimen in my life: I took up running.

I had bicycled and played and coached ice hockey for many years, but I soon found that running was great exercise as well, with no equipment needed. It was also a great way to relieve stress. I took it up in 1978 during my third year. I would wake up early in the morning and run five or six laps around Washington Square Park—three to three-and-a-half miles—then shower, dress and head to the office.

Later, during a long and hard-fought racketeering trial when I was in the court-room all day long, I switched to running at night. I would return to the office after court, have a sandwich delivered, and work until around ten. Then I would go to the University Place studio, do my five or six laps around the park, have a beer and go to bed around eleven. That allowed me to sleep soundly and get to the office by six to finish my trial preparations for the day. In addition to reducing stress I found that exercise was a great asset during long trials. Such trials are, to a significant extent, endurance con-tests—physical stamina is essential to the ability to keep performing at a high level over a prolonged period. Running every day helped me do that.

Naturally the minute they learned I was running around Washington Square Park, several of my AUSAs wanted to up the ante. Some of them were training to run the New York Marathon and dropped broad hints, if not outright challenges, that I might want to try it. I said I'd think about it.

In the meantime, however, I was keeping up my tennis game. I had started when I was a kid and still enjoyed it, never having been good enough at golf to go in that direction. Then in 1976 a game that started at the Second Circuit Judicial Conference in Buck Hill Falls, Pennsylvania turned into a long-running affair to match the "oldest established permanent floating crap game" in the musical *Guys and Dolls*.

It started when three of my AUSAs—all of whom had clerked for federal judges—and I decided to play a game of doubles at the Poconos resort where the conference was being held. It only had two courts, the other was occupied, and we were at two-one in the first set when we heard loud voices coming down the hill. They be-longed to two women we recognized as judges' wives, and it seemed they were meant for us. "How long do you think they've been playing?" one voice asked. The other replied, "I don't know, but I hope they finish soon." They were clearly planning to play doubles with their husbands. We got the message, told them we were just finishing, and left the court.

That night at dinner the four of us decided to resume our game when we got back to New York. So, the next week we looked around and discovered the Wall Street Racquet Club. Not quite as auspicious as its name, it was several courts laid end-to-end under a bubble on an East River pier at the end of Wall Street. We started playing there every Tuesday at seven in the morning, and soon learned that in the cold of winter its hard rubber surface made all our serves invincible. The game continued beyond our time at the U.S. Attorney's Office. It survived the demise of the Wall Street Racquet Club, went through several other venues, and continues to this day at Sutton South on East 59th Street with a rotating cast of former AUSAs.

That's why we borrowed from *Guys and Dolls* and called it "the oldest established permanent floating tennis game in New York." But other tennis players tell me their games are equally venerable, and even more so—a tribute to a game that men and women can enjoy long past their Grand Slam capabilities.

CHAPTER 16

Hands-On, Open-Minded, Tested by Washington

I THINK IT IS FAIR TO SAY I was a "hands-on" United States Attorney. I wanted to know as much as I could about what was going on and to be involved if I could be productive without undercutting the division chiefs and unit heads. I also wanted to let the assistants know I cared about what they were doing and was following their work.

To that end I visited their offices, often at night and on weekends, to talk and learn about their cases. If an AUSA won a motion or a trial or an appeal I would stop by, call or send a congratulatory note. If they lost, I would try to cheer them up. I used my own long-ago experience in the Grunewald case to tell them that they could learn the most from the cases they lost. I would try to be in the courtroom for every assistant's opening statement, at his or her first trial and I often went to the Court of Appeals to hear arguments.

Following the practice established by my predecessors, I made sure that each new AUSA's swearing in was a meaningful experience. All of the assistants would gather in the library at 9 a.m. After making a short speech about the new AUSA's background before coming to the office, I would administer the oath of office with the new AUSA's family standing alongside. Following that brief ceremony, the new AUSA would be greeted and welcomed by the entire group.

REVIEW OF INDICTMENT DECISIONS

I kept a close eye on criminal cases to assess whether investigations were progressing or if we should be using our resources elsewhere.

From the outset I felt that any person or entity under investigation should be able to have any decision to indict reviewed at higher levels in the Office including, as the final appeal, by me. This was important for two reasons. Fairness dictated that an individual or entity should be able to present his or her case all the way to the top before being indicted, and such a review might reveal any post-indictment surprises that could lead to an acquittal.

These review sessions were very much a two-way street. To the extent the suspect made a case against an indictment, we were avoiding doing an injustice. We were also avoiding losing a case that should not have been brought. When we decided to go ahead, as we did in the overwhelming majority of cases, we often learned facts that enabled us to adjust our approach and present our case more effectively.

I was still in my first month as U.S. Attorney when lawyers for two accountants at a major accounting firm appealed to me. The firm had been the auditors for a large company that had gone bankrupt, with large losses to its shareholders and creditors. Two assistants in the Criminal Division had conducted a lengthy investigation with the assistance of a lawyer loaned to us by the SEC and were recommending the accountants be indicted. The charges would allege that there had been significant "red flags" of falsity in the financial statements of the company to which they had been willfully blind. Tom Edwards, who remained Chief of the Criminal Division while Elkan Abramowitz was being vetted by the FBI, was strongly supporting their recommendations.

The accountants' lawyers argued to me that the facts constituting the "red flags" were either unknown to their clients or, if they were, were insufficient to make a case of willful blindness. When I asked if their clients would come in and tell their story, they said the AUSAs had told them they would have to do it in the grand jury. The lawyers were not going to allow them to do that. It would be close to malpractice, they said, to allow their clients to be questioned without the benefit of counsel by a hostile prosecutor who wanted to indict them.

The evidence told me this was a close case. I did not want to indict them and find out for the first time at trial what they had to say. So, I proposed to the lawyers that they bring their clients in for the equivalent of a civil deposition. They would be questioned by the AUSAs under oath, but the lawyers could be present and at the end could ask questions to elicit any information they wanted us to have that had not come out during the AUSA questioning. The transcript would then be given to the grand jury and made part of its proceedings.

This was a more formal procedure than the common "Queen for a Day," in which a prospective defendant is interviewed, but not under oath, with the agreement that what he or she says can't be used by the government unless the case goes to trial—and then only to impeach the testimony. The lawyers accepted my proposal. The questioning went forward, and I read the transcripts carefully.

At the end I concluded that there was not enough evidence to establish criminal intent, and told the line prosecutors and the SEC attorney that I would not approve the indictment.

This was difficult. I had only been there for a month; the investigation had consumed much time and resources; the SEC was heavily invested in it; and a lot of momentum for an indictment had built up. But I believed it was the right thing to do. I did not want to bring an indictment that would seriously damage the careers of two accountants and that I did not think we could sustain at trial.

Stanley Sporkin, Director of the Enforcement Division of the SEC, reacted angrily. He said to me, "We are going to stop lending you our people if they are just wasting their time." I mollified him—at least to an extent—by pointing out that the SEC now had the sworn testimony of the accountants for use in its investigation, when otherwise the accountants would have taken the Fifth. The AUSAs who had conducted the investigation were initially disappointed, but accepted and respected the decision—as did the Office as a whole.

It turned out to be extremely important. It demonstrated to the defense bar at the outset that I had an open-minded approach to criminal prosecutions, and it showed the AUSAs that exercising independent judgment is an important component of leadership.

MAINTAINING THE AUTHORITY OF THE SOUTHERN DISTRICT

The Southern District is often referred to as "the Mother Court" because it was the first federal district court when it was created in 1789, and it had the first United States Attorney. When he was the U.S. Attorney Judge Lumbard believed that his office should represent the government in any case brought in the Southern District. He had upheld that principle, with the support of then Attorney General Herbert Brownell, against several efforts by the Justice Department in Washington to take over certain cases. He warned me that Justice "will test every new U.S. Attorney and you need to be ready to hold your ground."

That happened early on. Our Civil Division had won a case in the District Court alleging improper conduct by some law enforcement officials on grounds of qualified immunity. A deputy assistant attorney general in the Civil Division in Washington informed Tag Adams that because of the national implications of the issue, Washington was going to handle the appeal. We pushed back and the result was a high-level meeting in Washington at which Rex Lee, the head of the Civil Division, and I presented our respective positions to the decision maker—Harold Tyler. I am sure the Civil Division thought it was not a level playing field, but we were successful. We won the right to handle the argument—and we won the appeal.

About a year later in the early days of the Carter administration, the issue came up again. Our Civil Division in the Southern District had defeated a constitutional challenge to a provision of the Public Works Employment Act of 1977 that set aside for minority businesses 10 percent of a $4 billion appropriation for the construction industry. The plaintiffs had appealed.

The case clearly had national implications and Drew Days, the Assistant Attorney General in charge of the Civil Rights Division, told us he wanted his attorneys to argue the appeal in the Second Circuit. We pushed back and, after some discussion, reached an agreement with Days. He said he would back off if I would agree to argue the appeal myself. I said yes.

I argued before a panel consisting of Judges James Oakes, who was presiding; Joseph Blumenfeld, from the District of Connecticut; and William Mehrtens, a visiting district judge from Florida. We had won at the trial level by arguing that the set-aside provision of the Public Works Employment Act was a valid exercise of congressional power because it remedied the effects of past discrimination in the construction industry. I was making the same point when Judge Mehrtens, clearly irritated, interrupted. He said, "Are you telling me that I have to lose business today because of something my grand-daddy did fifty years ago?"

Without waiting for an answer he swirled his chair around so he was facing the wall behind the bench with his back to me. I gave Judge Oakes a "what do I do now?" look and he smiled and gestured that I should continue. I made the remainder of my argument to Judges Oakes and Blumenfeld and Judge Mehrtens' back.

The decision, when it came down, was three to nothing in our favor.[28]

The plaintiffs appealed again. The Supreme Court granted *certiorari* and, with Drew Days arguing for the government, upheld the Second Circuit.

CHAPTER 17

Three More Years!
Senator Moynihan and My Full Term

I WONDERED WHEN I was appointed how long my tenure would be, and as 1976 went on it seemed likely to be short. President Ford's pardon of Richard Nixon had damaged his popularity and Jimmy Carter, chosen as the Democratic candidate that summer, seemed likely to win in the fall. It had been the practice up to then, whenever there was a change in administration, for the incoming president to replace all the United States Attorneys with appointees from his own party, so friends and professional colleagues believed I wouldn't be in office very long.

The *New York Post* pointed out the "intensely political" nature of the selection in a profile of me soon after my appointment, saying "it is customary for all U.S. Attorneys to tender their resignations to the new president."

"In Fiske's case . . . a changing of the White House guard would give him only nine months in office before he becomes a lame duck."

Carter won, as expected, and around the middle of November I began receiving calls from lawyers who all said versions of, "Bob, I am going to be the next U.S. Attorney. When can I come up and talk with you about the transition?"

After the first few calls, I began to be amused. I said, "Why don't we wait until one of you is nominated and do it then."

At the same time Carter won, Daniel Patrick Moynihan—having beaten Ramsey Clark and Bella Abzug in the Democratic primary—went on to defeat the incumbent Republican Senator James Buckley to become New York's junior Senator. Moynihan was a brilliant intellectual—a graduate of the London School of Economics who had served both in the Kennedy and Johnson administrations as an Assistant Secretary of Labor. Under Johnson he had helped formulate the policy for the "War on Poverty." He joined Nixon's White House staff in 1968, serving as his Counselor for Urban Affairs. In 1973 Nixon appointed him Ambassador to India, where he served until 1975 when President Ford appointed him Ambassador to the United Nations—the position he left when he ran for the Senate.

Moynihan had an extraordinary background in most of the areas he would be dealing with in the Senate, including economics, labor, social and foreign policy. However, he recognized from the outset that he had no background in law, and no experience in the selection of judges and United States Attorneys. So, he turned to the two lawyers who had been co-chairs of his "Republicans for Moynihan" Senate Committee. They were Leonard Garment, who had been Nixon's White House counsel, and John Trubin. He asked them to form a committee of lawyers and lay persons to recommend judge and U.S. Attorney appointees. There were four federal court districts in New York, each with an incumbent Republican U.S. Attorney appointed to a four-year term "at the pleasure of the President," meaning they can be terminated at any time. Moynihan told Garment and Trubin that he wanted to judge them on their merits instead of strictly on their politics. He said those who were doing well should be able to complete their terms.

In early January 1977 I received a call from Leonard Garment inviting me to lunch. He said the Committee had concluded I had been doing a good job, and he was prepared to recommend to Senator Moynihan that I be allowed to finish out my term—typically four years—if I would agree to leave at the end of it and allow him to pick a Democrat. I made that deal on the spot.

Moynihan Backs 3 G.O.P. Officials

The New York Times, *January 19, 1977*

The Committee and Senator Moynihan reached the same conclusion with respect to two of the other three U.S. Attorneys in New York. David Trager in the Eastern District, headquartered in Brooklyn, had eighteen months left in his term. Richard Arcara in Buffalo, the Western District headquarters, had just under two years remaining. I had more than three. To keep us on was courageous on Moynihan's part because it denied the spoils of victory to outraged Democratic politicians who could legitimately claim that without their help in delivering New York Carter would not have won the election. Moynihan, however, said it was important to place professionalism over politics in the aftermath of Watergate. Attorney General Griffin Bell supported him.

CHAPTER 18

Trials and Appeals

JUDGE LUMBARD BELIEVED trying cases and arguing appeals was an important part of leadership, and did both while he was United States Attorney. I felt the same way. In my four years, I tried three cases and argued eight appeals.

My first two appeals came in the first six months, while President Ford was still in office. Both presented issues that would affect the Office; its ongoing work in one case, and the success of an important trial and the morale of the assistants conducting it in the other. I thought it was important for me to argue both of them.

In July 1976 the Speedy Trial Act became effective, requiring that all criminal cases be tried within sixty days of arraignment. This put an enormous burden on the Office, as well as on the district judges, and created pressure to resolve cases through plea bargains.

UNITED STATES V. SANTOS-FIGUEROA

Harry Santos-Figueroa was one of three men charged with attempted armed robbery of the Bankers Trust bank on Madison Avenue earlier that year. His lawyer bargained for a sentence of ten years against the twenty-five year statutory maximum. The Office refused to agree, for one reason because Santos-Figueroa shot a bank guard during the holdup attempt. District Judge Henry Werker then entered into direct negotiations with defense counsel.

He said he would read the pre-sentence report, tell Santos-Figueroa what sentence he would impose if he pleaded guilty, and—if he agreed—that would be the sentence. We worried that if this were allowed district judges might offer lower sentences than some cases demanded to induce guilty pleas to meet the Speedy Trial deadlines. So, we filed a petition for *mandamus* to prevent Judge Werker from joining discussions regarding sentence until after a plea agreement had been reached. The defendant would have to plead guilty without knowing what the sentence would be unless it was by agreement with the government.

The Second Circuit agreed. It wrote, "the petition raised significant questions of the proper exercise of judicial power and the administration of criminal justice in the federal courts." It went on to find that Rule 11(e) of the Federal Rules of Criminal

Procedure prohibited the court from being involved in any discussion regarding sentence until after a plea.[29]

After the opinion came down I sent a bouquet of red, white and blue flowers to Judge Werker's chambers with a note that said, "May our future relations be more harmonious." They were.

UNITED STATES V. AMREP

The other early appeal involved a pre-trial ruling in a major mail fraud prosecution. It involved the sale of land and houses in a development called Rio Rancho, owned by the AMREP Corporation outside Albuquerque, New Mexico. The case was controversial—with disagreements in the Office as to whether it should be brought—and the indictment was not filed until Paul Curran's last day in office.

The case was assigned to Judge Charles Metzner, who from the outset was hostile to the prosecution—and to the individual prosecutors. Throughout the pre-trial proceedings he consistently expressed his skepticism about the case and gave the assistants handling the case, Patricia Hynes and Alan Kaufman, a very hard time. Ten days before trial he granted a defense motion to exclude three crucial pieces of evidence. This was a major setback both substantively and psychologically.

Title 18, Section 3731, allowed the government to appeal from an order entered pre-trial that excluded evidence. I argued the appeal and obtained a reversal of Judge Metzner's order.[30] Pat Hynes and Alan Kaufman tried the case and won a conviction of all the defendants.

As it turned out, the judge did us a favor. If he had excluded the evidence during trial and the defendants had been acquitted, the government would have had no recourse.

COL. MANUEL ALFONSO RODRIGUEZ

My first trial, in the fall of 1976, wasn't that much of a challenge. In fact I took some good-natured ribbing for how easy it was.

Colonel Manuel Alfonso Rodriguez, the head of the armed forces of El Salvador, had been caught in an undercover Alcohol, Tobacco and Firearms sting operation involving the illegal sale of guns to El Salvador. We had a videotape of him counting payoff money in a smoke-filled room in Mt. Kisco, New York.

The case went to the jury after just four days and they returned a quick conviction. Judge Kevin Duffy gave Rodriguez a ten-year sentence.

The next two cases weren't so easy. The trials stretched out over ten weeks in each one, but the superb managerial skills of Criminal Division Chiefs Fred Hafetz and John Doyle—and Frank Wohl and Naomi Reice Buchwald, their Civil Division counter-parts—gave me the freedom to concentrate on these complex, difficult and challenging contests, dealing at the end of each day or over the weekend with any issue any of them felt needed my attention.

CHAPTER 19

The Trial of Nicky Barnes

IN THE MID-1970'S Leroy "Nicky" Barnes was widely regarded in law enforcement circles—state and federal—as the most powerful drug dealer in New York. He was nicknamed "Mr. Untouchable" because he had been indicted four times by the Bronx and Manhattan district attorneys and acquitted every time.

On March 16, 1977, after two years of work with the DEA, the Office brought an indictment against Barnes charging that he was "the head of a loose-knit narcotics organization through which massive quantities of heroin and cocaine were distributed on the streets of New York."

Five of Barnes's top lieutenants and nine other members of the organization were indicted with him. Two experienced AUSAs in the Narcotics Unit, Tom Sear and Bob Mazur, obtained the indictment and they were to be the trial team along with a newly-appointed AUSA, Denise Cote.[31] But on Sunday, June 5, 1977, things changed.

The New York Times Magazine that day featured a cover picture of Nicky Barnes, striking an arrogant pose, with the caption "Mr. Untouchable." The subtitle was: "This is Nicky Barnes. Police Say He May Be Harlem's Biggest Drug Dealer. But Can They Prove It?"

A lengthy profile of Barnes followed in the magazine. It described an all-night operation in an anonymous apartment, with naked women cutting and packaging heroin bought from Italian suppliers and destined for Harlem and the Bronx. It estimated his drug profits at over $2 million per week, and went on to describe him as a legend on the streets "because of a spit-in-your-eye, flamboyant life style that is perceived by the street people as Barnes's way of thumbing his nose at officialdom."

The article said Barnes—according to police—had 300 new suits, 100 pairs of shoes, fifty leather coats and twenty-five hats as well as "at the very least, one Mercedes-Benz, perhaps more, and a Citroen Maserati, and is surrounded by gaggles of Thunderbirds, Lincoln Continentals and Cadillacs. At various times he has had [police report] apartments in upper Manhattan, Riverdale, Hackensack and across the Hudson in the forest of high rises in Fort Lee."

The New York Times Magazine, *June 5, 1977*

The article described a series of episodes in which he had flouted and taunted the police. One came during a trial the year before in which he was charged with "possession of hashish, a sawed-off shotgun, a .25-caliber automatic, a .32-caliber Smith & Wesson revolver, a .32-caliber Clerke revolver and a .38-caliber handgun, a collection police said they found in his upper Manhattan apartment in August 1973, along with $43,934 in small bills." During a break, according to the article, Barnes entered a washroom and encountered two narcotics detectives. He ran his hands under the water and pretended to search his pockets for a handkerchief—pulling out instead two big rolls of bills—then shook his hands dry and walked out with a grin at the detectives.

Knowing the police were tailing him, he led them on fruitless high-speed chases around Harlem and the South Bronx. As a result of his flamboyance and episodes like these, he became a folk hero in Harlem—particularly to young kids.

The article concluded with the information that Harlem's street people were skeptical about our effort—after his four New York acquittals—to put Barnes behind bars. He was still "Mr. Untouchable" to them.

I was in my office Monday morning when the phone rang. It was Attorney General Griffin Bell. He said he had just come back from a cabinet meeting where President Carter had described the article and said, "This is the most important case in the country. If we can't put someone like this away, there is something wrong with our criminal justice system."

Judge Bell told me the President had said, "I hope we have a good case," and Bell had assured him that we did. Judge Bell then said to me, "We do have a good case, don't we, Bob?"

I replied: "Well, it has its problems, but I think we'll be okay."

"I hope we're sending in the first team," he said to close the conversation.

I got the message. Later that morning I met with Tom, Bob and Dee and told them of the call. I explained that I felt obligated to come into the case and take the lead. They concurred, and we went to work preparing for a September trial.

Judge Werker drew the trial assignment. In a pre-trial conference he showed the same streak of independence with which he had entered plea negotiations in the Santos-Figueroa case. For the Barnes trial we had filed a motion asking for a sequestered jury, meaning that jurors would stay at an undisclosed hotel throughout the trial. We cited "the sordid history" of attempts to influence witnesses and jurors in big narcotic cases in the Southern District.[32]

Judge Werker granted our motion for sequestration. He then surprised everyone at the conference by announcing that in addition to being sequestered, the jury would be anonymous. Neither side would know their names or where they lived, and *voir dire* questions about their ethnic background would be prohibited. They would be known only by numbers.

A stunned silence fell over the courtroom. This was totally unprecedented; nothing like this had ever been done anywhere. The defense lawyers went ballistic, crying to be heard and to be permitted to file briefs.

Judge Werker was unmoved. "Sit down, I have ruled," he said. He was clearly sending a message to the fifteen defense lawyers that he was in charge; this was a tight ship; and he was not going to tolerate disruptions.

I had only a few seconds to decide what to do. I could see instantly that this would be a huge appellate issue if we won a conviction. One part of me said I should join the defense lawyers in asking for time to analyze and brief the issue. Another part of me said that if I did that, Judge Werker would tell me to sit down, too, and then the defendants would be able to say on appeal that the government also had doubts about the validity of this procedure. So, I said nothing.

The jury selection procedure went forward as Judge Werker had outlined it. We had the first-ever anonymous jury.

Judge Werker said he did not want any more than three government attorneys appearing in court, so Dee had to drop out. Tom and Bob played major roles—handling a number of witnesses—and Tom did the opening summation. I did the opening statement and the rebuttal summation—always a deadly weapon for the government.

The trial was held in Room 110, the largest courtroom in the federal courthouse on Foley Square. From the outset the atmosphere was grim and intense, dominated by the overriding presence of Nicky Barnes. *New York Post* writer Murray Kempton captured his aura in a column:

> "If a thousand of us stood in a crowd and Nicky Barnes was one among us, and the Martians landed, their commander would not say 'Take us to your leader;' he would go at once like pyrite to a magnet, to Nicky Barnes."

Barnes knew this himself. At the beginning of the trial he stationed himself next to his lawyer, David Breitbart, at the No. 1 position at the defense table—as close as possible to the jury.

In preparing for the trial we knew that our principal witness, Robert Geronimo, a DEA informant, had significant credibility issues. He had incriminating conversations with Barnes that he reported to the DEA, but the devices he used to capture the conversations failed repeatedly. Twice, a Nagra recorder strapped to his body mysteriously malfunctioned so that there was total silence on the tape. The DEA then had him feign a broken leg and embedded a transmitter in the cast. After that Geronimo reported another incriminating conversation with Barnes inside a bar, but all the agents heard through the transmitter was music. Geronimo told them that he and Barnes had been standing near the jukebox.

We needed corroborating evidence, and it needed to be compelling enough to persuade the jury to credit Geronimo's testimony, knowing it would be attacked on cross examination. We debated the sequence. Would it be better to have Geronimo testify and

then put on the corroborating evidence, or to put the corroborating evidence in first? We felt the latter approach would be more effective.

The first witness we called was the superintendent of a high-rise apartment building in Fort Lee, New Jersey. Direct examination established that the building had among its thirty-seven apartments a three-bedroom penthouse "with a beautiful view of the Hudson River." It also had a garage where the tenant in the penthouse kept two cars.

"What make are they?" I asked.

"A Maserati and a Mercedes Benz."

"Now, when you see this tenant in your building do you greet each other?"

"Yes."

"What does he say to you?"

"Good morning, Mr. Davis."

"And what do you say to him?"

"Good morning, Mr. Rice."

"Do you see Mr. Rice in the courtroom?"

"Yes."

"Could you point him out, please?"

The superintendent pointed to Barnes at the defense table.

The second witness was the superintendent of a second high-rise apartment in the Fort Lee area. The questions and answers were the same, except the cars were a Lincoln Continental and a Cadillac Eldorado and the name the superintendent greeted his tenant by was "Mr. Darling."

We next introduced Barnes's 1975 tax return in which he had reported over $500,000 of "miscellaneous income." This return was obviously calculated to fend off a "net-worth" income tax prosecution in which evidence of a high lifestyle suggests a greater income than reported and consequently tax evasion—the device the government used to finally put Al Capone in prison in 1931. The Detroit firm that prepared it had also prepared the returns of four other defendants. They, too, reported large amounts of "miscellaneous" or "other" income.

Then Inez Smart took the stand to testify that in 1974 she had sold large quantities of quinine, a substance used to dilute pure heroin for sale on the street, to Barnes for $25,000. She withstood a savage cross examination by Breitbart, who challenged her identification of Barnes. Her last answer was, "If it wasn't him, it was his twin brother."

So, on the first day of trial we had painted the picture of Barnes as a very wealthy individual, living under two separate false names in two fancy apartments and driving several fancy cars, with large amounts of unidentified income, who was purchasing a substance commonly used in the sale and distribution of heroin. We thought we had established a solid background to pre-condition the jury that Geronimo was telling the truth when he would testify that Barnes was a drug dealer.

Geronimo would need all the corroboration he could get.

Robert Geronimo had been enlisted by the DEA because he had grown up in the South Bronx and was friendly with several members of Barnes's drug ring, particularly Wally Fisher, the younger brother of Guy Fisher who was Barnes's chief lieutenant. He would hang out with the defendants and report back to the DEA on what had transpired. These reports were written down in a DEA 6, an account of an unrecorded interview, and were turned over to the defense.

Late on the second day of cross examination, Breitbart took Geronimo through the events of a weekend in which he had told the DEA he and Wally Fisher drove to Baltimore, checked into a motel and did the drug PCP, or "Angel Dust," with a man called "Jap." Breitbart's going into this was ominous, since this was not an event we had charged in the indictment and we had not elicited any testimony about it in the direct examination of Geronimo. Breitbart had Geronimo describe in great detail driving across the George Washington Bridge and down the turnpike to Baltimore, the motel (he couldn't remember the name) and finally asked him to describe "Jap."

By now it was almost 5:00 p.m. Breitbart then showed Geronimo a document and had him confirm that the signature on the bottom was his. It was a registration form for a hotel in the Poconos, and in the last few minutes before the jury went back to its hotel Breitbart forced Geronimo to concede that he and Wally Fisher, with two girls, had spent that weekend not in Baltimore but in the Poconos. There was no drive down the turnpike, no Angel Dust, and no "Jap." Geronimo had made it all up, and in the course of fifteen minutes had set some kind of speed record for lying with more than twenty lies told under oath.

The impact on our case was obvious. If Geronimo fabricated this entire weekend, he could have fabricated everything he was telling the jury as to his dealings with the Barnes organization. Judge Werker was furious. He made it clear that if we didn't address this false testimony we were not going to like what he would say to the jury in his charge. We satisfied the judge by pledging to present Geronimo's false testimony to the grand jury for a potential perjury prosecution once the trial was over.[33]

Our second most important witness was Promise Bruce, a convicted drug dealer. He had purchased narcotics from some members of the Barnes organization and had met with Barnes in the undercover operation. He also had credibility problems. At one point Tom Sear was asking him about a conversation he had with Barnes in 1974.

"When did that conversation take place?" Tom asked.

"That was around the fall, maybe March, middle. I don't remember, the latter part of March."

"Is March in the fall?" said Tom

"I really don't know."

Another bump occurred at the end of a long day in mid-November, more than six weeks into the trial. It involved Juror No. 2, a bank executive from Westchester who early on was dubbed "The Marlboro Man" by the defense. His expressions and body language from the outset telegraphed a pro-government position and the defense would have done anything to get him off the jury.

This particular day had been devoted to the testimony of a former drug dealer who testified as to drug purchases he had made from Guy Fisher in the early 1970's. We needed this proof as the case was otherwise weak against Fisher, who had been in jail serving a one-year sentence while the DEA undercover work was going on. But he had never mentioned those deals in his interviews with DEA agents at the time and Fisher's lawyer, Paul Goldberger, took him apart. The witness cost us some lost ground. But it got worse.

We were still in the office around 8 p.m., planning how we were going to recover, when I received a call from Judge Werker's law clerk: "You had better come over here right away. There is a big problem."

When we arrived at the judge's chambers, Goldberger was there with three other defense counsel, and they were upset. They told the judge the four of them had been walking down Pearl Street after court adjourned and passed the bus that was waiting to take the jurors back to their hotel. Juror No. 2 sat by a window in the rear, illuminated by a street light. "As we walked by," Goldberger told the judge, "he looked right at me and gave me the finger."

They argued that the man had obviously made up his mind, was clearly biased against the defendants and should be summarily excused from the jury. Judge Werker said no. They then demanded that he hold a hearing. Judge Werker said he was not going to do that either. He reasoned that the juror would deny it, and to pursue it further by asking other jurors if they had seen him might contaminate the jury. He said that all he would do was tell the jury the next day that if any of them had a negative opinion about any of the lawyers in the case they should not hold it against their clients. So, "The Marlboro Man" survived.

As did Geronimo's tattered credibility. One important piece of proof arose from his introduction of Wally Fisher to Louis Diaz, an undercover DEA agent. Diaz, Geronimo told Fisher, was his cousin from California who wanted to make big narcotics purchases. Fisher introduced Diaz to Leonard Rollock, who sold him a half-kilo of heroin. Fisher later told Geronimo that Barnes had asked why they went to Rollock, saying that for future purchases they should go to "Fat Stevie" Monsanto at the Harlem River Motors Garage. Both Rollock and Monsanto were charged as part of the drug ring.

Accordingly, Geronimo then bought a half-kilo of heroin from Monsanto at the garage. DEA surveillance agents identified Barnes driving into the garage shortly before the transaction and leaving shortly thereafter. Diaz himself also went into the garage, wearing a wire, to make a purchase of a half-kilo of heroin from Bo Hatcher, another of the co-defendants, and the heroin was delivered in the presence of Barnes.[34]

The case went to the jury at the end of November.

Three days later, they brought back convictions of Barnes and eleven others on the basic narcotic conspiracy count, and also convicted Barnes for being the supervisor of five or more persons in a "continuing criminal enterprise," which carried a maximum sentence of life without parole.

Two of the lesser defendants were acquitted and the jury was hung as to Guy Fisher, which would prove significant when the Second Circuit considered the defendants' appeals.

Judge Werker, when he sentenced Barnes to the maximum—life without parole—said he had affected thousands of lives and "the saddest part of all is that the great majority of the people he is affecting are people in his own neighborhood."

Barnes' three top lieutenants received sentences of thirty years. Taken as a group the sentences were the heaviest in the history of the Southern District. This produced a congratulatory note from President Carter, a complimentary note signed Juror No. 7 and widespread editorial praise. And the DEA agents sent me a framed and signed copy of *The New York Times Magazine* cover superimposed with the *Daily News* headline on December 3, the day after the verdict: "Barnes Guilty—Faces Life."

The significance of the convictions, as I said at the time, was not just that we had broken up what I described as "the largest, the most profitable and the most venal drug ring in New York," but that we might have sent a message to the young kids in Harlem and the South Bronx, for whom Nicky Barnes had been such a role model, that no one is "untouchable."

On appeal, ten anxious months after the argument, the Court of Appeals affirmed the convictions by a two-to-one vote, and later five-to-three on a petition for rehearing *en banc*, with a strenuous dissent from Judge Meskill on the anonymous jury. With respect to Juror No. 2, the court concluded there "was no basis for any conclusion that the juror was faithless to his jury commitment," noting that there was no verdict against Fisher, "whose counsel was allegedly the target of the juror's distasteful gesture," and noted that the acquittals of two defendants negated any claim of a spill-over effect.[35]

Two years later, furious upon learning that members of his organization were sleeping with his girlfriend, Barnes called Bill Tendy from prison and became a government witness against Guy Fisher and other ring members. As a result a number of them were convicted and served long jail sentences. For his cooperation Barnes was released from prison after serving twenty years and entered the federal Witness Protection Program. Word surfaced that Barnes was seeking a presidential pardon for his cooperation. I felt this was totally unjustified and said so, including in an interview with Mike Wallace on "60 Minutes." In the end I was persuaded that in light of what he had contributed to a number of successful prosecutions being released after twenty years was not an unreasonable result.

CHAPTER 20

The Trial of Anthony Scotto
and Anthony Anastasio

RICO, THE RACKETEER Influenced Corrupt Organization statute, became law in 1970 as a tool to keep legitimate business free of infiltration by criminal enterprises. In late September 1979 I stood before a jury in New York to launch only the second prosecution under the RICO Act by describing a payoff that took place in a restaurant bathroom.

"On an afternoon in August 1975," I told the jury, "two men got up from a table at Michael's restaurant here in New York and went into the men's room. After looking around to be sure that no one else was there, one man reached into his pocket and handed the other man a white envelope containing five thousand dollars in brand new one hundred dollar bills."

I was describing a payoff by the President of one of the largest stevedoring companies in the United States to the President of Local 1814 of the International Longshoremen's Association . . . "that man." I pointed to defendant Anthony Scotto, and continued, "the incident tells you in a nutshell the story of what this case is about."

"It is a story of corruption; it is a story of greed; it is a story of a powerful labor leader who, despite receiving a salary of one hundred and forty thousand dollars a year from his union, demanded and received over three hundred thousand dollars in cash in illegal payoffs from companies doing business on the waterfront."

The Taft-Hartley Act made it a misdemeanor for a union officer to receive payments of money from someone who employed members of his union. It also made it a misdemeanor for the employer to make such payments. The RICO statute included this type of payment as a predicate act that could be the basis for a felony prosecution for racketeering. Our indictment charged Scotto and his Local 1814 deputy Anthony Anastasio with both racketeering and conspiracy under the RICO statute, as well as a number of violations of the Taft-Hartley Act.

It would be a long and hard-fought trial. Judge Charles "Pete" Stewart presided and the jury was sequestered—but not anonymous. Our opponents were two of the best criminal defense attorneys anywhere—Jimmy LaRossa for Scotto and Gus Newman for Anastasio. The media covered it closely since Scotto was such a charismatic figure in New York labor and political circles, with newspaper stories every day and often front-page headlines. I tried the case with Alan Levine, who had led the investigation, and Scott Muller, a brand new AUSA from Davis Polk. They both handled a number of witnesses and Alan did the opening summation—as had Tom Sear in the Barnes case. I did the rebuttal summation.

The International Longshoremen's Association (ILA) operated at port cities along the East Coast from New York to Miami. The indictment had followed a long FBI investigation of the union that in New York had started when agents placed a microphone in the offices of a Brooklyn company called Quinn Marine Services. For six months they listened as William "Sonny" Montella, the General Manager of Quinn, freely discussed with others a wide range of criminal activity he was engaged in, including payoffs to Anthony Scotto and other labor leaders.

Scotto's Local 1814 was the union for longshoremen who loaded and unloaded cargo on ships at the Brooklyn docks. It was also the union for marine carpenters whose job was to go on a ship once the cargo was loaded and fasten it down, so when the ship

With Alan Levine (center) & Scott Muller

went to sea the cargo did not roll around and damage itself or the ship. Quinn Marine was in the marine carpentry business. It was important for Montella to have the best possible relationship with Scotto because Scotto could influence the shipping lines as to which firm they should hire.

The wiretaps revealed that beginning in 1976 Montella paid Scotto $25,000 a year in periodic installments. In May 1978 FBI agent Louis Freeh[36] confronted Montella with the evidence and persuaded him to cooperate. Wearing a wire, Montella continued to meet Scotto and make payments through the fall of 1978.

The other major payments to Scotto came from Walter O'Hearn, the President of McGrath Services, a company that employed longshoremen who loaded and unloaded the ships. In the spring of 1974 McGrath executives grew concerned about a sharp increase in workmen's compensation claims by members of Local 1814. They believed many of those claims were fraudulent and went to Scotto to see what could be done. As a result McGrath paid Scotto $60,000 a year and the number of claims dropped from $1,400,000 in 1974 to less than $300,000 in 1977.

Montella referred to McGrath's payments, which O'Hearn was making, in the conversations on the FBI wiretap. The FBI then confronted O'Hearn and he, too, agreed to cooperate. He would not wear a wire, but would testify as to the payments.

The evidence was clear, but Scotto was far from easy to attack. He was a powerful labor leader described during the trial as "influential, progressive, sophisticated and charismatic." He drew part of his power from the high regard of his members for whom he had negotiated a contract that paid them if they worked or not; they would report every morning for a "shape up" and those for whom there was work would report to the docks. The others would go home, but got paid anyway. They were thus intensely loyal and in large numbers would vote for—or contribute to—candidates at his command. High-placed Democrats usually benefitted, which made Scotto even more powerful. Shipping line executives were in his corner, too. They trusted him because he always kept his word and they believed he had improved conditions on the New York docks. He had lectured at Harvard on labor relations, and was a trustee of the Brooklyn Academy of Music.

LaRossa played these themes in his opening statement, calling Scotto a dedicated labor leader who had "won the respect of the political world from the President right on down." Indeed, President Carter, unaware of the investigation, had invited him to lunch before news of the indictment broke.[37] LaRossa said that Scotto was not going to deny receiving the payments. Rather, he would explain that he had raised large sums from shipping line executives, union members and others for a number of Democratic candidates. Why O'Hearn and Montella wanted to contribute to Mario Cuomo's 1977 mayoral campaign and Hugh Carey's 1978 gubernatorial campaign in cash instead of writing checks, the usual procedure, was known only to themselves.

From the outset two things were clear. The trial was not going to be about whether Scotto got the money; it was going to be about what it was for. And Scotto was going to take the stand.

Montella was not a model witness. His cooperation agreement with the government required him not to commit crimes beyond the two felonies he'd already pleaded guilty to. But just before trial he disclosed that he had stolen money from his company while he was cooperating, leading to an additional felony charge of tax evasion. Under cross examination he told the jury he could go to jail for a hundred years if he confessed all his past crimes. He explained how he had persuaded a reluctant bar owner to sign over his business: "You take a hair dryer, get it hot and put it on his neck until he signs."

"On the waterfront, no business is completely honest," Montella said.

Montella's escapades landed him in the federal Witness Protection Program because he was a crucial witness not only in the Scotto case, but in another case that involved major organized crime figures. While he was testifying his counsel Harold Baer[38] noticed several sketch artists at work. At the next recess he came into the robing room to protest that if those sketches appeared in a newspaper or on television where Montella was living his client could be identified and killed. Judge Stewart responded by banishing the artists from the courtroom.

Predictably, within an hour several First Amendment lawyers appeared. The leader of the group was Mark Monsky, the head of Channel 5 in New York, with whom I had a good relationship. He suggested a solution. He said, "Bob, you let my sketch artist stay in the courtroom and I will guarantee you the sketch will look nothing like Montella."

The others were less accommodating, so that didn't fly. Eventually, Judge Stewart let the artists stay but ordered them not to sketch Montella while he was on the stand. They had to do it during recesses, which—as a practical matter—reached the same result as the Monsky proposal.

O'Hearn was less vulnerable in cross examination. He had pleaded guilty to eight misdemeanor violations of the Taft-Hartley Act, but he had a sympathetic side. He was the CEO of a corporation confronted with the rising costs of what he believed to be fraudulent workmen's compensation claims. They had gone from $250,000 in 1972 to $1,400,000 in 1974 and threatened to put the company out of business.

O'Hearn testified that he went to Scotto asking for help and was told nothing could be done. But later, when he was discussing the problem with his partners, one of them said he had made a deal. For $60,000 a year Scotto would make the claims go down. O'Hearn testified that he thought they had no choice. The officers of McGrath agreed they would make the payments and O'Hearn agreed that he would be the one to make them.

O'Hearn's story was credible. Unlike Montella, who had committed other crimes and arguably had a motive to lie about Scotto to get leniency for those crimes, O'Hearn had no reason to plead guilty to illegal payoffs to Scotto unless it were true. And his testimony was corroborated by the fact that his three co-owners voted with him to have McGrath itself plead guilty to illegal Taft-Hartley payoffs, a more serious offense than making illegal cash contributions to a political campaign.

LaRossa prepared the jury for Scotto's testimony by bringing to the stand what had to be one of the most prominent group of character witnesses ever to testify at any trial. They included former New York City Mayors Robert Wagner and John Lindsay, State Senator Carl McCall, Appellate Division Judge William C. Thompson, AFL/CIO President Lane Kirkland, Seafarers Union President Paul Hall, Municipal Employees Local 37 President Victor Gotbaum, New York Postal Union head Morris Biller and finally, the then Governor of New York, Hugh Carey.

They were full of praise. Lindsay called him "a man of high integrity, whose handshake was always enough . . . when the public interest needed to be served, and help for New York he was there." Wagner called him "a man of integrity and ability, a friend for twenty years and a darned good labor leader." Carey called him "one of the outstanding young labor leaders in the United States" with "a rare quality about him. He chooses a course of conduct based upon his conscience for what is right and not what is popular."

Calling character witnesses can be dangerous. It allows the prosecution to ask "Did you know . . ." questions relating to acts of misconduct that might not otherwise have been admissible. LaRossa told me beforehand that he was going to ask Judge Stewart to preclude me from asking the witnesses if they had heard that Scotto was a member of organized crime. The FBI believed Scotto was a capo in the Gambino crime family. His wife's uncle was Albert Anastasia, known as "the Lord High Executioner of Murder, Inc.," who had been rubbed out in a spectacular barbershop shooting in the 1950's. I agreed because I believed we had enough such questions—from conversations picked up on a "bug" the FBI had planted in Scotto's office ceiling—to do serious damage and that we would come out ahead if the witnesses were called.

Cross examination of Carey, Wagner and Lindsay brought out how much money Scotto had raised for their campaigns. Then for them, and all the others, the cross also revealed that they knew nothing about the facts of the case, including whether or not Scotto had received payoffs from Montella or O'Hearn. They did not know he had told his friend Joey Laqua to burn his books if they were subpoenaed. They did not know that when Montella told him he had built a cabinet for a shipping executive—a crime under the Taft-Hartley Act—Scotto told him to lie and tell the FBI his father built it. They did not know that Scotto had an arrangement with a senior investigator at the Waterfront Commission whereby, using a false name, Scotto would call and get information about the investigation. And they did not know that when Montella told him he was committing the crime of defrauding his suppliers in generating the cash to make the payments, Scotto had told him that he didn't care.

Scotto took the stand immediately after Governor Carey. He admitted receiving the payments from Montella and O'Hearn, but claimed they were political contributions to Cuomo's mayoralty campaign in 1977 and Carey's gubernatorial campaign in 1978.

The story, from the contributions in cash to the fact that in many cases they fell outside the cycles of the two campaigns, was implausible. Could Scotto have been a contributor to candidates since 1972 without ever learning, as he claimed, that the election laws prohibited cash payments in excess of $100? And if that was true, why did a $5,000 cash contribution require the privacy of a restaurant men's room for delivery?

Scotto acknowledged he had given the money not to Carey or Cuomo's regular campaign committees, but to two longtime ILA union friends. They testified that Scotto had given them cash to be used as "street money" in the two campaigns, but they too claimed ignorance of the law prohibiting cash payments and, moreover, kept no books and had no record of the contributions. One of them was New York State Deputy Labor Commissioner Louis Valentino, who testified that Scotto had been behind his appointment to the post by Carey. Several photographs adorned his office walls: one of President Carter, one of Carey and five of Scotto. Carey admitted on cross examination that his campaign had no record of any cash payments from Scotto.

The proof against Anastasio, Scotto's number two at Local 1814, came from the third principal government witness, Nicholas Seregos. Seregos was the President of Jackson Engineering, a ship repair business. We indicted him for participating in a commercial bribery scheme between a shipping line and a stevedoring company involving a kickback for the rental of a crane. While Seregos was awaiting trial Montella told the FBI that Seregos had made a series of payments to Anastasio in order to buy his influence in getting

Cross examing Scotto

Jackson Engineering business from two shipping lines. Seregos refused to cooperate so we gave him use immunity—meaning his testimony and any leads it produced could not be used against him in the case against him—and compelled his testimony. Under that compulsion he testified that he agreed to pay Anastasio 10 percent of any business that his company received from the Presidential Lines and United States Shipping Lines. He said that after making this agreement, which he had discussed with Scotto, he received business from both lines and paid Anastasio $50,000 between 1976 and 1978.

Scotto, despite the holes in his story, was charismatic and charming. During the *voir dire* sessions that preceded jury selection, several women potential jurors had commented on how handsome he was. At the end when the five alternate jurors were excused, they left the jury box and exited the courtroom going past the spectator row where the Scotto family was seated during the trial. The last alternate stopped and hugged Mrs. Scotto in plain view of the entire courtroom. Mrs. Scotto later told the press the juror had said, "I was with you all the way."

Two of the *Daily News* reporters clearly favored the defense. While I was cross examining Scotto, Jimmy Breslin wrote that the jury's "sympathies were probably with

Scotto." After the jury retired to deliberate, in a column headed "Our National Bird: not the Eagle but the Stool Pigeon," Pete Hamill wrote, "There is something inherently dangerous about the growing practice of using wired stool pigeons," adding ". . . yesterday, as Anthony Scotto waited for the jury to make the decision that would affect the rest of his life, it was difficult to root for anyone but Scotto."

The deliberations lasted several days, during which the jurors asked to have read back portions of Montella's and O'Hearn's testimony, as well as the key tape recordings from the bug at Local 1814. There was a lot of waiting. At one point CBS radio reporter Irene Cornell voiced the news from the courtroom that "things are slow . . . so slow that the sketch artists are sketching the other sketch artists."

The jury returned on the morning of the fourth day and announced its verdict—guilty as to both defendants on the racketeering counts and a number of the individual Taft-Hartley counts. One juror told the press that the Scotto story of receiving the cash as political contributions "was fairy tale day" from the outset. Governor Carey, who had said he thought Scotto was innocent, issued a statement saying he regretted "that a person of such considerable talent and ability has violated our laws."

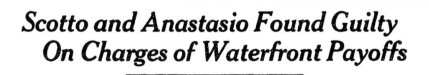

Scotto and Anastasio Found Guilty On Charges of Waterfront Payoffs

The New York Times, *November 16, 1979*

Judge Stewart, impressed by Scotto's record as a labor leader and the many testimonials on his behalf, gave both defendants what we considered very light sentences—five years for Scotto and three for Anastasio.

CHAPTER 21

Socialist Workers Party v. Attorney General of the United States

THE HIGH-PROFILE CASES weren't all criminal prosecutions. Civil cases, especially those that involve fundamental questions that will affect law going forward, can be just as hard fought. The third case of note I was involved in was one of these, in which we were defending a group of high government officials in a suit brought by the Socialist Workers Party (SWP).

The SWP was founded in 1938 as the principal Trotskyist organization in the United States. It was, according to its basic organizational resolution, "a revolutionary workers party . . . based on the doctrines of scientific socialism as embodied in the works of Marx, Engels, Lenin and Trotsky and incorporated in the basic documents and resolutions of the first four Congresses of the Communist International . . ." The resolution also called it "a combat organization which aims at achieving power in this country" and "models its organization forms and methods after those of Russian Bolsheviks . . ."

The FBI began an investigation of the SWP in 1940 and it continued into the 1970's. In 1974 an internal FBI memorandum said the SWP "has as its purpose the overthrow of the United States Government, the institution of a dictatorship of the working class and the eventual achievement of a communist society, and while the SWP is not known by the FBI to publicly advocate the use of violence at the present time, this organization maintains that eventual violent revolution is inevitable. SWP seeks to precipitate revolution when conditions are perceived by it to be ripe and seeks to seize control of and direct the revolution where it occurs."

In 1976 the party sued the United States and a number of high-ranking government officials under the Federal Tort Claims Act (FTCA). The officials included former President Nixon, former Attorney General Mitchell, John W. Dean, and several FBI agents. The suit claimed that in its investigation the FBI had engaged in a variety of unlawful activities, including electronic surveillance, burglaries, mail openings, manipulation and disruption of SWP's activities, undercover surveillance, interviews of third parties and use of informants. The SWP claimed that these actions had no valid law enforcement purpose since it had at all times been a lawful political party seeking to exercise its protected rights of free speech and association. It sought a total of $40 million in damages and various forms of injunctive relief.

The U.S. Senate's Church Committee, named for Senator Frank Church, had been looking into counterintelligence activities and found that the FBI, in thirty-six years, had uncovered no illegal activity by the SWP against the United States. That led Attorney General Levi to order a halt to the investigation in late 1976. But the suit also aimed to redress past wrongs.

The party alleged that the informants had been used by the FBI not only to gather information, but also to engage in disruptive and divisive conduct that would interfere with its activities. It charged that they had burglarized some party offices and purloined documents for disclosure to the FBI.

In March 1976 the SWP served interrogatories on the FBI asking—among other things—the agency to identify all chapters of the SWP where an informant had been located. The FBI answered, listing a total of 1,300 informants who had been placed in a number of separate chapters of the SWP since 1960—identifying the informants only by code numbers. The Denver chapter of the SWP was not on the list. A few weeks later an individual named Timothy Redfearn was arrested for burglary by the Denver police. As a result it was revealed that he was an informant in the Denver chapter. The interrogatory answers, by omitting Denver, were false.

The SWP lawyer was Leonard Boudin, a prominent civil rights attorney. Immediately following the Denver disclosure he moved for an order requiring the disclosure of the names of nineteen informants designated by the code numbers used in the interrogatory answers. He told a receptive District Court Judge—Thomas P. Griesa, a former Davis Polk partner—that this was "a representative cross sample," but made clear that he was going to make a future claim for all 1,300 names.

Our team, consisting of Frank Wohl, Tom Moseley and Stuart Parker, opposed the motion on several grounds. In an affidavit from a high-ranking FBI official they documented the damage that disclosure of the informants' names would do to the FBI's ability to gather information for law enforcement purposes. We argued that the party's need for the names was all but non-existent since there were several grounds under the FTCA upon which their claims based upon informant activity should be dismissed: the failure to state a claim; the statutes of limitation had expired; and Attorney General Levi's halt to the investigation made the matter moot.

Judge Griesa responded by ordering the government to compile and produce to him extensive summaries of the information contained in the files concerning the activities of each of the nineteen informants. After that was done he summarized the information for the SWP without disclosing their names.

The SWP was unwilling to settle for anything less than the names of the informants. Over our objections the court, on May 31, 1977, then directed the government to turn over the FBI files and summaries regarding the nineteen, including their names, to the party's lawyers, telling them not to reveal any of this information to their clients. In his ruling Judge Griesa said, "There are indications from the few files thus far examined that there may be a variety of tortious acts which were committed by the FBI, including trespass and conversion of property. The latter refers to removal of private documents for production to the FBI. The FBI and certain informants may have engaged in activities designed to intentionally destroy certain chapters of the SWP. The evidence about the FBI informants may reveal other activities giving rise to valid claims for damages."[39]

We appealed this ruling to the Second Circuit, with Chief Assistant U.S. Attorney Dan Murdock making the argument, asking for a writ of *mandamus*. The court denied the appeal, noting that discovery orders are ordinarily not appealable. The court held that "The order appealed from does not create an issue of first impression or extraordinary significance, nor was its issuance an abuse of discretion which warrants appellate review." However, the three-judge panel that included William Webster, later to be named director of the FBI by President Carter, went on to say, "We would be remiss if we did not express our concern that the course upon which the district judge has embarked will lead to disclosure for which there is no substantial need."[40]

The panel noted that motions to dismiss the complaint were pending, and suggested that the district court weigh "the serious prejudice to the government from compromising some or all of the informants for all time, even though the final determination of the action may be for the defendants." It said, "A decision as to the need for discovery of much privileged matter can be deferred safely until more fundamental issues, perhaps dispositive of the need, are decided on trial."[41]

Judge Griesa did not take up the suggestion that he decide the substantive motions. Instead, reading the decision as denying our appeal, he pressed on with the issue of disclosure of the informants' files.

We responded by stating that we might decide to accept issue-related sanctions rather than turn over the files. This produced an angry reaction from Judge Griesa. He made it clear he would not accept sanctions as a substitute for the production of the files. If we refused, he said, he would hold the responsible person in contempt with the possibility of imprisonment. He wanted us to tell him who that person was. After researching the Code of Federal Regulations, we advised the court and the SWP that the ultimate decision maker was the Attorney General, Griffin Bell.[42]

On April 9, 1978 we filed a petition for *certiorari* to the U.S. Supreme Court asking for review of the Second Circuit decision. We also asked the court to review the question whether appellate review of Judge Griesa's order could be obtained by any procedure other than our declining to comply.

On June 12 the Supreme Court denied the petition.[43] Judge Griesa convened a pre-trial conference the next day to find out our position. We submitted an affidavit from Attorney General Bell stating that "releasing these files to plaintiff's counsel would have a significant detrimental effect on law enforcement by undermining the pledge of confidentiality which the FBI makes to informants." The affidavit pointed out that the Supreme Court's denial of the petition for *certiorari* had left us in the position where the only way we could obtain appellate review was by declining to comply and accept sanctions under Rule 37 of the Federal Rules of Civil Procedure.

The SWP promptly filed a motion to hold Bell in civil contempt and to imprison him until he released the files. Judge Griesa heard arguments on June 28—over an hour from each side. I argued the government's case at the Attorney General's strong suggestion.

Two strong themes emerged from Judge Griesa's questioning. In his view the Court of Appeals had already ruled that requiring disclosure was up to him and so there was nothing further to appeal. And the sanction to be applied was also up to him and he did not think any issue-related sanction would work.

Two days later on June 30, he granted the SWP's motion in an opinion that reflected those themes in sharp language. He wrote, "The theory that full appellate review has thus far been denied . . . is simply invalid." The Court of Appeals, in dismissing the appeal but entertaining and ruling on the *mandamus* petition, "expressly resolved each relevant question of law," he added.[44]

Judge Griesa was equally harsh with respect to the issue of alternative sanctions. Those "suggested by the Attorney General," he wrote ". . . are nothing but attempts to avoid or drastically reduce the effect of the May 31, 1977 order. In other words, the government seeks to use the weapon of defiance of the order to dictate its own terms as to what it will or will not do in connection with providing evidence in this case. This position cannot be justified. The Attorney General has no 'right' to defy a court order for discovery, and accept sanctions of his selection. On the contrary, his duty is to obey the order . . ."[45]

> Stating, "It is not only in plaintiffs' interest, but in the broad public interest, that plaintiffs be afforded a fair opportunity to obtain and present the essential evidence about this alleged wrongdoing,"

Judge Griesa directed the Attorney General to comply with the order by July 7, 1978. He ruled that if he did not produce the files by then he would be in civil contempt until he purged himself by producing the files, and if he made no effort to purge himself the court would "entertain a motion for more drastic sanctions."[46]

Through all of this, the basic issue we had with Judge Griesa was that he would not accept the proposition that in every previous case requiring disclosure of informants the parties and the court had been able to work out an acceptable issue-related sanction. We pointed out that in criminal cases the government always retained the option to drop the case rather than disclose the name of an informant. We argued that the civil equivalent would be for us to agree to a default judgment rather than disclose the names, but that there should be sufficient issue-related sanctions short of that. We offered a specific proposal: if the SWP could prove actual damage at any chapter, such as loss of revenue or loss of members, we would stipulate that it was presumed to be the result of informant activity, and the burden would be on us to come forward with persuasive proof that the damages resulted from another cause. He rejected that out of hand and refused to consider any other issue-related sanction.

Judge Griesa kept stating that "the purpose of discovery is not to lead to sanctions; it is to lead to discovery." We felt that he placed improper emphasis on what he referred to as "the broad public interest," that is, the public's right to know what kind of improper abuses had been carried on by the FBI informants. This became more evident when we responded to his June 30 decision by submitting, on July 6, an affidavit from the Attorney General stating that in order to preserve the right to appeal he was declining to produce the files. We applied for a stay of the June 30 contempt citation pending appellate review.

Judge Griesa responded the same day, denying a stay and judging Attorney General Bell in civil contempt "unless and until he purges his contempt by compliance with the order." He set a one-week deadline before deciding what specific sanctions he would impose, and added: "In the considered judgment of this court . . . there is no legitimate ground for seeking further appellate review, and the attempt to do so constitutes a totally unjustified attempt to obstruct and delay.

In a recent address to a bar association, President Carter strongly warned about delays in litigation occasioned by litigants who have the power and resources to create obstructions. In the judgment of this court, the Attorney General's actions in the present case are virtually a classic example of this problem."

We immediately filed a notice of appeal and a petition for a writ of *mandamus* with the Second Circuit and applied for a stay of the contempt citation. The motion for a stay was assigned to Judge Murray Gurfein and I argued it the next day. The principal issue was whether Judge Griesa's order was appealable. The SWP argued it was a discovery order and thus was unappealable. I argued that it was appealable because the order was not directed to any of the parties to the lawsuit, but rather to Judge Bell in his individual capacity as Attorney General. Judge Gurfein accepted this argument and agreed that the order holding Judge Bell in contempt should be stayed until the appeal had been decided. He granted the stay, and I was able to come out and tell the assembled press corps on the courthouse steps that "The Attorney General is not in contempt."

> # BELL WINS REVERSAL OF CONTEMPT ORDER
>
> ---
>
> ## Ruling Against Attorney General on Informer Files Is Vacated
>
> ---

The New York Times, *March 20, 1979*

Leonard Boudin and I argued the case on November 15, 1978 before a panel consisting of Judges Lumbard, Friendly and Oakes in front of a standing-room-only audience in the Court of Appeals courtroom.

The decision came down four months later on March 19, 1979.[47] In an opinion written by Judge Oakes, the court started out by holding that the contempt order was not appealable. It rejected Judge Gurfein's appealability analysis, stating that the "third party" contempt rationale applied only when the discovery issue was "completely separate" from the merits of the action. The court felt that here the discovery issue was integral to the merits—not separate from it. But the court then went on to grant the petition for *mandamus* under the "extraordinary case rationale."

> "This . . . is an extraordinary case. It is, so far as we know, the first case brought by a political party against the government itself for damages as well as injunctive relief for allegedly illegal surveillance of that party. . . .

—⚋—

The case also involves a claim of privilege which includes the larger claim, to which Attorney General Griffin Bell has attested, that the failure to recognize the privilege would adversely affect the entire law enforcement and intelligence-gathering apparatus of the United States.

—⚋—

This case is unusually important for another reason—because the order for which review is sought adjudged the Attorney General of the United States in civil contempt. Although we unequivocally affirm the principle that no person is above the law, we cannot ignore the fact that a contempt sanction imposed on the Attorney General in his official capacity has greater public importance, with separation of power overtones, and warrants more sensitive judicial scrutiny than such a sanction imposed on an ordinary litigant . . ."[48]

The court then went on to the merits, and accepted the basic point that we had made to Judge Griesa:

"[H]olding the Attorney General of the United States in contempt to ensure compliance with a court order should be a last resort, to be undertaken only after all other means to achieve the ends legitimately sought by the court have been exhausted.

Judged by these standards, the action of the trial court unfortunately falls short, for in our view the court insufficiently considered issue-related sanctions. The Federal Rules of Civil Procedure permit many sanctions other than contempt, alternatives that the court did not sufficiently explore except to reject the government's proposals."[49]

The court then went on to direct the district court, with the aid of a special master, to review the informant files and produce a set of representative findings. It set out a form that included nine subjects including background information, method of recruitment, confidential relationship with the FBI, informants' relationship with the SWP, their method of obtaining information, activities, and compensation. It held that those findings would help the SWP both in prosecution of its case and in suggesting to the district court what, if any, issue-related sanctions would be appropriate.

The opinion concluded: "We grant the petition for a writ of mandamus, vacate the contempt order, and direct the district court to impose such issue-related sanctions as are consistent with this opinion. . . ."[50]

The case went back to Judge Griesa. He appointed Charles Breitel, a former Chief Judge of the State of New York, as a special master to produce the representative findings. They were prepared and given to the SWP. No motion for sanctions was ever made.

A lengthy trial finally occurred in 1981 after I had returned to Davis Polk. In 1986 Judge Griesa handed down his decision. He awarded the SWP $264,000: $42,500 for disruption activities; $96,500 for surreptitious entries; and $125,000 for the use of informants.[51]

CHAPTER 22

A Case That Didn't Happen

"BOLD-FACE NAMES" REFERS to the tabloid newspaper practice of highlighting celebrities on their gossip pages. Two of these, during the disco craze of the late 1970's, were Steve Rubell and Ian Schrager, the owners of the enormously popular Studio 54 on West 54th Street. Hailed as the "first pashas of disco," they hosted other celebrities and society figures—with their collections of hangers-on—employing rope lines at the door to keep lesser customers waiting and gawking.

At the height of disco fever a disgruntled employee revealed to the IRS that Rubell and Schrager had been taking in cash, hiding it in panels in the ceiling and obviously not declaring it on their tax returns. Based on this information we obtained a search warrant and found the cash in the ceiling. We indicted them in July 1979 for failing to report over $2.5 million skimmed from club receipts over a three-year period.

That August I received a visit from Mitchell Rogovin, a prominent Washington lawyer who represented Rubell. He told me that Rubell had damaging information about a highly-placed government official that would have severe political and national security implications. He would keep quiet about it if he got a favorable break on the tax charges, but would otherwise go public. The information was that Hamilton Jordan, President Carter's Chief of Staff, had used cocaine at Studio 54. I told him that we would not make any such agreement, and that if Rubell wanted to make the information public he should go ahead.

Rogovin then went to Attorney General Benjamin Civiletti, who had succeeded Griffin Bell, with the same proposal. Civiletti also rejected it out of hand, but initiated an FBI investigation into the allegations under the Ethics in Government Act. News of the investigation leaked to *The New York Times*, which published a front-page story on August 25. Civiletti then made the first application under the recently-enacted independent counsel statute and the three-judge appointing court, chaired by Judge Lumbard, named Arthur Christy—a former Lumbard AUSA and acting U.S. Attorney in 1958-1959 between Paul Williams and Hazard Gillespie—as the first Independent Counsel under the statute.

Jordan's lawyer was Henry Ruth, a Yale classmate of mine, who had succeeded Archibald Cox and Leon Jaworski as the chief Watergate prosecutor. He asked me, "Would your office prosecute someone who used two ounces of cocaine?" I said we would not. He took that to Christy and argued that if the Justice Department—through the U.S. Attorney in the Southern District of New York—would not prosecute this use of cocaine, the answer should be no different for the Independent Counsel just because the person using it was Hamilton Jordan.

Christy decided to go ahead and investigate the facts and concluded at the end, in a publicly-issued report, that there was insufficient evidence to substantiate the allegation against Jordan.

Rubell and Schrager both pleaded guilty to the tax evasion charges. They were sentenced to three-and-a half years in prison and fined $20,000 each.

CHAPTER 23

Assessments

THE ATTORNEY GENERAL'S ADVISORY COMMITTEE

The Attorney General's Advisory Committee of United States Attorneys (AGAC) was established in 1973 by then Attorney General Elliot Richardson, and was formally codified in the Code of Federal Regulations by Attorney General Edward Levi in 1976. It consists of fifteen U.S. Attorneys selected by the Attorney General to assure diversity in geography and the size of the offices represented.

The Committee exists to assure the maximum coordination between the Justice Department in Washington and the U.S. Attorneys' Offices around the country. It is charged with making recommendations to the Attorney General on "any matters which the Committee believes to be in the best interests of justice." These include establishing and updating policies and procedures, improving management, cooperating with state authorities, promoting greater consistency in applying legal standards, and aiding the Attorney General and top aides in formulating new programs for improving the criminal justice system at all levels.

Attorney General Levi, I am sure at Judge Tyler's suggestion, appointed me to the Committee in the summer of 1976. I went to one meeting in the late fall, after the election, in time to receive a plaque thanking me for my service along with the other fourteen members who had served for several years. In 1977 Attorney General Bell asked me to continue on—I was the sole survivor out of fifteen Republican U.S. Attorneys—and I stayed for the next three years, chairing the committee in 1979.

The group stayed the same for all three years. We met four times a year in Washington, for two days at a time—with a dinner after the first day. Our working days were taken up with a series of meetings with the Attorney General, the Deputy Attorney General (Ben Civiletti), the head of the Criminal Division (Phil Heymann) and various other criminal division representatives who had issues they wanted to discuss. We also had time to meet among ourselves at the outset (Committee members only) to be sure we had put together a list of the right items we wanted to bring up and at the end to discuss what we felt had been accomplished.

It was a great process. We accomplished a lot substantively, and we had a good time. We enjoyed each other's company—making for lively dinner table conversation. Also, sharing experiences was both entertaining and illuminating. I made lasting friendships with several of the U.S. Attorneys on the Committee.

ACCOMPLISHMENTS BY THE OFFICE

At the end of each year, for the benefit of the public, I wrote a report of what the Office had done that year. My last was a four-year report covering March 1, 1976 to March 1, 1980 chronicling the accomplishments of the Office during my term.

In the Criminal Division our Narcotics Unit obtained convictions of more than a hundred major narcotics traffickers who each received sentences of more than ten years, including the "untouchable" Nicky Barnes. Major Crimes was the unit that won the tax evasion convictions of Studio 54 owners Steve Rubell and Ian Schrager.

The Organized Crime and Racketeering Section, established by the merger of the Justice Department's Organized Crime Strike Force into the U.S. Attorney's Office,[52] obtained convictions not only of Anthony Scotto of the International Longshoremen's Association and his top deputy, but also officials of the International Brotherhood of Teamsters and the Newspaper & Mail Deliverers Union. Major organized crime figures the Section convicted included Tony Provenzano, widely believed to be behind the death of Jimmy Hoffa, as well as Russell Bufalino and Anthony "Fat Tony" Salerno. The Section also won convictions of several organized crime figures for infiltrating, taking over, and then looting into bankruptcy the well-known and once thriving Westchester Premier Theatre—convictions that demonstrated the control of organized crime over legitimate business. (In that case, the judge ruled out, as too prejudicial, a picture of one of the defendants with one arm around Carlo Gambino, head of the Gambino crime family, and the other around Frank Sinatra.)

The Business Fraud Unit obtained convictions of more than fifteen officers of major publicly-held corporations, as well as convictions of major corporations themselves, including United Brands for bribery of a foreign official, the Chemical Bank & Trust Company for violations of the Bank Secrecy Act, and PepsiCo for bribery of a labor official. It also brought the first-ever criminal insider trading case.[53]

Stemming fraud against the government was an area in which the Office had much success. Assistants pioneered a number of winning prosecutions to lead what later became a nationwide crackdown in Medicaid fraud. We also obtained major convictions in cases involving fraud in the New York City summer lunch programs, culminating in the conviction of Rabbi Leib Pinter of B'nai Torah Institute for bribing Congressman Daniel Flood of Pennsylvania and leading, through his testimony, to the conviction of Flood after which he was censured and resigned from Congress. In addition our assistants won convictions of a number of public officials, including the New York City Commissioner of General Services and the Regional Commissioner of the United States Small Business Administration.

In the Civil Division the significance of the cases we handled was demonstrated by the fact that in five of them the Supreme Court granted writs of *certiorari*. One of those was the case I had argued before the Second Circuit defending the constitutional validity of a 10 percent set-aside for minority businesses in public works construction contracts. The others involved the constitutional standards that should apply to the confinement of pre-trial detainees, the immunity standard applicable to federal executives in suits alleging violations of constitutional standards, the limits of the courts' ability to interfere with the discretion exercised by federal agency officials complying with the National Environmental Policy Act (NEPA), and whether a particular taxpayer was a tax-exempt business league. By long-standing practice and tradition these cases were all handled by the Solicitor General's office once they reached the Supreme Court.

Other major Civil Division cases included the defense of public officials in the Socialist Workers Party litigation, including the contempt citation against Attorney General Bell. Our assistants defeated an argument that an environmental impact statement regarding proposed relief under NEPA had to precede a Federal Trade Commission (FTC) antitrust investigation that—had the government lost—would have essentially sidetracked FTC enforcement efforts while agencies spent countless hours creating hypothetical impact statements. And the Division also successfully defended the old Department of Health, Education and Welfare's approval of amendments to NY State's Medicaid plan.

In the civil rights area the Office brought a number of suits against illegal discrimination by labor unions and urban real estate brokers and the use of racial quotas in public housing projects. In the environmental area assistants developed and brought actions to enforce the Federal Water Pollution Act and the Clean Water Act against New York City, which was discharging sewage into the East and Hudson Rivers, and against Westchester County, to require construction of facilities for on-shore sewage disposal. Affirmative efforts also included a suit against Congressman Bertram Podell, previously convicted of conflict of interest charges, to impose a constructive trust on the monies he had received as compensation for his illegal activities.

One of the things I was proudest of went beyond cases filed and convictions obtained. Continuing to hire on the merits, we saw an increase in the number of female AUSAs in my four years from eight to thirty-eight, with eight of those serving in executive positions. And the number of African-American lawyers in the Office went from one to eight during my tenure.

THE VALUE OF THE ASSISTANT UNITED STATES ATTORNEY EXPERIENCE

When I was appointed United States Attorney there were, for me, three principal reasons I found the position so attractive. I wanted the opportunity to set, and carry out, the law enforcement priorities for the Southern District of New York. I hoped to be able to personally try at least one important case.

And equally important I wanted the chance to have a positive influence—both in terms of professional skills and ethical values—on the highly-motivated and highly-talented young lawyers in the Office, many just starting their professional careers. In short, I wanted to be able to do for the young lawyers of the 1970's what Judge Lumbard had done for me and so many others two decades earlier. I had received, and wanted to provide, the best possible training in the skills of trial and appellate advocacy, and the early opportunity for responsibility vastly exceeding the norm in private practice. Hopefully, they too would develop a lasting belief in the importance and value of, and commitment to, public service.

In November 1989 a black tie dinner at the Plaza Hotel commemorated the 200th anniversary of the Southern District, the nation's first. Everyone who had been an Assistant United States Attorney under any of the United States Attorneys—starting with Judge Lumbard in 1953—was invited and several hundred attended. Every U.S. Attorney from Judge Lumbard to the recently-appointed Otto Obermaier was on the dais. They included, chronologically, Paul Williams, Hazard Gillespie, Robert Morgenthau, Whitney North Seymour Jr., Paul Curran, myself, John Martin, Rudolph Giuliani, and Benito Romano. Each of us was asked to say a few words.

When Paul Curran spoke he told a very appreciative audience: "The second best job in the country is being a United States Attorney. The best job is being an Assistant United States Attorney."

We all knew exactly what he meant.

Over 100 former AUSAs attended an April 2011 black tie dinner at the University Club celebrating the thirty-fifth anniversary of my appointment as United States Attorney. In my speech that night I summed up the unique opportunity afforded young lawyers as Assistant U.S. Attorneys, so much of it consistent with my own AUSA experience: the individual responsibility; important policy questions—often affecting millions; the chance to test their abilities against the best private litigators in the country; the teamwork; the friendships; the sense of great accomplishment; and the appeal of public service. I expressed it this way:

"What is it that makes being an AUSA such a remarkable experience—that brings so many of us back here thirty-five years later?

It is the great gratification that comes from the accomplishments achieved—

In the Criminal Division, trying high profile cases against the best criminal defense lawyers in the country.

In the Civil Division litigating cases involving important policy questions affecting the welfare of a large number of citizens around the country—again often against senior partners of the city's best law firms, cases on the cutting edge of the law. What law firm in the country in four years has five cases that go to the United States Supreme Court?

And that is only part of it. It is the esprit de corps that comes from being part of a group of team players whose only objective is to work together to do the right thing for the benefit of the public.

It is from this kind of experience that life-long friendships are forged that produce the kind of turnout we have tonight."

Looking back after more than thirty years, one of the most gratifying aspects of my time as United States Attorney was the chance to lead such a remarkable group of young lawyers. AUSAs in that group have gone on to become federal and state judges, an Attorney General of the United States, a United States Attorney—now Chairman of the SEC—high-ranking Justice Department officials, general counsels of the CIA and of the Director of National Intelligence, regional directors of the SEC, law school deans, bar association presidents, general counsels of major corporations, managing partners of major law firms and prominent practitioners in private practice. More than fifty of them have performed some form of public service since leaving the Southern District office.

When I left the Office in 1980 I told the AUSAs at the farewell dinner "I know that when I am eighty years old and I look back at my career, I will say that these were the best four years." They were.

UNITED STATES ATTORNEY'S OFFICE, JUNE 14, 1976

It had been four years to the day from my swearing-in on March 1, 1976 to the day I left on March 1, 1980. Janet and I took a three-week vacation, first visiting her parents in Florida and then mine, who were themselves vacationing on the island of Montserrat in the Caribbean. After that, I returned to Davis Polk & Wardwell.

SECTION VI

—⁂—

NEW CHALLENGES
AT DAVIS POLK,
1980–1989

IT WAS NICE TO BE BACK. I had many good friends at the firm, and as I made my rounds from office to office they welcomed me enthusiastically. The greetings were warm on a personal level, and I got the sense that among the partners there was the feeling that my experience as U.S. Attorney would prove beneficial to the firm. I expected to spend a little time to get settled and then a quiet period of reacquainting myself to private practice while I trained for the New York Marathon.

The marathon was an outgrowth of the running I had taken up earlier; several of my AUSAs had run in the 1979 marathon and I had decided, at their prompting, to try it in 1980. I knew it would take extended training to complete the twenty-six mile course that starts on Staten Island at the Verrazano Bridge and touches all five New York City boroughs before finishing in Manhattan's Central Park. I had about seven months before the November race. But as it turned out, my training schedule got some serious competition for my attention.

That was because, on my second day back at the firm, I was plunged into what became one of the most high-profile cases of the 1980's.

CHAPTER 24

Three Mile Island

A YEAR EARLIER, on March 28, 1979, a major accident at the Three Mile Island nuclear plant near Harrisburg, Pennsylvania resulted in a near meltdown of the nuclear core. The movie "China Syndrome" with Jack Lemmon and Jane Fonda had just come out, and its fictional account of a complete nuclear reactor meltdown intensified the public awareness—and alarm—over what happened in real life at Three Mile Island. The accident set back development of nuclear power in the U.S. for thirty-five years. Not a single new nuclear plant has been built since the accident.

On March 23, 1980, the day after I returned to Davis Polk, the company that owned Three Mile Island filed a $4 billion lawsuit in the Southern District of New York against Babcock and Wilcox, the company that designed and built the reactor. General Public Utilities demanded $1 billion for damage to the plant, $1 billion for clean-up costs, and $2 billion for the cost of replacement power.

The next day I received a call asking if I would take on the defense. It was a classic "Bet Your Company" case. Babcock & Wilcox was a subsidiary of J. Ray McDermott, which had a net worth of $1 billion. I agreed to do it.

A STEEP LEARNING CURVE

As I looked at the case from the firm's standpoint, I realized that an effective defense meant climbing a steep learning curve. We would have to know how a nuclear reactor works, the tasks employees were expected to fulfill, and how the basic responsibilities for the design, manufacture and operation of the plant were divided among the firms and personnel involved. We assembled a team that included Bob Wise, a partner, and six associates: Karen Wagner, Linda Thomsen, Bill Wurtz, Rod Benedict, Susan Johnston and Ann McDonald.[54] Together we embarked on a crash course in nuclear energy and the nuclear power industry that, in time, gave us a clear picture.

Babcock and Wilcox (B&W) built and provided the reactor and the equipment. General Public Utilities (GPU) was responsible for the basic training of the operators who ran the plant, but B&W was responsible for providing written procedures to guide them. B&W was also responsible for providing advanced training on simulators reflecting potential accident scenarios and was obligated to keep the plant owners advised of important developments affecting the operation of the plant.

The best way to understand how a nuclear reactor works is by using the diagram at the bottom of the page.

There are two systems, primary and secondary, both of which are in the reactor building.

In the primary system, which is fully enclosed (the green-shaded piping), water circulates clockwise in pipes through the reactor core (1) and is heated up to 605 degrees Fahrenheit. The heated water then passes through the steam generator, which is essentially a tank full of water (2)—that is the secondary system.

The heat from the enclosed primary pipes transfers to the water in the generator and two things happen. First, the transferred heat turns the water in the generator into

TMI-2 Schematic

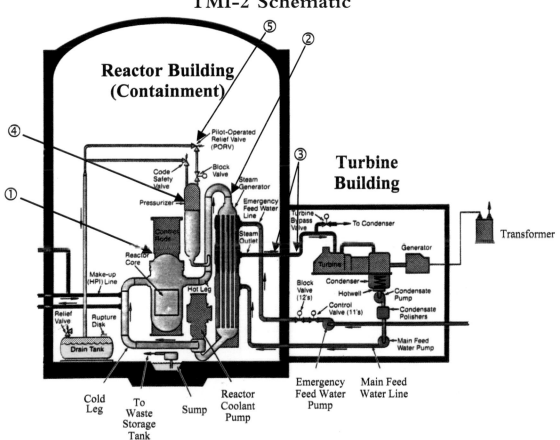

steam (the red section of the generator), which goes into the turbine building (3) and drives the turbine. Second, the transfer of the heat to the steam generator water cools the water in the enclosed primary pipes as it goes through the generator (blue section).

After passing through the generator the cooled water in the primary system then passes back through the reactor core. That, in turn, does two things: first, it heats the water in the primary system back up to 605 degrees; second, in the process it cools the reactor core. This is very important because if the core is not cooled it will overheat and eventually melt down.

Water boils at a temperature of 212 degrees Fahrenheit. The water in the primary system, which is at 605 degrees Fahrenheit, does not boil because it is kept under very high pressure of 2250 psi. The pressure is created by a pressurizer (4), which is an oval-shaped cylinder in which water is heated to the boiling point; that creates steam (gray area in the pressurizer) that, in the enclosed cylinder, pushes down on the water and produces the pressure that keeps the water from boiling.

With all of that in mind, it's easier to understand what happened on March 28, 1979.

THE EVENT

At 4 a.m. that day a problem occurred in the secondary system. Water got into the valves of the condensate polishers which shut down the flow of water into the generator. This meant that after the water that was then in the generator was turned into steam, the generator was dry and the water in the pipes in the primary system was not cooled down as it passed though. This caused a pressure spike in the primary system that caused the pressure operated relief valve (PORV) at the top of the pressurizer (5) to open, which it was supposed to do in such a situation.

The opening of the valve immediately caused a sharp drop in pressure in the primary system from 2250 psi to 1640 psi. At that point a high-pressure injection system (HPI) came on—as it was supposed to do—and began to pump water in to replace the water in the primary system that was going out the top as steam. This was crucial because without water circulating through the core, it would overheat and potentially melt down.

Everything had gone just as it should up to this point.

But then the PORV did not close as it was supposed to. If it had the pressurizer would have started to bring the pressure back up to 2250 psi. Rather, steam continued to escape through the open valve. The operators did not realize that the relief valve was still open—the indicator light had malfunctioned—and they turned off the injection system when the pressure was still at 1640.

The HPI would remain off for two-and-a-half hours, during which the water in the primary system was continuing to boil off with steam going out the top. This is known as a "loss of coolant accident." Two-thirds of the core was uncovered, which caused extensive damage to the core and other equipment. Radioactive material was released within the building.

It was a real disaster.

THE ISSUE FOR TRIAL

Everyone agreed that, except for the failure of the PORV to close, there was no problem with the equipment. The cause of the accident was the conduct of the operators in turning off the HPI and leaving it off as long as they did. General Public Utilities, represented by Kaye Scholer, waived a jury trial in return for our agreement to have a speedy trial before a judge. The question for the judge—Richard Owen of the Southern District—was whose fault it was that the operators acted as they did.

GPU'S "SMOKING GUN"

Two years before there had been a similar incident at another B&W plant, Davis-Besse in Toledo. No one had experienced an event like it before, but the Davis-Besse plant was at low power and the operators diagnosed the problem before any serious damage occurred.

B&W sent a team of engineers led by the head of its safety division, a man named Bert Dunn, to analyze what had happened. They concluded there was no problem with the equipment. The problem was that B&W had not given adequate instructions to the operators to deal with the situation that occurred.

Bert Dunn wrote a memo to eleven people at B&W in which he laid this all out and proposed specific instructions to deal with this kind of event which, it was now clear, could occur although it never had before.

Dunn's memo did not mince words. He wrote that it was fortunate that the Toledo plant was at extremely low power. "Had this event occurred in a reactor at full power . . . it is quite possible, perhaps probable, that core unrecovery and possible fuel damage would have resulted."

He went on:

"The incident points out that we have not supplied sufficient information to reactor operators in the area of recovery from LOCA [loss of coolant accident] . . . I,

therefore, recommend that operating procedures be written to allow for termination of high pressure injection . . . . [only when] . . . system pressure has recovered to
normal operating pressure (2250 psig) and system temperature within the hot leg is
less than or equal to the normal operating conditions (605° F)."

Dunn called the matter "very serious" and said it "deserves our prompt attention
and correction." But the operating procedures he recommended were never sent.

In 1979 following the near meltdown at Three Mile Island, Congress, the Nuclear
Regulatory Commission (NRC), and a specially constituted presidential commission—
headed by Dartmouth University President John G. Kemeny—all convened hearings.
In them, everyone agreed that if the Dunn instructions had been sent and followed the
accident would not have happened.

News coverage of the hearings fed a strong and widespread—indeed universal—
public perception that B&W's failure to send the instructions was inexcusable to the
point of being unconscionable. The NRC found that a "breakdown of communications"
and "crucial misunderstanding" within B&W were precursor events to the disaster.

In the year-and-a-half leading to the trial, while we were boning up on nuclear
power and various accident scenarios as well as deposing witnesses, I got a real sense of
what we were up against. Everyone I told that I was representing B&W had the same
reaction: "How do you defend this case?"

The answer lay in going on the offensive—attacking GPU for various acts of negligence, including the failure of the operators to diagnose the problem even without the
Dunn memo. In order to do that effectively we deployed our defense team in what the
American Lawyer would later call the "zone defense." Karen Wagner immersed herself in
operator training issues. Linda Thomsen's realm was the Dunn memo. Bill Wurtz was
in charge of all facts relating to the accident sequence. Rod Benedict was developing
evidence on leak rates. Susan Johnston was becoming the PORV expert. And Ann
McDonald was in charge of the facts relating to the condensate polishers. All of them
reported directly to me and Bob Wise, the partner who was trying the case with me,
so that we could each work with them, one on one, in learning that aspect of the case.

THE NEW YORK MARATHON

All the while, in those first months of getting up to speed on how nuclear reactors
worked, I was also trying to get up to a running speed that would allow me to complete
the New York Marathon in under four hours. My younger brother, John, had run the

Boston Marathon in 1978, finishing in three hours, fifty-nine minutes and fifty-eight seconds; I wanted to do at least as well. I trained hard, running with friends all spring and summer, and when November came I was ready.

The start of the marathon in Staten Island is a crowd scene. The elite runners get their own start but the rest of us—16,000, more or less—jostled together until there was enough room to actually move our feet and head across the Verrazano Bridge. When I finally hit Brooklyn it was a thrill to find spectators lined three deep along the streets. Boom boxes were blasting the theme from "Rocky" and volunteers held out cups of water.

A strong wind was blowing from the west. That had been a great help at the start, a tailwind that pushed us across the Verrazano. But it was in my face as I crossed the 59th Street Bridge from Queens into Manhattan. Then as I turned up First Avenue toward the Bronx I passed some friends whose cheers prompted an injudicious burst of speed. At about the twentieth mile, coming down from the Bronx along Fifth Avenue, my thighs were killing me and I was mustering all my determination to keep going.

Suddenly, about thirty yards ahead, a very large man stepped out of the crowd and stationed himself in the middle of the road in what I saw as a confrontational pose. My first thought was, "I can't deal with this." Then he raised his right hand, slapped mine in a high-five and said, "You can do it, dude!"

With the distraction I forgot how bad my thighs were hurting. I got my second wind and made it down Fifth Avenue and into Central Park and across the finish line in under four hours.

That was my one marathon. It was a challenge, and I had wanted to see if I could do it, but I had promised Janet it would be a one-time event and not the start of a series of marathons in New York and elsewhere—as some of my friends and colleagues were doing. But I continued to run to relieve stress, as the Three Mile Island case was proving complicated beyond the details of nuclear power generation.

Running the NY Marathon

THE PENNSYLVANIA STATUTE

This was a diversity of jurisdiction case and the law of Pennsylvania, where the accident occurred, applied. The governing statute, combining contributory and comparative negligence, offered two alternatives. If the plaintiff's negligence is more than 50 percent responsible for the accident, the plaintiff loses. If it is 50 percent or less, then the loss is apportioned according to the negligence assigned to each party.

As the November 1982 trial date drew closer, Judge Owen had already eliminated half of GPU's monetary claims against B&W. In pre-trial motions he tossed out the claim for $2 billion for the cost of replacement power because of contractual clauses preventing consequential damages. So, that meant either GPU would lose, or get a percentage of $2 billion that by definition would be anywhere between $1 billion and $2 billion. Even the lower figure was more than the net worth of J. Ray McDermott.

DEFENSE BY OFFENSE

As noted earlier we decided that our best course was to go on the offensive. First we would attack GPU and the operators to show that even without the Dunn instructions they should have figured out what was happening and turned the HPI back on in time to prevent the damage. Only secondarily would we defend B&W's conduct in not sending the Dunn memo.

The trial started on November 1. David Klingsberg of Kaye Scholer, representing GPU, devoted almost all of his opening to the Dunn memo, telling the judge:

"It is a frightening episode because of the horrendous damage which Babcock's misconduct caused and the unthinkable risks to human life which it created."

I cited the Pennsylvania statute and said we would prove that GPU's negligence was overwhelmingly more than 50 percent responsible for the accident. I described the different ways GPU's conduct had caused the accident and didn't mention the Dunn memo at all until the end.

Our best way to prove our case was by attacking their witnesses; their best way to prove their case was by attacking our witnesses. As the plaintiffs, they had to go first. The key people at B&W, like Bert Dunn, were located out of state in Lynchburg, Virginia and were not at the management level. GPU could not compel us to produce them for its case and we declined to do so. We said we would produce them in our case. Meanwhile, we prepared to go after their witnesses on cross examination.

GPU's expert witness

GPU OPENED THE DOOR

Early on GPU called Robert Arnold, the person in charge of servicing all of GPU's nuclear operations. He testified persuasively as to what a well-run place GPU was. However, his broad testimony opened the door to cross examination on several damaging points that emerged from the depositions we had taken.

One of these came from a man named Richard Zechman who was in charge of training. Zechman was not himself a licensed operator. He was spending half his time training operators to become licensed and half his time studying to get his own license.

The night before we were scheduled to take his deposition, GPU delivered four large boxes of previously requested documents to our office around 8 p.m. We were pretty sure they thought we would never have time to thoroughly review them before the deposition started. But Karen Wagner and two legal assistants stayed up all night and, around 4 a.m., one of them found a document showing that Zechman had taken the operator's test—and flunked it. Early in the deposition we confronted him with the document. The other side immediately asked for a break. After about ten minutes they came back and said the witness was sick and the deposition would have to be adjourned.

When it resumed a month later we asked him about the failed test. We also showed him one of the procedures drafted by B&W and given to the operators: a heatup/cooldown curve reproduced on the facing page.

Heatup/Cooldown Curve with Saturation Line

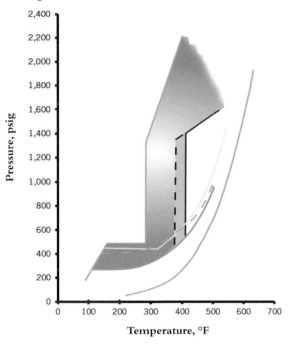

The blue curve at the right is called the saturation line—it shows the temperature/ pressure ratios at which the water will boil or—in the parlance of the operators—become saturated. The procedure prescribes that the pressure/temperature ratio must be at all times in the gray shaded area to the left of the curve—a comfortable margin above saturation. But when asked, Zechman said he did not know on which side of the saturation curve the operators were supposed to be.

At a later deposition we confronted GPU Vice President James Herblein with Zechman's answer. He said he did not think it was important that the head of training know that.

James Floyd was the head of operations at TMI-1, one of the two reactors at the Three Mile Island complex. The accident had occurred at TMI-2. Floyd also had to have a license from the NRC and had to pass a test in order to obtain it. From deposing him we learned that the test was a take-home exam in two parts and that Floyd had someone else take one of the parts for him. GPU sent the test in and Floyd got his license.

GPU had been cavalier about this in the depositions, so much so that I was able to say in my opening statement, "We asked people from GPU about this in the depositions and their answer was, 'We didn't consider that cheating,'" I said.

"They didn't consider that what?" was Judge Owen's sharp comeback.

"Cheating."

We cross examined Robert Arnold on the stand about Zechman's test failure and Floyd's phantom co-test taker. GPU objected that these things were irrelevant because they happened after the accident. Judge Owen overruled, saying, "I got the impression that all was right with the training department . . . Now it seems to me highly probative . . . Isn't this a cover-up, arguably . . . a cover-up of another incompetent at the supervisory level? Doesn't this clearly show the quality of the people that were in charge of training?"

GPU'S NEGLIGENCE

We contended that GPU caused the accident with several acts of negligence, three before the accident and two while it was going on.

We brought out on cross examination that before the accident GPU manipulated leak rates to avoid having to shut the plant down. Leakage is serious because it can indicate a crack in the system presaging a major eruption. The NRC requires a shut-down if leakage exceeds one gallon per minute. GPU falsely reported rates of less than a gallon a minute. They had an economic motive.

Of the company's two plants at Three Mile Island TMI-1 had been shut down for repairs for several weeks before the accident. Shutting down TMI-2 would have taken both plants off-line and cost GPU up to $500,000 per day in replacement power, although by happenstance TMI-1 was scheduled to reopen less than twelve hours after the accident sequence started. We argued that if GPU had told the truth to the NRC the plant would have been shut down and there would have been no accident.

The second pre-accident act of negligence involved the condensate polishers, a piece of equipment on the secondary side. On an earlier occasion water had gotten into the valves of the polishers which had shut down the flow of water into the generator. GPU ignored internal recommendations on a way to fix the problem and it happened again on March 28, 1979, starting the sequence that caused the accident.

GPU's operator training—or lack of it—was the third act of neglect before the accident. The company was responsible by contract for the basic training of the operators in how the system worked. That was 90 percent of the required training. B&W was responsible for advanced training, which included the use of simulators to create various accident sequences—although not this one—and it had a duty to keep plant owners updated on important developments relating to the operation of the reactor.

We stressed that GPU's operator training—including the basic pressure/temperature ratios necessary to prevent boiling—was deficient, and that was why they did not diagnose the accident.

NEGLIGENCE DURING THE ACCIDENT SEQUENCE

To prove GPU's negligence during the accident sequence, we had to show that the symptoms were so obvious that the operators should have figured it out without the Dunn memo. This was a major challenge: how could all four operators misdiagnose the problem if the diagnosis was so obvious?

This was our impetus for having to learn how a nuclear plant works. The defense team spent almost a year in lengthy sessions with B&W personnel to be able to effectively cross examine the operators.

The operators claimed that the only loss of coolant accident they had been trained on by B&W—and the only kind they ever envisioned—was a break in the system, with water running out the bottom of the reactor. In that case the water level in the pressurizer would drop, and they would keep the HPI on until it resumed its original level.

They testified that they always thought you could measure water level in the reactor by the pressurizer level. It showed normal in this case because water was boiling and going out the top keeping the level up, and so they thought that the level of water in the primary system was where it should be. They stressed that if the level was where it was supposed to be they were taught to avoid "going solid." The term means continuing to add water when the pressurizer level was normal which could fill up the pressurizer and destroy its ability to create pressure from the steam at the top.

We challenged them on two basic points—two different ways in which they negligently failed to diagnose the problem. First, they failed to diagnose that the pressure operated relief valve was open. Second, they turned off the high-pressure injection system when they should have known that the water was boiling.

In fairness to the operators there was a light on the control panel that was supposed to go off when the PORV was closed. But it only showed that the power was on to the solenoid that was supposed to close the PORV, not that the valve actually closed. Further, we argued that the symptoms were so unmistakable that even if the light was off they should have known the PORV was open.

The first indication was the drop in pressure. A B&W drafted procedure said that a psi of 1640 was a symptom of an open PORV. The psi went down to that level in the first few minutes. The second indication was the temperature on the discharge pipe downstream of the PORV.

At his deposition and at the trial the chief operator, William Zewe, testified that he had no reason to think the PORV was open because of the temperature readings on the discharge pipe. He claimed he was told when the accident started that the temperature on the pipe was 280 degrees and that when he checked later he was told it was 230 degrees. That indicated to him that the pipe was cooling down—which would mean that the PORV was closed.

A CRUCIAL FIND

But we had learned that the NRC had conducted and recorded interviews at Three Mile Island about two weeks after the accident. The tapes were on file, but not transcribed. We went down to the NRC, found the tapes and Ann McDonald listened to them for many hours. She heard Zewe telling the NRC that he had been told the initial reading was 225 degrees, not 280, which would mean the pipe was not cooling down.

We were pretty sure the team representing GPU didn't know about the tapes, so we made a key tactical decision not to cross examine Zewe about this at his deposition. Then at the trial we sought and won a ruling—over strenuous objections—barring substantive discussions between him and the GPU lawyers once his cross examination started. That kind of directive is common in criminal cases, but was very infrequent in civil trials.

Zewe testified on direct, as he had in his deposition, that the first temperature reading was 280 degrees and when he heard the lower temperature of 230 degrees he thought the pipe was cooling down and the PORV was therefore closed. On cross examination we had him repeat the testimony and then played the tape. Both he and the judge heard him say that the first temperature he heard was 225 degrees.

We challenged him, saying, "Isn't it a fact that you changed your story (to 280) because a temperature of 225 would have shown that the PORV was open?" He denied it, but we were sure the judge got the point.

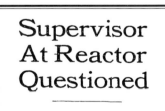

Supervisor At Reactor Questioned

Testimony on Data Attacked

The New York Times,
November 24, 1982

The operators testified that they were trained to turn off the high pressure injection system once pressurizer level came back to normal, as they thought it had. A B&W procedure given to them actually said not to turn it off until pressurizer level and pressure had both come back to normal, which had not happened.

We cross examined them extensively on their failure to recognize obvious signs of trouble. There were instruments right in the center of the control panel that, side by side, showed pressure and temperature. We stressed to them that it had to be obvious from the fact that temperature was over 600 degrees and pressure was 1640 psi instead of the normal 2250 that the water in the primary system was boiling.

GPU tried to rehabilitate its operators by asking to call an expert witness to explain why their conduct was reasonable. Judge Owen refused saying, "I don't need an expert witness in stupidity."

SETTLEMENT

That comment and others showed GPU the writing on the wall. By now it was January 1983 and the trial was in its third month. GPU had not finished its case when its business people approached B&W about a resolution. A settlement was reached just as we started the defense case with Bert Dunn on the stand. It was announced on January 24 as the trial came to an abrupt end.

GPU dropped its $2 billion lawsuit in return for a contract giving it the right to buy from B&W services and equipment used in the continuing cleanup of Three Mile Island at a discount off the list price totaling $37 million. The discount was still above cost, and B&W stood to make a large profit if GPU bought the hundreds of millions of dollars' worth of equipment and services necessary to reach a total of $37 million off the list price. That would have been a bonanza for B&W in light of the depressed state of the industry after the accident.

We asked that the contract require GPU to make the purchases. They declined. We asked that it require GPU to use its best efforts to make the purchases. They declined. In the end they actually bought almost nothing. In short, the suit had been dropped in return for a contractual option which, if exercised by GPU, would have been a huge benefit to B&W.

LESSONS IN ADVOCACY

In the aftermath we had cause to reflect on the success of our "zone defense." Giving each associate responsibility for a discrete subject area had worked extremely well in bringing the team up to speed for both depositions and the trial.

That was among the lessons in advocacy I recounted years later, in May 2009, when I was asked to speak in Toronto at a program sponsored by the American College of Trial Lawyers and the Canadian Advocates' Society. Using the Three Mile Island trial as my example, I stressed thorough preparation not just in the way we deployed our associates, but in the long hours learning how a nuclear reactor worked; finding and listening to the NRC tapes; and staying up all night to find the Zechman failed test results.

Another significant lesson was the importance of litigating on the offense—attacking GPU and only secondarily defending the Dunn memo.

Tactical decisions are also important, I said. The example I used was saving the damning Zewe tape from the NRC interview to use in cross examination at the trial, rather than at his deposition.

Finally, I told the Canadian lawyers that in my experience a mistake even experienced trial lawyers make is becoming infatuated with the testimony that a particular witness can give without thinking through what damaging information could be elicited on cross. (We had made that mistake with the Guy Fisher witness in the Barnes case.) Juries and judges think that whoever calls a particular witness is vouching for the proposition that the witness will help that side's case. If cross reduces the weight of evidence to 50-50, the side that called the witness will have lost. GPU's star witness, Robert Arnold, was an example—opening the door as his testimony did to the Zechman and Floyd debacles.

—∞—

The TMI case exemplified the rewards of private practice in three separate ways. First, the opportunity to make a difference for a client: to make a potentially bad situation better, with the gratification that comes from making that happen—in some cases by a total vindication and in others by a favorable settlement. Second, the opportunity to learn the intimate details about a wide variety of industries ranging from nuclear power to the auction markets in tobacco and art. The fact that you have to master the facts to be successful isn't a burden; it's a series of windows opening into interesting new worlds. And third, the opportunity—as in government service—to work and bond as a team with the many exceedingly smart and highly motivated young lawyers whom it was my privilege to help train.

CHAPTER 25

USFL v. NFL

THE SAME YEAR THAT General Public Utilities agreed to the settlement with Babcock & Wilcox in the Three Mile Island case, a new football league launched play in the United States with a spring schedule that avoided direct competition with the established National Football League (NFL). But before long the new league called an audible and the two leagues wound up in a jury trial that produced a strange but eminently fair result.

The United States Football League (USFL) was conceived to play competitive, crowd-pleasing football with high-quality players just short of NFL caliber—comparable to baseball's Triple A-level teams. Its founders believed that the public demand for football was not satisfied by fall football at the NFL and college levels, and that cable television, which could not televise NFL games under the existing network contracts, would offer the USFL games. There was little competition for football viewers in the spring and there were enough good players for both leagues. The new league intended to use major stadiums and hire well-known coaches.

The USFL began play in 1983 with teams in Birmingham, Boston, Chicago, Denver, Los Angeles, Detroit, New Jersey, Oakland, Philadelphia, Phoenix, Tampa and Washington, D.C. The teams' location in major television markets allowed the league to obtain multi-million dollar network and cable television contracts with ABC and ESPN.

The first year was a mixed success. Its ratings were good but not great—6.23 on ABC and 3.28 on ESPN, compared with NFL ratings around 14. Average attendance was a respectable 25,000. Both figures jibed with the league and networks' pre-season projections.

The picture was not so bright on the financial side. The USFL lost almost $40 million, an average of $3.3 million per team, principally because teams exceeded the budgeted player salary guidelines of $1.3 to $1.5 million per team. Detroit's Michigan Panthers won the championship and lost $6 million dollars, leading owner Alfred Taubman to tell students at the Harvard Business School his formula for becoming a multi-millionaire: become a billionaire and buy a professional football team.

In its second year the USFL expanded from twelve to eighteen teams, four teams changed cities and five of the original owners left the league. Several of the new owners, led by New Jersey Generals owner Donald Trump, believed the league should go head-to-head with the NFL and play in the fall. This produced a heated, divisive debate among the owners throughout the 1984 season. That August, despite renewed television contracts for spring football with more money going forward, the owners voted to move to the fall beginning with the 1986 season. Two months later the USFL filed an antitrust suit against the NFL.

The suit charged the NFL had monopolized the business of professional football by signing contracts with all three major networks for televising its games. It said the league, by pressuring and threatening the networks to keep them from televising the USFL in the fall, had used its monopoly power to prevent the USFL from getting a television contract for fall football.

The complaint alleged the NFL had unfairly prevented the USFL from competing for players by expanding team rosters and creating a "supplemental draft" that coincided with the USFL recruiting season. It also charged the NFL had tied up the best officials and stadiums with full-year contracts, even though the NFL had no need for them in the spring. Finally, it accused the NFL of unfair disparagement of the USFL and the quality of its players and football products. The complaint asked for $1.32 billion in damages and an injunction.

Donald Trump's good friend, the notorious Roy Cohn, represented the USFL when the complaint was filed. Arthur Liman of Paul, Weiss, Rifkind, Wharton & Garrison represented the NFL. Cohn and Liman disliked each other intensely, and Cohn took great pleasure in moving to disqualify him and Paul Weiss on the ground that they had a conflict because the firm had negotiated stadium leases for the USFL. Judge Peter K. Leisure, who was Liman's good friend, ruled in Cohn's favor.

About a week later I returned to the office late in the afternoon and found a telephone message slip by my phone: "Please call Jay Moyer, Executive Vice President and general counsel, NFL."

The next day I went up to the NFL headquarters on Park Avenue where I met Moyer and Commissioner Pete Rozelle. They retained me to defend the case. Shortly thereafter, Roy Cohn withdrew in failing health and was replaced by Harvey Myerson of Finley, Kumble, Wagner, Heine, Underberg, Manley, Myerson & Casey.

Harvey Myerson was a high-flying, high-profile lawyer. *Fortune* magazine listed him in October 1985 as one of the top five trial lawyers in the country. His style was flamboyant—in and out of the courtroom. News clippings referred glowingly to "Heavy-Hitter Harvey," a gravelly-voiced "pit bull" litigator. *Fortune* nicknamed him

"Master of Disaster" for rescuing troubled companies from their legal problems. Outside the courtroom he was notorious for his raccoon coats, his big Cuban cigars, his Rolls-Royces, racing cars and high-priced art, with a "to die for" office at the firm's "Hall of Kings" corridor on Park Avenue. Trump thought he would be a worthy successor to Roy Cohn.

So instead of Cohn v. Liman, it was now to be Myerson v. Fiske.

Before the trial Myerson approached me with a settlement proposal. I presented it to the NFL owners at the spring meeting for their consideration, and they rejected it unanimously. Following that meeting, at the urging of several owners who wanted to fight the case all the way and were upset that a settlement proposal had been presented, the NFL brought Frank Rothman of Skadden, Arps, Slate, Meagher & Flom in as co-counsel.

The trial started in May 1986. Judge Leisure wanted an efficient trial, and at the outset he gave each side four weeks to present its case. He broke it down to an estimated six hours a day for twenty days, or a total of 120 hours. They could be used in either direct or cross examination, but when they were used up that side would be through no matter how much time the other side had left.

The USFL's principal evidence consisted of testimony as to the anti-competitive effect of the NFL having television contracts with all three networks. This included testimony from Commissioner Rozelle that one league on all three networks put rivals at a competitive disadvantage, that he had no problem in putting the USFL at a "major competitive disadvantage," and that all dominant sports leagues are natural monopolies. He said he believed that the only league playing fall football should be the NFL. The USFL also introduced an internal memorandum written by Moyer during network contract negotiations in 1973 that "an open network may well be an open invitation to a new league." The USFL claimed that the NFL, which had previously been on both CBS and NBC on Sunday afternoons, had signed up ABC for Monday night football to create a monopoly that precluded a new league.

Further to the same point was a June 1984 CBS business study suggesting that the fall broadcast of USFL games on Sundays would reduce the networks' advertising resources from NFL games between $49 million and $53 million over three years. The USFL argued that this "dilution effect" created a $50 million barrier to entry by a new league.

Prominently featured in the USFL's evidence was a presentation to the NFL, made at its request by Professor Michael Porter of the Harvard Business School. Porter captioned it "How to Conquer the USFL." His suggestions included bankrupting the weakest USFL teams by driving up player salaries, pressuring ABC not to continue USFL broadcasts by giving it an unattractive schedule for Monday night games,[55] showing highlights of NFL games at times that conflicted with USFL telecasts, and co-opting important USFL owners by offering them NFL franchises.

To the same effect was an internal memorandum by NFL labor negotiator, Jack Donlan, entitled "Spending the USFL dollar" which urged NFL owners to bid high for USFL players to drive up USFL costs.

The USFL offered proof from Al Davis, owner of the NFL's Los Angeles Raiders, that the league had conspired with the City of Oakland to destroy the USFL's Oakland Invaders in return for an NFL promise that Oakland would receive an NFL team. Davis was the odd man out among NFL owners since he had moved his Oakland Raiders to Los Angeles without NFL approval and defeated the NFL's suit challenging the move. The USFL had sued every owner but him, which encouraged him to testify.

The new league also offered proof—from Senator Alphonse D'Amato and Vincent Tese, Chairman of the New York State Urban Development Corporation—that Leon Hess—owner of the Jets—had promised them he would return the Jets to New York from New Jersey. The USFL claimed that this was part of a conspiracy to block Donald Trump's New Jersey team from moving to a new domed stadium in New York.

Frank Rothman and I agreed that, as in the Three Mile Island case, the best defense was a good offense. And we found much to work with in the USFL's own documents, particularly those of the original owners who did not like the direction that Donald Trump and the others were taking the league. It was clear that in urging the USFL to move to the fall Trump had in mind the success of the American Football League (AFL) in forcing its 1970 merger with the NFL. We contended that it was that strategy, not any monopolistic tactics of the NFL, that had caused the USFL to suspend its operations for 1986. It had said it would resume in 1987 but that seemed unlikely.

We were able to show that two particular USFL strategies had backfired on the league. The first was that it was the USFL—not the NFL—that was bidding up players' salaries, as the old AFL had done to put pressure on the NFL. This caused player salaries in both leagues to almost double what the NFL had been paying in 1982. Well-financed owners like Donald Trump and Alfred Taubman could afford these salaries, but many of the more marginal USFL owners could not.

Second, in order to position itself for a merger the USFL moved several franchises out of larger television markets to cities that did not currently have an NFL team. These included Baltimore, whose Colts had moved to Indianapolis in 1984, Oakland, which had lost the Raiders to LA, and Orlando and Phoenix. Eddie Einhorn, the USFL owner responsible for negotiating the television contracts, had warned that these moves might impair the league's ability to get a television contract by replacing larger markets with smaller ones. He was right. ABC withheld a significant portion of the USFL's rights fees for the 1985 season, and ESPN demanded a renegotiation of its proposed 1985–87 contract. Tad Taube, the original owner of the Oakland Invaders, summed up the situation in a memo to his fellow owners that borrowed the famous line from the Pogo comic strip: "We have met the enemy and he is us."

Finally, there was evidence from within the USFL that the lawsuit itself was part of the "force a merger" strategy. Myles Tannenbaum, the original owner of the Philadelphia franchise, wrote an internal memorandum citing his view of the three ways to make money in professional football: "tickets, television, and treble damages."

The USFL tried to keep the "force a merger" evidence out of the trial. They claimed it was an impermissible *in pari delicto,* or unclean hands defense.[56] That argument was rejected by Judge Leisure and upheld on appeal with some cogent language from Second Circuit Judge Ralph Winter:

> "It quite simply defies logic for the USFL to assert on the one hand that it was denied a network contract indispensable to its survival because of the NFL's anticompetitive acts and to argue on the other for exclusion of evidence that the owners of the USFL franchises knowingly lessened the value of their product to television. *Courts do not exclude evidence of a victim's suicide in a murder trial.*" (Emphasis added.)[57]

The USFL's damage testimony came from economist Nina Cornell, who estimated the league's losses primarily by assuming that the gate and television revenues of an unhindered USFL could be estimated by comparison with the old AFL. She estimated the USFL's damages by this method at $565 million (before trebling).

Relying heavily on a deposition taken by my partner Guy Struve, my cross examination exposed several flaws in her calculations. She had assumed that illegal NFL conduct was the reason the USFL did not get a network contract for fall football. She did not allow for the possibility that the USFL caused damages by its own mismanagement in bidding up salaries and moving out of television markets into merger cities. And she had assumed that despite enormous projected increases in television revenue and gate

Cross examing Nina Cornell

receipts resulting from the shift to fall play, player salaries would remain the same from 1986 to 1992.

She projected attendance at the USFL games based on growth rates in attendance at the old AFL. The New York Jets, for example, had a 188 percent increase in attendance during their first year and the Oakland Raiders had a 6 percent increase. She split the difference and projected a 97 percent increase for all twelve USFL teams that would be playing in NFL cities.[58] By that calculation her attendance figures by 1992 substantially exceeded stadium capacities; the Jets would have drawn by then 230,000 fans a game. Thus she was forced to produce a revised number called "constrained attendance," which was the actual maximum capacity of the stadiums.

This, of course, produced the hypothetical anomaly of the New York Generals (Trump's team) playing in Shea Stadium in 1992 with 65,000 people in the stands—and another 165,000 who couldn't get in—gathered to watch a group of players who hadn't had a salary increase for seven years.

After two months of trial, a timetable that fit Judge Leisure's timetable almost exactly, the case went to the jury with the instruction to answer a set of specific interrogatories.

After several days of deliberation they announced they had reached a verdict. They gave their interrogatory answers to Judge Leisure, who proceeded to read them one by one to a standing room-only audience in the courtroom.

Harvey Myerson and the Finley Kumble team were at the front table. We were at the table right behind them. The first question was: "Do you find that the NFL monopolized the business of professional football, yes or no?"

"Yes." This produced some elbow bumping at the USFL table.

A series of twenty-seven questions followed, one as to each NFL club—except Al Davis's Raiders—asking whether that club was part of the monopoly.

"Yes," twenty-seven times. More elbow bumping.

"Do you find that this caused injury to the USFL?"

"Yes." By now they were almost jumping out of their seats ahead of us.

"In what amount?"

"One dollar." We watched the whole table in front of us collapse like air going out of a balloon.

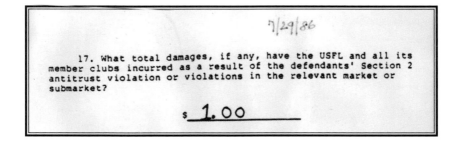

WCBS Radio was broadcasting live each interrogatory response as it came in. Pete Rozelle, having heard there was a verdict, called his driver and they headed to the courthouse down Park Avenue with the radio turned on. When they reached 23rd Street and heard that the USFL had suffered injury, he told the driver to turn around. They had retreated a block north when the amount of the damage was broadcast.

"Turn around again," the Commissioner told his driver.

So, back they went, down to the courthouse. Donald Trump was in the courtroom for the verdict. He was sitting next to John Mara, the son of New York Giants owner Wellington Mara. When Judge Leisure announced the jury's $1 damage verdict, John Mara reached into his pocket, pulled out a dollar bill and handed it to Trump.

Following the verdict the USFL retained Ira Millstein and Jim Quinn at Weil Got-shal & Manges to represent it in a motion for injunctive relief. Based on the monopolization finding they asked Judge Leisure to direct that the NFL could be on only two networks. Judge Leisure denied that request, and any other injunctive relief, a holding that along with the jury verdict of $1.00 damages was upheld on appeal. As Judge Winter put it:

> "Notwithstanding the jury's evident conclusions that the USFL's product was not appealing largely for reasons of the USFL's own doing and that the networks chose freely not to purchase it, the USFL asks us to grant sweeping injunctive relief that will reward its impatience and self-destructive conduct with a fall network contract. It thus seeks through court decree the success it failed to achieve among football fans. Absent a showing of some unlawful harm to competition, we cannot prevent a network from showing NFL games, in the hope that the network and fans will turn to the USFL. The Sherman Act does not outlaw an industry structure simply because it prevents competitors from achieving immediate parity."[59]

The USFL finally won a victory, of sorts, when it persuaded Judge Leisure and the Second Circuit that it should be awarded its attorneys' fees. Both courts concluded that the Clayton Act makes clear that all that is required for an award of attorneys' fees is injury to the plaintiff.[60] So, while the USFL obtained no injunctive relief and only $1.00 in damages, Harvey Myerson and his Finley Kumble colleagues were paid $5,529,297.25 by the NFL.

—⁓—

PROFESSIONAL SERVICE, POLITICAL PERIL

CHAPTER 26

The American College of Trial Lawyers

THE LAW IS an intensely collaborative profession. It takes teamwork and that's one reason why it has generated such an array of volunteer groups and associations to explore and improve the administration and pursuit of justice.

Every profession has its tiers of achievement and for trial lawyers one of those tiers, at the top, is membership in the American College of Trial Lawyers (ACTL).

The ACTL dates its origins to April 5, 1950, when two prominent California trial lawyers, Emil Gumpert and Les Cleary, were riding a Pullman car from San Francisco to Los Angeles to attend a California Bar Association meeting. Gumpert woke up in the middle of the night and from his upper berth asked Cleary, "Les, are you a member of the American College of Trial Lawyers?"

Cleary told him to go back to sleep. But Gumpert persisted, saying, "There is an American College of Surgeons. Why don't we have an American College of Trial Lawyers?"

Gumpert asked the question again the next night in Los Angeles over dinner at the home of Grant and Phyllis Cooper, well-known trial attorneys. The idea took fruit and the American College of Trial Lawyers was born, conceived as an organization for a very limited group of the nation's most outstanding trial lawyers comprising no more than one percent of the lawyers in any state or Canadian province.

Cody Fowler also played a major early role. He was the President of the American Bar Association (ABA) and was in Southern California for a meeting when he entered a room where the local ACTL contingent was sitting around drinking whiskey. He joined in and, as the story goes, after some discussion and more whiskey told them, "I am the best goddamned trial lawyer in this room." They inducted him and that year, traveling around the country as President of the ABA, he identified a group of leading trial lawyers from each area he visited, thus quickly expanding the College into a nationwide organization.

Over the years the College grew to its present membership of over 5,000 fellows—the term used for members—throughout the United States and Canada. Its presidents have included some of the country's most prominent lawyers, including Simon Rifkind, Leon Jaworski, Whitney North Seymour, Lewis Powell and Griffin Bell. All members of the United States Supreme Court and the Supreme Court of Canada, as well as a number of British jurists, have accepted honorary memberships.

No one applies for membership. Lawyers have to be proposed by an individual, which requires two seconders, or a state or province committee. The candidate is not supposed to know he or she is being considered. The extensive vetting process includes interviews with opposing counsel and judges. A lawyer is not approved by the state committee—and thereafter by the governing Board of Regents—unless he or she meets strict criteria. It's not enough to be good. High ethical and moral standards—professionalism and excellent character—are indispensable, and the most frequently asked question when the Regents consider a new member is, "Is this candidate just a very good trial lawyer, or is he/she really one of the very best in the state/province?"

I was admitted to the ACTL in 1975 and was inducted in Atlanta, Georgia during the period when Emil Gumpert was still delivering the induction charge. The ceremony is impressive—a black tie dinner for fellows and spouses at which the new inductees line up on stage facing ACTL past presidents while the charge is read.

As Past President Lewis Powell put it in a 1993 talk to ACTL fellows, "I doubt that the literature of our profession contains any more eloquent statement of the role and duty of a trial lawyer than Emil Gumpert's induction address," which he then quoted:

> "You, whose names are freshly inscribed upon our rolls, have, by your mastery of the art of advocacy, by your high degree of personal integrity, your maturity in practice and your signal triumphs at the bar of justice, earned the honor about to be conferred upon you.
>
> By your ability, learning and character you have added lustre to the legal and judicial annals of your state and nation, and have helped to strengthen and preserve the mighty fabric of our law.
>
> We are confident that in the days to come, the lofty objects and purposes of this organization will be further advanced by the application of those rare qualities and virtues which nature, fortune and laborious days have bestowed upon you."

With Janet at the Palace of Versailles

The charge concludes with the welcome to new fellows "as sages of our craft" and the wish, "Long and happy may be our days together."

Over the years the College has been a strong, impartial, non-political voice for improvements in the administration of justice. Its Code of Pre-Trial and Trial Conduct, with an introduction by Chief Justice John Roberts (and, in a previous edition, by Chief Justice Rehnquist), is frequently cited in court opinions. Its fellows volunteer to teach trial advocacy at law schools and to legal aid and other public interest organizations. And its thirty-five standing committees, chosen with an eye to balance, produce reports on issues of interest to the judiciary and to the trial bar that carry great weight because of their recognized impartiality.

The ACTL honored me in 1987 with election to the Board of Regents, and in 1991 to a one-year term as President. Elections are held at annual meetings, with the outgoing president presiding, and the end of my term coincided with the 1992 meeting that was held in London and Paris. Past President Alston Jennings from Little Rock delivered the invocation at the London session. He was missing for my final act, presiding over the closing banquet held at the Hall of Battles in the Palace of Versailles on November 3. Alston was back home in Little Rock by then watching the election night returns with his former law partner, William Jefferson Clinton.

Now approaching its sixty-fifth year as I write this, the American College of Trial Lawyers has fulfilled Emil Gumpert's initial sleepy vision of a rare meritocracy bringing together the very best practitioners to exchange ideas and propose improvements in trial practice and in justice itself. It has been one of the most rewarding and enjoyable experiences of my career, both for the opportunity to serve and for the friendships that I have made and kept over the years.

ACTL Officers, Regents and Past Presidents 1992

ACTL Officers, Regents and Past Presidents 2012

CHAPTER 27

The Federal Bar Council

THE FEDERAL BAR COUNCIL was organized in 1928 as the New York chapter of the national Federal Bar Association. In 1932, the New York chapter withdrew from the Federal Bar Association because it refused to admit African-Americans. In 1968 it became the Federal Bar Council, focusing on the courts within the Second Judicial Circuit—New York, Connecticut, and Vermont.

Spearheaded by a group of Judge Lumbard's former assistants—Peter Brown, Whitney N. "Mike" Seymour Jr., Harold Tyler, George Leisure and Fred Nathan—a number of significant changes were made beginning in 1961. Its programs were significantly enhanced and its leadership envisioned it as an advisory council to the Second Circuit, acting as barristers did in England as a law council of Inns of Court, a professional association emphasizing legal skills and ethics.

Today it has over 3,700 lawyers primarily from the Second Circuit states who practice regularly in their federal courts, although lawyers from all over the country belong. As described in its mission statement the Federal Bar Council "is dedicated to promoting excellence in federal practice and fellowship among federal practitioners [and] committed to encouraging respectful, cordial relations between the bench and bar."

The Council has had for many years two traditional events that always draw near-sellout crowds of judges and lawyers. These are a luncheon on the Wednesday before Thanksgiving at which the Council bestows the Emory Buckner Award for Outstanding Public Service and a Law Day dinner in May at which it bestows the Learned Hand Medal for Excellence in Federal Jurisprudence.

Since 1969 the Council has also sponsored an annual Winter Bench & Bar Conference, held in a warmer climate, that has become an extremely popular event. The friendly, laid-back atmosphere engenders great collegiality among the judges and lawyers who attend it, and it offers programs of exceptionally high quality thanks primarily to Mike Seymour. When Mike was President in 1982, he persuaded Court of Appeals Judge Walter Mansfield to head up a program committee that would select the topics for discussion and the proposed panels of judges and lawyers to present them. The panelists rarely said no when Judge Mansfield asked them. That structure, and the programs' high quality, have continued ever since.

The Council has a number of hard-working, productive committees on issues affecting judges and lawyers in the Second Circuit and sponsors a series of meaningful CLE programs. There is also an annual fall retreat, an annual reception for judges and an Inn of Court.

The Federal Bar Council has grown steadily in size and stature over the years, with a series of prominent New York lawyers serving as its president. I was privileged to serve as President in 1983 and 1984, the two years following Mike Seymour. Over twenty former trustees of the Council have gone on to serve in the federal judiciary, including Associate Supreme Court Justice Ruth Bader Ginsberg.

CHAPTER 28

The ABA Committee on Federal Judiciary
and Judge Robert Bork

AMONG THE FRIENDS I made in the American College of Trial Lawyers were four other past presidents who served with me on the American Bar Association's Committee on Federal Judiciary.[61] The ABA's Judiciary Committee, its abbreviated name, rates prospective federal judgeship nominees. It is a committee that I believed was the most important and powerful committee of any bar association. But when politics intrude, its workings can become the subject of partisan attacks. This happened in the time I served from 1981 to 1987, first as a member and then as the Committee's chair.

The Committee dates to President Eisenhower's first term, when he told his Attorney General, Herbert R. Brownell, that he would never select a general in the army without first obtaining the views of his military colleagues. From that comment there evolved the concept of a group of prominent and well-respected lawyers from around the country who would evaluate prospective nominees for the federal bench.

As it took shape, the Committee consists of fourteen members appointed by the President of the ABA: one from each of the twelve judicial circuits, one additional from the sprawling Ninth and a chair who can be from anywhere. The Committee never affirmatively proposes any person for a judgeship; its role is solely to evaluate the names submitted to it. It has a unique standing in order to assure its integrity and independence. Within the ABA no one has any supervisory authority over the Committee's work and its judgments are final.

The Committee's evaluation of a prospective nominee is directed solely to professional qualifications including integrity, professional competence and temperament. During my tenure its "not qualified" rating amounted to a *de facto* veto power. This fact, over time, led to harsh criticism from those displeased with some of its findings.

Candidate evaluations begin at the circuit level. After receiving the name of a prospective nominee from the administration the investigation is assigned to a circuit member who conducts an investigation that typically includes an analysis of the candidate's legal writings, interviews with lawyers who had worked with and against the candidate and judges before whom the candidate has appeared. In addition, interviews

152

may be conducted with law professors and deans, government attorneys, legal services and public interest attorneys and representatives of professional legal organizations and community leaders.

Committee members expect and receive reliable, frank and candid assessments from the interviews. Their standing in the bar in their respective circuits practically dictates it. They make their own phone calls and conduct their own interviews. The information they receive is confidential, a pledge the FBI—for example—cannot make because its reports are subject to the Freedom of Information Act.

Results in hand, the member then meets with the candidate for a lengthy personal interview to explore in depth the candidate's qualifications and give him or her the opportunity to respond to any negative information obtained during the investigation. The circuit member then prepares an informal written report to the chair reflecting the results, an evaluation of the nominee's qualifications and a recommended rating: well qualified, qualified, or not qualified.

The chair passes this on to the administration contact who floated the name. During my time we dealt with the Justice Department, usually either the Deputy Attorney General or the Assistant Attorney General for Legal Policy. The chair's report provides the basis for the evaluation and a tentative rating the candidate would receive if a formal report were requested.

A request for a formal report almost always happened when the initial report was favorable. The circuit member would then circulate to the Committee a written report setting forth everything the investigation had developed and ending with a recommended rating. The members would then communicate their votes to the chair, who would inform the Attorney General's Office of the rating and whether it was unanimous, by a "substantial majority" or simply a majority. The minority rating would accompany any rating that was not unanimous.

The Justice Department gets nothing in writing. To preserve confidentiality all copies of the report except the chair's are destroyed. Once the candidate is nominated the Committee would advise the Senate Judiciary Committee of its rating.

This exhaustive process had advantages. The informal reports gave a "heads up" when the investigation produced negative information the administration didn't know about. That might signal the administration not to go forward with the nomination to avoid embarrassment to itself and to the candidate, as happened in a number of cases over the years.

Going ahead in the case of a "not qualified" rating invited controversy because then the Committee would be invited by the Judiciary Committee to explain and the matter would become public. That happened in the Committee's early days in one highly-publicized case involving the 1965 nomination for a federal district court judgeship in Massachusetts of Francis X. Morrissey, a municipal court judge who was a long-time friend of the Kennedy family. The ABA Committee delivered a report of "not qualified" based on a lengthy investigation by the prominent Boston lawyer, Robert Meserve. The Johnson administration, pressed by Senator Kennedy, went forward with the nomination.

At the hearing before the Senate Judiciary Committee, the Committee revealed that Morrissey had acquired a law degree from a school that was unaccredited at the time he attended it, that he had failed the bar examination twice and that he had very little significant legal experience prior to becoming a municipal judge. ABA Committee Chairman Bernard Segal testified, "From the standpoint of legal training, legal experience and legal ability, we have not had any case where these factors were so lacking."

Opposition mounted and in the face of it Judge Morrissey eventually asked that his nomination be withdrawn. So, by the time I became the Committee's Second Circuit representative in August 1981, the Committee had great stature with both the Senate Judiciary Committee and the administration. Particularly during times when the Senate was controlled by the opposite party, it was very hard for the administration to get a "not qualified" rated nominee through the Judiciary Committee.

The Reagan administration, which took office in 1981, had three principal criteria for appeals court judges. They had to be smart, conservative and young, thus assuring the maximum impact on the development of the law in the years going forward. The nominees for the appeals courts during my three years as the Second Circuit representative were people like Robert Bork, Antonin Scalia, Richard Posner, and Ralph Winter. There was no issue as to their being qualified. The one bone of contention with the Reagan Justice Department was the clause in the Committee's backgrounder calling for "substantial trial experience (as a lawyer or a trial judge)" in prospective nominees to both appellate and trial courts.

All of these nominees deserved our highest rating, except for the issue of trial experience—all of them had virtually none. The Committee felt that in reviewing trial records for error by a district judge, an appellate judge with trial experience would make a better evaluation. That led to a "substantial majority" or a majority vote of "well qualified" for some of them, with a minority vote of "qualified." This produced a negative reaction from the Justice Department, which had a philosophically different view on the importance of trial experience for appellate judges.

That was the only major difference we had during the time I was the Second Circuit representative. Then in 1984 I was asked to chair the Committee and I assumed that role at our August meeting. I told those assembled that I was borrowing my guiding slogan from A. Whitney Griswold, who was appointed President of Yale during my sophomore year. The undergraduates had assembled to hear his inaugural address one early afternoon in Woolsey Hall, and he said he had searched without success to find some guiding words until he had stopped to make a sandwich just before coming over to speak to us. He found his inspiration on the Hellman's mayonnaise label: "Keep cool, but do not freeze."

Subsequently I was asked to serve two additional one-year terms, so I ended up serving a total of three years as chairman. And those three years were considerably more tumultuous than the first three.

The number of controversial candidates, especially for the circuit courts, increased. The administration continued to select young, extremely smart conservatives, but three years of such appointments had largely exhausted the pool of those who didn't send up warning flags. The informal reports we sent to Steve Markman, then the head of the Office of Legal Policy, rated several potential nominees "not qualified" because of issues relating to judicial temperament or professional qualifications. The administration decided—after much discussion—not to pursue these nominations. This generated a sharp backlash against the Committee from conservatives who charged that the ABA—and the Committee—had a liberal bias and that the candidates had been rejected because of their ideology.[62]

That was not true. The Committee had approved, often with "well qualified" ratings, a number of judges who were equally conservative as those we had rejected, but it became a recurring theme in those three years.

The Committee had always considered, in evaluating temperament, whether the candidate had evidenced any prejudicial views against minorities or women. It had for many years sought input from the National Bar Association, comprised primarily of African-American lawyers. Early in my first term as chair I was approached by Nan Aron, the president of a liberal organization called the Alliance for Justice, asking if the Committee would also give the names to her organization for their feedback. The Committee discussed it, and agreed.

This turned out to be a really bad mistake. The Alliance for Justice provided information that produced a "not qualified" rating for at least one potential nominee. But in the fall of 1986 Nan Aron went public, making a statement to the effect that "[W]e used to get the names after the candidate had been nominated and could weigh in only at the Senate Judiciary Committee hearing. Now we are getting the names before the nomination is made and we can be much more effective."

Conservatives were outraged. One right to life group demanded that it receive the names in advance so it could provide the Committee its views on the candidate's position on the rights of the unborn. The Washington Legal Foundation sued the Justice Department claiming that its use of the ABA Committee to evaluate judicial candidates violated the Federal Advisory Committee Act (FACA) which required that covered committees give public notice of their meetings in advance, open meetings to the public, and have a "fairly balanced" membership in terms of points of view to be considered.

We denied the right to life group's request and announced that going forward we would no longer provide the names to any outside group. With respect to the lawsuit, the Justice Department vigorously defended it and the Supreme Court eventually held, unanimously, that the FACA did not apply to the Committee.

So we dodged that bullet, but the Committee remained under attack from conservatives. They charged that by giving the names to a liberal group—like the Alliance for Justice—the Committee intended to dredge up negative information to derail conservative potential nominees. Our relationship with the Justice Department took a hit as well. At the Committee's traditional dinner during the ABA annual meeting in August 1987—when my three-year term ended—Steven Markman, the Assistant Attorney General for Legal Policy who had been our principal contact, stood up and said—not altogether facetiously—"A substantial majority of the Justice Department wish you well."[63]

At the time of that August meeting there was pending before the Committee the nomination of Robert H. Bork, then on the D.C. Circuit Court of Appeals, to fill the vacancy on the Supreme Court created by the resignation of Lewis Powell. President Reagan had announced Bork's nomination on July 1 and the Senate Judiciary Committee asked for our evaluation. The Committee started right away, hoping to complete an investigation and vote on a proposed recommendation at the August meeting. But it became very clear, very soon that that would not be possible.

There was an instantaneous outpouring of opposition to Judge Bork, led by Senator Kennedy's incendiary condemnation:

"Robert Bork's America is a land in which women would be forced into back-alley abortions, blacks would sit at segregated lunch counters, rogue police could break down citizens' doors in midnight raids, schoolchildren could not be taught about evolution, writers and artists could be censored at the whim of the government, and the doors of the Federal courts would be shut on the fingers of millions of citizens for whom the judiciary is—and is often the only—protector of the individual rights that are the heart of our democracy... President Reagan is still our president. But he should not be able to reach out from the muck of Irangate, reach into the muck of Watergate and impose his reactionary vision of the Constitution on the Supreme Court and the next generation of Americans. No justice would be better than this injustice."

The Committee received a barrage of white papers from organizations including the AFL-CIO, the American Civil Liberties Union, Common Cause, the NAACP and the National Organization for Women, all strongly protesting his nomination. It became clear by the time of our August meeting that there would be more. To allow a full opportunity for comment, and for Judge Bork to be able to respond, we decided to defer the decision to September. Harold Tyler, then the Second Circuit representative on the Committee, succeeded me as chair at the August meeting. He asked me to stay on in an unofficial capacity through the completion of the investigation.

Judge Bork had graduated from the University of Chicago Law School, worked for a Chicago law firm, taught at the Yale Law School and served as Solicitor General of the United States. That was his position in October 1973 at the time of the so-called "Saturday Night Massacre" when first Attorney General Elliot Richardson and then Deputy Attorney General William Ruckelshaus were fired in rapid succession by President Nixon for refusing to fire Archibald Cox, the Watergate Independent Counsel who had infuriated Nixon by pressing for production of the White House tapes. Bork, as Solicitor General, was third in line. Richardson and Ruckelshaus both urged him to follow the President's order, reasoning that they had made the point and that sooner or later—down the line of succession—someone would decide to follow the order and stay on as Attorney General and that person would be nowhere near as qualified as Bork. Bork followed the order, fired Cox, appointed Leon Jaworski to succeed him and—as they say—the rest is history.

President Reagan had nominated Bork for the D.C. Circuit Court of Appeals in 1981. The Committee member from the D.C. Circuit at that time was William Coleman, a Republican who had been Secretary of Transportation during the Ford administration. He recommended that Bork be found "exceptionally well qualified"—a superlative commendation that was rarely bestowed and was later discontinued. The Committee, of which I was then a member, voted unanimously in support of the recommendation.

Judge Tyler and I interviewed Judge Bork on two separate occasions in August 1987. During the interviews we went over all the allegations against him, his judicial opinions and his writings. He dismissed the controversy and said he was confident he would be confirmed. His example was Colonel Oliver North, who earlier in the year had won public support in the wake of the Iran/Contra scandal by appearing before Congress in full uniform and defending selling arms to Iran to finance Nicaraguan rebels he saw as "freedom fighters." Judge Bork told us he thought he would be able to do the same thing in the intellectual arena—that he would win over his critics by his performance at the Senate hearing. That did not turn out to be the case.

Our Committee met in September. There were fifteen of us, including Chairman Tyler and myself. It found Judge Bork "well qualified," the highest rating available under the then existing rules for Supreme Court Justices, but by a divided vote. Four members voted him "not qualified" because of temperament. I did not have a vote, but Judge Tyler asked for my opinion. I said I had been on the Committee when it found him "exceptionally well qualified" for the D.C. Circuit and that in the six years since then I had seen no evidence that he had gone downhill in integrity, temperament or professional qualifications. Therefore, I said, if I had a vote it would be "well qualified."

I, together with others, disagreed with the interpretation of the Committee's definition of temperament by the four members who voted "not qualified." As set forth in the Backgrounder:

> "In investigating temperament, the Committee considers, among other factors, the prospective nominee's compassion, decisiveness, open-mindedness, sensitivity, courtesy, patience, freedom from bias and commitment to equal justice."

The majority believed that freedom from bias, compassion and sensitivity were meant to refer to the candidate's interpersonal relationships. And on that score our interviews had produced positive testimony, including a very strong endorsement from a former law clerk of Judge Bork, an African-American woman. The majority believed that the Committee was not supposed to consider judicial philosophy as it may have been reflected in opinions or speeches. The minority did that by applying the definition to Bork's written decisions, many of which had raised the bar against women and minorities in employment discrimination cases.

A firestorm greeted the announcement of the Committee's evaluation. Senator Metzenbaum had written Judge Tyler to ask for confirmation that the Committee's evaluations did not consider ideology, and he did so. When the vote was announced Metzenbaum, an Ohio Democrat, immediately proclaimed that for the first time in its history of evaluating candidates for the Supreme Court members of the Committee had found the candidate "not qualified" based on professional qualifications, temperament or integrity. Senator Hatch immediately attacked the minority evaluation, charging that the dissenters on the ABA panel were politically motivated.

Indeed, the reaction followed political lines. The year before, when Republicans controlled the Senate and Strom Thurmond chaired the Judiciary Committee, the ABA Committee had testified twice, once on the nomination of William Rehnquist to be Chief Justice of the United States and a second time on the nomination of Antonin Scalia to fill the vacancy created by Rehnquist's elevation. Gene Lafitte had presented the Committee's report on Justice Rehnquist during the time that I was on trial in the NFL case, and I had presented the report on Judge Scalia. The Committee had been unanimous in finding both "well qualified," and Thurmond and Orrin Hatch had praised our work while Senator Kennedy attacked us.

The following year was the diametric opposite. The Democrats now controlled the Senate and Senator Joseph Biden chaired the Judiciary Committee. Judge Tyler asked me to join him when he testified.

We were not looking forward to the experience. We knew that the minority finding had been damaging to Judge Bork, and that the Republican members of the Judiciary Committee were angry about it. We expected very intense and probably hostile questioning on national television about the justification for the minority position.

The first panel was comprised of four very strong anti-Bork witnesses: Atlanta Mayor Andrew Young, Texas Congresswoman Barbara Jordan, former head of the DOJ Civil Rights Division Burke Marshall and William Coleman—the same William Coleman who as the D.C. member of the ABA Committee in 1981 had written the report finding Bork "exceptionally well qualified." He testified that he had come to believe that Bork deserved opposition based on ideology which he had not considered in 1981.

Senator Biden let this panel go all day, keeping the second panel, a pro-Bork group of four former Attorneys General—Edward Levi, William French Smith, Nicholas Katzenbach and William Rogers, waiting in the wings past the evening television news deadlines. Their testimony started late and continued on into the evening. It was 11 p.m. by the time they were finished. We were next and Senator Biden graciously offered to let us come back in the morning. But we noticed that except for C-Span, the television cameras had all departed and we seized the opportunity to go forward with a very limited late-evening television audience.

This time, instead of praising the Committee for its selfless contribution to the administration of justice, Senator Hatch attacked the credentials of the Committee members he believed were the dissenters. The Committee had never revealed how individual members voted and Judge Tyler maintained that position, but Hatch took aim at "at least three members who have been pretty active . . . on behalf of politically liberal causes . . ." He said the minority had acted "basically for political reasons."

In the end Judge Bork's nomination for the Supreme Court was rejected, first in the Judiciary Committee by a vote of nine to five. He insisted on a vote by the full Senate and, on October 23, 1987, lost by a vote of fifty-eight to forty-two. His defeat left both Judge Bork and Republicans in the Senate extremely bitter.

Following his failure to be confirmed Bork resigned his seat on the U.S. Court of Appeals for the D.C. Circuit and was for several years a senior fellow at the American Enterprise Institute for Public Policy Research, a conservative think tank. Until his death in December 2012, he served as a visiting professor at the University of Richmond School of Law and was a professor at Ave Maria School of Law in Naples, Florida.

CHAPTER 29

Deputy Attorney General
and the Bork Fallout

JUDGE BORK'S REJECTION would reverberate for a long time. It would steel the resolve of conservative Republicans to add conservative judges to the federal court system at all levels. And it sent ripples beyond the courts to other areas of government as they exacted revenge for his rejection.

More than a year later, in January 1989, I began to see first-hand just how serious they were.

The string of events dated back to the end of 1987. That December, E.R. Wallach, a California lawyer was indicted on charges of conspiring to defraud the United States in actions related to his work for Wedtech Corporation, by then a defunct Bronx, NY defense contractor. The indictment charged that he had accepted $3 million in payments from Wedtech in return for improperly influencing federal government officials, including his friend—then Attorney General—Edwin Meese.

An Independent Counsel, James McKay of Covington & Burling, was appointed to investigate the allegations against Meese.

In March 1988 Deputy Attorney General Arnold Burns and Assistant Attorney General William Weld told White House Chief of Staff Howard Baker that President Reagan should remove Meese because the criminal investigation had put an ethical cloud over his head and was distracting him from doing his job. When Baker told them the President would not ask Meese to resign, Burns and Weld resigned giving rise to a new phrase in counterpoint to Nixon's "Saturday Night Massacre." This, said a Justice Department official, "is a Monday Night Suicide."

In August 1988 McKay filed a report in which he concluded that there was credible evidence supporting a prosecution of Meese for conflict of interest and tax violations, but that a combination of facts and circumstances presented compelling reasons not to prosecute him. Meese resigned declaring himself vindicated, and President Reagan appointed Dick Thornburgh to succeed him.

Thornburgh had been the Assistant Attorney General in charge of the Criminal Division in the last years of the Ford presidency, the position for which I also was in the running before I decided the timing wasn't right and voluntarily withdrew. He had then gone on to become a very successful, two-term governor of Pennsylvania. He led the State at the time of the Three Mile Island accident, and his cool reassurance calmed fears of a widespread release of radiation. His selection as Attorney General drew acclaim, and when George H.W. Bush was elected President in the fall of 1988, he announced that Thornburgh would stay on.

In January 1989 after Bush had been inaugurated, I received a call from Thornburgh. He asked if I was interested in coming to Washington. I replied that I didn't want to head the Criminal Division, a position I had already turned down twice—the second time when I was U.S. Attorney for the Southern District which I thought was a better job—and I told him I wasn't really interested. He said, "Well, I was thinking of Deputy Attorney General."

That was a whole different story. The Deputy Attorney General was, for all practical purposes, the operational head of the Justice Department. It was he, someone once said, who "made the trains run on time." Judge Tyler had held the position when I was United States Attorney. As the number two position in the Department of Justice the person who held it was—to many—the presumptive successor as Attorney General.

Earlier when I had debated the move to Washington the main factor against it was that Bob and Sue, our two younger children, were still in school and it wouldn't have been fair to them. Now time had passed and things had changed; Linda was working in New York at an art/photography gallery; Bob was at Vermont Law School; and Sue was married and working in Boston for Addison Wesley book publishers. They and Janet all supported the idea of a move.

I went down to Washington and had several discussions with Thornburgh; I told him in early February that I was ready to do it. Before Thornburgh could make it public, however, the news leaked out through a *Wall Street Journal* editorial writer, Gordon Crovitz, who had worked with me when he was a summer associate in 1985, and who had heard about it through sources at the Department of Justice.

Crovitz wrote an editorial on March 24, 1989 criticizing then U.S. Attorney Benito Romano for his decision to retry a case after a conviction had been reversed by the Court of Appeals. The editorial criticized Rudolph Giuliani, his predecessor, for bringing a series of what Crovitz termed "lousy cases"—which Romano inherited—and lamented the lack of Department of Justice supervision. The editorial went on to comment, "we . . . understand that Mr. Thornburgh has asked New York attorney Robert Fiske to become Deputy Attorney General. Mr. Fiske was the Manhattan federal prosecutor in the pre-Giuliani era under President Ford ... and could help Justice regain control over loose-cannon prosecutors."

Immediate howls of protest went up from the right, led by the Washington Legal Foundation and several other conservative groups that had been critical of the ABA Judiciary Committee's rejection of conservative candidates during my tenure as Chairman and especially the minority votes against Judge Bork. Thornburgh defended his choice and told the White House that he should be able to pick the person he wanted. A key player in the White House disagreed.

John Sununu was President Bush's Chief of Staff. He was a very conservative former governor of New Hampshire and embraced the complaints about my selection. He told the President that there must be a lot of qualified candidates for Deputy Attorney General and that it was not worth offending the right wing of the party.

I had allies in the Bush cabinet. Nick Brady, a Yale 1952 classmate, was Secretary of the Treasury and a close friend of the President. Sam Skinner, a former United States Attorney in Chicago, was Secretary of Commerce. Burt Lee, another Yale 1952 classmate, was the President's personal physician, and John Robson, another Yale classmate, was Under Secretary of the Treasury. They supported me on the merits and on the principle that Thornburgh should be able to pick the person he wanted. I also had strong support from Steve Markman, who was head of the Office of Legal Policy and had been my principal contact at the Department of Justice while I was head of the ABA Judiciary Committee. He was cited in a supportive *Wall Street Journal* editorial to the effect that at the ABA I was "part of the solution, not the problem."

The battle raged on throughout the spring of 1989. At one point Thornburgh's Chief of Staff, Robin Ross, told me he thought I should meet directly with representatives of the groups opposing my nomination. I went down and met with about twenty of them. They grilled me on my views on a wide range of ideological issues. After over an hour of this, I asked, "Does anyone have any questions about my professional qualifications?" There were none.

The shape of the battle grew clearer when my friend and law partner Dick Moe, a prominent Democrat who had been Vice President Mondale's Chief of Staff and was respected on both sides of the aisle, passed on something he'd been told. His source was Paul Kamenar of the Washington Legal Foundation who told Dick that he had just discovered a bombshell that was going to be the death knell of my candidacy. I spent two days in suspense wondering what it could be. Then Kamenar announced it: I had made a contribution to a Democrat.

This was true. The candidate was William Gray, a former United States Attorney from Vermont who during my time as U.S. Attorney had been an Associate Deputy Attorney General heading the Executive Office of United States Attorneys under Judge Tyler. He and I had become good friends during that period and I had a high regard for his character and abilities. So, when he ran for the Senate in Vermont in the fall of 1988, I—along with several other Republicans, including Judge Tyler—contributed to his campaign. For me it was simply a question of contributing to a friend who I felt was the most qualified person. For my conservative opponents it was an act of disloyalty to the Republican Party.[64]

As they had two years earlier—when Judge Bork was up for the Supreme Court— in 1989 the Democrats controlled the Senate Judiciary Committee. Judiciary would have to consider my nomination if it were made. The Republicans had six senators on the Committee. They were Strom Thurmond of South Carolina, Orrin Hatch of Utah, Alan Simpson of Wyoming, Arlen Spector of Pennsylvania, Charles Grassley of Iowa and Gordon Humphrey of New Hampshire. Humphrey was the most outspoken opponent of my nomination, based on his views of the ABA Judiciary Committee. Grassley was a close second. Both made public statements urging the President not to make the nomination. Through Thornburgh's staff I asked to meet with them to explain what I believed to be the true facts with respect to the ABA Committee. Humphrey never agreed to meet and Grassley said he would not meet unless Humphrey also attended. So, those meetings never happened.

I had two enthusiastic Republican supporters in the Senate. One was Alphonse D'Amato from New York and the other was John Danforth from Missouri, whom I had known when he was an associate at Davis Polk in the 1960's. D'Amato lobbied the conservatives on my behalf and issued a public statement calling the charges "unfounded." He said, "They are doing a great disservice to a fine, outstanding lawyer." Danforth organized a meeting of Republican senators that included Hatch, Simpson and Thurmond but not Grassley or Humphrey. I had a chance to answer questions and address the arguments against me. Afterward Danforth, sensing that a lot of the opposition stemmed from Bork's rejection, solicited a letter from Judge Tyler recalling my statement to the Committee—that if I had had a vote it would have been "well qualified." He distributed the letter to my conservative opponents and later told me many of them were dismissive. "It doesn't matter," they said, "he allowed a climate to develop in the ABA Committee that produced the 'not qualified' votes on Bork."

Fourteen Republican senators sent a letter to President Bush on June 20, 1989. Thurmond, Grassley and Humphrey were among them; Hatch, Simpson and Spector were not.

The letter urged the President not to nominate me for Deputy Attorney General. It questioned my loyalty to the Republican Party on the ground that when I chaired the ABA Committee it had "improperly applied ideological criteria to thwart the nominations of various well-qualified candidates." Danforth and D'Amato immediately produced a letter signed by thirty-four Republican senators supporting my nomination.

Around the same time President Bush spoke at a conference of United States Attorneys. He described federal prosecutors as "a breed apart" and went on to say, "We hope to see yet another, Bob Fiske of New York, joining our ranks here soon." I learned of this when *Washington Post* reporter Ruth Marcus called me to say, "Well, it looks like you are going to get the job." But then Ross, Thornburgh's Chief of Staff, called saying that Sununu was furious and was complaining that a Thornburgh staffer must have persuaded Bush to ad-lib the remark because it wasn't in the prepared text. Actually, somebody who was there told me that it was.

Nevertheless, Sununu redoubled his efforts. In early July Thornburgh called to say he'd discussed the situation with the President at a social gathering, and that Bush had decided to follow Sununu's advice rather than his. He told me that, under these circumstances, the appropriate thing for me to do was to withdraw.

I wrote to Thornburgh on July 6, 1989 withdrawing from consideration "with a great deal of regret." I said I had wanted to help him and President Bush further "our goals of enhancing the nation's law enforcement capabilities and . . . improving the administration of justice." I said that while I thought the Senate would have approved me overwhelmingly, given the controversy and delay, it was better that he move on to another nominee.

His reply was gracious, and added, "Unfortunately, your volunteer efforts as Chairman of the American Bar Association's Standing Committee on Federal Judiciary have been misstated and misunderstood . . ."

The New York Times carried a front-page story about my withdrawal that included Senator Danforth's remark echoing Thornburgh's. A supportive *Wall Street Journal* editorial said it "proves most of all that conservatives still excel at spiting their own faces."

President Bush's hand-written note, dated July 8, contained the empathy of a long-time government servant who had risen to the highest office in the land: "I write this letter to tell you of my personal distress about what you have been through. Sometimes public life is great and rewarding—sometimes it is ugly and unkind."

Several years later, in his autobiography *Where the Evidence Leads*, Dick Thornburgh took responsibility for the fact that my nomination had not gone forward. He called

THE WHITE HOUSE
WASHINGTON

July 8, 1989

Dear Bob,

We don't know each
other you - I, but we
have many mutual friends
all of whom unanimously
sing your praises.

I write this letter
to tell you of my
personal distress about
what you have been
through. Sometimes

public life is great
and rewarding — sometimes
it is ugly and unkind.

I saw your very
unselfish letter to Dick
Thornburgh. That simply
re-inforced my view that
you're a very good man.
Someday we'll meet and
I will tell you then of
my respect.

Sincerely,

Gy Bush

President George H.W. Bush letter

it "one of my first and most costly mistakes" and wrote, "The eventual defeat of his appointment underscored the harshness of the Washington environment as well as my own naiveté in seeking to act without laying the proper foundation." He summarized my role with the ABA Judiciary Committee and the Bork episode, and then turned to the opposition:

"Conservative members of the Senate Judiciary Committee, encouraged by conservative think tanks and legal foundations committed to strict constructionism, chose to see a Fiske appointment as the new administration's affirmation of the approach that had resulted in Bork's nomination being rejected. They were also determined to mount a charge against the ABA itself and saw Fiske as a symbol of that group. I failed to take the appropriate sounding and thus missed the opportunity to rebut this case until far too late. A complicating factor, I suspect, was my failure to court the support of the White House staff, specifically Chief of Staff John Sununu.

By the summer of 1989, Sununu's opposition, it was reported, had solidified (partly, I suspect, because of a desire to 'put me in short pants') . . . Finally, Bob asked that his name be withdrawn from consideration . . . The president later sent me a handwritten note expressing his dismay that Fiske had been 'done in by rumors, fiction and half-truths,' but adding that 'there would have been too much blood letting if we had proceeded.'

In the final analysis, I was driven to agree with the editorial writers of the *National Law Journal*: 'Sometimes it's a wonder anyone would even consider relinquishing—even briefly—a successful legal career to enter public service . . . [Deputy attorney general] is a job for which Mr. Fiske is perfectly suited: few in this country have the knowledge and integrity he has gained in his years in the law. [H]e is an extremely capable and reasonable professional whose addition to the Department of Justice would give it a new level of quality. The public deserves no less.' But neither the public nor the department got what it deserved . . ."

—⁓—

DAVIS POLK, 1989–1994

I WAS DISAPPOINTED with the outcome, but I found that almost becoming Deputy Attorney General had enhanced my attractiveness to potential clients. And after my exposure to Washington politics it was almost a relief to concentrate on the equally rigorous but less partisan demands of litigation. But if I thought that intrigue and infighting were unique to our nation's capital, the next case I was involved in demonstrated beyond a doubt that these were facts around the world.

CHAPTER 30

The America's Cup

LIKE MOST SAILORS, I had long been aware of the America's Cup. As a boy growing up on Five Mile River in Darien and sailing with my brothers in our 19-foot, wood-hulled Lightning, knowledge of the world's oldest international sporting trophy was inescapable. Later, when Janet and I moved from Tarrytown to Darien in 1961, we joined the Noroton Yacht Club, one of the premier one-design racing clubs on Long Island Sound. We only raced as crew for friends, but we owned a series of cruising sloops that got bigger as our family grew—from a 28-foot Triton to a 36-foot, cutter-rigged Cape Dory. We'd spend a week or two each summer sailing to Nantucket and back with stops at Block Island, Newport and Martha's Vineyard. Sailing together on a small boat is a sure-fire prescription for family togetherness and—most of the time, at least—harmony. Among our sailing friends the Cup, and the long history of American skippers defending it against all challengers, was a mark of quiet pride. Still, I was about to learn that I knew barely a fraction of its history.

At the Wheel of Baloo

The story of the America's Cup dates to August 1851, when a radical looking schooner ghosted out of the afternoon mist and sailed swiftly toward the royal yacht stationed in the Solent, the water that lies between the Isle of Wight and the southern coast of England. Queen Victoria was watching from the yacht.

As the schooner, named *America*, passed in first position and saluted by dipping its ensign three times, Queen Victoria is said to have asked one of her attendants to tell her who was in second place. "Your Majesty, there is no second," came the reply. That day *America*, representing the New York Yacht Club, beat the best the British had to offer and won the Royal Yacht Squadron's 100 Guinea Cup.

169

Baloo

After the race New York Yacht Club Commodore John Cox Stevens and the rest of his ownership syndicate sold the celebrated schooner and returned home to New York as heroes. They donated the 100 Guinea Cup to the New York Yacht Club under a Deed of Gift which stated that the trophy was to be "a perpetual Challenge Cup for friendly competition between nations." Thus was born the America's Cup, named after the winning yacht. The silver trophy itself is the corpus of a charitable trust created under the laws of New York.

Pursuant to the Deed of Gift, the Cup's holder—not the winning skipper but the skipper's yacht club—is its sole trustee. If it is won by a challenger the trusteeship passes to the winner's yacht club along with the Cup itself. Unless otherwise agreed by the parties, the terms of the challenge are specified in the deed. Any foreign yacht club can mount a challenge "with a yacht or vessel propelled by sails only and constructed in the country to which the Challenging Club belongs, against any one yacht or vessel constructed in the country of the Club holding the Cup." The challenger must give ten months' notice and provide prospective race dates, the name of the challenging boat's owner and its name, rig, and dimensions.

The construction requirement meant that the America's Cup would be a contest of yacht design as well as sailing skills. Thus, there was no restriction on design other than the boat's length at the waterline which could not be more than 90 feet. The challenger was required to give the defender this dimension: the beam (width of the boat) at the waterline, extreme beam and the draft, or how far down into the water it extended. The defender was subject only to the waterline limitation but could play with the others. This was not "one-design" racing.

The Royal Thames Yacht Club issued the first challenge in 1870 but finished eighth in a fleet of seventeen schooners behind the American yacht *Magic*. After another unsuccessful British challenge the Royal Canadian Yacht Club entered the fray, only to be defeated twice by different American defending yachts sailing under the banner of the New York Yacht Club.

There then followed a series of one-on-one match race challenges from 1885 to 1937, in which the defending New York Yacht Club repeatedly prevailed in a variety of different boats against a series of British challenges, culminating in the victories in 1934 and 1936 by Harold S. Vanderbilt's J-Class boats *Rainbow* and *Ranger* over the Royal Yacht Squadron's *Endeavor* and *Endeavor II*.

World War II then intervened and twenty years passed until the next challenge. In the post-war economic climate no one could afford to challenge in the hugely expensive J-Class boats, which were 125 feet long (80 on the waterline) and had 150-foot masts. What had cost $500,000 to build in the 1930's now cost over $3 million. So, the New York Yacht Club looked for a cheaper alternative to resume the competition. A clause in the deed permitted its terms to be varied by "mutual consent," so all contenders agreed that the Cup races would be sailed in 12-meter class boats which were roughly 60 feet in length with 85-foot masts. Their waterline length was 44 feet, less than the previously specified minimum of 65 feet, but a petition to the court won permission for the change.

The British challenged in 1958 and the New York Yacht Club again prevailed in races held off Newport, Rhode Island. There then followed a series of Australian challenges, seven race events held from 1962 to 1980, with the New York Yacht Club winning each in Newport.

In the meantime, interest in the competition was expanding. In 1964 two American boats contended for the right to defend the Cup against an Australian challenge. Both skippers hailed from Darien and had been commodores of the Noroton Yacht Club. Janet and I had been Noroton members for three years at that point, and sailed a 28-foot sloop named *Hornet* after the Darien Hornets, the Commuter League ice hockey team that was my winter recreation. *American Eagle*, skippered by Bill Cox, and *Constellation*, skippered by Bob Bavier, had more lofty names. Bavier prevailed and went on to successfully defend the Cup against the Australian challenger, *Sovereign*.

Starting in 1970 multiple countries began to express interest in mounting Cup challenges. As in 1964 there had often been competition on the defender side, but now a challenger selection series began with the French malletier Louis Vuitton as the sponsor. The Vuitton Cup series was designed, among other things, to produce the best boat and the strongest competition in the races for the America's Cup, which had for the most part been one-sided American victories. The lack of spectator appeal had caused Red Smith, the legendary New York *Herald Tribune* sportswriter, to write that "watching an America's Cup race is like watching grass grow."

In 1983 there was a major breakthrough. The Australian challenger *Australia II* defeated the New York Yacht Club defender *Liberty*, skippered by Dennis Conner, in an exciting series of seven races off Newport. The last race was a true thriller with *Liberty* leading all the way until the last leg, a spinnaker run, in which *Australia II* caught up, took the lead and held on despite Conner's ferocious, last-gasp effort.

This defeat not only broke a 132-year winning streak for the Americans, it removed the New York Yacht Club as America's representative in the Cup races. The honor of defending the Cup now went to the Royal Perth Yacht Club of Australia.

In 1987 Conner, now representing the San Diego Yacht Club, defeated thirteen other American challengers in the Louis Vuitton Cup series and won the right to challenge the Aussies. The races were sailed off Fremantle, on the west coast of Australia, with Conner sailing *Stars & Stripes* against the Australian defender *Kookaburra III*. These races were high entertainment with the famous "Fremantle Doctor" blowing up giant white-capped seas that tested both sailors and equipment. ESPN mounted cameras on the boats to provide dramatic close-up coverage that had American viewers glued to their sets in the pre-dawn hours to watch the action halfway around the world. *Stars & Stripes* won four straight races in February to bring the Cup back to the United States. There was a presidential welcome and a ticker tape parade in New York City, but for the first time the Cup's home in America was now the San Diego Yacht Club.

The next challenge was a complete surprise. Typically, under the "mutual consent" provision of the Deed of Gift, the defender would work with a challenger of record to set details of the next competition. But after Conner waffled on selecting a lead challenger and a racing site, Michael Fay, a New Zealand merchant banker, decided to bypass the elimination format and within six months of Conner's victory issued a provocative but legal direct challenge to San Diego to race in 1988. This shocked the sailing world, but not so much as the boat he chose to do it with.

Fay thought 12-meter racing had become boring and it was time for some innovative design. He wanted to bring back the grandeur of the massive J-Class boats, and with his wealth cost was not a problem. He had taken his ideas to Bruce Farr, the uncontested design specialist of light displacement boats.

The boat Fay wanted had to meet the limits of the Deed of Gift, so Farr designed a narrow hull that was 90 feet at the waterline, the longest allowed, with a minimum of wetted surface. He fitted a 160-foot mast that would carry almost 2,000 square feet—almost a half-acre—of sail. To balance against this massive amount of sail, his design called for a deep hull, and a wide deck allowing a crew of up to forty men to act as additional ballast. The launch ceremony took place in Auckland, New Zealand in front of a crowd of over 100,000. The boat, named *New Zealand*, challenged for the America's Cup under the auspices of the Mercury Bay Boating Club.

America's Cup racing was always a millionaire's club. J. P. Morgan is supposed to have said, "Anyone who complains that the America's Cup is too expensive is playing the wrong game." The yachting community was dismayed by Fay's challenge nonetheless. Yacht clubs around the world were preparing to challenge in 12-meter yachts in the Vuitton Cup format. The 12-meters were expensive as it was; the top sailing teams were tank-testing hulls and building multiple yachts in search of peak performance, and moving from part-time amateur crews to full-time professionals. Corporate sponsorships were displacing individual backers as costs rose. Boats like Fay's *New Zealand* would be beyond the reach of many challengers and stretch the resources of the defending San Diego Yacht Club.

Fay's timetable was another problem. Conner had anticipated next defending the Cup in 1991, a three or four-year cycle that the racing world expected. Fay wanted to race on September 19, 1988, shrinking the defender's preparation time.

San Diego announced that Fay's terms of challenge were unacceptable. Fay and the Mercury Bay Boating Club promptly filed suit in New York for an order declaring the validity of its challenge and enjoining San Diego from considering any other challenge. On November 25, 1987 Justice Carmen Ciparick of the New York Supreme Court— New York's term for its trial courts—granted the motion and declared the challenge valid. She held that San Diego's options were "to accept the challenge, forfeit the Cup, or negotiate agreeable terms with the challenger."[65]

1988 America's Cup New Zealand

1988 America's Cup Stars & Stripes

After declining Fay's offer to postpone the races to give it time to build a boat similar to his, San Diego then announced that it would defend the Cup in a catamaran, a completely different type of boat. A monohull sailboat gains its stability from weight below the waterline, usually in the form of a heavy blade-shaped keel. A catamaran stays upright in the wind because of its widely spaced twin hulls and is naturally lighter and faster than a monohull. The San Diego boat's dimensions would fall within the Deed of Gift, although it would be smaller than New Zealand's. This brought cries of protest from the Kiwis, who claimed that racing a catamaran against a monohull violated the concept that the America's Cup should be a "friendly competition" between nations in a "match" that required that the defending boat be "like or similar" to the challenging vessel.

There was more legal wrangling about that, and whether a British yacht club should be allowed to join the competition, but the two-boat match went forward. The races were held in San Diego in early September 1988. The outcome was a foregone conclusion: there was no way a monohull was going to beat a catamaran.

Knowing they had no chance, the Kiwis fought back with friendly mockery. During pre-match practices the American *Stars and Stripes* flew a spinnaker with a Marlboro logo from its sponsor Philip Morris, followed by *New Zealand* with a spinnaker proclaiming "Smoking is Bad for Your Health." The races themselves came off as predicted. San Diego won by a wide margin in the best two-out-of-three series, with Conner accused by the Kiwis of deliberately slowing his boat to narrow the lopsided margin of victory.

Mercury Bay promptly went back to court claiming that San Diego's catamaran violated the Deed of Gift. It moved to set aside the race results, have *New Zealand* declared the winner and have the Cup turned over to it. The issue, as framed by both parties, was whether the Deed of Gift required the trustee to defend the Cup with a vessel "like or similar" to the challenging vessel.

Judge Ciparick ruled in favor of New Zealand.[66] She found that San Diego had violated the spirit of the Deed of Gift's friendly competition clause in hosting a competition on its own terms and not the challenger's. Holding that San Diego's defense deviated from the donor's intent that the competing boats be "somewhat evenly matched," she disqualified San Diego's catamaran and declared New Zealand's boat the winner.

At this point San Diego, which had been represented by Latham & Watkins, added Harold Tyler to its legal team. He was the former Deputy Attorney General who had been instrumental in my appointment as United States Attorney, and was then at Patterson Belknap Webb & Tyler. He argued the case in the Appellate Division and was successful. In a four-to-one decision, the court held that Judge Ciparick's finding had "promulgated a rule that is neither expressed in, nor inferable from, the language of the Deed of Gift."[67] The appellate judges noted that the only design constraint imposed by the deed was the length on the waterline—a minimum of 44 feet and a maximum of 90. They dismissed New Zealand's argument based on the "friendly competition between foreign countries" clause as precatory only, and "not imposing any obligation on San Diego to use any particular vessel in defense of the Cup."[68]

The reversal came as a shock to Michael Fay and his New Zealand team. Not long afterward he commissioned one of his principal advisors, a prominent barrister named David Williams,[69] to find new counsel to argue the case in the New York Court of Appeals. Williams approached my partner Taggart Whipple to see if I would be willing to take on the case.

I had to think about it. I thought it might be unpatriotic to take a case against my own country's sailing fortunes. But as a sailor myself, I decided that what San Diego had done was wrong and I agreed to take the case. As Tyler had with Latham & Watkins, I joined the team at Condon & Forsyth, headed by George Tompkins, who had been handling the case up to that point.

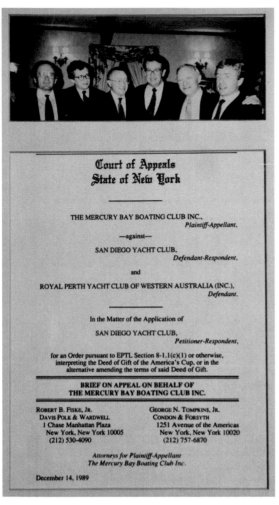

Court of Appeals
State of New York

THE MERCURY BAY BOATING CLUB INC.,
Plaintiff-Appellant,

—against—

SAN DIEGO YACHT CLUB,
Defendant-Respondent,

and

ROYAL PERTH YACHT CLUB OF WESTERN AUSTRALIA (INC.),
Defendant.

In the Matter of the Application of

SAN DIEGO YACHT CLUB,
Petitioner-Respondent,

for an Order pursuant to EPTL Section 8-1.1(c)(1) or otherwise,
interpreting the Deed of Gift of the America's Cup, or in the
alternative amending the terms of said Deed of Gift.

BRIEF ON APPEAL ON BEHALF OF
THE MERCURY BAY BOATING CLUB INC.

ROBERT B. FISKE, JR.   GEORGE N. TOMPKINS, JR.
DAVIS POLK & WARDWELL   CONDON & FORSYTH
1 Chase Manhattan Plaza   1251 Avenue of the Americas
New York, New York 10005   New York, New York 10020
(212) 530-4090   (212) 757-6870

Attorneys for Plaintiff-Appellant
The Mercury Bay Boating Club Inc.

December 14, 1989

With David Williams, Jim Kerr, George Tompkins,
Michael Fay, and Andrew Johns

The first step was to apply for leave to appeal to the New York Court of Appeals. Ordinarily it would have been up to the Court of Appeals itself to decide whether it was a case that deserved their review. But because there had been a dissent in our case, we were able to apply in the first instance to the Appellate Division. They granted the application, which was what we needed. However, it meant that the case was in the Court of Appeals without that court having had any say in the matter. As it turned out this grated heavily on Chief Judge Sol Wachtler, who did not see any broad issue of New York law that justified the court's review.

The sailing community submitted several *amicus curiae* briefs supporting our appeal. Most significant was a brief signed by virtually every living American skipper of the previous America's Cup challengers and defenders. They all attested to the basic unfairness of the race. Only one of the seven judges on the panel was a sailor; Judge Stewart Hancock had done one-design racing on Lake Onondaga near Syracuse and knew, as a friend of his said, "the bow from the stern and one hull from two hulls." Preparing for the argument I searched for a way to demonstrate to the six non-sailors why a race between a monohull and a catamaran was such a travesty. I consulted Bruce Kirby, a fellow member of the Noroton Yacht Club and a prominent boat designer.[70]

Bruce proposed a simple demonstration to show what prevents a boat from tipping over when the wind hits the sails broadside. I stood with my feet apart to show how that enabled me to take a push from the side and stay upright—that was the catamaran. Then I stood with my feet together and showed how I would not be able to sustain a push without falling over—that was the monohull, which could only preserve its stability by having a heavy keel protrude downwards into the water. The keel's extra weight obviously made the monohull much slower. Simply stated, these were two radically different boats, with the catamaran a foregone winner every time. This was not "friendly competition" or a "match." To the contrary, it was a gross mismatch.

On February 8, 1990, almost fifteen months after the actual racing, we argued the case in front of a standing-room-only audience. Reports later described it as the largest crowd ever to witness any argument in the Court of Appeals. I was given thirty minutes. I stood up and said, "May it please the Court, I am Robert Fiske, counsel for Mercury Bay, and I would like to save five minutes for rebuttal." Chief Judge Wachtler said, "That is fine, Mr. Fiske, and now tell me, where in the Deed of Gift does it say that the defender can't sail a catamaran?"

There then followed a barrage of intense questions. I literally spent the entire time answering questions, doing my best to incorporate all of the points I had intended to make into my answers. Judge Tyler was interrupted frequently, but not as much. The questioning made clear that, with the exception of Judge Hancock, most of the court was unsympathetic to the notion that, as Judge Wachtler put it, the finish line of the race should be on Eagle Street. They seemed to feel that a sporting event should be resolved on the field—or on the water in this case—and not in the courts when the loser cried "foul."

Mercury Bay v. San Diego was the first case on the calendar. After our argument concluded the standing-room-only crowd dwindled to a few. Judge Wachtler was overheard proclaiming, "Now that the international yachting community has left us, we can get down to the business of the court."

There is a tradition in the Court of Appeals that on decision day the clerk of the court calls the winner first with the result. On April 26, 1990 at 9:00 a.m. in the morning, I received a call from the clerk: "Congratulations, Mr. Fiske, you won."

I said, "We did?"

He said, "Yes. You do represent San Diego, don't you"?

That cruel twist was bad enough, but then I had to call my client, Michael Fay, in Auckland, New Zealand—waking him up in the middle of the night—to give him the bad news.

The five-to-two opinion largely tracked the Appellate Division decision. It held that nowhere in the deed did the donors express an intention to prohibit the use of catamarans or require the defender to race an "evenly matched" vessel of the same type as the challenger. It held that the deed makes clear that the design and construction of the yachts, as well as the races, are part of the competition. It held that the "friendly competition between foreign countries" clause referred only to the spirit of cooperation in working out the details of the matches and pointed out that it was in this spirit that the competitors since 1958 had agreed to race in 12-meter yachts until New Zealand departed these conditions by issuing the challenge. And, finally, it held that San Diego, as the trustee of the America's Cup, did not breach any fiduciary duty to the beneficiaries (challengers) because the trustee was expressly obligated to use its best efforts to defend the Cup in competition with the beneficiary challenger.[71]

Chief Judge Wachtler filed a concurring opinion, in which he noted that although the case "has caught the public eye like few cases in the Court's history," it has "little or no significance for the law."[72] He concluded:

> "It is tempting, of course, to confuse our authority to construe the trust instrument with a license to mold the America's Cup competition in accord with our notions of sporting ideals. Ultimately, however, it must be the contestants, not the courts, who define the traditions and ideals of the sport. No one wishes to see the competition debased by commercialism and greed. But if the traditions and ideals of the sport are dependent on judicial coercion, that battle is already lost."[73]

Judge Hancock, joined by Judge Titone, filed a lengthy dissent spelling out his view that San Diego, as the trustee of the Cup, had breached its fiduciary duty to the challenging beneficiary:

> ". . . [T]here can be no doubt that San Diego chose the catamaran to race against the monohull for one reason: to be certain that there could be no reasonable possibility of losing."

—⁓—

> ". . . Can it be consistent with the duties of a holder and defender as trustee of the America's Cup to meet a lawful challenge by a monohull with a catamaran for the express purpose of avoiding the very competition which the gift of the Cup was intended to promote?"

—⏳—

". . . [I]t is unthinkable that the donors could ever have intended that the trophy holder and defender could construe the Deed of Gift in its favor for the express purpose of creating a mismatch to retain the trophy, thereby subverting the very purpose of their gift in trust. We therefore dissent."[74]

Judge Wachtler answered by saying it wasn't the court's job to impose a duty "on the defender to—well, to do just what? To not try too hard to win, it seems."

The case was over, but the debate raged on. A few months after the decision Judge Edmund Thomas of the New Zealand High Court wrote a lengthy article for the *New Zealand Bar Journal* praising Judge Hancock's opinion. He invited Judge Hancock to New Zealand, where he went bungee jumping in Queensland at age sixty-seven and the two became good friends. Judge Hancock reciprocated the invitation and when Judge Thomas came to the United States hosted a dinner in Albany for him with the entire Court of Appeals, with Judge Tyler and myself as special guests.

In the wake of the ruling the America's Cup races returned to the Louis Vuitton Cup format for challengers. Potential defenders vied in a similar round-robin race series. From 1992 to 2007, following a mutually-agreed upon modification of the Deed of Gift, the race boats followed design specifications for the International America's Cup Class, which made them longer and lighter and gave them more sail area than the old 12-meters. In the five matches in that span, New Zealand and Switzerland each won twice and the United States once. After another battle in the New York Court of Appeals set up a one-on-one match between Switzerland and the United States, the competitors sailed trimarans off the coast of Spain in 2010 and San Francisco's Golden Gate Yacht Club brought the America's Cup back to the United States.

In the 2013 America's Cup races in September the focus once again fell on radical yacht design. The boats were 72-foot catamarans called AC-72s, built so light that with special daggerboards and rudders they were capable of actually lifting off, and sailing with only these fins in the water could reach speeds over 50 miles an hour. They were also dangerous, with the crewmember of one challenger killed when his yacht went stern over bow attempting a maneuver. Sailors on competing yachts wore helmets and body armor because the forces were so powerful.

Contention revisited the Cup as well. The defending American team, called Oracle and backed by software billionaire Larry Ellison, was penalized two races by an international jury for illegally modifying smaller catamarans in runups to the Cup. That meant the Americans started two races down, and they quickly fell behind still further to a New Zealand team that jumped out to an eight-race to one lead with nine needed to win. But the Oracle team staged an amazing comeback, taking the last eight races on San Francisco Bay to retain the Cup.

These boats that seemed to levitate brought even non-sailors into the television audience for America's Cup racing. Whatever else can be said for the court battles, the spirit of "friendly competition" among nations, and the march of technology in a time-less sport, few will now repeat Red Smith's old line that "watching the America's Cup is like watching grass grow."

REMEMBERING A SEAFARER

My father died on the Fourth of July, the year after the America's Cup ruling against Michael Fay. He had an abundant sense of fairness and while we didn't discuss the case at length he agreed with the position that the Americans should have sailed a similar boat to the Kiwis. He knew first-hand the joys of sailing and the demands of being at sea, and he appreciated—as few other men I've known—the rigors sailors and seamen face when the chips are down. He wasn't one to favor an uneven contest.

For his funeral on July 11, 1991 we returned to the Old Lyme Congregational Church where we had said goodbye to my mother in August 1984. She had been eighty when she died; Dad was two weeks short of his ninety-first birthday, and lucid to the end. Having seen it coming, he had joined in making the arrangements. So, it was no surprise that one of the hymns he selected for the service was a prayer for his fellow seafarers:

> "Eternal Father, strong to save,
> Whose arm hath bound the restless wave,
> Who biddest the mighty ocean deep
> Its own appointed limits keep;
> Oh, hear us when we cry to Thee,
> For those in peril on the sea!"

CHAPTER 31

In Praise of the Outdoors:
New Zealand, Fly Fishing, and Vermont

IN THE SPRING OF 1991 Janet and I spent three weeks in New Zealand at the invitation of David Williams and another of the New Zealand lawyers, Andrew Johns, from the Russell McVeigh firm. Johns was an avid sailor and had been part of the crew on *New Zealand*.

New Zealand, two rugged and beautiful islands that between them have half the inhabitants of New York City, is an outdoor lover's paradise. We hiked the Milford Track on the South Island, fished for trout, rode horses, visited sheep farms and landed on glaciers in ski planes. Not that we needed it, but that trip was yet another reminder of the strong attraction the outdoor life has always held for me, and the need to do what we can to preserve our natural resources.

Maybe that is part of my genetic makeup. My father, in his autobiography, described the joys of trout fishing on the Beaverkill River in the Catskills in part by evoking "the trees, the flowers, the occasional deer, fox, mink and porcupines and unafraid birds of many varieties" he encountered while on the stream at the Balsam Lake Club. I maintained our family's membership in the fishing club and when my son Bob was about twelve I started taking him to Balsam Lake so the three of us could fish the trout beats together. Janet, too, after some schooling by Orvis and Joan Wulff, turned out to be an avid and skillful fisherman and we have gone to the Balsam Lake Club over her birthday in June and many other times over the years.

In 1988 we bought a house in Barnard, Vermont, close to Woodstock and Hanover, the home of Dartmouth College. We bought it as a vacation home, primarily for downhill and cross-country skiing in the winter, but for summer use and the spectacular fall foliage as well. It was a great springboard for bicycling trips around the state and for hiking in the Green Mountains. We created a conservation easement with the Vermont Land Trust for the 100 acres of woods we have on the property. After several years there Janet followed my parents' example at Hamburg Cove and designed a small log cabin for the children and grandchildren overlooking our one-acre pond that has made the property a magnet for family reunions.

The Milford Track

A birthday cast at the Balsam Lake Club

When I was U.S. Attorney I had worked with Douglas Costle, who headed the Environmental Protection Agency during the Carter administration. He had later become dean of the Vermont Law School, a small independent school in South Royalton that was founded in 1975. It quickly developed a stellar reputation in environmental law, an area where it is usually ranked No. 1 by *U.S. News and World Report*, and has a solid general practice curriculum as well. Costle called me in 1990 and asked if I would join the board, and I readily agreed. I served until 2000 and rejoined the board in 2011 at the request of Geoffrey Shields, who was the dean at that time—succeeded in 2013 by Marc Mihaly. I was proud to receive an honorary degree in 2005, presented by Dean Shields.

With Linda in Vermont

Hiking the Long Trail with Bob

In between my board terms I served for six years as a trustee of the Vermont Natural Resources Council at the request of its Executive Director, Elizabeth Courtney, who I had met when she was also serving on the law school board. The Council is the leading environmental organization in Vermont and has, over the years, worked closely and effectively with the state legislature and various state agencies to maintain the state's forests, upgrade water quality, preserve open space and meet important climate change and energy goals.

As much as I have enjoyed the outdoors as a sportsman and a traveler throughout my life, it seems only appropriate to give back in a small way to help Vermont preserve its natural beauty and its resources.

CHAPTER 32

Building a White Collar Crime Practice

BY NOW IT must seem as if all my big cases fell into my lap, and the rest of the time I was being courted for government jobs and doing bar association service. But when I came back to Davis Polk in 1980, I thought I saw an area of law that no major firm except possibly Paul Weiss[75] was involved in—a white collar criminal practice.

Most of the big firms had not considered it respectable. But that was changing thanks to a cadre of lawyers like Bob Morvillo, Peter Fleming, and Charlie Stillman, who had served as prosecutors in the Southern District under Robert Morgenthau. They— and lawyers who had served in the local DA offices—knew criminal law, made criminal defense their careers when they went out on their own, and were highly regarded in the profession. They were mostly with "boutique" firms, but the ice was breaking in the big firms by the 1980's.

Jack Cooney had come to Davis Polk out of Duke Law School, left to serve as an AUSA and, when I was U.S. Attorney for the Southern District, headed the Narcotics Unit. He had returned to Davis Polk in 1978 and became a partner in 1981. He was as interested as I was in the opportunities, to say nothing of the excitement and challenge of these high-stakes cases, and we set out to build a white collar defense practice. We did, with the encouragement of our Davis Polk partners, and set a trend that other big firms followed.[76]

In 1982 Bob Morvillo asked us to represent a partner in a New York law firm that was under investigation by the United States Attorney's Office in Charleston, West Virginia. The firm had given tax opinions in connection with coal mining tax shelters that contemplated a traditional ratio of deductions to investment; however, it later put together a very highly leveraged coal tax shelter that was designed for clients and friends of the law firm and reflected a ratio of deductions to investment of eighteen-to-one. The thrust of the investigation was that this latter transaction was a sham—there was no coal to be mined—and the lawyers, including our prospective client, knew it. He and three other partners had all received target letters advising them that the U.S. Attorney's Office intended to indict them. Morvillo was representing the firm along with Cono Namorato, a former high-ranking member of the Tax Division at the Department of Justice. Former Watergate prosecutor Jim Neal and two other prominent criminal defense lawyers, Paul Grand and Seymour Glanzer, were representing the other three partners.

We agreed to take the case, our first in the new practice. Jack and I worked as a team together with Scott Muller, who had just come back to Davis Polk from the U.S. Attorney's Office. We and the other defense lawyers met with prosecutors from the U.S. Attorney's Office in Charleston to try to persuade them not to indict our clients. We argued that they had legitimately believed that there was coal to be mined and that the tax shelters were valid—the firm had hired experts and had relied on them as to the quantity and quality of the coal and the economic viability of the mining operation. The prosecutors rejected our arguments and told us they intended to proceed with indictments of all four of them. We then went to Washington to the Tax Division of the DOJ, which had the final say.

Our appeals went through several levels of the Tax Division, and each provided feedback. The first report was positive. The reviewer agreed with the West Virginia prosecutors as to two of the defendants, but agreed with us and with Glanzer as to our clients. They were out, or so it seemed. The other two appealed to the next level where one of them was dropped as well. So, while we knew that the remaining partner was taking his appeal to the final level—review by the head of the Tax Division—we assumed that our client had avoided prosecution. By now it was 1983.

Davis Polk held an annual summer outing at the Rockaway Hunt Club in Cedarhurst, Long Island. This year it was in June, and I was riding a golf cart to the sixteenth tee when the clubhouse sent a messenger to say I had received an urgent phone call that I needed to return immediately. I left the course, went back to the clubhouse and called the number. It was Cono Namorato. He told me that the head of the Tax Division, Robert Edwin Davis, had decided the government should not go to trial against one partner alone. He wanted another partner as a defendant and, without giving us a chance to be heard, had put our client back into the case.

This was devastating: unpredictable, unjustified, but also unappealable. If it was devastating news for us, it was worse for him. He thought the tax evasion charges were behind him. Now he was going to be indicted and his life would never be the same.

Charleston, West Virginia was a badly depressed area in the early 1980's. It took only one visit to convince us that four lawyers from New York were not going to do well in a highly-leveraged tax shelter case before a jury there. So, when the indictment was filed, we moved to dismiss the substantive counts for lack of venue, since our clients had committed no acts there, and to transfer the conspiracy count to New York.

There were three defendants in the case at this point; the third was one of the promoters of the tax shelters. Scott Muller drafted the motion on behalf of them all, so impressing Jim Neal that he told me he'd make Scott a partner if I didn't. (We did, two years later.)

The Federal Rules of Criminal Procedure allow for transfers of venue "for the convenience of the parties, and in the interests of justice . . ." Scott's motion argued that twenty-three of the thirty-eight potential witnesses at the trial lived in the Southern District of New York and only five in West Virginia; that all but two of the twenty-eight overt acts alleged occurred in New York; that counsel for two of the three defendants lived in New York (Jim Neal lived in Tennessee); and that it would be a hardship for the defendants, their lawyers, and the witnesses to have the case tried in West Virginia.

District Judge Charles H. Haden II of West Virginia agreed with us in a ruling filed on October 21, 1983.

In the meantime the government had gone to trial in West Virginia against the experts who had given favorable opinions of the tax shelters. The prosecutor argued that the opinions were intentionally false and that those false opinions had misled both the investors and the lawyers. In her opening and in her summation she told the jury exactly what we had been saying all along; that the lawyers didn't know anything about coal and had relied on experts they trusted. The experts in turn, she said, wrote opinion letters that "misled [the investors'] lawyers . . . into believing that the coal . . . could be mined at a profit." Of one expert she said, he "had a very good reputation, and he was very believable, and those investors and those lawyers relied on him." And in emphasis by repetition, she said the lawyers "didn't see coal except when they were in the army, so they hired an expert, and they believed him."

As soon as the case was transferred to New York we renewed our efforts to exonerate our clients, making the argument now to Southern District U.S. Attorney Rudolph Giuliani as well as Roger Olson, who had succeeded Davis as head of the Tax Division. The case, we said, "is not a prosecution worthy of the Southern District of New York." In our support, we had not only all the facts we had presented earlier to the West Virginia U.S. Attorney and the Tax Division that our clients had no reason to believe the tax shelters were a sham. We now had the overwhelmingly powerful fact that the government prosecutor had agreed with those facts in her summation.

A 1935 case, *Berger v. United States*, established that the government's interest in a criminal prosecution "is not that it shall win a case but that justice shall be done." That's what we told Giuliani and Olson. We argued that the government could not go into one courtroom in the United States and represent to a jury that the lawyers knew nothing about coal and had been deceived by the experts in order to convict the experts, and then go into another courtroom somewhere else and take the exact opposite position in order to convict the lawyers. And, as it turned out, the experts had also been acquitted in two separate trials, so we were handed an additional argument: if the government could not prove that coal mining experts didn't know there was no coal, how could two New York lawyers be expected to know?

Giuliani and Olson agreed with us and directed that the indictment be dismissed. So, our client was finally vindicated after what was a very unfair indictment, and we had won our first white collar crime case.

CHAPTER 33

E.F. Hutton and George Ball

OUR SECOND CASE AROSE from shady practices that the brokerage firm E.F. Hutton followed in the early 1980's to boost its interest income. They were sophisticated versions of check kiting schemes, and Hutton had generated massive profits through their use.

The practices involved the company's system for collecting funds received by its domestic branch offices and transferring those funds to central accounts, where they were used to meet corporate cash needs. Essentially, Hutton was obtaining its large interest income by misusing the "float" that arises in the banking system in the interval between the time a check is deposited in a bank and the time the depository bank collects funds from the bank on which the check was drawn. Electronic banking would make such a scheme impossible today.

In banking terms the two practices were "excessive drawdowns" and "multiple transfers." Excessive drawdowns means writing excessively large checks against deposits before the deposited checks cleared, in effect creating interest-free loans from the banks to the company. Multiple transfers means transferring branch funds successively through several banks on their way to the company's central bank which allowed the company to earn interest income from potential increases in float that might arise from random delays in the check-clearing system.

The scheme was uncovered in 1983 when the Genesee County Bank in Batavia, NY discovered that the large deposits made by Hutton's four-person office there were far more than the office's banking requirements. Genesee also discovered that the checks Hutton was using to make the deposits were drawn on two Pennsylvania banks. When the Genesee officials learned that Hutton did not have enough money in the Pennsylvania accounts to cover the checks they stopped honoring Hutton checks and asked the FDIC to investigate. In 1984 the matter was forwarded to the U.S. Attorney's Office for the Middle District of Pennsylvania, which started a criminal investigation led by AUSA Albert Murray.

When news of the investigation broke the late night TV comics had a field day with an E.F. Hutton ad that was appearing at the time. The ad showed a group of people

188

talking over one another until one says, "My broker is E.F. Hutton," and they all fall silent. The tag line was, "When E.F. Hutton talks, people listen." The comics changed this to, "When E.F. Hutton talks, people lose interest."

George Ball had been the President of E.F. Hutton during the time period involved. By the time the investigation started he had left to become CEO of Prudential Bache Securities, taking with him Loren Schechter, a Hutton assistant general counsel, to become general counsel at Prudential Bache. Cahill Gordon, led by Tom Curnin and Tom Kavaler, was representing E.F. Hutton, and had lined up a number of lawyers to represent the individuals under investigation. Schechter called to ask if I would represent George Ball, which I agreed to do along with Jack Cooney.

Ball had been Hutton's National Sales Manager prior to becoming President. In that position his responsibilities were not expanded and he remained in charge of the sales network. He was not Hutton's chief operating officer and had no responsibility for non-sales operations, including financial affairs, accounting and operations. However, prosecutor Murray had Ball very much in his sights because of a series of emails he had sent to the sales force encouraging them to try to increase interest income.

Typical was a memo sent to all regional VPs and regional sales managers that emphasized "an examination of the P&Ls [profit and loss statements] indicates that those offices paying particular attention to their interest profits tended to be standouts." But the one of greatest concern was a memo sent to Ball citing the example of an office that had been earning $30,000 per month "from overdrafting of the bank accounts," but where the branch dropped to $10,000 per month after the branch manager changed cashiers. The message was to emphasize the value of effective branch cashiers. Ball recirculated this memo to all regional VPs, sales managers and branch office managers, with the comment, "A point well worth remembering and acting on."

In a series of meetings with AUSA Murray we argued that there was nothing wrong in stressing the desirability of increasing income from interest, since there were a number of perfectly legitimate ways to do that. We also argued that overdrafting is not *per se* illegal, and that the overdrafting referred to in the memo was not synonymous with the excessive overdrafting that Hutton had engaged in, which Ball was totally unaware of. At the end of the day after fifty seven immunized witnesses had testified in the grand jury without a single one indicating Ball was aware of the abuses, and Ball himself had testified, without immunity, to his unawareness, the government did not charge him with any wrongdoing. Nor did they charge any other individual.

After Hutton pleaded guilty to 2,000 counts of mail and wire fraud and was fined $2 million, without any charges being brought against any individuals, William Safire of *The New York Times* wrote a column comparing Hutton to bank robber Willie Sutton. He said Hutton's draws against uncollected funds made Sutton's bank jobs look like "small change" and called for the Senate Judiciary Committee to look at the lack of individual prosecutions saying, "There's a Sutton at Hutton who beat the rap."

The hue and cry led to a very contentious hearing at which top DOJ officials were called upon to justify their decision not to prosecute any top-ranking officials at Hutton. It also resulted in Hutton's CEO retaining former Attorney General Griffin Bell, then a partner at King & Spalding in Atlanta, to investigate the conduct that led to the plea. Ball testified before Congress and gave interviews to Bell's investigators. In his report Bell supported the DOJ decision as it related to Ball, by concluding that while Ball had "the responsibility as a senior corporate officer to report improprieties in overdrafting or gaps in accounting controls once he was put on notice," there was "no substantial evidence that he was put on notice" of these problems.

So, Davis Polk's white collar crime practice now was two for two as a defense team. More importantly, the practice that we started from whole cloth was gaining praise in the legal community and other firms were beginning to take notice.

CHAPTER 34

Paul Thayer

BY 1985 OUR WHITE COLLAR criminal practice at Davis Polk was established and growing. It had also produced an unexpected bonus by bringing me into contact with some of the most larger-than-life people you could ever hope to meet.

Paul Thayer led an incredible life. To say he lived in the fast lane was an understatement. "Dynamic," "charismatic," "tough" and "wily" were just a few of the adjectives used to describe him. He was born in Oklahoma in 1919 and worked as a roughneck in the oil fields before entering the University of Kansas where, in 1940, he enrolled in the Civilian Pilot Training Program. He entered the Naval Aviation Cadet Program in 1941 because he wanted the challenge of landing on aircraft carriers, was commissioned in 1942, and quickly became one of the navy's ace pilots. His service in World War II included six confirmed and nine probable kills of Japanese aircraft, three Distinguished Flying Crosses and two Presidential Unit Citations.

After the war he started as a commercial pilot for TWA, but missed the action and decided to become a test pilot for experimental aircraft for Chance Vought and Northrop. He was the first pilot to break the sound barrier in a navy-production fighter and the first to use an ejection seat, which he did when his plane caught on fire during an air show. He survived seven crashes, four as a fighter pilot and three as a test pilot.

He developed some business expertise along the way, managing sales and service at Chance Vought as well as his job as chief of flight test. He was there ten years when, in 1961, Ling-Temco-Electronics merged with Chance Vought to become Ling-Temco-Vought, Inc. Thayer became President of Chance Vought Aircraft, now a subsidiary. Four years later when the company was reorganized, Thayer was named President and CEO of LTV Aerospace Corporation, the successor to Chance Vought. Under his leadership the company's sales grew four-fold from $195 million to $800 million annually.

My relationship with him began in 1968 when I was asked to represent him and two other executives of LTV, the Dallas-based conglomerate over the aerospace and other operations. They were charged in a derivative suit brought to recover for the company profits they made by selling restricted stock issued under a stock option plan. The other defendants were James Ling, LTV's CEO, and James Weldon, Chairman of the

Board of another LTV subsidiary. Each man had taken the stock "for my own account for investment" and declared he had "no present intention of selling" the shares, but each had sold all or large portions of the stock within a few months of receiving it.

The plaintiff relied on an SEC pronouncement that it would not take action in such a case if the stock were held for three years as meaning that the SEC believed that an earlier sale was illegal. We argued that they had intended to hold the stock, as they had represented, and had sold it only because their circumstances changed.

The case went to trial in the Southern District of New York before Judge Lloyd MacMahon without a jury. Each of the defendants took the stand and testified as to the reasons for his sale. Thayer's explanation was the one that intrigued the judge the most. He was an inveterate gambler[77] and he told the court that shortly after receiving the stock and making the representation he went to Las Vegas and lost $60,000, on credit, at the crap table. He said he had to sell his stock to pay the gambling debt. Judge MacMahon accepted his explanation as well as the less colorful but also persuasive explanations of the other two defendants, and we won the case.[78]

In 1970 Thayer was elected chairman and CEO of the LTV Corporation, which was in the midst of a major financial crisis. He steered the company into new ventures, including development of the Steamboat Springs ski area and its golf course. Within two years Thayer brought LTV's operations back into the black and by 1974 the company was reporting record sales and earnings.

In 1983 President Reagan selected him to become Deputy Secretary of Defense. In that role he oversaw the day-to-day operations of the Defense Department and crafting of the Department budget. He had publicly criticized the military's waste and cost overruns and had said that he could cut the budget by 20 percent without sacrificing readiness. This produced sharp clashes with military leaders, especially Navy Secretary John Lehman, who did not appreciate having their budgets cut. And he did something no other Defense Secretary has done before or since—he test flew new proposed military aircraft before deciding how much money to budget for them.[79]

Paul Thayer in his Corsair Fighter

In the spring of 1983, still early days for our white collar practice, I received a call from Paul. He had gotten a subpoena from the SEC, which was investigating insider trading by a Dallas stockholder named Billy Bob Harris. The SEC was looking at a large volume of purchases emanating from Harris's firm, AG Edwards & Co., just prior to two major corporate acquisitions. These were Anheuser-Busch's purchase of the Campbell Taggart Company and Allied Corporation's acquisition of Bendix. Thayer explained that he had been subpoenaed because he and Harris were good friends and he, Thayer, was on the Boards of both Anheuser-Busch and Allied.

He sent me a copy of Harris's deposition taken by Bettina Lawton and Suzanne Mishkin, both young attorneys in the Enforcement Division of the SEC. In his testimony Billy Bob denied receiving any inside information from Thayer and maintained that he had made the purchases based on his own research. I knew we were in trouble when I read the last page of the deposition which contained the following statement by Harris after it was suggested he might have to come back for more questions: "I think you all are darling, but I don't want to come back over here."

Jack Cooney, Scott Wise and I went down to the Pentagon to prepare Thayer for his testimony. His impressive office contained numerous pictures of Thayer in flying regalia and several of the planes he had flown. It also included a stuffed lion, which he had shot on a safari in Africa, an autographed $5 bill he had won on the golf course from Arnold Palmer, and a Dallas Cowboy football helmet that Cowboy coach Tom Landry had thought might come in handy in his budget negotiations. His fast lane life was on full display.

Billy Bob Harris was another character out of central casting, the stockbroker equivalent of fictional "Dallas" oilman J. R. Ewing. Thayer's actress daughter, Brynn—then starring in "One Life to Live"—had introduced them. A local writer had called him a "regular celebrity groupie" and the description was dead-on. Harris hobnobbed with former Cowboy quarterback and "Monday Night Football" star Don Meredith, former quarterback Craig Morton and Country and Western singer Kenny Rogers. He gave parties known for wall-to-wall girls, champagne, hot tubs and more girls. He was a celebrity himself with a radio show every afternoon at 5 reporting on the day's stock market activity. He had a girlfriend, Julie Williams, who taught aerobic dancing at a local health club.

And it emerged in our deposition prep session that Paul Thayer also had a girlfriend. Married since 1947, starting in 1979 he developed a relationship with Sandra Ryno, an LTV receptionist. The two couples spent a lot of time together, along with Thayer's doctor Doyle Sharp and his girlfriend Julia Rooker. An avid motorcyclist, Thayer used to take long rides with Ryno on the back.

As he later told the SEC, Thayer said he had not told Harris about either the Anheuser-Busch/Campbell Taggart or the Allied/Bendix acquisition. He said he had not given him inside information of any kind. He said shortly before each deal, when rumors were circulating, Harris had asked him what he could tell him about Campbell Taggart and later, Bendix. "I can't talk about that," he reported he said each time, but had added that each was a good company "and anyone who bought that stock wouldn't get hurt."

We thought that was dangerously close to the line, but our research developed a line of cases that gave considerable leeway to someone who has inside information and is suddenly surprised by a question where a truthful answer would reveal it. So, we thought we were probably okay.

When we went to the SEC to testify I approached Bettina Lawton, the lead SEC attorney taking the deposition, and asked her not to ask Thayer about Ryno. I explained that his wife was unaware of the relationship and I was concerned that the deposition, through a FOIA request, might become public whether or not the SEC ever brought a case. I said we would acknowledge the relationship's existence if it became important later. She agreed and the deposition went forward. We did not finish the deposition that day and a second appearance was scheduled. When we returned, Gary Lynch, Deputy Director of Enforcement,[80] told us that he would not go along with the deal we had made and that Thayer would have to answer questions about his relationship with Ryno, which he did.

Several months later, in late 1983, the SEC told us they were considering bringing charges against Thayer, Harris, Sharpe, Ryno, Williams and Rooker. At that point Harris's lawyer had him take a lie detector test in which he denied Thayer had given him any information about either acquisition. He not only passed, the test's administrator issued a statement saying how exceptionally credible he was. The United States Attorney in Dallas also wrote a letter certifying to the administrator's outstanding credentials.

We submitted all this to the SEC—to no avail. They advised us they were going ahead. Thayer refused to discuss any resolution of the charges and several days later, in early January 1984, the SEC brought the case. The complaint, with its descriptions of the defendants' relationships, made front-page headlines in *The New York Times*, *The Wall Street Journal* and *The Washington Post* and was the subject of feature articles in *Time* and *Newsweek*.

The *Time* article quoted the complaint as to Thayer and Ryno's "private personal relationship" and called her "a show stopper brunette" whom he provided, again quoting the complaint, with "monetary support." It reported the accusation that Thayer shared "lunches, dinners, trips, vacations, and social gatherings with a small circle of high-living southerners and their women friends" as well as "stock tips worth $1.9 million."

Thayer resigned as Deputy Secretary of Defense, saying he had to devote time to "defending myself against these meritless allegations" and to limit political damage to the Reagan administration and the Defense Department.

The SEC complaint included an allegation that Thayer had tried to "impede and obstruct the SEC investigation" and the Justice Department was looking into possible perjury charges. While we were preparing to go to trial against the SEC, Justice was moving forward aggressively. Sandy Ryno learned that the FBI had been visiting her neighbors and telling them she might go to jail. It became ominous when her lawyer stopped returning our phone calls.

At the same time the sledding was getting heavy on another front. Davis Polk had represented Anheuser-Busch in the Campbell Taggart acquisition. When Thayer first called me I reached out to the Anheuser-Busch general counsel, Walter Suhre, and asked if he had any objection to our representing him in the SEC investigation. Suhre said he did not, spoke highly of Thayer and wished us well. But once the complaint was filed, with its detailed allegations of phone calls between Harris and Thayer right before the acquisition, Anheuser-Busch concluded that Thayer was guilty and its attitude changed. Suhre called to say he and a Williams & Connolly partner, named Paul Wolff, would like to come to New York and meet with us. When they arrived they told Jack and me that Davis Polk had to withdraw from representing Thayer because it conflicted with our prior representation of Anheuser-Busch. They said that the heavy purchasing of Campbell Taggart just before the acquisition had driven its stock up several points, forcing Anheuser-Busch to pay more for the company, and that they had a claim against Thayer.

We said we had obtained their consent in the beginning, that Thayer had relied heavily on us, and that he would be severely prejudiced if we were to withdraw now. They insisted that we think it over. Jack and I consulted with our managing partner, Henry King. After a thorough discussion he agreed with us. Several days later Henry and I flew to St. Louis and delivered our decision to Suhre and Wolff: we would continue to represent Thayer against the SEC and DOJ, but would not represent him in any suit brought by Anheuser-Busch. They said they could not accept that answer.

A few days later, after consulting with Henry, I called Suhre and told him we were going to seek independent advice from another law firm and would follow whatever course of action it advised. We selected Merrell "Ted" Clark of Winthrop Stimson Putnam & Roberts, a prominent New York attorney who had been President of the Bar

Association of the City of New York. Ted wrote an opinion concluding that we had an obligation to continue to represent Thayer because of Anheuser-Busch's initial consent and the prejudice to him if we were to withdraw. We sent the opinion to Suhre and said we were not going to withdraw.

In early 1985 we were approached by Charles Roistacher, the AUSA in the District of Columbia who was heading the criminal investigation. He told us they had a compelling perjury case and offered to let Thayer plead to one count.

The case was indeed compelling. As the evidence was described to us Thayer had given Harris very specific information about the two acquisitions, as well as advance information concerning LTV's earnings and a prospective acquisition of Grumman Aircraft that later did not go through. He gave the inside information about Grumman to someone he and Harris both trusted, who bought Grumman stock and sold it for a large profit. Ryno had testified to a celebratory dinner she and Thayer had attended with Harris and his girlfriend. She described piling the profits—in cash—into a "breadbasket" that went around the table as they laughed, "Let's pass the bread."

Harris had led Thayer to believe that he would use the information he received discreetly, making only limited purchases for Ryno, Williams and Rooker that would give them a "nest egg" but would keep the level of transactions below the SEC's radar screen. Instead Harris had put virtually all of his customers into both Campbell Taggart and Bendix, thus producing the high volume of transactions that triggered the SEC's suspicions and Thayer's eventual demise.

In March 1985 Thayer and Harris each pleaded guilty to one count of perjury. Thereafter they reached a settlement with the SEC in which Thayer agreed to pay $555,000 and Harris $275,000. Charges against Ryno, Williams, Sharpe and Rooker were dropped. On May 15 we appeared before Judge Charles Richey in the District of Columbia for sentencing. We had assembled a powerful set of letters, including many from the military, industry and government.

Senator Barry Goldwater wrote that he knew of no one "living in this country who has been as dedicated, patriotic and such a willing and constant servant to our government and our Constitution."

Former President Gerald Ford said of Thayer, "I have always found him to be honest and forthright." Additional letters of high praise for Thayer—his integrity and his many contributions to the country—came from, among others: General John W. Vessey Jr., then the chairman of the Joint Chiefs of Staff; two former chairs; the U.S. ambassador to Britain; CEOs of LTV; Rockwell International, Hughes Aircraft, Martin Marietta, Chrysler and Boeing; and former Secretary of Defense Clark Clifford.

Judge Richey was not moved by the letters or by my argument that they showed his criminal conduct was "an aberration." He said Thayer deserved no medals "for the breach of trust, for the false statements, and the obstruction of justice you have engaged in in recent years," and sentenced him to four years in prison. This was before the sentencing guidelines that eliminated parole, and Thayer was released after serving fifteen months.[81]

Thayer's wife Margery stayed with him all the way despite the lurid revelations. After he was released from prison in 1986 Thayer picked up his life and went on as before. At age eighty-six he flew his F4V-Corsair fighter in air shows, and at least twice circled the globe—once in a record-setting Learjet marathon with four pilots, and again on a continent-hopping golfing trip in a Cessna 414. He visited Antarctica and, according to his daughter Brynn, at age eighty became the oldest man ever to bungee-jump at New Zealand's AJ Hackett Bungy.

He died in May 2010 at age ninety and remains to this day, despite the fatal flaws that probably were linked to his gambling and his love of danger, one of the most dynamic persons I've had the opportunity to know.

CHAPTER 35

United States v. David Brown

OUR NEXT CASE provided another graphic demonstration of how prosecutorial over-reach and judicial prejudice can devastate careers and lives, and how a spirited defense determined the only path that led to justice.

David F. Brown grew up in Queens, New York. He attended public schools and graduated from Flushing High School in 1958. He worked his way through Rutgers University as a dishwasher and a summer lifeguard, graduating in 1962. He went on to Rutgers Law School, aided by a scholarship and work as a research assistant, and graduated in 1966.

After graduation he became the first Rutgers law grad to get a job in a large New York law firm, Cravath, Swaine & Moore, where he worked as a corporate associate. He left Cravath in 1972 to take a position as Vice President and general counsel of City Investing, a large conglomerate holding company with over $8 billion in assets and $7 billion in annual revenues and more than twenty separate businesses. One of those businesses was a Florida company called General Development Corporation (GDC), which was in the business of developing planned communities in Florida.

In 1984 City Investing decided that the separate value of its businesses was much greater than the stock value of the company. It decided to sell the companies and give the proceeds to the stockholders. So, in 1985 GDC and the other businesses were sold or spun off; GDC was spun off and sold to the public and its shares were listed on the New York Stock Exchange. At the insistence of Merrill Lynch, which managed the public offering, David Brown agreed to move to Florida as Chairman of the Board of GDC. As a new public company GDC would have to deal with all the issues that came with that status—dealing with financial institutions, the capital markets, the SEC, and so forth. Brown was an ideal candidate. He had no operating responsibilities. These remained under the President, Robert F. Ehrling, who had been running the company for several years.

GDC was one of the first major community developers in Florida. Going back to 1954 it had bought up land and built communities populated by people from the north who wanted to come south to enjoy "the Florida dream." Over thirty-five years it developed nine separate communities in Florida covering a total of 270,000 acres, including Port Charlotte—a city of 100,000 people—and Port St. Lucie, the winter home of the New York Mets.

Its business model wasn't cheap. GDC had to make the prospective community an attractive place to live. This meant roads, water and sewer lines, and development plans that included the size and location of the building lots, as well as areas for parks, lakes, tennis courts, swimming pools, and community centers, all of which were built by GDC. It had to carve out areas for retail stores and office buildings. These basic development costs topped $500 million.

To lure residents to its communities GDC employed a sales force in the north of over 2,000 people. Using direct mail and magazine ads, reaching out to friends and relatives and even building a model home mock-up in New York's Grand Central Terminal, they identified prospective customers and paid them home visits equipped with maps and videos of GDC's communities and floor plans and photos of GDC-built homes. The sales pitch stressed the values of the Florida experience in a GDC house in a GDC community. If that sparked sufficient interest, the company paid for a three-day "SoHo" trip to Florida to show the customer around. SoHo stood for "Southward Ho."

GDC also sold building lots without houses. As time went on local builders began to buy lots and build spec houses in GDC's growing communities. Their houses were comparable to GDC's, but less expensive since they didn't bear the additional costs of the community's infrastructure or the large sales force. At times what would cost a GDC customer $75,000 could be bought from a local builder for $50,000 to $60,000 even though GDC was essentially selling the house for a break-even price.

Over time GDC buyers began to learn about this price disparity, usually when they tried to sell or refinance their houses only to discover that the local market value—set by the builders' houses—was often less than they owed. Enraged at GDC for selling them houses they could have bought for $20,000 less, a number of disgruntled customers brought suit against the company.

They alleged that GDC had concealed the price disparities beginning with the tightly-controlled SoHo trips in which salespeople stayed with customers at all times and used tour routes that avoided billboards and other price comparison displays. The concealment continued, the suits charged, when buyers sought financing and were encouraged to use a GDC subsidiary called GDV. This kept them away from local banks where they would not qualify since the mortgage would be higher than the houses' fair market value. The next act of concealment, according to the suits, lay in the use of appraisers who used only GDC houses as price comparisons for appraisals that would be used by GDC in selling the mortgages to institutions such as Fannie Mae.

In addition the suits claimed that GDC salesmen made factual misrepresentations in claiming that the land was a good investment, that values of GDC houses were appreciating and that the houses could be rented for more than the monthly payments on the mortgage.

When David Brown came to GDC in 1985 and learned of the customer complaints and lawsuits, he turned to a friend he knew from his days at Cravath. Paul Dodyk was a partner at the firm, a Rhodes scholar and a former Columbia Law professor. Brown told Dodyk that he wanted him to investigate the allegations being made. He placed all GDC documents and personnel at his disposal because he wanted to know, he told Dodyk, "Are we doing anything wrong because if we are I will stop it immediately."

Dodyk visited Florida with a team of Cravath lawyers and spent several months reviewing the charges. When he was finished he advised Brown and the GDC Board that "there is nothing legally or morally wrong with what you are doing." His rationale was simple: if a customer comes to a Chevrolet dealer to buy a car the dealer has no obligation to tell the customer that he can buy a comparable car from the nearby Ford dealer for $5,000 less. And if the customer wants to take a test drive, it is perfectly acceptable if the Chevrolet salesman takes him on a route that does not go by the Ford dealer's sign advertising its lower price. The appraisals were not used as a sales tool and were never shown to the customer, thus they were not a problem. Dodyk made clear that GDC could not condone affirmative misrepresentations by its sales force, but also made it clear that its basic method of doing business was perfectly lawful.

Fortified and reassured by this advice GDC continued what it was doing. Then, in 1989, GDC received a grand jury subpoena from the United States Attorney's Office in Miami. Brown again turned to Dodyk who told him, in essence, not to worry; GDC's authorized sales practices did not constitute a civil fraud and were certainly not a criminal fraud. The first subpoena focused on whether GDV was defrauding the government by using its appraisals to support mortgages sold to Freddie Mac and Fannie Mae. GDC's lawyers were able to convince the government that there was no fraud because Freddie Mac and Fannie Mae knew the appraisals were based on GDC comparables.

The government then served a second subpoena that focused on GDC's house purchasers, and that part of the investigation continued for over a year into the fall of 1990. David Brown and Robert Ehrling, along with GDC, received target letters advising them that the U.S. Attorney was planning to indict them for mail fraud.

At this point Dodyk reached out and assembled a first-class defense team. He asked Lloyd Cutler of Wilmer Cutler and Jack Miller of Miller, Cassidy, Larroca and Lewin to represent GDC; Vincent Fuller of Williams & Connolly, best known for his successful insanity defense of John Hinckley against assassination charges in Ronald Reagan's shooting, to represent Ehrling; and me to represent Brown.

We tried to prevent the indictment by presentations to line prosecutor Norman Moscowitz, U.S. Attorney Dexter Lehtinen, and the DOJ in Washington in the person of Deputy Assistant Attorney General Jack Keeney, making essentially the same arguments that had formed the basis for Paul Dodyk's opinion. The presentations fell on deaf ears and the prosecutions went forward. The indictment was filed in March 1990 charging that GDC had sold over 10,000 homes for over $700 million and caused customer losses of around $150 million. The case was assigned to Judge Lenore Nesbitt.

By that time GDC was in serious financial difficulty. Because of the high costs of its houses and its attempt to deal with the price disparity, it had lost money for several years. Faced with a criminal conviction and the potential costs of fines and restitution—let alone what an indictment would do to its business—GDC entered a guilty plea. Because the indictment to which it pled guilty alleged that GDC's basic business model violated the law, GDC found its access to the capital markets disrupted and went into bankruptcy. The government then offered Brown and Ehrling a plea deal—one count of mail fraud with a maximum sentence of five years.

We agonized long and hard over whether to accept it. The two men fervently believed they had done nothing wrong and were innocent. But with a potential loss of over $150 million, they faced sentences under the sentencing guidelines that could put them away for the rest of their lives. After some tortured analysis and several mind changes they decided to accept the proposal. Judge Nesbitt accepted the pleas pending a pre-sentence report. Several weeks later the prosecution and defense teams gathered in the courtroom to hear her decision. She shocked everyone by refusing to accept the plea because, she said, "I am not satisfied that the penalty that could be imposed for the single count of the indictment is commensurate with the alleged . . . massive fraud and the crimes that are set forth in the government's indictment."

This was a stark preview of the intensely hostile anti-defendant attitude that she would manifest throughout the trial.

She set the trial down for January 7, 1991. In the meantime the government filed a superseding indictment on December 15, 1990, with a total of seventy-two counts of mail and wire fraud and a conspiracy count. It named Ehrling and Brown and added two defendants: Tore DeBella, head of sales, and his deputy, Richard Reizen. The court adjourned the trial to October 19, 1991.

We began to prepare our defense. The stellar Davis Polk team included several fine young lawyers, all of whom would go on to have great success in their careers. In addition to myself the team consisted of Carey Dunne, then a fourth year associate,[82] and two younger associates: Pat Smith[83] and Sheila Sawyer.[84] We had a strong group of co-counsel: Vince Fuller for Ehrling; Roy Black for Reizen; Seth Waxman and Stan Mortenson for DeBella; and Steve Edwards, a former Cravath associate, helping all of us.

In June, with the trial three months away, we received some devastating news. Up to then the defense was being funded through GDC's directors and officers insurance policy, which provided coverage for wrongful acts while in office. The coverage excluded fraud, however, and the carrier—National Union—suddenly not only refused to continue to advance the costs of defense, but filed a suit to rescind the policy claiming the insureds had not disclosed they had engaged in fraud when the policy was issued. National Union's about-face brought on our counterclaim seeking the continuation of the attorneys' fees and a motion to stay the rescission complaint until after the trial. Fuller, Black, Waxman and Mortenson all withdrew from the case. I stayed on, believing I had made a commitment to David Brown, and was prepared, with Davis Polk's support, to try the case even if we ended up not getting paid. Ehrling, DeBella and Reizen got new lawyers, all members of the local bar in Miami—Joel Hirschhorn for Ehrling; Clark Mervis for DeBella; and Richard Sharpstein for Reizen.

After filing the counterclaim we immediately moved for summary judgment. National Union argued that while they were obligated to pay the costs of defense, they were not required to advance the costs, but could await the outcome of the trial. If the defendants were acquitted the company would pay the costs, but if they were convicted they would not have to pay because of the exclusion for fraud.

We took the position that under the language of the policy the legal obligation to pay occurred at the time the defense costs were incurred. Further, we argued that it was unfair—indeed unconscionable—for National Union to cut off funding, thereby preventing an effective defense and making the invocation of the fraud exclusion a foregone conclusion.

We argued the motion and on October 4, two weeks before the trial was due to start, Judge Edward Davis issued an opinion upholding our arguments in all respects and ordering National Union to continue advancing the costs of defense.[85]

The trial began on October 19, 1991. Its opening coincided with two other major events that left me few slivers of free time. As the President-Elect of the American College of Trial Lawyers I began my one-year term as President a week before the trial. The job included travel and a lot of mid-week dinner meetings, but I could only make the meetings that were held on weekends. And Janet and I had scheduled some major internal renovations to our house in Darien that took the kitchen out of commission. Anybody who's done a renovation knows they take twice as long and cost twice as much as estimated. In this case it took three times as long, a fact that also applied to the trial. It was expected to last three months—it ended up lasting nine. Between October 1991 and August 1992, I would fly in from Miami to the trial lawyers' meetings. Janet would fly in from New York to meet me and at the end of the weekend, we would fly back to our separate destinations.[86] But at least I missed the disruptions of the renovation, except on the weekends I went home.

The government witnesses were primarily GDC homebuyers and former GDC executives and salesmen.

Twenty-one homebuyers testified about their experiences with GDC. They all said they were unaware, at the time they made their purchase, of the substantial difference between GDC's prices and those of the competition. Virtually all of them testified that the value of their house turned out to be less than the amount owed on the mortgage. All complained that, while they were on the SoHo tour, their time had been so monopolized that they had no opportunity to shop around. All testified they had relied on GDC's size and reputation, as well as its promotional literature touting the benefits of "one-stop shopping" and the advantages of Florida life, in deciding to buy from GDC. Finally, nearly all of the purchasers testified they had been told that a GDC house was a good investment that would appreciate in value and that they could make a profit in the rental market.

None of these witnesses had one word to say about David Brown.

Three former salesmen testified that while conducting the company sponsored SoHo tours, community salespeople routinely took steps to prevent their customers from finding out about competitors' prices. They said salespeople drove along circuitous routes to avoid other builders' models, arranged with local hotels to bar other real estate agents from the premises, and removed local newspapers from hotel vending machines. These three witnesses claimed that such practices were meant to maintain "control" of the customers and were known to, and encouraged by, some members of GDC's management.

Again, however, none testified that such practices were known to or condoned by David Brown.

The only former GDC employee who testified about any substantive contact with Brown was its former CFO, who testified he told Brown he thought it was "unethical" to sell a house priced in excess of its resale value.

In addition to the live witnesses the government introduced over 200 complaint letters written to GDC by customers who felt they had been defrauded. Many of them were highly emotional and tragic. "I have lost all my money on this investment. You people are a multi-billion dollar corporation. I am a poor man. I have nothing to lose but my life," said one. Another lodged claims of "genocide" of "minorities." Many told of lost health, lost jobs and lost peace of mind, all as a result of a GDC purchase. One man wrote that he was "but a vegetable" because of GDC and that it would cause his death.

We objected that the letters were hearsay. Judge Nesbitt rejected our argument and agreed with the government that they were not being offered for the truth, but only to show that the defendants were on notice of alleged misconduct. She also rejected our Rule 403 argument that the probative value of these letters solely for the purpose of notice was outweighed by the prejudice to the defendants. We unsuccessfully argued that this was especially true in the case of Brown, who only was aware of three of the 200 letters that came into evidence.

The prosecution case took four long months, exceeding the original estimate for the entire trial. With other delays it was April 1992 before we began the case for the defense. We presented witnesses who described the costs of the communities' development, how the price differential came about and why it was legitimate, and GDC's training programs that were designed to detect and deter misrepresentations by the sales force. In addition all of the defendants except Reizen testified on their own behalf as to their good faith.

Brown's testimony as to his good faith stressed his reliance on the advice of counsel. He told of retaining his friend Dodyk at Cravath as soon as he learned of the allegations in the civil cases, and of relying on Dodyk's advice that the basic sales practices engaged in by GDC were completely lawful. He testified that he neither knew of, nor condoned, any misrepresentations by salespeople.

Paul Dodyk testified as the last defense witness. He confirmed his advice had been given to Brown and explained the rationale that supported it. He forcefully stated that he had been given access to all relevant information—a key element of an advice-of-counsel defense. At the close of his testimony he said that knowing everything that had come out at the trial he would give the same advice again.

Moscowitz, the prosecutor, attacked him on cross examination using the information that GDC, under Brown, had paid Cravath over $8 million in legal fees over several years. He called Dodyk "the $8 million dollar man" and argued that Dodyk would say anything that Brown wanted him to.[87] The government also argued that the advice was so unreasonable on its face that no one should be able to rely on it.

The defense continued to encounter Judge Nesbitt's hostility. During Brown's testimony we had sought to demonstrate that his reliance on Dodyk's advice was reasonable by showing that in three of the civil cases, involving the same allegations as the indictment, Cravath had won summary judgment rulings that, as a matter of law, there was no fraud. We wanted to be able to argue that Dodyk's advising Brown of these rulings squarely refuted the government's argument. As we put it, "How can it be unreasonable to rely on the advice when the conclusion that there is no fraud is coming not just from Dodyk but from opinions by three separate Florida judges?"

The court excluded this testimony under Rule 403, noting that these rulings came late in the conspiracy period and ruling that, in her opinion, the prejudice to the government's case from this testimony outweighed its probative value. On the same grounds, she barred Brown and the other defendants from testifying that in believing the GDC sales practices were lawful they had relied on the fact that the FTC had opened an investigation into the sales practices and had concluded its investigation without bringing any charges. She made this ruling notwithstanding the fact that during the cross examination of DeBella, she allowed the government to bring out that he was aware that the FTC had brought charges against another company, Amrep, which had engaged in allegedly similar practices. These were all examples of the intense anti-defendant bias we faced throughout the trial.

Proceedings were delayed in May when Ehrling's lawyer Joel Hirschhorn needed back surgery and four weeks of recuperation. The court refused to sever Ehrling out and instead suspended the trial. It was August before the case went to the jury.

Going into the deliberations I thought we had the ideal advice-of-counsel defense. It would be hard to imagine a better one given Dodyk's background, Cravath's history and reputation, and Brown's testimony that he believed it was "the best law firm in the world." And it was a consummate stand-up performance by Paul Dodyk, culminating in his testimony that he would give the same advice again.

The government had argued in summation that legal advice in this case was irrelevant and made a clear appeal to anti-lawyer sentiment by saying, "No one needs a lawyer to tell you what's right and what's wrong. All of us are expected to know that on our own. And one lawyer, two lawyers, ten lawyers, a hundred lawyers telling you it's okay doesn't make it okay. We all know it's wrong to cheat, to mislead, to conceal." Admission of the civil summary judgment rulings would have stripped this argument of credibility.

The jury was out four days. When they came back the foreman handed the verdict to the clerk to read. He began his recitation with the counts charging mail and wire fraud. David Brown was the first defendant named in the caption and the verdicts as to him were read first. "Not guilty" continued through all seventy-two of the substantive counts. But on the final count, conspiracy: "Guilty."

We were devastated. Reizen was also convicted on the single conspiracy count, while Ehrling and DeBella were convicted on multiple counts.

As sentencing approached we knew that the five-year statutory maximum was a foregone conclusion. Indeed, that was the sentence Brown and Reizen both received, and Ehrling and DeBella received ten-year sentences. The big issue then was bail pending appeal.

The criteria for release pending appeal are threefold: no danger to the community; no flight risk; a substantial issue on appeal. The government agreed with the first two, but maintained there was no substantial issue on appeal. Judge Nesbitt agreed—refusing to acknowledge that any of her rulings presented a serious issue on appeal—and all of the defendants were remanded. We appealed this decision to the Eleventh Circuit where a three-judge panel affirmed it.

We differed about what to do next. Several of the lawyers wanted to petition for rehearing *en banc* before the entire Eleventh Circuit Court. I disagreed, believing our chances were slim and if we lost we would have set a bad precedent for the appeal: no matter which group of three judges was assigned to hear the appeal on the merits, they would have previously prejudged the merits by participating in a ruling which held there was no significant issue on appeal. In the end that reasoning prevailed. We did not file the petition and the defendants went to prison pending appeal.

Our briefs on appeal were filed in October 1993. We argued that the convictions should be vacated because the conduct did not constitute fraud. In addition we argued for a new trial because of errors by the court in disallowing the evidence of the civil summary judgment rulings, disallowing the evidence of the FTC investigation and allowing the 200 complaint letters into evidence, which we argued the government had used for the truth despite her ruling that they constituted only notice of alleged misdeeds.

In January 1994 I was appointed Independent Counsel for the Whitewater/Madison Guaranty investigation of President Clinton by Attorney General Janet Reno and took a leave of absence from the firm to move to Arkansas (see pp. 220 *infra*). In August 1994, after the independent counsel statute was renewed and I was replaced by the independent counsel court, I returned to Davis Polk in time to argue the appeal in the spring of 1995.

The panel was Judges Kravitch and Edmondson from the Eleventh Circuit and Judge Eisele, a visiting judge from Arkansas (who, coincidentally, was the judge before whom I moved the admission of our Whitewater team to the Arkansas bar). The day of that argument was one of the most gratifying days of my legal career.

After all defense counsel had made their arguments Norman Moscowitz stood up to argue for the government. He started out by saying, "I would like at the outset to give the court an overview of the government's position." At that point Judge Edmondson, who was presiding, interrupted. "Mr. Moscowitz," he said, "maybe it would be helpful, before you start your argument, to give you a preview of my position. Simply stated, 'Where is the crime?'" When Moscowitz started to explain Judge Edmondson interrupted him again, saying, "Do you mean to tell me that you are claiming someone can commit fraud by concealing the price of real estate in Florida?"

The government's argument went straight downhill from there. Near the end Judge Edmondson put a series of questions to Moscowitz, beginning by asking him if the defendants were in jail.

"Yes, your honor."

"Did the defendants make a motion for bail pending appeal?"

"Yes, your honor."

"Did you oppose the motion?"

"Yes."

Edmondson then asked, incredulously, "Did you take the position that there was no substantial issue on appeal?"

"Yes."

In my rebuttal it was a no-brainer to tell the court that I would like to renew the defendants' motion for bail pending appeal. The next morning the panel ordered that the defendants be immediately released.

Developer convictions overturned

Court says GDC's buyers not bilked

The Miami Herald,
April 17, 1996

Several months later the opinion came down, unanimously reversing the convictions of all four defendants on the basic ground that they had not committed any crime.

"No allegation is made that customers who knew they were traveling to Florida at GDC's expense on SoHos for the express purpose of shopping for a home were barred from looking for better deals either before or after their trip to Florida. Where a company pays for customers to visit, pays for their meals, provides their transportation and pays for their rooms, not every step requiring customers to discover a better bargain through the customers' own investigation is unlawful. Under the circumstances in this criminal case, no reasonable jury could find that GDC prevented . . . people of ordinary prudence from discovering what houses in Florida sold for and rented for and how the price of GDC homes compared to comparable properties in Florida.

Looking at the evidence in this case, our worry is that the criminal fraud statutes were used to convict four people simply for charging high prices—all allegations of misconduct in this case involved the prices customers paid for their homes, not the physical qualities of these homes. The government tries to draw a distinction; they say these men were convicted for deceptions about these high prices. For us, at least in the context of home sales and of the openness of the Florida real estate market, this distinction is a distinction without meaning."[88]

The court concluded by stating, "We reach none of the other assertions of error in this case, except to note that we think they might have considerable merit."[89]

The government, pressed hard to do so by a furious Judge Nesbitt, asked the Solicitor General to file a petition for *certiorari* to the Supreme Court claiming the Eleventh Circuit had applied the wrong test in determining whether the victims were defrauded. We took our objections directly to the Solicitor General's office in the person of Deputy Solicitor General Michael Dreeben, without whose approval the petition could not be filed. It was an unusual step at the time. Both in writing and in person at a meeting attended by the prosecutors, we argued that this was not an appropriate case for Supreme Court review. We pointed out that the government itself had asked that the test used by the Eleventh Circuit be used in the charge to the jury.

Our written submission concluded:

"The appellants have been under indictment over six-and-one-half years. Their lives and careers have been irreparably harmed. Most importantly, all four appellants—as a result of the Government's unjustifiable insistence that there were 'no substantial issues on appeal'—have spent over two years in jail for crimes which the Eleventh Circuit Court of Appeals has held they did not commit. As a matter of simple fairness, it is time for this to end."

Shortly thereafter I received a very curt telephone call from the U.S. Attorney's Office in Miami: "The Solicitor General has told us that we cannot file a petition for *certiorari*."

It was finally over.

CHAPTER 36

Clark Clifford

ONE OF THE MOST powerful letters of support at Paul Thayer's sentencing in 1985 came from former Secretary of Defense Clark Clifford. At that time Clifford was admired as an extraordinary lawyer and statesman to whom politicians—including three presidents—and business leaders turned for advice. Little did he know that a few years later he himself was going to become embroiled in a controversy that threatened to destroy his career and reputation.

Born on Christmas Day, 1906, Clark Clifford grew up in St. Louis, Missouri and started his career as a trial lawyer. He set his sights on becoming the best trial lawyer in Missouri and was on his way until World War II intervened. In 1943, at the age of thirty-seven, he left his practice and enlisted in the navy reserves. He was commissioned a second lieutenant and assigned to the Chief of Naval Operations in Washington.

In 1945 a St. Louis friend and former client, who was President Truman's Chief Naval Aide, asked Clifford to come on as his assistant. Clifford took the job and, as one of his responsibilities was organizing—and joining—poker games on the presidential yacht, came to know Truman and others in the game, including Winston Churchill. Eventually he became Truman's Chief Counsel and was a key architect of Truman's come-from-behind presidential win over Thomas Dewey in 1948. The same year, he successfully advocated U.S. recognition of the new State of Israel in the face of intense opposition from General George Marshall.[90] He wrote many of Truman's most important speeches, and won credit for drafting the basic legislation establishing the CIA and the Department of Defense.

Clifford left the White House in 1950 and began what became an extraordinarily successful and lucrative law practice advising major U.S. corporations, in many cases on matters involving the federal government.[91] This took up only half his time; he spent the rest advising Democratic presidents. He chaired the Foreign Intelligence Advisory Board established by President Kennedy. When the big steel companies moved to raise prices after Kennedy thought they'd agreed not to, the President called on Clifford to persuade them against it. He was one of the first people Lyndon Johnson turned to for advice and counsel after Kennedy's assassination—they met for five hours during

Johnson's first twenty-four hours in the White House. Thereafter, Clifford served as Johnson's unofficial advisor on a number of the most sensitive issues he encountered. Prominent among those was the Vietnam War.

From the beginning Clifford thought the war was fruitless and counseled against the commitment of more troops. Johnson raised troop levels nonetheless and Clifford supported his position until January 1968 when the president named him Secretary of Defense to replace Robert McNamara. By that time Clifford's views on the war had changed and he told Johnson in a series of discussions, many of which involved other advisors as well, that he should try to bring it to an end. On March 31, 1968 Johnson delivered a speech remembered mostly for its famous line, "I shall not seek, and I will not accept, the nomination of my party for another term as your President." Johnson called for a de-escalation of the war and a curtailment of the bombing, saying he hoped that this would open up the way to peace talks. Clifford continued his opposition to the war throughout the rest of Johnson's term. On his last day in office, January 20, 1969, Johnson awarded Clifford the Presidential Medal of Freedom—the country's highest civilian award.

In 1969 Clifford returned to his law practice with his reputation even greater than before. A Washington publication described him as "a symbol of elegance"—six-feet-two, trim, wavy-haired, his French cuffs always a half-inch longer than the sleeves of his impeccably tailored double-breasted suits. He had a deep, melodious voice—he sang in choral groups—and was extraordinarily articulate, all of which enhanced his courtly aura. To most people who knew him, he stood for probity itself. One commentator called him "The Washington Monument." For people with serious problems in the capital, he was the go-to guy.

In 1977 Clifford was retained to represent President Jimmy Carter's friend Bert Lance, the Georgia banker who headed the Office of Management and Budget. The Comptroller of the Currency had issued a report criticizing his conduct while acquiring and becoming President of the National Bank of Georgia, and pressure was building for his resignation. Clifford persuaded Carter that Lance should stay in office and be allowed to defend himself before the Senate Banking Committee. To help him prepare Lance for his testimony Clifford brought in one of his young partners, Robert Altman, a rising star who was married to "Wonder Woman" actress Lynda Carter. Altman drafted Lance's testimony which turned the tables by sharply criticizing Committee members for attacking him in the days leading to the hearing. Members ended up challenging one another during the televised proceedings, and some publicly apologized to Lance for inaccurate statements they had made. The public loved it and opinion polls ran heavily in Lance's favor.

Lance's testimony was a success, but short-lived. Senate Majority Leader Robert Byrd told Carter that Lance would have to resign to avoid a long battle, and he did—only to face a federal indictment in Atlanta. Clifford and Altman advised the defense behind the scenes. They suggested the use of character witnesses including the Rev. Martin Luther King Sr. and President Carter's mother Lillian, and Altman arranged their testimony. The case ended with an acquittal on all charges. For helping to save his reputation Lance wanted to reward Clifford beyond his legal fee. That opportunity came a few years later when Lance brought Clifford a new client: The Bank of Credit & Commerce International, known as BCCI.

BCCI came to Clifford through its CEO, Agha Hasan Abedi, in connection with a proposed takeover of Financial General Bankshares located in Washington. BCCI was advising four Arab investors who had bought shares in Financial General and were then sued by a hostile management. The investors—two sons of the ruler of Abu Dhabi who at the time was President of the United Arab Emirates, a Saudi royal who had headed Saudi intelligence and a prominent Kuwaiti businessman—decided to buy control of the bank with their own money. Financial General's management opposed the takeover and years of litigation followed involving Armand Hammer of Occidental Petroleum, Jack Stephens of Stephens Inc.—who would later head the Augusta National Golf Club—and Lance himself. Finally, the parties reached a deal that allowed the acquisition to proceed.

The takeover required approval of several regulators, including the Federal Reserve and the New York State Banking Department (Financial General had a branch in New York). From the outset there were questions about the role of BCCI. BCCI was chartered in Luxembourg, headquartered in London, and operated through a complex corporate structure that included subsidiaries all over the world. It was not subject to regulation by the Federal Reserve. Moreover, unlike most large financial institutions, its network of banks was not regulated on a consolidated basis by any central bank, and its deposits were not guaranteed by any government. All of this concerned U.S. regulators—they did not want an American bank to be owned or controlled by BCCI.

On April 23, 1981 Clifford and Altman testified at a Federal Reserve hearing on the proposed takeover in their capacities as counsel to the four investors. The regulators wanted to know the ongoing role of BCCI and to be assured it was the four investors, not BCCI, who were buying the bank. Clifford and Altman assured them that was the case, and that no relationship or connection existed between BCCI and the investors' holding companies. Rather, BCCI acted as an investment advisor and "communications link" to the investors following the acquisition.

In connection with the Federal Reserve's investigation the CIA and State Department confirmed to the regulators that the four investors were prominent, wealthy, and respected. Clifford also offered a personal testimonial for the principal proposed shareholder, the Saudi royal Kamal Adham. He described their contacts in the preceding years and said, "I have come to have the deepest respect for his character, for his reputation, for his honor and for his integrity. . . . He is the kind of man with whom I like to be associated."

The New York State Banking Department received similar assurances.

Anticipating approval Clifford traveled to London for a series of meetings with Kamal Adham, Agha Abedi and Abedi's principal assistant Swaleh Naqvi at BCCI's headquarters in London. They praised Clifford for the work he had done in executing the takeover of Financial General and reported that the Arab shareholders wanted him to become the Chairman of the new bank, which was to be renamed First American Bankshares. Clifford accepted because, at age seventy-five, he wanted a new challenge. The approval came through and in the next nine years, under his leadership and that of Robert Altman who became its President, First American grew into the largest bank holding company in the Washington area.

But during this same time period, BCCI ran into serious trouble. In 1988 the bank was indicted in Miami, Florida on charges of helping Panamanian leader Manuel Noriega launder drug money through various U.S. banks including First American. First American denied knowledge of any money laundering and was never charged. Meanwhile, Clifford and Altman, in their role as counsel to BCCI, selected lawyers who negotiated a deal under which BCCI pled guilty and paid a $14 million fine.

But that was not the end of BCCI's troubles. Through the 1980's, the bank had lost millions of dollars in bad loans and bad trades in the commodities market, which it covered up by falsifying the books. All of this was revealed in 1990 when BCCI's founders, including Abedi, were replaced and the bank was taken over by the ruler of Abu Dhabi, Sheik Zayad al-Nahyan.

And then an audit by PricewaterhouseCoopers revealed that the takeover of First American by the four Arab investors in 1981 had been secretly financed by loans

from BCCI, with the First American stock pledged as collateral. When they missed interest payments BCCI had taken control of their shares. Around the same time a tape
recording surfaced. A BCCI banker named Amjad Awan was talking with someone
posing as a businessman, but who was actually a DEA undercover agent who was part of
the operation that produced the BCCI indictment. Awan told him:

> "We own a bank based in Washington. It's called First American Bank. . . . Bought
> out by BCCI about eight years ago. BCCI was acting as advisor to [the sharehold-
> ers], but the truth of the matter is that the bank belongs to BCCI. Those guys are
> just nominee shareholders."

The Federal Reserve accused BCCI of illegally acquiring control of First American.
The Department of Justice opened a criminal investigation into whether Clifford and
Altman had misled the Federal Reserve in their 1981 testimony. First American had a
branch in New York and Robert Morgenthau, the Manhattan District Attorney, also
launched an investigation into whether Clifford and Altman had lied to the New York
Banking Department.

In June 1990, based on what I later learned was a recommendation from Marty
Lipton at Wachtell Lipton, Clifford retained me to represent him, Altman and First
American in these investigations. I enlisted Jack Cooney. Several months later Clifford
and Altman also retained Bob Bennett and Carl Rauh of Skadden Arps in Washington to work with us in dealing with what—by then—had become three simultaneous
high-pressure investigations: Morgenthau in New York and the DOJ and the Federal
Reserve in Washington. Later there would be a fourth front—Congress, with hearings
in both the House and the Senate. And throughout, the media comprised a fifth front
that was unrelenting it its pursuit of what it viewed as a would-be scandal involving one
of Washington's most prominent figures. In the late spring of 1991 we heard from Morgenthau, the DOJ and the Federal Reserve that they all wanted testimony from Clifford
and Altman on an accelerated schedule. We agreed to dates in late June and early July.
Preparation was going to be a monumental challenge.

On Memorial Day weekend Jack Cooney and I went down to Washington and
moved into the Watergate Hotel. Julie O'Sullivan and Grace Rodriguez from our Washington office joined us, together with Bennett and Rauh and two of their associates,
for a series of lengthy preparation sessions at Clifford's office. These sessions continued

non-stop—weekends included—for over six weeks. Clifford amazed me. He was now eighty-five, and insisted we start every day at eight-thirty and work until eight-thirty or nine every night, with only a short break for a delivered-in lunch. He was ready to go even longer, but we said twelve hours a day was enough.[92] He and Altman obviously had no obligation to testify, but for them the Fifth Amendment was never an option, even in the D.C. grand jury where the prosecutors insisted they go in cold, with no office interview in advance.

All of this was extraordinarily difficult for Clifford. After near-iconic status for nearly fifty years he suddenly found himself in the position of having to admit he was either a crook or a dupe. Either he had known all along that the representations of the four Arab shareholders that they were independent of BCCI were false, or else they had fooled him. Cynics found it hard to believe that Clifford, whose entire reputation was built upon seeing around corners and anticipating problems for his clients, could have been duped by front men for BCCI.

Clifford grasped his situation very well. "It's easy to say I should have known," he mused in a comment to the press,

> "... but a client tells his lawyer what the client wants the lawyer to know. I have to admit that they came to me because of my standing and reputation. If you think of that, then you'd understand better that I'd be the last person they'd divulge this stuff to. I gave them standing. Why would they jeopardize that? They knew if they told me, I'd be out the door."

The timing was painful for Clifford as well. For several years he had been working on a book chronicling his career. Entitled *Counsel to the President*, it was being serialized in the *New Yorker* beginning in the early spring of 1991 before its May release accompanied by a promotional campaign and a book tour. As the media frenzy escalated, Clifford was forced to add a long footnote that read in part.

> "I knew nothing of any secret loans or other financial arrangements between First American investors and BCCI ... If the Federal Reserve Board and other authorities had been deceived, so had I. It was possible that I had been used, I realized with a combination of outrage and deep concern, by a group of foreign investors. The operations of First American, for which I had been responsible, had been honest,

ethical, and successful, as I stressed to reporters; no depositors had ever lost a penny. Nor had there been any misappropriation of funds from First American, no 'bailout' by the government, as in the colossal savings-and-loan scandals. But I realized that even while successfully running a large group of banks, it was possible that I had been deliberately misled. No event in my entire career caused me greater anger and outrage."

In June within a space of two weeks, Bennett and I went with Clifford and Altman for separate sworn appearances before the Manhattan DA's office, the Washington, D.C. federal grand jury, and the Federal Reserve.[93] Clifford and Altman said the same thing in all three forums. They did not know whether the allegations concerning BCCI's ownership of First American were true, but they never knew of any such control. They met often with Abedi, Naqvi and others at BCCI in its capacity as an investment advisor and communications link to the Arab stockholders of First American, but the management of First American was totally under the control of Clifford and Altman and at no time had BCCI made any decision affecting its affairs. Comprehensive audits of the First American banks conducted by teams from the Federal Reserve, Office of Comptroller of the Currency, and state bank regulators in connection with the investigations had concluded First American had been honestly run, and there was no transaction or any evidence of BCCI influence or control over First American. Clifford and Altman had said all of this under oath at the televised hearings held by the Senate and the House Banking Committees. Amid much political grandstanding, it all seemed to fall on deaf ears.

A hard charging, aggressive prosecutor, John Moscow, was leading Morgenthau's investigation. In May 1992 we learned that he was recommending an indictment of both Clifford and Altman. We were given the chance to present our arguments to Morgenthau. We prepared a memorandum and exhibits demonstrating that there was no case. We showed there was no evidence that Clifford or Altman knew anything about the alleged ownership of First American by BCCI and no evidence that BCCI had in any way controlled the management of First American. We showed that Clifford and Altman had run the bank and done it well. An audit of First American by the Federal Reserve had found no manipulation by Clifford and Altman of First American for BCCI's benefit and showed that no First American depositor or customer had lost a cent. Buttressing our argument, Federal Reserve president Robert P. Black had testified before the House

Banking Committee that "no connection between the banks' lending practices and their unauthorized ownership by BCCI has been uncovered."

He continued, "The one who really lost out on this First American deal was BCCI. You have to wonder why they did it. They put in over $500 million; they never took dividends. Now BCCI is bankrupt and they appear to have gotten nothing out of it."

We went to the DA's office in early June 1992. I was only available because the David Brown trial in Florida was suspended for Joel Hirschhorn's back surgery. We met for three hours with Morgenthau; one of his top assistants, Michael Cherkasky; and John Moscow along with two other assistant DAs who worked for him. Bob Bennett and I made all the arguments as to why there was no case. We would later learn that Cherkasky agreed with us, but Moscow and his two deputies disagreed. Morgenthau by then had become a legend in law enforcement circles. Former Police Commissioner Robert McGuire had said, "He will go down in history as the finest district attorney in the country." He had received widespread acclaim for his investigation and conviction of BCCI and its top executives, in what was called "the biggest banking fraud in history." However, on this issue, he sided with Moscow instead of Cherkasky. On July 29, 1992 while I was still in Miami in the closing days of the Brown trial, indictments of Clifford and Altman were filed simultaneously by Morgenthau in New York County Supreme Court and by the Justice Department in the District Court for the District of Columbia.[94]

The New York indictment charged Clifford and Altman, along with Abedi, Naqvi and three of the four Arab shareholders of First American, with crimes on two fronts. It alleged a scheme to defraud state and federal regulators by concealing the true roles of Abedi, Naqvi and BCCI in the ownership and control of First American, and charged a series of commercial briberies based upon non-recourse loans and profitable sales of First American stock in return for which Clifford and Altman were alleged to have allowed BCCI to influence the management of First American. The Washington indictment was much more limited. It did not charge that BCCI secretly owned First American, but contained one count of conspiracy and two counts of concealing material facts from federal regulators relating to BCCI.

When the indictments were announced the DA's office took the draconian step of obtaining an *ex parte* freeze order on all of Clifford's and Altman's assets. Clifford and Altman were handed the freeze order when they appeared for their arraignments in New York. Clifford's check to pay the men who cut his lawn was rejected. Altman's wife tried to use a credit card to pay for medicine for their sick child and it was rejected.

If this was a pressure tactic to force a plea, there was no way that was going to happen. Clifford and Altman came out swinging. They issued a joint statement denouncing the indictments as "cruel and unjust" prosecutorial abuse. "We totally and categorically deny all charges," they said. "They are the result of mean-spirited suspicion and unfounded speculation . . . We shall fight to establish our innocence."

There was a fight over which case would go first. Clifford and Altman wanted to try the federal case first because the charges were narrower and because an acquittal there would make the state case barred by double jeopardy, whereas it did not work that way if the state case went first. Clifford's health issues also played a role—it was a lot better to be tried in a place where you could go home at night. Moscow wanted to go first and pressed a receptive state judge, John Bradley, for an immediate trial date.

At that point Clifford and Altman announced that they each needed new counsel because up to then Jack and I had represented them both and they said that this would present a potential conflict at trial. This produced a delay in the New York trial so their new counsel would have time to prepare. The new date was set for March 23, 1993. The DOJ sat on its hands in the meantime, perhaps sensing the weakness of the case, and the New York case still went first.

For the New York trial Altman retained Gus Newman, one of the best criminal defense lawyers in the country, who had extensive experience in the New York criminal courts. I had known him for years, since he represented Anthony Anastasio in the Scotto trial. Altman's defense team was supplemented by William Shields—a former prosecutor in the Manhattan DA's office—and Mitchell Ettinger, an associate at Skadden Arps who had worked with Bennett and Rauh, knew the case well and had extensive trial practice in the military before going into private practice. Clifford, who took the position early on that he could not appear in New York because of his deteriorating health, retained Charlie Stillman, another excellent and highly experienced criminal defense lawyer.

I continued on as their counsel fighting against the freeze order, now limited to New York where most of their assets were, which was before a different judge. I succeeded in easing it so they could pay their living expenses and attorney's fees.

Before the trial Clifford had open-heart surgery. His doctors, and doctors selected by Morgenthau's office, agreed that his health did not permit him to attend the trial. He was severed and the trial of Altman went forward. Although only Altman was now on trial, everyone knew that Clifford was on trial in *absentia*. If Altman were acquitted Clifford would be vindicated. If convicted, Altman faced a lengthy prison term in the New York State system.

The trial started as scheduled on March 23 and continued until August 14. The case the DA's office presented turned out as Bennett and I had told Morgenthau it would. Judge Bradley dismissed the bribery counts without letting them go to the jury. Gus Newman, deeming that no defense case of any kind was needed, rested after the prosecutor's case. Altman never took the stand, and the jury deliberated for four days before returning with an acquittal on all counts. The jury forewoman wept as she read the verdict and the jury burst into applause along with Altman's family. They then joined the family in hugs in the courthouse.

From his home in Rockville, Maryland Clifford said the verdict was "deeply gratifying. It is not just the end of a trial. It is the end of a two-and-a-half year nightmare."

Morgenthau issued a statement saying, "We accept the verdict, of course. Justice has been served. However, our investigation of BCCI continues." The Department of Justice dropped its case and the asset freeze against both men was vacated.

Clifford continued on, in extremely ill health—bedridden much of the time. While he felt vindicated by the acquittal, he was wise enough to realize that his reputation, battered by reams of inflammatory press coverage, would never be the same. He died six years later on October 10, 1998—just short of his ninety-second birthday.

Altman told the press after the verdict, "Banking has very little appeal to me." He returned to the practice of law but gave it up several years later. He has since had a successful business career, currently serving as Chairman and CEO of ZeniMax Media, a video game publishing company he founded outside Washington, D.C.

—꘏—

WHITEWATER INDEPENDENT COUNSEL, 1994

AS I WROTE earlier the torturously long case against David Brown and GDC, while on appeal, was interrupted for me by the appointment to serve as Independent Counsel in the Whitewater case in the second year of Bill Clinton's presidency. By the time of my appointment in January 1994, Whitewater had become shorthand for Republican accusations of shady real estate dealings by the Clintons back home in Arkansas culminating in the death of Deputy White House Counsel Vincent Foster in Washington the year before.

CHAPTER 37

How It Came About

THE INDEPENDENT COUNSEL ROLE dated back to 1974, when Attorney General Elliot Richardson used the Code of Federal Regulations to appoint Archibald Cox to investigate President Nixon and others in his administration for their role in Watergate. In the aftermath of Watergate and Cox's firing in "the Saturday Night Massacre,"[95] Congress enacted the Independent Counsel Act designed to insulate future Independent Counsels from termination by the President. It gave a specially appointed three-judge court the power to appoint an Independent Counsel when credible allegations were made against a high-level administration official, and provided that the counsel could only be terminated "for cause," which was reviewable by the three-judge court. The statute had a "sunset" provision under which it expired after five years unless renewed. It was renewed several times, but when it was due to expire in late 1992 Republicans—irate at Independent Counsel Lawrence Walsh over his Iran/Contra investigations—refused to reenact the statute. So, in late 1993 when the Whitewater allegations—fueled by Foster's apparent suicide—reached a fever pitch, the law was not in effect.

Attorney General Janet Reno still had the authority that Richardson had had to appoint an Independent Counsel under the Code of Federal Regulations, but she refused, saying that any appointment would be criticized for the appearance of a lack of independence since she reported to the President. She told the Republicans that if they wanted an Independent Counsel they should reenact the statute. But in the New Year spurred by a spate of editorials, Senator Moynihan of New York—followed quickly by eight other Democratic senators—urged her to make an appointment. With that mounting pressure President Clinton announced, while traveling in the Czech Republic, he would ask her to name an Independent Counsel and she said she would honor the request.

Attorney General Reno's two top deputies, to whom I assumed she would turn for advice, were both people I knew and had worked with closely when I was the U.S. Attorney for the Southern District of New York. Philip Heymann, the Deputy Attorney General, had been the Assistant Attorney General in charge of the DOJ's Criminal Division during the Carter administration. We had interacted on a number of matters, most

often at meetings of the Attorney General's Advisory Committee of United States Attorneys, which I had chaired. Jo Ann Harris headed the Criminal Division under Janet
Reno, and she had been an Assistant United States Attorney in the Criminal Division
at the U.S. Attorney's Office during all four years of my term in the Southern District.
Because of these relationships I suspected it was likely that I was one of the people they
would be considering.

This gave me time to think what I might say if I were asked. There certainly were
negatives. It was bound to become very political—no matter what I did I was sure to
be criticized, either by the Clintons if they perceived me as too aggressive or by conservative Republicans if they perceived me as not aggressive enough. It would mean a
full-time commitment in which I would have to live in Arkansas away from home and
my law practice, perhaps for several years. On the other hand it was hard to conceive of
anything more important—the President of the United States was under a cloud and it
was vital to the country that either the allegations be substantiated or that he be exonerated as quickly as possible. It would be an extraordinarily interesting and challenging
experience. I consulted with Janet, of course, as I had at every step of my career. She
supported it completely. I decided that if I were asked, I would accept.

On January 13 my daughter Sue called from Wayland, Massachusetts where she
lived. Her cousin, my niece Addie, had told her that she had been driving to work listening to NPR and heard Nina Totenberg, known for her reliable sources within the Justice
Department, reporting that the choice had come down to two people: Bob Fiske or Dan
Webb, who had been a highly-regarded U.S. Attorney in Chicago during the Reagan
administration. I waited all day and around 5 p.m. the phone rang. It was Jo Ann Harris.
She said, "Bob, is there any way that you could do this?"

I said, "Jo Ann, how could I possibly say no?"

The following day and over the Martin Luther King weekend, I had a series of telephone conversations with Jo Ann and her principal deputy, Merrick Garland,[96] whom
she had put in charge of this process. We talked mostly about potential conflicts. There
were none, and I went down to Washington on the morning of Wednesday, January 19
to work out the terms of my appointment.

The broad outlines of the case were well known at that point. Bill Clinton, growing
up in Hope, Arkansas, became friends with another Arkansas native, James McDougal—a successful land developer—in 1968 when they worked together on Senator J.
William Fulbright's re-election campaign. After graduating from Yale Law School in
1973 and marrying Hillary Rodham in 1975, Clinton returned to Arkansas and became

a professor at the University of Arkansas Law School while she went to work at the Rose Law Firm in Little Rock. In 1976 Clinton was elected Attorney General of Arkansas. Two years later, at age thirty-two, he was elected as Arkansas' youngest governor and brought Jim McDougal into his administration as an aide for economic development.

While Clinton was running for governor in 1978 he and McDougal, together with their wives, became partners in the purchase of 230 acres of land on the White River in north-central Arkansas, near the Missouri border. They borrowed the $212,611.12 purchase price from two local banks and deeded the land to the Whitewater Development Corporation. The plan was to subdivide the land and sell lots for vacation homes.

In 1980 Jim McDougal, along with others, took control of the Kingston Bank in Madison County, Arkansas, changing its name to Madison Bank & Trust Company. And in 1982 McDougal and his wife, Susan, acquired a controlling interest in the Woodruff County Savings & Loan Association, changing its name to Madison Guaranty Savings & Loan Association. In 1980 Madison Bank, prohibited by banking regulations from loaning money to any entity owned by the McDougals—they were already at the regulatory limit—loaned $30,000 to Hillary Clinton.

In March 1992 *The New York Times* published a lengthy front page article by reporter Jeff Gerth headlined "The 1992 Campaign: Personal Finances: Clintons Joined S&L Operator in an Ozark Real-Estate Venture." The article raised a number of issues. It noted that Whitewater was heavily subsidized by McDougal, leaving the Clintons at little risk; that Whitewater had made the payments on the $30,000 loan taken out by Mrs. Clinton; that the Clintons improperly took tax deductions for interest paid on a portion of the $30,000 loan payments that Whitewater had made; that "missing records" obscured some questions about the Whitewater relationship and the Clintons' role in it; that Madison Guaranty allowed Whitewater to keep making payments even when its accounts were overdrawn; and that in 1985, when Madison Guaranty was insolvent and subject to closure under state regulations, a new securities commission appointed by Governor Clinton allowed it to stay open while Mrs. Clinton and other lawyers at the Rose Law Firm asked that Madison Guaranty be allowed to raise additional capital until, in 1986, federal regulators took control, ruled the banks insolvent and ousted McDougal.

Jim McDougal was no stranger to financial trouble. In the late 1980's, he had been indicted for a "cooking the books" fraud at Madison Guaranty, an accusation that had not involved Whitewater or the Clintons. He was acquitted after raising an insanity defense. He had been unemployed for several years, subsisting on Social Security payments and living rent-free, in a deep depression, in a trailer. Once Clinton emerged as a presidential candidate, the revelation of the Whitewater partnership between the Clintons and McDougals triggered intense media scrutiny and many questions, including whether McDougal used money from Madison Guaranty to pay off a loan Clinton took from another bank to help finance his 1984 gubernatorial race.

Clinton had been in the White House for exactly six months when, on July 20, 1993, Vincent Foster was found dead in Fort Marcy Park in McLean, Virginia, just outside Washington. He had a gun in his hand and a fatal gunshot wound in his mouth. The park police said it was a suicide, but the tabloid press and radio talk shows pumped up speculation that he had been murdered because he knew too much. They insinuated that if indeed Foster had killed himself, it was because he was depressed over the true facts relating to Whitewater. In August, *The New York Times'* columnist William Safire asked if Foster was "dreading the exposure of malfeasance yet unknown," and "if dread of further scandal [was] a triggering cause of the apparent suicide." On July 22 *The Wall Street Journal* editorial page called for the appointment of a special prosecutor to determine the true reasons for his death.

On the same day Foster died a federal magistrate in Little Rock issued a search warrant for the offices of Capital Management Systems (CMS). The warrant was based on an FBI affidavit alleging that CMS, as a Small Business Investment Corporation (SBIC) funded and regulated by the Small Business Administration (SBA), was supposed to be making loans to the economically disadvantaged and instead was lending money to owner David Hale's business and political allies including Susan McDougal, who received a $300,000 loan. Hale, a Little Rock municipal judge, was indicted in September by the United States Attorney in Little Rock. He and two Little Rock attorneys, Charles Matthews and William Fitzhugh, were charged with conspiring to defraud the United States through the SBA. After unsuccessful plea negotiations Hale went public with allegations that Governor Clinton had asked him to make the $300,000 loan to Susan McDougal to help the McDougals and the Clintons pay down the Whitewater loans. If true, this would have made Clinton a participant in a federal crime.[97]

After Foster's body was discovered the park police went to his office to take possession of his papers. White House Counsel Bernard Nussbaum barred them, insisting that he first be allowed to screen out any documents he considered personal or privileged. This caused a ruckus, with the park police complaining they were stonewalled and the media insinuating that there must have been something to hide. These disclosures led Congressional Republicans to demand an Independent Counsel, which Attorney General Reno did only when Democrats joined in and Clinton saw the need to clear the air.

It remained, on my trip to Washington in January 1994, to work out terms that would let me get to the bottom of the case. As I saw it, if the overall responsibility of the Justice Department was a large pie, whatever jurisdiction I had as Independent Counsel would be a piece out of that pie. Within that jurisdictional area I would be the Attorney General of the United States; all of her authority and power would be ceded to me.

Jo Ann Harris showed me a draft of the language they had written and told me to revise it any way that I wanted, to be sure that I was satisfied with its scope. She said she was confident that anything I drafted, within reason, would be accepted by the Attorney General.

By that time the trial of Hale, Matthews and Fitzhugh in the CMS loan matter had been set for March 19 in Little Rock, and I knew that would be one of my responsibilities. So, the language I drafted gave me jurisdiction and authority to investigate any violation of federal criminal law "relating in any way to James B. McDougal, President William Jefferson Clinton or Mrs. Hillary Rodham Clinton's relationship with Madison Guaranty Savings & Loan Association, Whitewater Development Corporation, or Capital Management Services."

A crucial second paragraph gave me jurisdiction and authority to investigate

COUNSEL GRANTED A BROAD MANDATE IN CLINTON INQUIRY

TO EXAMINE SUICIDE

President and First Lady Are to Be Questioned on Land Dealings

Reuters
Robert B. Fiske yesterday.

The New York Times, *January 21, 1994*

any "other allegations or evidence of violation of any federal criminal law . . . developed during the Independent Counsel's investigation referred to above and connected with or arising out of that investigation."

A third paragraph gave me jurisdiction to investigate any obstruction of justice or false statement as I probed the allegations. But it was the second paragraph, with its potential expansion of my jurisdiction, that grew more important as the investigation progressed.

Jo Ann agreed, and she took me up to see Attorney General Reno. Our meeting was brief. She asked me two questions: "Are you satisfied that you have all the authority you need?" and "Are you satisfied that you have all the independence you need?" I answered "yes" to both questions. She thanked me for being willing to do this, and then said, "You will not be hearing from me again until it is over."

The announcement was scheduled for the next day, January 20. The string of coincidence was eerie—it was six months to the day since Foster's body was discovered, and exactly one year after Clinton's inauguration. Adding to the portents, a severe ice storm swept down on Washington. Temperatures in the single digits shut down the Justice Department to save power, and the news conference took place at the nearby Willard Hotel which, coincidentally, was hosting a conference of United States Attorneys.[98]

Janet Reno opened by announcing my appointment. She said, "A week ago I said I was looking for someone who would be fair and impartial, who had a reputation for integrity and skill, someone who would be ruggedly independent. I think Mr. Fiske fits that description to a T." She then turned it over to me.

The questions came fast and furious. I assured the reporters that I had personally drafted my charter to achieve a broad mandate and total independence. I said that while I respected the career Justice Department prosecutors who had conducted the investigation so far, to maintain the appearance of independence I would bring in a new team of experienced prosecutors from around the country. I said I knew the country wanted and deserved answers to the questions Whitewater had raised, and that I was taking a leave of absence from Davis Polk to work "flat out" to complete a "thorough and impartial investigation." The answer that drew headlines, though, was my intention to question President and Mrs. Clinton under oath. The *New York Daily News* rose to the occasion, screaming in large type: "Special Prosecutor—I'll Grill Bill and Hill."

After the conference ended and the reporters left, I had a moment to reflect. This was a daunting moment. Yesterday I was a private lawyer working on a number of matters for different clients. Today I was, in effect, the Attorney General of the United States responsible for the highest profile investigation imaginable. And I had no office and no staff. I had to move quickly.

The first step—lining up the full support of the FBI—was easy. Director Louis Freeh had been the case agent on the Scotto case as a young agent, and we had remained good friends. He pledged the full resources of the Bureau for what they had code-named "MOZARK."

CHAPTER 38

The Independent Counsel Team

TO FORM A CORE STAFF I turned to four experienced prosecutors whom I knew and could trust. Denis J. McInerney, Julie O'Sullivan and Mark Stein had all clerked for federal judges (Julie for Sandra Day O'Connor on the Supreme Court). I had worked with them closely as associates at Davis Polk, and in January 1994 they were serving as AUSAs in the Southern District of New York, where they had tried and won significant cases. Mark and Denis had been appointed Deputy Chiefs of the Criminal Division by U.S. Attorney Mary Jo White. They were all persons of great ability and—equally important—were team players with judgment and impeccable integrity. I knew I would have their complete loyalty from day one.[99]

I selected Rod Lankler as Deputy Independent Counsel to head up the Washington office. He was a good friend and I was confident of his total loyalty as well. Rod was a lawyer who had earned an outstanding reputation in New York legal circles. He had been a star in the Manhattan District Attorney's Office, serving as a Deputy Chief of the Homicide Bureau under Bob Morgenthau and John Keenan and then had headed the Trial Bureau. He was an experienced homicide investigator and a great trial lawyer, ideally suited to lead the investigation into Vincent Foster's death, which was now fodder for conspiracy theorists spurred on by tabloid headlines such as the *New York Post's*, prompted by its own investigation: "Doubts Raised Over Foster Suicide."

Rod and Mark went down to Washington to find space, open an office and begin the Foster investigation. They had two basic questions to answer: Was it suicide or murder? If it was suicide, had concerns about Whitewater led him to take his own life?

Little Rock, however, was "the center of gravity," as I had said at the news conference. I gave Denis responsibility for getting the case of Hale and his two co-defendants ready for trial on March 19. I did not want to ask for an adjournment. Julie's job was to find office space in Little Rock and get as quickly as possible on top of all the Madison Guaranty/Whitewater issues. The fifth member of the group was Pat Smith, then a fourth-year Davis Polk associate. He had worked very effectively with me on both the Clark Clifford case and the David Brown trial in Florida. He was assigned to Little Rock to work with Julie.

Julie and I went down to Little Rock the Monday after my appointment. An ice storm followed us there, making it too slippery to walk or drive, so with rooms at the AmeriSuites and office space at Two Financial Centre down a hill 100 yards away, the only way to get to work the next morning was to slide down the hill on our raincoats. That was how the FBI agents we were on our way to meet got their first sight of the Independent Counsel.

The agents gave us a fuller briefing on what the investigation had developed to that point. I then turned to increasing the staff and broadening it to create a team that was national in its scope. I had over 300 resumés from lawyers all around the country who wanted to work on the investigation. Several of them looked good on paper, but what was missing were the intangibles that I knew would be vital to success—qualities like judgment, collegiality and loyalty. So, I again turned to people I knew and trusted.

First, I called Griffin Bell, then King & Spalding's senior partner in Atlanta, and asked who among his partners he would want as a close aide if he were in my job. He consulted with Frank Jones, another King & Spalding partner who was at that time the president of the American College of Trial Lawyers. They recommended Bill Duffey, a young partner at the firm. He came out for an interview, we hit it off, and he joined the team.[100]

The second person I called was Bob Mueller, a former AUSA in Boston and Jo Ann Harris' predecessor as Assistant Attorney General in charge of the Criminal Division. He had served in the Bush administration and returned to private practice at Hale & Dorr. He would later head the FBI for twelve years beginning in 2001. I told him I was looking for a woman lawyer with five or six years' experience. He said he had just the right person—Gabrielle Wolohojian, one of Hale & Dorr's rising stars, who also played violin in the Boston Civic Symphony Orchestra. She also came down for an interview, found a rapport, and signed on with the team.[101]

Now I needed someone from the Arkansas area who could take the lead in trying the Hale/Matthews/Fitzhugh case with Denis. I felt that having a New York lawyer as lead trial counsel would be a mistake with an Arkansas jury. I quickly learned that practically everyone in Arkansas was disqualified, because of some relationship with the Clintons or some other person involved in the investigation. So, I reached out to my friends in the American College of Trial Lawyers in the six states that bordered Arkansas—Missouri, Texas, Oklahoma, Mississippi, Tennessee and Louisiana—and asked for recommendations. Harry Reasoner at Vinson & Elkins, and David Beck at Fulbright & Jaworski both suggested Houston's Russell "Rusty" Hardin. He had just left the

Houston District Attorney's Office where he had a record of 113 convictions—thirteen in first-degree murder cases—and had been voted Texas "Prosecutor of the Year" in 1989. He turned out to be the perfect choice.

Finally, from friends in Cincinnati, Ohio came a strong recommendation for Carl Stich. Carl, then in private practice, had been an assistant district attorney investigating savings and loan frauds in Ohio and Kentucky. That was valuable experience for our investigation. Just as important, he was known for his skill, judgment and fairness by the lawyers who had defended clients in those investigations. He, too, proved to be a valued addition to the team.[102]

While all this was going on my assistant, Michele Corelli, asked if she could come down to Little Rock with me. I asked her what her husband, Vinny, thought about it. She said, "The day you were appointed he told me, 'You have to go. Don't worry, we'll work it out.'" It was an easy decision. I had come to know Michele when she was working for Mike Leisure, a young litigation partner who died suddenly while jogging in Washington Square Park. When I was chosen to be U.S. Attorney for the Southern District, I asked her if she wanted to go there with me. She started in March 1976, proved to be invaluable and we have worked together ever since. I knew she could make a great contribution in Arkansas in a number of capacities including managing our office, and she also had a deft touch at dealing with the press. Denis McInerney's assistant, Joyce Golliver, also decided to come down, and she too made a valuable contribution.[103]

To round out the team, we brought on board two paralegals: John Bryck, who had excelled as a paralegal on the Brown case in Florida, and Frances Impellizzeri, a star paralegal in the U.S. Attorney's Office recruited by Denis and Mark.[104]

With Michele in the U.S. Attorney's Office

CHAPTER 39

An Early Breakthrough

WE HAD A BIG BREAKTHROUGH early on that validated some of my hiring instincts. Randy Coleman, David Hale's lawyer, had disparaged the indictment we inherited, and said publicly that New York lawyers weren't likely to have much success in Arkansas. He changed his tune at the first pre-trial conference we had before Chief Judge Stephen M. Reasoner of Arkansas's Eastern District, to whom the case had been assigned, in early February. I introduced Rusty Hardin to the court, explained that he would be lead trial counsel in the case, and Rusty handled the conference from there. After listening to Rusty, and after talking with him after the conference was over, Randy Coleman decided that he was not going to take Rusty on in front of a Little Rock jury.

That led to plea negotiations, and what Hale could tell us as a cooperating witness. Rusty and Denis, together with two FBI agents, met first with Coleman, and then intensively over three weeks with Coleman and Hale. During those discussions Hale provided details of the CMS $300,000 loan to Susan McDougal, including his conversation with Governor Clinton. He also opened a new door with information about a potential tax and bankruptcy fraud involving Governor Jim Guy Tucker.

On the scheduled trial date, March 19, David Hale waived indictment and pleaded guilty to two felonies. The first was the one charged in our inherited case, the second a new conspiracy charge alleging a fraud on, and false statements to, the Small Business Administration in connection with the $300,000 loan to Susan McDougal. The uncontested indictment charged Hale with conspiring with "others to the grand jury known and unknown" but did not publicly name the co-conspirators. Judge Reasoner put off Hale's sentencing, intending to assess the extent of his cooperation and the information he provided when his cooperation was complete. He adjourned the trial of the remaining defendants, Matthews and Fitzhugh, until June.

Hale's information moved us forward on two fronts. The first was to determine whether there was corroboration for his testimony about Clinton's role in the $300,000 loan to Susan McDougal. No responsible prosecutor would bring a case against anyone solely on the uncorroborated testimony of David Hale, and the fact that the potential defendant was the President of the United States raised the corroboration bar far higher. The second front was the allegation of potential tax and bankruptcy fraud against Governor Tucker. And that brought to bear the second paragraph of the jurisdictional statement that extended my authority to investigate "other allegations or evidence of violation . . . arising out of the investigation."

During the course of my tenure there were many such allegations. The question as to each was whether we should take it on ourselves, or refer it to the Justice Department or the local prosecuting authorities. Most of them we declined to investigate as being too remote from our basic charter.

But Hale's allegations against Tucker were different. They had nothing to do with Whitewater, Madison Guaranty or Capital Management, but they involved Hale as a witness against the sitting governor of Arkansas. He was also the principal potential witness against President Clinton, so we thought it was important that we not hand him off to another prosecutor to build a case against Tucker. Hale's lawyer had told us that Hale had agreed to plead guilty and cooperate with us after he had rebuffed the local U.S. Attorney in the fall of 1993 because he believed we were honest, professional and non-political. He wanted the judge to hear a fair account of his cooperation when it came time for his sentencing. We in turn thought the best way to build and keep his trust was to be his one point of contact as a witness.

Around the same time other events were unfolding that expanded our original mandate. One involved Webster Hubbell, a partner of Hillary Clinton's at the Rose Law Firm who had moved to Washington with the new administration and held the number three job in the Justice Department— Associate Attorney General of the United States. The other involved contacts that came to light between the White House and the Resolution Trust Corporation (RTC), which had made several criminal referrals to the Justice Department.

The issue with Hubbell involved discrepancies in his billing practices at the Rose Law Firm that his partners discovered after he left for Washington in the spring of 1993. They had sought explanations, but Hubbell claimed repeatedly that his vitally important job at Justice made him too busy to respond. He would get back to them later. "Later" never came and in March 1994 the firm filed a grievance with the Arkansas Bar Association that, by its rules, immediately became public. Questions relating to the firm—its role in representing Madison Guaranty and the destruction of some of its files within days of my appointment—were already an important part of our investigation. So, after discussing it with Jo Ann Harris, we announced that we also were looking at whether Hubbell had criminally defrauded his clients, his partners or both.

During this same period in early March, Deputy Treasury Secretary Roger Altman, who was acting head of the RTC in the absence of a permanent appointment, told a Congressional hearing that he had briefed the White House on how the RTC would proceed on potential civil claims arising out of the failure of Madison Guaranty.[105] Republicans attacked the disclosure as an "ethical umbrage" that compromised the RTC's independence. *The Washington Post* ran a front-page story headlined "Treasury Officials Told White House Status of S&L Probe." The article described two meetings in the fall of 1993 at which Treasury officials, including Jean Hanson, had updated White House officials on the status of several criminal referrals made by the RTC to the Justice Department—specifically including the fact that two of the referrals had mentioned the Clintons as potential beneficiaries of illegal actions at Madison Guaranty.

CHAPTER 40

White House Subpoenas

NEW TURMOIL ERUPTED after this disclosure. President Clinton said the meetings should never have occurred. We decided that we should investigate whether anyone in the White House had tried to influence the ongoing RTC investigations and, therefore, obstructed justice. We wanted to do it swiftly, with a minimum of opportunity for those being questioned to coordinate their stories. Eric Holder, the U.S. Attorney for the District of Columbia (and later U.S. Attorney General under President Obama), cooperated by allowing us to use one of his existing grand juries and we issued subpoenas, returnable on March 10, to all of the White House and Treasury Department officials involved in the meetings. They included—at the White House—Deputy Chief of Staff Harold Ickes; Hillary Clinton's Chief of Staff Margaret Williams; Communications Director Mark Gearan; White House Counsel Bernard Nussbaum; and Bruce Lindsey, senior advisor to President Clinton. The Treasury officials were Roger Altman; Jean Hanson, Josh Steiner; and Jack Devine, RTC press secretary.

The White House disclosed the subpoenas and a new firestorm of publicity erupted. While an administration official told *The Washington Post* their arrival at the White House had created an atmosphere that was "unbelievable," Republicans demanded that Congress hold public hearings into the contacts. Congressman Jim Leach of Iowa, ranking minority member of the House Banking Committee, said the participants "should not only be sanctioned for their breach of public trust, they should be brought before Congress to provide full disclosure of their actions and discussions."

This was a moment I had feared. I didn't want Congressional hearings and had said so the day I was appointed. I noted that the history of relationships between Independent Counsel and Congress had been "an uneasy one." In Iran/Contra, for example, Independent Counsel Lawrence Walsh won convictions of Oliver North and John Poindexter, only to have them reversed because Congress had granted them immunity to obtain their testimony. The grant of immunity protects the witness against not only the direct use of the testimony in any future prosecution, but also from the use of any information derived from that testimony. In the case of both North and Poindexter, although Walsh had effectively screened off the prosecution teams from any knowledge of the testimony, the Court of Appeals reversed the convictions because some witnesses who had heard or read about the testimony testified that they were influenced by it.

The demand for hearings had gone into remission after my appointment but now, with the disclosure of the White House/Treasury contacts and news of the subpoenas, it re-emerged stronger than ever. Rep. Leach was the principal advocate. My immediate response was to reach out to the congressman to tell him that I felt hearings would interfere with my investigation and ask that he defer them. That provoked a very strong letter in response. He advised me that I had an "obligation not to interfere with the legitimate oversight responsibilities of Congress," and said he was concerned that my position "has the effect of sending a chilling precedent for Congressional oversight and a fatuous pretext for the majority party which controls Congress to delay, defer, or avoid its Constitutional responsibilities."

He assured me there would be no grants of immunity. I wrote back to say that was not my sole concern. I also worried that witnesses would tailor their testimony to what they had heard others say. In addition, I was concerned that important witnesses in our investigation would be testifying under oath prematurely.

Ordinarily in a criminal investigation, prosecutors would not put a potential witness under oath until they had a full opportunity—using documents and other testimony—to find evidence of culpability. This produced more truthful witnesses. If, for example, Jim McDougal had been an accomplice to the alleged conversation between David Hale and Governor Clinton about the $300,000 loan and was asked about it in a sworn appearance before Congress, he would probably deny it. If it turned out later that he in fact had been an accomplice to the transaction, his credibility as a witness against Clinton would be severely damaged by a prior denial under oath. Prosecutors do not want their potential witnesses testifying under oath in another proceeding because of the development of potential impeachment material.

I hoped to explain this to Representative Leach, but he declined my request to meet with him. He told the press, "I [do] not want him to compromise my work and I [do] not want to compromise his."[106] But two key Republican senators, Alphonse D'Amato of New York, the ranking Republican on the Senate Banking Committee, and William Cohen of Maine, did agree to meet with me to see if we could work out an acceptable resolution.

So, on the evening of March 16 I flew to Washington for a meeting the following day. It had been announced, and I was swarmed by reporters and TV cameras when I changed planes in Memphis. I deflected their shouted questions as best I could and hurried to catch my Washington-bound flight.

At the meeting with Senators D'Amato and Cohen, we agreed that hearings would go forward, but not until I had finished my investigation into whatever the subject matter of the hearing was going to be. In the case of the White House/Treasury contacts, I said I thought we would be finished in "several months." About a week later, Rod Lankler and I had a similar meeting with members of the House, including Speaker Tom Foley of Washington, Majority Leader Richard Gephardt of Missouri, Minority Leader Newt Gingrich of Georgia and Congressman Leach. That meeting produced a similar agreement.

CHAPTER 41

Taking the Fiske

SENATORS D'AMATO AND COHEN had said they were satisfied, but many others were not. Treasury Secretary Lloyd Bentsen appeared before a House subcommittee to testify on other subjects and was, inevitably, asked about the meetings. He said, "On the advice of Mr. Fiske, the Special Counsel, I refuse to answer." House Republicans were quick to call that "taking the Fiske."

Senator Bob Dole was particularly outraged. As time went on, he compared me to "a congressional traffic cop." He said "he has commanded Congress when to go and when to stop, insisting that hearings take a back seat to his own investigation and exercising an almost complete veto over congressional oversight . . . To our own discredit, both the Senate and the House have willingly gone along with this charade." He said historians would look back on 1994 as a year when the Congress forfeited its power. He concluded by saying, "Mr. Fiske may be a fine person and a fine lawyer, but he is without a doubt one of the most powerful bureaucrats ever seen in American history."

What we had was a legitimate difference of opinion based upon our different responsibilities. Mine was to conduct the most effective criminal investigation I could—and I felt that testimony by key witnesses before Congress would interfere with that. Those who wanted public hearings felt that it was more important that there be an airing of all the facts so that the public could make political judgments of the propriety of the conduct of high level administration officials.

I said repeatedly that I had no power to tell Congress what to do. It was up to Congress to decide how to resolve the competing considerations. Was it more important to preserve the maximum potential for an effective criminal prosecution or to shed sunlight on the conduct of public officials? It was solely their decision, but the outcome hinged on politics. In March 1994, with the Democrats in control of Congress and concerned that hearings might embarrass the administration, they readily deferred to my request not to hold them. But elections were coming in the fall.

Among the voices critical of my position was *The Wall Street Journal* editorial page which, because of my representation of Clark Clifford, had criticized my appointment from the outset.[107] Its news pages were different. The *Journal's* front-page story digest on March 14 displayed the stark contrast in two consecutive headings. The first was a news article headed, "Fiske Gets Off To Fast Start in Whitewater Probe By Moving Aggressively on All Fronts." Immediately under it was the heading for an editorial: "The Fiske Cover-up."

The news article appeared on page 16. It recounted the investigative steps we had taken after six weeks, mentioned my "reputation for fierce independence," and said my "show of prosecutorial muscle . . . was a stern warning to the White House, Congress, and Hillary Clinton's former law firm that he won't tolerate anything that impedes his investigation."

While the news department praised "a show of prosecutorial muscle," the editorial page saw a "cover-up." The editorial charged that "in practical terms, Mr. Fiske's crusade against Congressional hearings has become an all-purpose political shield for all the President's Men . . ." The editorial went on to say, "The main public interest here is not in putting the likes of Roger Altman in jail, but in finding out what the Clinton/Little Rock/Rose presidency is all about."

"[Congress] should tell Mr. Fiske that they ultimately don't care whether someone goes to jail; for our own part we hope no one does. The most important responsibility is to give the public the facts it needs to judge the performance of its government; deciding whether to indict is less important than deciding whether to throw the rascals out."

CHAPTER 42

The Investigation Continues

AS OUR WASHINGTON OFFICE pursued its investigation of the contacts between the Treasury Department and the White House, Congress continued to withhold hearings on that issue. And now two new issues arose from those contacts. Questions surfaced about whether Roger Altman had told the truth in his congressional testimony that first described the White House/Treasury meetings. The second issue involved George Stephanopoulos, one of Clinton's high-level aides, and whether he had tried to force the firing of a lawyer hired by the RTC to pursue its civil investigation into the Whitewater/Madison Guaranty matter.

Time magazine focused on the Stephanopoulos allegation in an early April cover story. The cover photo showed President Clinton and Stephanopoulos, both looking somber and Clinton holding his head with his hand under the heading: "Deep Water: How the President's men tried to hinder the Whitewater investigation." Clinton had said in a news conference, "We certainly know that no one in the White House, at least to the best of my knowledge, has tried to use any information to in any way improperly influence the RTC or any federal agency." But the article said, ". . . his words do not quite jibe with a story that Special Counsel Robert Fiske and a Whitewater grand jury were hearing almost simultaneously."

The appointment that Stephanopoulos had problems with was the RTC's choice of former District of Columbia United States Attorney, Jay Stephens, to head up its Whitewater civil investigation. He had complained bitterly to Altman's deputy, Josh Steiner, about it. Stephens, a Republican, had openly criticized Clinton when, at the outset of his administration, he had fired all ninety-four U.S. Attorneys. Stephens claimed he

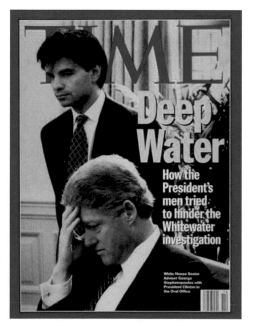

Time Magazine, *April 4, 1994*

was being fired because he was investigating House Ways and Means Committee Chairman, Dan Rostenkowski, a key Clinton ally in the battle for healthcare reform. The issue, as *Time* phrased it, was whether Stephanopoulos was simply venting or whether, perhaps at the insistence of Clinton himself, he was trying to get an outspoken Clinton critic replaced. The article quoted one administration official: "Based on the facts we believe Fiske has developed during his grand jury sessions, it's possible that at least one and perhaps several [obstruction of justice] indictments could issue."

We proceeded expeditiously, calling everyone who had been involved into the grand jury.

CHAPTER 43

The Death of Vincent Foster

MEANWHILE, OUR INVESTIGATION into the circumstances surrounding the death of Vincent Foster continued. Here, unlike our probe of the Treasury/White House contacts, we decided with one or two exceptions not to put the witnesses in the grand jury. We interviewed them all subject to U.S. Code provisions that made it a felony to make false statements, but I wanted to avoid the reporting limitations we faced with grand jury testimony. We could still make a public report of our conclusions, but under the Federal Rules of Criminal Procedure we had to apply to a federal judge first. That was an unpredictable process that might involve delays. Foster's death—suicide or murder—remained an open question generating enormous public interest—even more so than the White House and Treasury contacts—and we felt it was vital to answer that question fully and on the record as soon as we were confident of our conclusion.

As we proceeded the conspiracy theorists kept up their steady drumbeat of allegations that Foster had been murdered and his body transported to Fort Marcy Park to make it look like a suicide. In early June, while answering other questions about the investigation, I told a reporter that I thought we would be finishing our Foster investigation and announcing the results shortly. Within days our office in Little Rock was inundated with hundreds of identically worded postcards, all from Orange County, California. To paraphrase: if we found it was a suicide it would be the biggest cover-up in modern history.

What follows (pp. 240–245) is taken from the public report we issued on June 30, 1994:

Fort Marcy Park, where Foster's body was found the year before, was one of a ring of fortifications built during the Civil War to defend Washington against Confederate attack. As a national park its terrain of earthwork walls and trenches is well preserved. The person who discovered the body found it amid dense foliage at the top of a raised berm. Without touching the body he notified two uniformed Park maintenance officials, who in turn notified the Park Police. They arrived to find the body lying on a slope, feet down, with its head near the top of the berm. At first neither the witness nor the Park officer had seen a gun because the foliage concealed the hands. But the emergency medical crew that arrived on the scene a few minutes later found a gun in his right hand. Foster was lying with his arms straight down by his sides. His clothes were neat, and there was no sign of a struggle. Police and EMS photos showed bloodstains on Foster's face and on the right shoulder of his white shirt, covering the top of his shoulder to his arm. The blood on his face was on his right cheek and jaw, what the FBI lab report later described as a "contact stain."

The autopsy by the Park police medical examiner found a contact bullet wound entering the soft palate inside the mouth, extensive gunpowder residue on the soft palate, and gunpowder-like residue on the lateral portion of both index fingers, with a greater concentration on the right index finger.

The U.S. Park Police is part of the Department of the Interior, and it had jurisdiction over the investigation rather than the FBI because the death occurred in a national park. In the weeks afterward they interviewed family members, White House staff and others; reviewed documents obtained from the White House and Foster's personal belongings; and took other investigative steps, including fingerprint analyses and an unsuccessful search in the Park for the bullet fired from the gun. Their conclusion that Foster had put a gun in his mouth and killed himself was entirely reasonable based on the evidence.

But the alternative theories had taken hold and continued to gain traction with a segment of the public. Our investigation went forward, conducted by Rod Lankler, Mark Stein and Carl Stich of our Washington office, together with seven experienced agents from the FBI, the FBI Laboratory and the Bureau's National Center for the Analysis of Violent Crime. In addition Rod retained a four-member panel of experienced forensic pathologists to review the results of the investigation. They included New York City's Chief Medical Examiner Charles Hirsch; Seattle's Chief Medical Examiner Donald Reay; Charles Stahl, the Chief Medical Examiner for the U.S. armed forces; and James Luke, a clinical professor of pathology at Georgetown and George Washington universities who also consulted with the FBI.

We interviewed 125 people, including close friends and confidants of Foster who provided insight into his activities and state of mind during the weeks prior to his death, people who worked with and for Foster in the White House, and everyone who was known to have been in Ft. Marcy Park on the afternoon and evening Foster died.

We also reviewed documents obtained by the Park police from Foster's wallet and his car, documents from his office that had been turned over to the Foster family attorney or the Clintons' private attorney, photographs of his body taken in the Park and during the autopsy and, of course, the autopsy report.

Finally, FBI lab technicians analyzed the physical evidence. They looked at the gun, and compared chemically and physically the gunpowder and lead residue on Foster's clothing with that found in the gun. They analyzed photographs taken by the Park police for patterns of bloodstains, gunpowder and the presence or absence of physical matter on Foster's clothing and body. They performed a full battery of blood tests comparing Foster's blood with that found on his clothing and a DNA comparison of Foster's blood with the blood found near the muzzle of the gun. They analyzed mineral deposits on the clothing, his fingerprints and the handwriting on a torn-up note discovered in his briefcase.

Their conclusion was that Foster had committed suicide by firing a bullet from a .38 caliber revolver into his mouth. Clinching factors included no signs of a struggle and marks and powder evidence that showed Foster had pulled the trigger himself. The forensic panel agreed unanimously. Our report said the evidence was "typical and characteristic of such findings in deaths due to intentional and self-inflicted intraoral gunshot wounds." Or, as Charles Hirsch put it less formally, "We do this all the time—it is always a question of suicide or homicide. On a scale of one to a hundred, this one is a ninety-five."

Importantly, the forensic panel also determined from the position of the body that it could not have been moved into the Park from somewhere else. This was clear as soon as he was moved from the downward incline in the Park to a gurney; the level position redistributed the blood that had collected in his legs and lower body so that it soaked his shirt and undershirt. Had he been killed elsewhere and moved to the Park, his clothing and body would have been far bloodier.

Of this Hirsch had no doubt. I asked him how certain he was, and he replied "One hundred percent. It is impossible that he was murdered elsewhere and brought to Ft. Marcy Park." I said, "Dr. Hirsch, I have dealt with a lot of expert witnesses in my career. It is always on the one hand this, on the other hand that before coming to a measured conclusion. This is the first time I have ever heard someone say, 'I am 100 percent right and any other conclusion is impossible.'" He smiled and replied, "I am sure that may be true, but I have absolutely no doubt about this conclusion." Later in a Senate Banking Committee hearing into Foster's death, he told the senators the same thing: "It is my unequivocal, categorical opinion that it was impossible for him to have been killed elsewhere."[108]

FOSTER'S STATE OF MIND

It remained to figure out if Whitewater had driven Foster to suicide. He had been severely depressed, but was Whitewater the cause? We gradually learned that political attacks and some press coverage were among the factors contributing to his depression. Foster believed his integrity was being unfairly sullied, and nothing was more important to him than his reputation.

In May 1993 Foster gave the commencement speech to the Arkansas Law School graduating class. He spoke, in a voice that his sister recalled being unnaturally strained and tense, about the importance—and the frailty—of reputation. "The reputation you develop for . . . integrity will be your greatest asset or your worst enemy," he said. "There is no victory, no advantage, no fee, no favor which is worth even a blemish on your reputation . . . dents to the reputation in the legal profession are irreparable . . ."

Witnesses told us that he had worked himself to near exhaustion. Foster's position at the White House required a fourteen-hour work day, six or seven days a week. He had taken no vacation, or even a weekend off, until the weekend immediately prior to his death. Friends and relatives commented on the signs of stress he showed—difficulty sleeping, weight loss and anxiety attacks—and said he worried constantly.

Those closest to Foster stated that the single greatest source of his distress was the criticism he and others within the Counsel's office received following the firing of seven employees in the White House travel office after an investigation into allegations of financial impropriety, including embezzlement and kickbacks. Foster assigned responsibility for the investigation to his fellow Rose Law Firm partner, William Kennedy. Kennedy retained an accounting firm to audit the travel office books, and contacted the FBI to discuss the possibility of a criminal investigation. The White House received heavy criticism for its handling of the matter, one more blast in a season of blame. Allegations that the FBI was pressured to open an investigation in order to justify the firings led to an internal FBI review of the meetings between the agents and the White House Counsel's office. The Bureau's report to the Attorney General included statements attributed to Kennedy that he denied making. After reviewing the report, on July 2, the White House reprimanded Kennedy. There was some discussion within the White House about reprimanding Foster, but that did not occur.

By what we were told, Foster was deeply disturbed by the reprimand and by what he believed were distortions in the press. He told family members that he believed the FBI agents had lied about the meeting with the Counsel's office and that the office had been "set up" by the FBI. His wife, Lisa, reported that the reprimand triggered an "anxiety attack."[109] Foster told his wife, as well as his sister and Kennedy, that he was considering resigning. Both his wife and sister believed that the personal humiliation he would have felt if he had returned to Arkansas prevented him from doing so. He told Webb Hubbell that in Washington you are assumed to have done something wrong even if you have not.

The press coverage that bothered Foster was a series of *The Wall Street Journal* editorials. The first, on June 17, was entitled "Who is Vincent Foster?" and criticized him for "carelessness in following the law." It cited as examples his refusal to give the *Journal* a photo of himself, and then not responding within the required ten-day period to a Freedom of Information Act request. "Who ensures that this administration follows the law, or explains why not?" the paper asked. A second editorial, a week later, with the title "Vincent Foster's Victory," criticized a D.C. Circuit Court of Appeals decision agreeing with the Counsel's office position that Hillary Clinton was the functional equivalent of a federal employee and, therefore, the Health Care Task Force she headed did not need to meet in public pursuant to the Federal Advisory Committee Act.[110]

The editorials distressed Foster. He told people we interviewed that they were mean-spirited and factually baseless. He said he believed the *Journal* would continue attacking him and others in the administration until someone from Arkansas was forced out of the White House. He told his brother-in-law that he had spent a lifetime building a reputation and now it was being tarnished.

On July 19, 1993 the *Journal* ran a third editorial, this one criticizing the speed at which the administration was moving to replace FBI Director William Sessions and compared it to the handling of the travel office matter. It noted that Foster was involved in the latter and said, "The mores on display from the Rose alumni are far from confidence building." It ranks as tragic irony that Louis Freeh's appointment to succeed Sessions was announced the next day, the same day Foster killed himself.

Several days after his death, a lawyer in the White House Counsel's office found a torn-up note in his briefcase that chronicled his feelings on these issues. The note, whose handwriting was confirmed to be Foster's, included the following statements, four of which related to the the travel office matter:

> "No one in the White House, to my knowledge, violated any law or standard of conduct, including any action in the travel office."

> "The FBI lied in their report to the AG."

"The press is covering up the illegal benefits they received from the travel staff."

"The WSJ editors lie without consequence."

"I was not meant for the job or the spotlight of public life in Washington. Here ruining people is considered sport."

Foster's sister told us that she had urged him to see a psychiatrist for his depression. She wrote down several names on a paper that was found in his wallet on the day he died. He never made an appointment. Speculation suggested that one reason might have been that he had not yet completed his formal written application for the position of Deputy White House Counsel on a form that, like many other applications for government positions, asks, "Have you ever seen a psychiatrist?" Since then the form has been changed to include a disclaimer in bold type: "**Mental health counseling in and of itself *is not a reason* to revoke or deny a clearance.**" (Section 21 of the SF86.)

While Foster's state of mind was troubled, we had found no evidence after extensive interviews with family members, friends, White House colleagues and others that concerns about Whitewater were the causes of his suicide. White House workers in the first half of 1993 all stated that Whitewater was not an issue of any significance during that time; it was not until the fall of 1993, when the RTC referrals became public, that the matter received significant attention. Each of Foster's family and close friends whom we questioned stated that he had never mentioned Whitewater or Madison Guaranty as a cause of concern. So, our report concluded that, while it was impossible to know exactly what was in his mind and we could not rule out the possibility, we had found no evidence that Whitewater had factored in his suicide.[111]

FOSTER'S WHITE HOUSE PAPERS

The final piece of the Washington puzzle had to do with the treatment of Vincent Foster's papers in his office following his death, when White House Counsel Bernard Nussbaum refused to turn them over to the Park police, or to let the Justice Department lawyers look at them until he had reviewed them to screen out personal or privileged documents. This prompted questions as to whether Nussbaum was trying to hide incriminating documents. His position was that he was acting as any good lawyer would to protect the interests of his clients.

CHAPTER 44

I Question the Clintons

THE *NEW YORK DAILY NEWS* headline from my announcement as Independent Counsel had painted an over-dramatic picture of my intention to interview the President and First Lady in my investigations. But as we looked at the contacts between Treasury officials and the White House, Foster's death, and the White House handling of his papers, we decided we needed to question both the President and Mrs. Clinton on all three of those issues. So, I doubt it was a big surprise to David Kendall, President Clinton's personal lawyer, when I called him to set up the interviews. I added, "I think it is better for everyone if it is under oath."

Kendall and I discussed the format and the scope of the testimony. Rod Lankler and I had decided that while we should take the testimony under oath, in deference to the position of the presidency we would not ask them to appear before the grand jury. Instead we would take what amounted to a deposition under oath, and then read the testimony into the record before the grand jury. This was a protocol established by Paul Curran when he, as Independent Counsel, deposed President Jimmy Carter about loans made to the Carter family's peanut warehouse by Bert Lance's National Bank of Georgia. Secondly, I agreed with Kendall that we would concentrate on the Washington issues and leave the Arkansas matters for another day.

We arranged to take the testimony at the White House on the afternoon of Sunday, June 12. We needed a trustworthy court reporter, and the FBI put us in touch with Elizabeth Eastman, who had the highest security clearances and had been used before in sensitive situations. To keep the matter confidential we did not tell her who the witnesses were going to be. Rod Lankler and I picked her up around 1:00 p.m. and on the way over told her we were going to the White House to question the President and the First Lady. She almost went into shock, but recovered by the time we arrived.

We were taken to a small room in the West Wing called the Treaty Room, where we started with the President at 2:00 p.m. We had allotted two hours for each of them, which was enough considering the limited questioning we would be doing at this point. I finished questioning the President around 4:00 p.m. and Mrs. Clinton about six-thirty. When I returned to the hotel room where Janet had joined me for the weekend, she announced, "You know, you weren't the only one who was with President and Mrs. Clinton this afternoon." With that she pulled from her purse a photograph that showed her posing, with a smile, next to department store cutouts of the pair.

Our office and the White House had managed to keep advance word from leaking out. But the White House released the news late Sunday after both depositions were completed. This produced front-page articles in several newspapers including *The New York Times* and *The Washington Post*. The *Times* article, headlined "Special Prosecutor questions Clintons, Setting a Precedent" said the questioning "represented the first time that a sitting President has given a deposition about his official conduct." That overlooked Curran's questioning of Carter, which generated far less publicity, but it was correct in saying, "It was apparently the first time a sitting First Lady has ever been interviewed by law enforcement officials about her conduct while in the White House."

CHAPTER 45

The Results

WE MADE THE RESULTS of our work public on June 30, 1994. That was the day we filed reports on two investigations—into the contacts between the Treasury Department and the White House over Resolution Trust—and Vincent Foster's death. As required, the first report of 150 pages was submitted under seal to the Independent Counsel Court. The second, fifty-eight pages long, was the report on Foster's death. It was also filed with the Independent Counsel Court but available to the public because it was not under seal. We announced the results of both investigations in a news release issued the same day.

In the first case we said, "After a review of all the evidence, we have concluded that the evidence is insufficient to establish that anyone within the White House or the Department of the Treasury acted with the intent to corruptly influence an RTC investigation." The release went on to say that we found no evidence to justify an obstruction of justice prosecution or any other federal criminal prosecution. That afternoon we advised Roger Altman's counsel that we were not going to charge him with false testimony before Congress.

On Foster, the release said simply, "Vincent Foster committed suicide in Ft. Marcy Park on July 20, 1993. Although the contributing factors to his depressed state can never be precisely determined, there is no evidence that any issues relating to Whitewater, Madison Guaranty or CMS played any part in his suicide."

At the same time we announced that the investigation into the handling of the papers in Foster's office had not been completed and was continuing.[112]

CHAPTER 46

Outcry

THE CONSPIRACY THEORISTS immediately attacked the credibility of our report on Foster's death. They trumpeted the fact that searches of the area where Foster's body was discovered had not found the bullet that killed him. They argued that security guards at the Saudi-Arabian Embassy 100 yards away had not heard any gunshot. Republican Representative Dan Burton of Indiana—one of the most vocal critics—offered proof by shooting a watermelon in his back yard and reporting that his wife—stationed 100 yards away—had heard the shot. More arguments picked at the condition of Foster's body when it was found, including discrepancies between what the person who found it saw and what the Park police saw when they arrived and whether there was dirt on Foster's shoes.

It did not seem to matter that our report had dealt with all the important issues. We described Foster's body and the site in detail, what people saw and why and explained how it all fit with a verdict of suicide. Interviews with the security guards at the Saudi Embassy revealed that noise from traffic on the Chain Bridge and heavy construction machinery in the area were among the sources of noise that could have drowned out the sound of a shot already muffled by heavy foliage and the fact that the gun was inside Foster's mouth when it was fired. There was indeed dirt on Foster's shoes; the FBI found mica particles on his shoes and socks consistent with soil in Ft. Marcy Park, but his shoes weren't clumped with dirt because it was a dry day and there was no exposed dirt where he was found. The missing bullet wasn't critical because there was no way to know the angle at which the gun was fired or the speed and trajectory of the bullet as it exited his skull.

Finally, and most important, on the basic issue of whether the body had been shot elsewhere and moved, we relied on what we considered the irrefutable conclusion by Dr. Hirsch and the other pathologists that it would have been "impossible" for that to have happened without his white shirt becoming bloodstained the way it was after he was lifted up from the incline and put in a level position. Based on this, and the pathologists' conclusion that on a homicide/suicide scale of 100 this was a 95, we had reached what we believed to be a solid conclusion. I remember Rod Lankler saying, "If we keep this investigation going much longer people are going to think there is a real issue here." So, we issued our report hoping to put the matter to rest.

That it did not put the matter to rest did not come as a total surprise.

Coincidentally, June 30 was not only the day we announced our results and issued the report on Foster. On the same day Congress had passed and President Clinton had signed into law a reenactment of the independent counsel statute. Attorney General Reno immediately asked the three-judge court to make an appointment, and recommended me, an action the law permitted.

But a number of conservative Republicans led by Senator Lauch Faircloth of North Carolina began to publicly urge the court not to reappoint me, claiming conflicts of interest. None of those claims, in my judgment, were legitimate. For example, the land for the Whitewater Development had been bought in 1978 from the International Paper Company, a Davis Polk client. No one ever said there was anything wrong with this transaction and Davis Polk had not been involved in it, but this produced one far-fetched claim of conflict. Another centered on my having been co-counsel for Clark Clifford with Bob Bennett. Bennett more recently had been Clinton's counsel in the Paula Jones matter. This was not part of our investigation, but even if it had been the notion that a lawyer cannot ever oppose a lawyer he once worked on the same side with was as untenable as the International Paper claim.

Faircloth and his allies also said I had conflicts involving Bernard Nussbaum. I had, in fact, worked as co-counsel with him on several matters, and had recommended him to my partner Lawrence Walsh for the number two position when he was assembling his team for the Iran/Contra investigation. Nussbaum had consulted me—among many others—on the appointment of Louis Freeh as FBI director. I had reviewed these connections with Phil Heymann before my appointment. He concluded that we were professional, not social, friends—neither of us had ever been in the other's home—and there was no reason the professional relationship should prevent my appointment. Moreover, newspaper reports had said the outcry over the White House/Treasury contacts, which was inflamed by our grand jury subpoenas to White House officials including Nussbaum, had prompted Clinton to request that he step down as White House Counsel. This should have demonstrated that whatever my relationship with Nussbaum, it was not standing in the way of my doing my job as Independent Counsel.

But it was clear to me that my critics were not concerned about any perceived conflicts. Rather, I had blocked hearings that the Republicans wanted to hold and completed two investigations without finding criminal wrongdoing by anyone in the administration. This, to them, showed I was not sufficiently "aggressive."

I found this exceedingly frustrating. I felt that in the very short period of five months, February to June, we had made extraordinary progress. We had already obtained three convictions. David Hale had pleaded guilty in March to two counts of conspiring to defraud the SBA. On June 23, after three days of trial conducted by Denis McInerney and Jim Ed Reeves[113] before Judge Reasoner in Little Rock, we obtained guilty pleas from Hale's two co-defendants, Charles Matthews and William Fitzhugh, on the original charge of defrauding the SBA. And what my critics didn't know was that we were well on our way to a number of significant indictments.

First and foremost of the prospective indictments was that of Associate Attorney General Webb Hubbell, Hillary Clinton's former law partner in Little Rock and the President's close friend. Julie O'Sullivan had developed powerful evidence that Hubbell had defrauded both his clients and his partners through falsified expense reports that gave him hundreds of thousands of dollars of unlawful income. We had the crime established and could have brought the indictment in July, but Julie was developing further evidence of false billings and we needed to determine what the final amount would be. In addition our legal advisors in the Justice Department told us that under their reading of a provision in the independent counsel statute, we should not bring any indictment or negotiate any guilty pleas while the application for the appointment of an Independent Counsel was pending.[114]

A second major investigation that was well on its way to an indictment was a bankruptcy tax fraud scheme involving cable television properties owned by former Arkansas Governor Jim Guy Tucker and a businessman named William Marks. By July Gabrielle Wolohojian had developed substantial evidence that Tucker, his lawyer and Marks had devised a series of sham corporate transactions and filed a fraudulent bankruptcy action in order to falsely inflate the tax basis of the corporation's assets—thus reducing the amount of tax owed when those assets were sold. The scheme defrauded the government of approximately $1 million in tax revenues.

Hale's cooperation had also launched a third investigation that was well on its way to an indictment. This involved an $825,000 loan from Madison Guaranty to a nominee of Hale—purportedly for a land purchase, but actually to inflate Hale's books to show profits—that when matched by the SBA allowed his company, CMS, to make four separate fraudulent loans totaling the same amount in a scheme to benefit Jim and Susan McDougal. The Little Rock team of Denis McInerney, Pat Smith and Tim White[115] had developed evidence that tied Tucker and Jim McDougal to the scheme, which included the $300,000 loan to Susan McDougal to which Hale had already pleaded guilty.

That investigation and others had produced several other prospective indictments involving illegally inflated land appraisals, false loan application statements and the failure to file required currency transaction reports on money borrowed for Bill Clinton's 1990 Arkansas gubernatorial campaign. At least one of these was ready to go but for the restrictions imposed by waiting for the Independent Counsel Court to act.

We had also devoted substantial time and resources to the core Whitewater real estate transaction and related Madison Guaranty issues that we were charged with investigating. We had subpoenaed thousands of documents and had interviewed a number of key witnesses.

We worked through July on all of these investigations, continuing to develop evidence but now unable to issue subpoenas or bargain for guilty pleas as we waited to hear from the Independent Counsel Court on Attorney General Reno's application. We had expected quick action when she asked for my appointment on June 30.[116] But as time went on and nothing happened, we all began to wonder.

On August 4, a Thursday, I flew to Washington to meet with the team there. It had a new member in Beth Golden, an associate in the Davis Polk Washington office who—together with Michele Corelli's counterpart, Debbie Gershman—had been highly recommended by Scott Muller.[117] The next day, around noon, I flew from Washington to Orlando to spend the weekend with Janet and her mother, who was then ninety-one and had been in the hospital with congestive heart failure. I arrived around three and as I was walking off the plane my beeper went off, telling me to call our Washington office. Janet was waiting and I said, "I have to call the Washington office—this will just take a minute."

Mark Stein answered when I called. He said, "You won't believe this—you have been replaced by Ken Starr."

CHAPTER 47

The Independent Counsel Court

THE INDEPENDENT COUNSEL COURT, all appointed by Chief Justice William Rehn-quist, consisted of David Sentelle from the District of Columbia Court of Appeals, Joseph Sneed from the Ninth Circuit Court of Appeals and John Butzner from the Fourth Circuit Court of Appeals. Sentelle and Sneed were conservative Republicans and Butzner was a Democrat. Judge Butzner strongly opposed replacing me, as professor Ken Gormley later wrote in *The Death of American Virtue: Clinton vs. Starr.*[118] Sentelle and Sneed outvoted him. According to Gormley the opinion subsequently issued was unanimous, despite Butzner's opposition, because he believed that a dissent would have been seen as politicizing the court.

Starr had been a judge on the D.C. Circuit Court of Appeals and served as Solicitor General in the George H. W. Bush administration. The appointment conferred upon him exactly the same jurisdiction, in exactly the same language, that was in Janet Reno's order appointing me under the Code of Federal Regulations. The rationale expressed in the opinion for replacing me was the same rationale the Attorney General had expressed in her initial reluctance to appoint an Independent Counsel:

"...The Court, having reviewed the motion of the Attorney General that Robert B. Fiske, Jr., be appointed as Independent Counsel, has determined that this would not be consistent with the purposes of the Act. This reflects no conclusion on the part of the Court that Fiske lacks either the actual independence or any other attribute necessary to the conclusion of the investigation. Rather, the Court reaches this conclusion because the Act contemplates an apparent as well as an actual independence on the part of the Counsel... It is not our intent to impugn the integrity of the Attorney General's appointee, but rather to reflect the intent of the Act that the actor be protected against perceptions of conflict. As Fiske was appointed by the incumbent administration, the Court therefore deems it in the best interest of the appearance of independence contemplated by the Act that a person not affiliated with the incumbent administration be appointed...."

I was not totally surprised. As July stretched toward August I had become concerned that something like this might be in the works. But I was angry, frustrated and above all disappointed that I was not going to be able to carry through and finish bringing the indictments that we had brought nearly to fruition in such a short time. I was looking forward to answering the conservatives who had complained that because my first two investigations concluded there was no criminal wrongdoing, I was not sufficiently aggressive. My staff had the same reaction.

CHAPTER 48

Calming Troubled Waters

AFTER THE WEEKEND in Orlando with Janet and her mother, I flew back to Little Rock to find a mini-revolt among the team. They had come to the airport carrying signs saying "Ken who?" and "Bob is the real Star." They were ready to quit *en masse* and go home.[119]

We talked about it at length on Monday. I understood and appreciated how they felt. But I urged them to stay on under Starr, at least long enough to pass the baton to the people he brought in so they could run as much as possible with the momentum we had generated. I said, "You have an obligation to the country to continue and finish what we started."

Next I had to meet with the agents. The lawyers had told me that both the FBI and the IRS agents we had been working with were extremely demoralized. They thought that everything we had accomplished was in jeopardy.

So, I brought the whole team—lawyers and agents—together on Tuesday, August 9th. I told them that based on our work together I had expected we would return eight indictments, involving eleven defendants, in the fall of 1994 and winter of 1995. I assured the agents that the lawyers they'd been working with would stay on at least through the transition to the team that Starr would put in place. And I told them that Ken Starr was a person with integrity who would do the right thing with the evidence we had developed.

I said, "He has no experience as a prosecutor, so things may move a little slower, but these indictments will happen."

That prediction turned out to be true. The indictments I referred to all were brought and resulted in convictions. They are described in the final report of Independent Counsel Robert Ray, who took over from Ken Starr in October 1999. His report recognized our role: "By early August, 1994 Mr. Fiske's investigation stood poised to charge Hubbell for billing fraud and Governor Tucker for conspiracy and tax fraud."[120] The Code of Federal Regulations required a report from me, which I filed under seal with the Independent Counsel Court in October 1994 describing our activities before I was replaced.

CHAPTER 49

An Assessment

WHILE I WAS UPSET about being replaced, I felt good about the experience. I was proud on a professional level that we had accomplished an enormous amount in a very short time with a relatively small but extremely cohesive team that worked extraordinarily well with one another. Potential conflicts limited our contacts with the Little Rock community,[121] but our team bonded socially as well as professionally to create a very close-knit group.[122]

And we did find ways to become involved with life in Little Rock. Gabrielle Wolohojian played violin with the Arkansas Symphony Orchestra. Gabrielle and Julie O'Sullivan took oil painting classes at the Arkansas Arts Center. Bill Duffey's twelve-year-old son Charles, an accomplished fiddler, jammed with other bluegrass aficionados at Reed's Music Store in Pickles Gap. And Bill got us four seasons tickets at $55 each to the Class B Arkansas Travelers baseball games, where they played bingo between innings and hot dogs were free after the seventh.

As for me, the *Arkansas Democrat Gazette* revealed early on in my stay in Little Rock that I had played semi-pro hockey while at Yale. This was a bit of an overstatement, but the next day I received a call at the office from a Little Rock lawyer who had read the article and invited me to play in his weekly pick-up game at the only ice rink in the State of Arkansas. So, the next time I went home I brought back my hockey equipment and played in the Wednesday night game. That was my principal exercise outside the Little Rock Athletic Club, a fitness center located in the Westside Creek garden apartment complex—almost all of us lived there—where several of us used to go every morning before work.[123]

The *Democrat Gazette* also published an August 15 post-mortem, based largely on an interview with me, that captured our need to stay apart that brought the team together, our hard work of twelve and fifteen hour days, and the pride at what we were able to accomplish.

"It was a wonderful team," I told the writer, "the kind of team that you remember the rest of your life. We're very upbeat about what we've accomplished, how much we've

The Whitewater Team

been able to do in six months, how much there is waiting for Ken Starr to come in and capitalize on . . . we have a good feeling about how much we've done."

I left Arkansas for the last time on August 10 and took some well-deserved time off, decompressing, before going back to Davis Polk. Janet and I relaxed in Vermont, celebrated our fortieth wedding anniversary in Bermuda, cruised on our sailboat and just basically regained our equilibrium.

Starr's investigation went on for three more years. In the end, in the contacts between the White House and the Treasury, including the issue relating to Stephanopoulos, and in the cause of Vincent Foster's death, he reached exactly the same conclusions we had.[124] And his conclusions did little more than ours had to quiet the disbelievers. Starr, too, was excoriated by Foster conspiracy theorists for not producing the results they wanted.

But, as time went on, it seemed increasingly clear that Ken Starr's public legacy as Independent Counsel was destined to be shaped much less by Whitewater or Vincent Foster than it was by the 1998 revelation of President Clinton's dalliance with Monica Lewinsky and Starr's subsequent perjury charge against the President that led to articles of impeachment being voted in the House.

Receiving the FBI Honor Cup from Director Freeh in October 1995
after my tenure as Whitewater Independent Counsel

—⚍—

Whitewater team at 20th reunion

—⚬—

DAVIS POLK, 1994–2010

CHAPTER 50

Judge John H. McBryde

I FOUND ONCE AGAIN, as I had after being considered for Deputy Attorney General, that my Whitewater experience had made me more attractive to potential clients. Back at Davis Polk in mid-October I became involved right away in a number of matters. One of the most interesting was an assignment from the Judicial Council of the United States Court of Appeals for the Fifth Circuit, involving a district judge in Fort Worth, Texas. But it all started with a hunting trip to the bayou country of Louisiana.

I was fortunate to enjoy friendships with lawyers all around the country stemming from my work for the ABA Committee on Federal Judiciary and the American College of Trial Lawyers. One of the closest of those friendships was with a lawyer from New Orleans, who served with me on the Judiciary Committee for six years and was a fellow past president of the trial lawyers group. His name was Gene Lafitte, not to be confused with Jean Lafitte—the notorious and long-dead Pirate of New Orleans. We had traveled with our wives, bicycling in Burgundy, cruising the Great Lakes, visiting Prague and Budapest with a Danube River trip built in, and lastly a trip to Venice with a cruise down Croatia's Dalmatian coast. He also was an avid duck hunter.

In January 1995, roughly a year after I'd begun my six months as Independent Counsel, Gene invited me to go duck hunting at a lodge in Gueydan, Louisiana—a spot deep in Cajun country about three hours west of New Orleans. His law firm, Liskow & Lewis, had a lease that allowed them duck hunting privileges, and they had lined it up for a weekend. There were fourteen of us. Gene and six of his partners were the hosts. The guests included four oil company general counsels, Chief Judge Henry Politz and Judge Eugene Davis from the Fifth Circuit Court of Appeals, and me.

With Gene Lafitte

Duck hunting is an early riser's sport. We got up at four in the morning, dressed and stumbled down to the dock where seven "mud boats" waited. A Liskow partner and a guest climbed into each boat with a guide and his dog, the motors revved and we took off in pitch darkness on a high-speed trip through a maze of narrow canals. At some point we left the mud boats and climbed into long, narrow and very tippy boats called pirogues, which the guides poled through shallow water until we reached the blinds.[125] Gene and I shared a pirogue and at this point he handed me a flashlight and told me to look down into the blind. "Why is that?" I asked.

"Just to check for water moccasins," he said with a grin in his voice.

We were not allowed to shoot until ten minutes before sunrise. We sat, watching the sky turn from dark to gray to lighter gray to red with the sun's first light from below the horizon. As the red lightened we could hear the ducks all around us. Just as it was light enough to see—literally at daybreak—we were allowed to shoot. Crouching in the blind in dark clothes and not showing our faces, we waited for the magic word from the guides: "One coming in on the left, take him!" It was amazing how fast these ducks flew—the first few times they were gone and out of range before I pulled the trigger. But eventually I got the hang of it and performed respectably.

I don't remember how many, if any, I took back that first morning. In future years sometimes we reached our limit quickly and sometimes not at all.[126] No matter what, we always returned to the lodge about eight. We would then have a huge breakfast, and most of us would go back to bed for a nap. There was a second round of hunting in the late afternoon in the rice fields and then we would come back for dinner. We would go out again early the next morning and then, after breakfast, pack up the ducks we were taking home and leave.

Those were wonderful times. Camaraderie develops among men who get up at 4 a.m. together. One of the Liskow partners was a great duck hunter who took me under his wing—no pun intended—and significantly improved my skills. There was a lot of dead time during the day that we spent sitting around the lodge and talking, and the more lubricated evenings were a definite highlight—a lot of people with good senses of humor that produced lively repartee about the day's events, and Judge Politz's deep well of Cajun jokes delivered with great flourish and the Cajun accents he'd grown up around.[127] I enjoyed his company, and that of Judge Davis.[128]

With Judge Politz

Gene invited me back in the fall of 1995, the first of several repeat invitations, for a weekend in early November at the very start of duck season. During the Saturday afternoon lull Judge Politz came over to me and said, "Let's take a walk." We did, and he described a serious problem that the Fifth Circuit had with a district judge in Fort Worth, Texas. His name was John McBryde.

As we walked Judge Politz described two separate incidents. In the first, McBryde had held an Assistant U.S. Attorney from Arizona, Darcy Cerow, in contempt of court for failing to provide information that he said he needed in order to sentence a defendant named Satz who had also been indicted in Arizona. Other defendants in the Arizona case had pled guilty and were cooperating, but the fact of the cooperation was not publicly known because aside from the guilty pleas, the proceedings had been put under seal by the Arizona Judge, Paul Rosenblatt.

Cerow had said the sealing order prevented her from providing McBryde the information he wanted. He rejected her position in scathing terms: "I find . . . that the contention that she was prevented by a sealing order is a fabrication and is not true." He also suggested that Cerow and Judge Rosenblatt were trying to manipulate the order of sentencing to prevent the defendant from invoking double jeopardy.[129] Finally, he unsealed motion papers in his court that revealed the fact of the co-defendants' cooperation. The U.S. Attorney for Arizona, Janet Napolitano,[130] said this had "undermined the Arizona investigation [with the result that] several persons will probably avoid prosecution altogether."[131]

Judge Politz next described McBryde's harsh treatment of Nancy Doherty, the Clerk of the Court in the Northern District of Texas. A case involving Grecia Torres, a Mexican minor, had been settled and Judge McBryde had ordered that the funds to be paid to Torres be invested in an interest-bearing account. Torres's attorney had advised a financial deputy in the Clerk's office that depositing the funds in the U.S. could have an adverse tax effect and had asked him to hold the money until he could set up a Mexican trust fund. Neither the attorney nor the deputy followed up and the money stayed in the court's treasury for three years without earning interest.

When Doherty learned of the error she contacted the Administrative Office of the United States Courts and was told that the only remedy was through the Federal Tort Claims Act (FTCA). When Doherty informed McBryde he entered an order excoriating her for suggesting the plaintiff had to go through an FTCA proceeding and stated that enforcement of his order should be the only redress. After asking the District's Chief Judge, Jerry Buchmeyer, for advice she wrote McBryde a letter reiterating the FTCA remedy and expressing disappointment that Judge McBryde had felt it necessary to enter an order to resolve the matter. McBryde then issued a second order, labeling Doherty's letter "so unprofessional and so disrespectful of the undersigned judge . . . and manifestly such a high degree of insolence, that it borders on, if it does not constitute, contempt of court . . ."

By now it was getting to be a long walk with Judge Politz, and he continued the story.

Judge Buchmeyer learning about both situations entered an order, pursuant to 28 U.S.C. § 137,[132] transferring both cases to himself, vacating McBryde's second order in the Torres case and the contempt finding against the Arizona AUSA, Cerow. Buchmeyer stated that while the code did not give him power to reassign a case because of a disagreement with how a case was handled, he felt this was "an extraordinary situation" because of an unwarranted attack on Judge Rosenblatt and because Judge McBryde had jeopardized a grand jury investigation. He justified the reassignment of the Torres case as necessary "to avoid public humiliation and damage to the District Clerk as well as to the reputation of this Court."[133]

But McBryde was not finished, said Judge Politz. At that point he filed a "request for assistance in resolution of dispute" before the Fifth Circuit Judicial Council. Each of the twelve U.S. judicial circuits has such a council. They are an administrative body, chaired by the Circuit's Chief Judge and include equal numbers of appeals court and district judges. They are charged, among other things, with acting on complaints charging judges with disability or misconduct.

Chief Judge Politz directed that McBryde's request be heard by a special investigatory committee consisting of himself, two circuit judges and two district judges. The committee heard testimony from Judges McBryde and Buchmeyer, AUSA Cerow and

Nancy Doherty. Based on its report, the Judicial Council denied McBryde's request for assistance. The order stated, in part:

> "Our review of the record along with our independent investigation in these two cases overwhelmingly demonstrates that Judge Buchmeyer's factual predicate, on which he based his orders, was correct. Judge McBryde's conduct in both cases was unwarranted."

Judge McBryde then filed a petition for a writ of *mandamus* to the Fifth Circuit, and that is where matters stood in early November 1995 when Judge Politz invited me to go for what had turned out to be a very long walk.

He said that the Fifth Circuit Judicial Council needed to retain counsel to deal with the *mandamus* petition, and more broadly, with Judge McBryde. He wanted a lawyer with a national reputation who needed to be from outside the Fifth Circuit. He asked me to think about it, and give him a list of five names, which I said I would be glad to do.

The next morning, as I was in my room packing up to leave, he stuck his head in the door to tell me that he was looking forward to receiving my list. After a pause he added, "And by the way, be sure your name is one of the five."

I sent Judge Politz the list, with four other distinguished candidates on it, when I got back to New York. I was not surprised when he called and said he wanted me to do it. This was obviously going to take a lot of time and I knew, with the money coming from the federal judicial budget, we would get paid a fraction of what we normally would. But that was never a serious issue—for me, or my partners. It was clearly an important matter—it would be interesting and challenging, and I unhesitatingly said yes.

As Judge Politz explained the situation, it had two prongs: one was to defend the action of Judge Buchmeyer and the Judicial Council in the *mandamus* petition; the other was to deal with McBryde more generally. And that got us into a very thorny—and largely uncharted—area: how far, and for what type of conduct, can the Judicial Council, an administrative body, go in regulating the conduct of a district judge? Article 3 of the Constitution grants life tenure to federal judges "during good behavior" to assure their independence. The sole remedy in the Constitution for regulating the conduct of federal judges is provided in Articles 1 and 2, which allow Congress to remove them from office on impeachment for "treason, bribery or other high crimes or misdemeanors." So, what power does the judicial branch itself have in administrative proceedings to regulate the conduct of judges short of impeachment? That issue would be resolved by judicial opinions upholding the actions taken by the Judicial Council in this case.

We proceeded on both tracks simultaneously. For the legal issues I enlisted one of Davis Polk's smartest lawyers, Gordon Harriss. For the development of the facts, I recruited Bill Wurtz, a partner whose dogged thoroughness had been so valuable in the Three Mile Island case. We were assisted by two associates, Arthur Burke and Michael Flynn, who both later become partners. We had a very formidable and tenacious adversary: Bill Jeffress of the Miller Cassidy firm in Washington, who fought us with great skill, tooth and nail, all the way and earned the great respect of Judge Politz and everyone on our side.

I argued the *mandamus* petition against Bill Jeffress before a Fifth Circuit panel of Patrick Higginbotham, Emilio Garza and James Dennis, none of whom were on the Judicial Council. Higginbotham was one of the most respected judges on the circuit, with a national reputation that had earned him the prestigious Samuel E. Gates Award from the American College of Trial Lawyers.[134] He was also a very gracious person. While we were in the courtroom waiting for the judges to come on the bench—we were the only case on the docket that day—we were told that the court wanted to see us in the robing room. We went back there and found all three judges, in their robes, waiting for us. Judge Higginbotham welcomed us to the Fifth Circuit. He said they were pleased to have such distinguished counsel appear before the court, commented on what an interesting case it was, complimented us on the briefs we had written and told us how much they were looking forward to the oral argument we were about to have. With that we shook hands with all three judges and returned to the courtroom for a very lively argument that lasted well over an hour and a half.

Several months later the panel issued a lengthy and unanimous opinion. It granted the writ of *mandamus* and vacated the reassignment orders. Essentially the court held that neither Judge Buchmeyer nor the Judicial Council had the power to reassign the cases because of what the court found to be no more than a disagreement with Judge McBryde's substantive rulings.[135]

That was a big loss. But, meanwhile, acting under then 28 U.S.C. § 372 (now 28 U.S.C. § 351), we had been moving full speed ahead on the other front. Section 372 provides that if a person files a complaint alleging that a judge "has engaged in conduct prejudicial to the effective . . . administration of justice," the complaint goes to the Chief Judge of the circuit. Unless the Chief Judge finds the complaint is frivolous or "directly relates to the merits of a decision or procedural ruling,[136] he must appoint a special committee to investigate the complaint, consisting of himself, two circuit judges, and two district judges." The code provides that if a judge has engaged in conduct "prejudicial to the effective administration of justice," the committee can stop the assignment of cases to a judge "on a temporary basis for a time certain" and/or issue a public reprimand.

Two complaints had been filed against Judge McBryde in November 1995. One came from an attorney who claimed that McBryde's conduct during a trial had been "abusive and hostile." The other, which Judge Politz treated as a complaint, was a letter from the Department of Justice referencing his treatment of Arizona AUSA Cerow in the Satz case. Judge Politz's committee included Circuit Judges Eugene Davis of Louisiana and Robert Parker of Texas; and District Judges William Barbour of Mississippi and Edward Prado of Texas; in addition to himself.

Politz was concerned from the outset that McBryde's conduct in the Satz and Torres cases reflected a psychiatric problem. At his suggestion we sent transcripts and documents to two prominent psychiatrists for their review. One was Dr. Herbert Pardes, the dean of the Columbia University School of Medicine and chair of its Department of Psychiatry, who also directed psychiatric services at the Columbia-Presbyterian Hospital.[137] The other was Dr. Melvin Sabshin, chair of the American Psychiatric Association. They found sufficient basis to suggest that Judge McBryde should submit to a psychiatric examination.

We told Bill Jeffress the committee wanted McBryde to have a psychiatric test. Predictably, McBryde unequivocally refused. So, on behalf of the committee, we asked the Judicial Council to order him to do so, and the Council entered an order over McBryde's strenuous objection.

Judge McBryde then brought an action in the Northern District of Texas seeking declaratory and injunctive relief that the investigation under Section 372(c) was unconstitutional and that the Council's order that he undergo an examination was invalid.

During this time we had begun to learn about more incidents of abusive conduct by Judge McBryde towards litigants and lawyers in his courtroom. Talking with the special committee, we decided to defer pushing for a psychiatric exam. Instead we would proceed with a hearing before the committee and bring in witnesses to McBryde's behavior. We would retain a new psychiatrist to sit in on the hearings, hear the testimony and decide whether McBryde needed to be examined.

We notified Jeffress and Judge McBryde of that decision and, a month before the hearing, sent them a list of the witnesses who would testify and a brief summary of the subject matter. The hearing went forward in two stages. We put our witnesses up during the last week of August in New Orleans. A month later, from September 29 to October 2 in Fort Worth, the committee heard McBryde's witnesses. More than forty witnesses, including Judge McBryde himself, testified during those two weeks with direct and cross examinations conducted by Bill Wurtz, Michael Flynn, Art Burke[138] or myself. The new psychiatrist, Norman Osofsky, listened and took notes.

The complaining witnesses recounted some twenty incidents of McBryde's intimidation and abuse. Among them were:

- He had held an attorney in contempt of court for being too slow to start a conference call with him and opposing counsel when the problem was a phone system malfunction.
- After his chambers told a public defender that a deliberating jury had recessed for lunch, the defender left the courthouse. But the jury wasn't out to lunch; it reached a verdict, but the defender was unavailable for almost an hour. McBryde then ordered that the attorney, and every other attorney in the public defender's office, wait on his floor of the courthouse through jury deliberations in any case before him—including lunch breaks and recesses in deliberations. The order stayed in effect for sixteen months.
- The head of the Enforcement Division of the SEC testified that McBryde threatened him with sanctions because during settlement discussions with the defendant's counsel he would not agree that the enforcement order that had been negotiated would be placed under seal. He said McBryde angrily rejected his explanation that the need for public disclosure was a principle critical to the law enforcement efforts of the SEC, accused him of negotiating in bad faith and berated him to the point that he feared he would be held in contempt and jailed.
- A prisoner had sued the government for an injury suffered while playing baseball in the prison yard. Two government lawyers refused to make a settlement offer because they believed the suit was frivolous and wanted to discourage such suits in the future. McBryde ordered them to show cause why they should not be held in contempt for not negotiating in good faith. He then held a hearing in which he belittled and attacked the attorneys with sarcastic and abusive language, and questioned the integrity of the entire Civil Division of the U.S. Attorney's Office.
- McBryde had scheduled a pre-trial conference that included an attorney who was trying a case at the same time before a state judge and jury. The lawyer filed a

motion with McBryde in which he explained the situation and asked for a continuance. McBryde denied the motion. The state judge called McBryde to assure him that the attorney was in fact on trial before him. When McBryde failed to return the call, the judge told his jury to wait and his court reporter drove him to the federal courthouse so he could explain the situation to McBryde. At the judge's chambers he was sent to a conference room to wait with the lawyers in the pre-trial conference. Moments later an embarrassed law clerk came in to deliver a message: "Judge McBryde told me to tell you that you are not welcome here and you are to leave." Stunned, the state judge left after asking McBryde to release the lawyer as soon as possible since his jury was waiting.

The special committee also heard from attorneys who said they stifled their better litigation judgment, bypassing questions and foregoing arguments, because they felt intimidated by McBryde or feared he would undermine them openly before a jury.

When the hearings were over the special committee issued and sent to the Judicial Council a lengthy "Report and Recommendations." The incidents it chronicled formed the basis for recommending the most extreme sanctions that had ever been imposed upon any judge in any disciplinary proceeding since the Judicial Conduct and Disability Act became law in 1980.[139]

The committee of five judges emphasized the breadth of "Judge McBryde's negative effect on the Fort Worth legal community . . ." They knew the sanctions they suggested were severe, but they underscored the fact that McBryde's intemperate and abusive behavior could only be dealt with through the kind of disciplinary channel contemplated by the Act. The committee wrote that "the effect of Judge McBryde's pattern of conduct—the failure of lawyers to act; the decision to forgo asking questions or moving for relief; the sleepless nights; the refusal to accept cases; the decision to seek employment elsewhere; the compromising of advocacy as a form of self-protection—cannot be remedied through the appellate process and often cannot even be articulated in isolation. Nevertheless, the harm to the administration of justice is palpable and must be redressed."

The committee recommended that the Judicial Council publicly sanction McBryde "for conduct prejudicial to the effective and expeditious administration of the business of the courts within the Circuit," and that he be barred from taking new cases for a year.

Dr. Osofsky, meanwhile, concluded after the hearing sessions that McBryde needed to be examined for psychiatric problems. But he and the special committee agreed that an examination would be ineffective without McBryde's cooperation.

The Judicial Council acted on the last day of 1997. It rejected Judge McBryde's objections and entered an order imposing the recommended sanctions.

McBryde pursued two separate avenues of review. He first appealed to the Committee to Review Circuit Council Conduct and Disability Orders, an administrative tribunal appointed by Chief Justice Rehnquist to hear appeals from Judicial Council orders except issues raising constitutional questions.[140] He claimed that the sanctions were improperly based on the merits of his rulings, that the committee acted improperly in expanding the investigation to include matters that had not been the subject of a complaint and that the evidence was not sufficient to support the sanctions. When the review committee rejected those arguments in September 1998, I told the Dallas *Observer*, "We were very, very pleased by the decision."[141]

That put an end to the administrative case, but McBryde had also made constitutional arguments in a suit filed in the District Court for the District of Columbia. He claimed there that the only disciplinary remedy prescribed in the Constitution is impeachment by Congress, so allowing the judicial branch to discipline judges violates the separation of powers. He also argued that judicial independence rests primarily in the unfettered autonomy of individual judges and that no judge has the power to sanction any other judge for any kind of conduct. Judge Colleen Kollar-Kotelly of the D.C. District Court rejected these arguments as well,[142] and her opinion was upheld by the D.C. Court of Appeals in a two-to-one vote after oral arguments heard on Election Day, 2000.[143]

Of the team members who worked for the Fifth Circuit Judicial Council in this case, the real star was my partner Gordon Harriss. Chief Judge Politz and the other special committee members said time and again how much they admired his extraordinary intellect, both in guiding the steps taken during the investigation and in writing what turned out to be the winning briefs at all stages. Chief Judge Carolyn Dineen King recognized this by singling him out in a letter she wrote to the two of us on October 25, 2002 on behalf of the Judicial Council, after the case was over. She thanked us for our legal work "of superb quality." She added, "Best of all, you were wise counselors . . ." and went on to thank the many Davis Polk lawyers who worked with us on the case.

Judge Eugene Davis was grateful enough that he made a special trip to New York to thank Gordon for everything he'd done.

CHAPTER 51

Public Service While in Private Practice

IT WAS CLEAR to me that I had been selected by Judge Politz for the McBryde matter in large part because of my public profile resulting from my very recent Whitewater experience. That was a good demonstration of how government service not only raises your profile among potential private clients, but also produces opportunities while in private practice to serve in other public capacities. These inevitably address needs of the legal and other communities, as well as providing fresh challenges apart from the day-to-day demands of private practice. A number of these came my way thanks, I am convinced, to my government service.

NEW YORK STATE COMMISSION ON DRUGS AND THE COURTS

In 2000 the Chief Judge of the State of New York, Judith Kaye, asked me to chair a judicial commission to study the impact of drug cases on the New York courts. I worked for eight months with judges, court administrators, prosecutors, defense attorneys, substance abuse experts, academics and others from the private and public sectors to produce a report that made sweeping recommendations for a statewide expansion of drug treatment courts. DPW partner Carey Dunne served as Chief Counsel to the Commission and Angela Burgess, David Massey, Ola Rech and Brian Weinstein, all then DPW associates, served as Deputy Counsel.

The concept was that with the consent of the prosecutor, a non-violent person convicted of selling drugs to finance his or her own use—who might face up to six years in prison under the mandatory sentencing provisions of the Rockefeller drug laws of the 1970's—would be eligible for treatment instead of jail. If, after pleading guilty and receiving a deferred sentence, the defendant completed a two-year treatment program under court supervision, the plea would be vacated and the conviction expunged. The program was not for drug dealers, just for addicts selling for their own use. For such defendants, we concluded, treatment instead of jail would have three important consequences: it would save lives, reduce crime by significantly reducing the recidivism rate, and reduce state spending by saving some of the money spent incarcerating inmates.

The commission's report received front-page coverage in *The New York Times*, praise on editorial pages statewide and applause from the court system. Judge Kaye sent it to the National Association of State Judges and it became a model for similar programs in other states.

COMMISSION FOR THE REVIEW OF FBI SECURITY PROGRAMS

In March 2000 FBI Director Louis Freeh asked former Director William Webster to make recommendations for improving the agency's internal security following the arrest for treason of former special agent and counter-intelligence expert Robert Hanssen, who for over twenty years had given the Soviet Union valuable national security information. In response to that request Attorney General John Ashcroft appointed Judge Webster to head up a seven-member commission consisting of former Attorney General Griffin Bell; former Secretary of Defense William Cohen; former U.S. Trade Representative Carla Hills; former House Speaker Tom Foley; former Army Secretary Clifford Alexander, and myself.

We worked for two years and in April 2002 released a report recommending several steps. It called for the creation of a new security division reporting only to the Director with responsibility for restructuring the FBI's information security system and significantly tightening access within the Bureau to sensitive information. Other remedial steps included increased use of polygraphs and review of financial information for FBI employees.

ATTORNEY GENERAL CUOMO AND THE STATE POLICE INVESTIGATION

In March 2008, shortly after taking office following Elliot Spitzer's resignation, Governor David Patterson asked Andrew Cuomo, then New York's Attorney General, to investigate allegations that the state police harbored a rogue unit that was conducting political espionage against elected officials. Cuomo asked a former Assistant United States Attorney, Sharon McCarthy, to come in and lead the investigation working with lawyers in his office. He also asked Mike Armstrong, former counsel to the Knapp Commission that had investigated corruption in the New York City Police Department in the 1970's, and me to serve *pro bono* as "special advisors" to him on the investigation.

Mike and I, helped by DPW counsel Rebecca Winters and associate Jane Yoon, worked closely with Sharon and her team of investigators, met frequently with Cuomo's top advisors and Cuomo himself over an eighteen-month period. In September 2009 he issued a report that found "no significant evidence of wrongdoing by rank and file state troopers," but found repeated instances in which top officials at the agency had taken actions to benefit political figures.

NEW YORK STATE JUDICIAL COMPENSATION COMMISSION

For a period of twelve years, from 1999 to 2011, state judges in New York did not receive any increase in compensation—not even a cost of living adjustment. At New York's trial level, called the Supreme Court, a justice was earning the same $136,500 he or she had earned in 1999, an amount that because of inflation by 2011 had lost almost half of its purchasing power. New York was last among all fifty states in judicial compensation.

In 2010 the New York Court of Appeals held that the legislature's failure to remedy this situation—because legislation proposing judicial salary increases had been improperly linked to other unaccomplished legislative objectives, including legislative pay raises —was an unconstitutional violation of the separation of powers clause of the New York State Constitution. In response the legislature established a seven-member Commission on Judicial Compensation, with three members including the chair to be appointed by the Governor, two by the Chief Judge of the state, and one each by the temporary President of the Senate and the Speaker of the Assembly. The Commission was to recommend compensation levels for state judges for each of the four years beginning April 1, 2012. These would have the force of the law and, unless repealed by a specific act of the legislature, would go into effect on April 1, 2012. The bill also provided for similar commissions to be established every four years going forward.

Andrew Cuomo, now the governor, appointed William Thompson—former New York City controller and mayoral candidate—to chair the Commission. I was one of the two appointees by Chief Judge Jonathan Lippman; the other was Kathryn Wylde, President of the Partnership for New York City. The Governor's other appointees were Rick Cotton, General Counsel of NBC, and William Mulrow, Senior Managing Director of the Blackstone Group. Senate President Dean Skelos appointed his law partner, Mark Mulholland, and Assembly Speaker Sheldon Silver appointed James Tallon, President of the United Health Fund and a former member of the Assembly.

The Commission received numerous submissions from civic groups and bar associations and then held a one-day public hearing in Albany. Following the hearing, assisted by DPW counsel Rebecca Winters and associate Michael Scheinkman, I took the position that judges should be raised to $195,734 in 2012, the level they would have reached if they had received costs of living increases every year since 1999. I pointed out that each judge had lost over $300,000 in twelve years without cost of living increases and said, "We cannot give them the $300,000 back, but we can put them in a position where they will not lose any more."

A majority of the Commission—James Tallon and the Governor's three appointees—relied heavily on testimony from the State Budget Director as to the State's economic hardship and rejected that approach. They voted to award a three-step increase that by 2014 would put the state judges at $174,500, the same level as their counterparts in the federal system. I could not argue that an increase to the federal level was unreasonable, but I said I did think it was unreasonable to make the state judges wait until the third year to get there. Kathryn Wylde and Mark Mulholland joined with me in that position, so the final result—by a four to three margin—was a 27 percent pay increase, going from $160,000 in 2012 to $174,000 in 2014.

Chief Judge Lippman issued a statement to the State's judges after our report was released. He said that while the increase was not what he had hoped for, or what he believed was fair, "the nightmare is over and the miserable situation that we have endured for so long will shortly be a thing of the past." He also commended the fact that there was now in place, through the establishment of the commission structure, a process by which in the future political figures would be required to evaluate judicial salaries on a regular basis.

—⚜—

All four of these experiences presented interesting and stimulating challenges, and it was gratifying for me to be able, in each case, to make a significant contribution to the resolution of an important public issue. I am confident I would never had any of those opportunities if I had not had public service experience and credentials.

I was also fortunate to be able to serve my town of Darien. For 13 years, I was a member (and for the last 4 the Chairman) of the Darien Police Commission, which selects, promotes and supervises the 50 member Police force. And for 6 years (the last 3 as President) I served on the Darien Land Trust, which over the years has acquired and preserved (through ownership or conservation easements) over 200 acres of open land in Darien.

CHAPTER 52

The Suzuki Samurai:
Kathryn Rodriguez v. Suzuki

ONE OF THE FEATURES, if not peculiarities, of our court system in the United States is that given appeals, remands, and the generally but necessarily slow pace of appellate rulings, cases can linger far beyond the events that triggered them. They can outlive the need for actions originally sought by plaintiffs and fought by defendants. But they're often brought for other reasons in the first place—for business survival, for example—or to establish principles that guide future jurisprudence.

I was involved at the appellate level in a pair of such cases that set Japan's Suzuki Motor Corporation against Consumers Union, the organization that publishes *Consumer Reports*.

In 1985 Suzuki produced what was essentially the first sports utility vehicle, the Suzuki Samurai. Priced at $6,200 the little SUV became an instant hit, especially in California and Arizona. It was light and came with an optional convertible soft and hard top, and offered excellent four-wheel drive off-road performance. Suzuki sold 47,000 Samurais in the first year, with sales increasing to 150,000 by 1988.

Then in July 1988 *Consumer Reports* came out with an article headlined "Warning: The Suzuki rolls over too easily." The article described a test conducted by Consumers Union in which its drivers drove the Samurai through a double lane-change avoidance maneuver. The Samurai tipped up onto outriggers attached to the vehicle for safety reasons, leading to the judgment that "the Suzuki Samurai is so likely to roll over during a maneuver that could be demanded of any car at any time that it is unfit for its intended use." It slapped the Samurai with its worst rating: Not Acceptable.

This article destroyed the car's commercial viability. Sales plummeted, and by 1995 the Samurai was withdrawn from the market. In the meantime Suzuki had been hit with a wave of 240 lawsuits based upon accidents where the Samurai had rolled over, with 8,200 injuries and 213 deaths reported—to the point where the company's financial viability was threatened. The most serious of these was a case brought in St. Louis County, Missouri by Kathryn Rodriguez.

Rodriguez was one of three young women who left St. Louis on a Sunday morning in February 1990, headed west for an outing to the wineries located in Herman,

Consumer Reports, *July 1998*

Missouri. She and Lisa Nunnally were passengers in a Samurai driven by their friend Deborah Dubis. The women arrived at the Hermannhof Winery in the early afternoon and spent about an hour and a half sampling several wines. Dubis drank at least three sampler glasses and two full-sized glasses of wine totaling about half a bottle. Rodriguez and Nunnally also each had several glasses of wine.

When the winery closed they decided to go on to another winery located in St. Charles County. They proceeded west on Highway 94 with Dubis at the wheel, Rodriguez in the front seat and Nunnally in back. After traveling a few miles the vehicle went off the right side of the road, traveled about ninety feet in a ditch and struck an embankment—a dirt "headwall" extending down into the ditch from a cemetery driveway. What happened next was disputed. According to the driver and passengers the Samurai returned to the roadway, crossed the center line, and when Dubis turned sharply right to correct, the vehicle rolled over. According to Suzuki the Samurai never returned to the roadway. Instead the impact with the headwall launched it into the air over the cemetery driveway, where it landed in the ditch and rolled. Rodriguez was thrown from the car and sustained serious permanent injuries that made her a quadriplegic, paralyzed from the mid-chest down.

Rodriguez sued Suzuki in the Circuit Court of the City of St. Louis using Jim Butler of Atlanta, a flamboyant and successful plaintiff's product liability lawyer. Among his high-profile verdicts against automobile companies, the most noteworthy was a $105 million verdict against General Motors for the death of a driver who burned alive when his pick-up truck was hit by a GM truck that caught fire after the collision.[144]

His case against Suzuki was based largely on the Consumers Union findings. He also introduced communications between Suzuki and General Motors, which had considered marketing the Samurai under one of its brands. Butler argued that Suzuki knew that GM had rejected the Samurai because of rollover concerns and had gone ahead and marketed the vehicle itself without making the modifications GM had said were needed to deal with the problem. And he used an accident reconstruction expert, Dr. Andrzej G. Nalecz, to support his claim that the Samurai had returned to the road after hitting the headwall and overturned when Dubis turned the wheel to correct.

After a trial of several weeks the jury returned a verdict of $90 million, $30 million in compensatory damages and $60 million in punitive damages. Missouri is a comparative negligence state. The jury assessed the fault as all Suzuki's, placing no responsibility on Dubis or Rodriguez.[145]

Suzuki's lawyers included Ken Starr and Paul Cappuccio from Kirkland & Ellis in Washington, D.C., Carter Phillips and Gene Schaerr from Sidley & Austin in Washington, and Frank Gundlach and Jordan Cherrick from Armstrong & Teasdale in St. Louis. They came up with a strategy to take the appeal directly to the Missouri Supreme Court, which they felt would be a more favorable forum than the intermediate appellate court.[146]

The Missouri Constitution provided that "the Supreme Court shall have exclusive jurisdiction in all cases involving the validity of . . . a statute . . . of this state." Suzuki challenged the constitutionality of three statutes, all of which related to the punitive damage claim, on the ground that they violated the Due Process Clause by giving the jury unlimited discretion in assessing punitive damages.

The Missouri Supreme Court accepted the appeal based upon the challenge to those three statutes. But in the brief and in the oral argument, the appeal was based primarily on two non-constitutional arguments.

Suzuki's brief said the trial court had erred by excluding evidence of the wine drinking by Dubis and Rodriguez. Under Missouri law evidence of a driver's alcohol consumption was admissible only if coupled with evidence of erratic driving or some other circumstance that might suggest that the driver was impaired when the accident occurred. The rationale, stemming from the *Doisy v. Edwards* case in 1968, was that a mere reference to drinking could prejudicially and improperly enflame the jury. It meant that the courts required some evidence that the drinking had had an impact before they would allow it to be admitted. Suzuki argued that the evidence had met that standard.

Suzuki also claimed that the court had given the jury the wrong instruction when it said punitive damages could be based on a "preponderance of the evidence." Such damages are imposed to punish and deter, the company said, and because the remedy is extraordinarily harsh a higher standard—"clear and convincing evidence"—should be required.

After Rodriguez, now represented by Butler and a highly regarded appellate specialist, Maurice Graham of St. Louis, had filed her opposition brief, George Ball, general counsel of Suzuki, approached me and asked if I would come into the case. He explained that Suzuki's financial survival was at stake and it wanted to send a strong message that it would fight these cases to the bitter end. The spearhead of this strategy was getting the Rodriguez case reversed. I agreed to argue the appeal, and to take a leadership role in formulating Suzuki's overall strategy in defending the rollover cases. Davis Polk associates Frances Bivens—now a partner—and Mike Quinn—now a litigation counsel at Time Warner Cable—helped with the reply brief and the argument. Partner Michael Carroll and Counsel Sharon Katz, later to become a partner, helped with the overall strategy planning.

The Rodriguez jury had obviously agreed with the plaintiff's version of the accident sequence. That scenario fit with the Consumers Union conclusion that the Samurai was likely to roll over during extreme corrective maneuvers. We wanted to revisit that question on appeal. If the Samurai launched into the air after it hit the headwall and rolled when it landed in the ditch there would be no basis to impose any liability on Suzuki because, as its lawyers had argued, any vehicle would have rolled under those circumstances.

Suzuki had prepared a video of crash testing by a Suzuki expert. It showed several different types of vehicles going through the same sequence as Dubis' Samurai and rolling after impact with the ditch. The trial court had excluded the video. We argued this was an additional error and told the Supreme Court Clerk's office that we wanted to play the video at the oral argument. This had never been done before in the Missouri Supreme Court and the Clerk told us we would have to make a special application. We made the application and it was granted, but not until the morning of the argument.[147]

I argued the appeal against Maurice Graham, using the video, as well as several poster boards to demonstrate the accident sequence. It was a lively argument, with a number of questions to both of us throughout. When it was over I was cautiously optimistic that we would win—and we did. On December 17, 1996 the Missouri Supreme Court, by a vote of six to one, reversed the judgment and sent the case back for a new trial.[148]

The court's main reason for reversing was that the evidence of wine drinking had been excluded. The court held that while the Doisy standard may have been appropriate when Missouri was a contributory negligence state, it had been a comparative negligence state since 1983. Therefore, "since the apportionment of fault and damages is factual by nature, a jury should be as fully informed as possible in order to determine the relative fault of the parties." That meant a new standard: "Evidence of alcohol consumption is admissible if otherwise relevant and material." Having established that standard the Supreme Court had little trouble deciding that evidence of Dubis' wine drinking should have been admitted. Secondly, the court accepted our argument that the punitive damage instruction should have required "clear and convincing evidence," not simply a preponderance. The court never reached any of the constitutional arguments.

When the case went back for a new trial George Ball brought in a new team of trial lawyers from California. But while Suzuki had new lawyers, it still had the same judge, whose rulings in the first trial Suzuki felt were biased in favor of Rodriguez. The result was not much better in the new trial. Butler used essentially the same evidence. Even with the evidence of the wine drinking admitted and the "clear and convincing" evidence instruction given as to punitive damages, Butler won a verdict of $25 million compensatory damages and $11.9 million punitive. The jury assessed fault at 99.85 percent for Suzuki, 0.15 percent for Dubis and zero for Rodriguez.[149]

Once again, George Ball asked me to handle the appeal. Again we went straight to the Missouri Supreme Court, raising the same constitutional issues that were raised but not decided in the first appeal. Two other Davis Polk associates, Jennifer Newstead[150] and Laura McNeill,[151] worked with me this time around. As in the first appeal we primarily argued improper evidentiary rulings made during the trial. The first was the trial court's exclusion of affirmative evidence supporting Suzuki's position. The second was a restriction on the cross examination of Rodriguez' expert, Dr. Nalecz.

The excluded evidence consisted of a series of official reports from the United States National Highway Transportation Safety Administration (NHTSA) and the British Transport and Road Research Laboratory (TRRL) that criticized the Consumers Union "modified accident avoidance maneuver" that had been used to create the unacceptable rating for the Samurai. These reports concluded that the test "did not have a scientific basis and cannot be linked to real-world crash avoidance needs or actual crash data." The trial court had excluded these conclusions and opinions as hearsay.

The cross examination issue with Dr. Nalecz related to the computer simulation he had designed to present Rodriguez' reconstruction of the accident sequence as she claimed it occurred. He called it the "Advanced Dynamics Vehicle Simulation," or ADVS. Suzuki's trial counsel had attempted to cross examine Nalecz, a former university professor, about two memoranda he had written. One, from 1992, questioned the ADVS as a tool for investigating "the handling behavior and stability of modern vehicles which use the latest technologies." The other, from 1993, agreed that the ADVS had been discredited in other studies and was "practically useless" since no one could use it effectively. The trial court sustained Butler's objection to Suzuki's line of cross examination questioning, and the introduction of the memoranda, on the ground that ADVS had been modified to eliminate the problems. The court refused to allow Suzuki's counsel to confront Nalecz with evidence that the new ADVS contained virtually the same deficiencies.

We recognized going into the argument that it was a highly unusual situation. Frank Gundlach of St. Louis said it was unprecedented in his experience. The Missouri Supreme Court only had jurisdiction because of the alleged constitutional invalidity of the three punitive damage statutes. They had reversed the first judgment on evidentiary rulings without any discussion of the constitutional issues during the argument, and without reaching them in their opinion—and now we were asking them to do that again.

I thought I needed to do something to stimulate the court's interest in what was going to be—again—a solely evidentiary argument. To that end, I thought it was important to say why we were back in front of the Supreme Court. So, I opened my argument by saying,

> "The cardinal principle of this Court's opinion reversing the judgment in the first trial was that 'a jury should be as fully informed as possible in order to determine the relative fault of the parties.' Unfortunately, Mr. Butler[152] and I are back here a second time because the trial court failed to follow this basic instruction."

I then proceeded to make the argument on the two evidentiary issues we had emphasized in the brief. This time the argument was more one-sided. The court gave Butler a hard time in his defense of the trial court's rulings, and it was not a surprise when on June 1, 1999 the Supreme Court, again by a six-to-one margin, reversed the judgment based on these two issues.[153]

The court acknowledged that the NHTSA reports were hearsay, but concluded they were admissible under the express provisions of a Missouri statute that made admissible "all records and exemplifications of office books, kept in any public office of the United States, or of a sister state." This language, said the court, was all-encompassing, making no exception for opinions or conclusions as the trial court had ruled.

The court also held that it was an abuse of the trial court's discretion to limit the cross examination of Dr. Nalecz. "The error committed in this instance," said the court, "compounds the error in disallowing the government reports and reconfirms the earlier conclusion that the reversal is required."

As had been the case the first time the Court did not reach the constitutional issues. This produced a lengthy and vehement dissent from Judge Ronnie White. He had dissented the first time, largely on the basis that the new rules resulting from the majority's rulings should have been applied only prospectively. In this dissent Judge White lashed out at the majority for having taken the appeal in the first place, claiming that the constitutional challenges were "tenuous" and a "pretext" and did not present the requisite "real and substantial controversy" to confer jurisdiction on the court. He also sharply criticized both of the majority's substantive rulings.[154]

After this second reversal the Chief Administrative Judge with responsibility for the Circuit Court in St. Louis had had enough. He summoned Butler and George Ball to his chambers and told them that the court was not going to go through this a third time. He told them to settle it. And under his supervision Butler and Ball arrived at a settlement for an amount that remains confidential, but which Suzuki felt was fair and reasonable.

That result in the Rodriguez case emerged as a turning point in Suzuki's fight against the rollover cases. Meanwhile in 1996, while the first appeal in Rodriguez was still pending, George Ball had decided to take on Consumers Union over the testing methodology that had produced the original article that had so devastated Suzuki in both showrooms and courtrooms around the country. I eventually became involved in that litigation as well.

CHAPTER 53

The Suzuki Samurai:
Suzuki v. Consumers Union

THE CONSUMERS UNION Automotive Testing Division (ATD) conducted its first test of the Samurai on April 20, 1988. The Suzuki SUV was among a group that included the Jeep Cherokee, Isuzu Trooper II and Jeep Wrangler. The test occurred on the ATD's standard long course, a double lane change avoidance maneuver test course that Consumers Union had used since 1973. The course was designed to replicate an emergency situation in which a driver suddenly steers a vehicle left into the opposing lane to avoid an obstacle and quickly back into the original lane to avoid oncoming traffic.

Several Consumers Union personnel attended the April 20 test, including Robert Knoll, the head of the ATD, Dr. R. David Pittle, Consumers Union's Technical Director and Senior Vice-President, and Irwin Landau, the Editorial Director of *Consumer Reports*. Landau had been assigned as the initial writer and editor of the article that would report the test results.

Consumers Union driver Kevin Sheehan drove the Samurai first, putting it through the course sixteen times at speeds reaching over fifty miles per hour. The Samurai did not tip onto two wheels during Sheehan's runs. His evaluation notes read: "rubbery, slow response, rocks a bit, but never felt like it would tip over."

A Consumers Union driver named Small drove the Samurai next. He went through the course twenty-one times at speeds similar to those achieved by Sheehan. Again, there were no tip-ups.

Pittle took the wheel after Sheehan and Small had completed their test runs. He was not a test driver, but he began to drive the Samurai through the long course because, he said, he had never driven a small SUV and wanted to get a feel for how it handled. Pittle drove the course ten times. On his tenth run the Samurai tipped up onto two wheels. Pittle said he hadn't set out to cause the Samurai to tip up, and he'd been startled by it.

After the long course testing, Knoll redesigned Consumers Union's avoidance course to replicate the situation that caused the tip-up. This new modified short course shortened the distance for the first lane change and moved the obstacle to be avoided three feet to the left, guaranteeing sharper and more violent turns. This was the first time in years of testing vehicles on the long course that Consumers Union had ever used a shorter course.

Consumers Union ran tests on the new course on April 26 and May 12, 1988. Both times the Samurai tipped up on one of the runs.

Then came the July issue of *Consumer Reports* carrying the article and the "Not Acceptable" rating that caused Suzuki's sales to tank. The article described the steps Consumers Union took to test the Samurai, the Isuzu and the two Jeep models. After detailing other evidence of the Samurai's safety problems, the article then described the long course testing noting that Pittle, "a staff member who does not normally drive the course," tipped the Samurai after making "a slight steering misjudgment" that should not have "put daylight under the tires of any car." The article continued by highlighting the results of both short course tests and concluded with its damning judgment.

Almost eight years later, in early 1996, with the Samurai now off the market, George Ball retained Louise LaMothe, a California lawyer, to bring a product disparagement suit against Consumers Union in the Central District of California where Suzuki's headquarters were located. *Consumer Reports* had published a sixtieth anniversary issue that month that recounted the Samurai episode, which reset the statute of limitations clock. Consumers Union moved to dismiss the complaint for failing to state a cause of action, and the motion was granted by District Judge Alice Marie Stotler. George Ball brought us into the case at that point. We filed an amended complaint, which survived a second motion to dismiss.

My partner Michael Carroll took the lead in this assignment. He retained Kroll Associates, which sent an investigator named Adam Deutsch to interview former Consumers Union employees who had been involved in the testing. What emerged was a conversation that cast doubt on Consumers Union's objectivity. Ronald Denison told Michael and Deutsch that during the initial long course testing he had overheard Landau, the *Consumer Reports* Editorial Director, tell driver Kevin Sheehan, "If you can't find someone to roll this car, I will." Mike also developed evidence that suggested a reason: Consumers Union had incurred substantial debt for a new headquarters and was overextended. It needed a blockbuster story to raise its financial profile and increase donations, and it had used the Samurai rollover story in its fundraising solicitations.

Mike obtained more incriminating evidence in the video tapes of the actual testing. Pittle's drive that put the Samurai on two wheels was accompanied by victory shouts. One onlooker yelled, "Yeah!" Another shouted, "I think I got that. I think I got that." On the first day of the short course testing, when Sheehan tipped up the Samurai on his final run, Knoll was heard on the tape saying, "That's it. That looked pretty good." And when Rick Small tipped up the Samurai on his second run, Consumers Union technician Joseph Nappi was heard on the tape saying, "All right, Ricky baby!" Finally, on the last day of testing, during a run before the one that produced a tip-up, Pittle said in what sounded like despair, "Can't you just see it, we get no lift off the ground. Oh God."

After discovery was completed Consumers Union moved for summary judgment. It argued that under the relevant legal standard a reasonable jury could not conclude that it acted with actual malice. We argued that a jury could find malice at three stages—the background comments that suggested the tests were rigged,[155] Consumers Union's need for a blockbuster story to raise its revenues and the organization's refusal to reconsider the reliability of its testing despite NHTSA's conclusion that the "test procedures . . . . do not have a scientific basis and cannot be linked to real-world crash avoidance needs, or actual crash data."[156] Judge Stotler, however, granted the motion.

She ruled that based on information Consumers Union had gathered before the testing began it had developed concerns about the safety of the Samurai[157] and that this was "not an impermissible mindset for a publisher, particularly one which proclaims its mission as protecting the consumer." And she dismissed the fact that Consumers Union had ignored NHTSA's findings, saying "part of the First Amendment's protection has to do with disagreeing with the government."[158]

Suzuki appealed Judge Stotler's decision to the Ninth Circuit Court of Appeals, and I argued the appeal before a panel consisting of Judges Tashima, Graber and Ferguson. The argument was in February 2002 and the decision came down in June—a two-to-one reversal of the District Court.[159] Judge Tashima wrote the opinion, joined by Judge Graber, with a strong dissent by Judge Ferguson. The majority held that:

> ". . . [A]lthough the dissent provides a plausible view of the evidence—that CU acted in good faith as a skeptical consumer watchdog should—it is not our role, at this stage, to take sides in this way. As we discuss below, there is also another plausible view of the summary judgment record—that CU 'rigged' a test to achieve a predetermined result in order to serve its own pecuniary interests. Because a jury would be entitled to believe the latter view of the evidence, Suzuki's case survives summary judgment."[160]

The majority found that Suzuki had met the standard for actual malice—whether the defendant had "a high degree of awareness of probable falsity."

Judge Ferguson's dissent criticized the majority for not applying the independent examination rule, which in a First Amendment case requires an appellate court to independently review the whole record "so as to assure (itself) that the judgment does not constitute a forbidden intrusion on the field of free expression" (*The New York Times v. Sullivan*). His disagreement with the majority was that it had not tried to determine which of the two explanations for the short course testing—Suzuki's or Consumers Union's—was more plausible; it had left that to the jury.[161] Judge Ferguson said that is exactly what the "independent examination" rule required, and when he applied the rule, he found that "the actions and words of Consumers Union were appropriate."[162] He found that "at most the comments of Consumers Union employees give rise to an inference of bias against the Samurai." But he noted, "Bias alone cannot support a finding of actual malice," since Consumers Union had disclosed its course changes and given reasons that

> ". . . are completely consistent with the benign explanation that they were simply seeking confirmation of the existing accusations of rollover propensity against the Samurai, which it had exhibited in the early stages of testing."[163]

Consumers Union filed a petition for rehearing *en banc*. Almost a year went by. Then on May 19, 2003 an opinion came down denying the petition. It was a close vote, fourteen to thirteen, with a long and vociferous dissent by Judge Kozinski.[164]

Like Judge Ferguson his principal quarrel with the majority opinion was that, in his view, while recognizing the validity of the independent examination rule after a verdict, it refused to apply it at the summary judgment stage:

> "The practical effect of the panel's decision is that our review for sufficiency at summary judgment is now governed by one standard, while our review after a jury verdict is governed by another. Cases will now often proceed to trial, even though the court can tell ahead of time that the plaintiff's evidence will not support a jury verdict under New York Times."[165]

He then proceeded to analyze the full record under the independent examination rule and, again like Judge Ferguson, concluded that the evidence was insufficient to demonstrate actual malice. With regard to the change to the short course, he said:

> ". . . Even assuming CU wanted to make the Samurai tip and designed its short course to achieve that result, so what? The fact remains that the Samurai did

tip—several times—while every other vehicle run through the same course did not tip even once. This is certainly something consumers would want to know before deciding which of these vehicles to put their families in."[166]

And he dismissed the comments made during the testing, which he called "fleeting remarks"—three of which were "no more than inane schadenfreude"—as insufficient to support a finding of actual malice." He continued, "If a tabloid sends an investigator to dig up dirt on a celebrity, the fact that it deliberately attempts to find damaging information and is pleased when it succeeds hardly proves it's lying. Forcing CU to stand trial for statements that show nothing more than bias ignores these settled First Amendment principles."[167]

Our razor-thin Ninth Circuit victory brought us to the next question: would the Supreme Court take the case? It seemed likely that it would. Consumers Union's petition for *certiorari* was supported by an *amicus* brief submitted by twenty-four news organizations, including *The New York Times*, *The Washington Post*, *The Wall Street Journal*, *Time* and *Newsweek*. *Newsweek* warned that if the decision stands, "virtually any product evaluation is at risk, and this valuable journalistic genre is seriously compromised." And on October 31, 2003, the day the Supreme Court was scheduled to decide the petition, the *Times* ran an editorial urging the court to take the case. Under the headline, "A Crucial Case for the Supreme Court," the editorial stated:

> "The [Ninth Circuit's] refusal to reject this flimsy libel case and avoid an expensive jury trial has set an awful First Amendment precedent that threatens to chill reporting about important public issues, especially health and safety.
>
> Left to stand, the Ninth Circuit's standard for getting libel cases dismissed before trial would wreck the protective framework of Times v. Sullivan and its progeny. For the sake of free speech, not to mention consumer safety, this is one case the Supreme Court must not pass up."

But the justices apparently were not listening. *Certiorari* was denied, and the case was now back before Judge Stotler for trial.[168] At that point, George Ball decided to bring in a California lawyer, Marshall Grossman, to try the case.

But there never was a trial. Judge Stotler told the parties that she had serious doubts about whether Suzuki had suffered any meaningful damages within the statute of limitations period. The rapid fall-off in sales had happened earlier, after the 1988 article, not in the five years before the 1996 anniversary article that reset the clock. She suggested to Consumers Union that it file another motion for summary judgment on that issue. With this development, the Suzuki management in Japan apparently had had enough and they instructed Ball to settle the case.

Suzuki and Consumers Union reached an agreement in 2004. The settlement contained a "clarification" by Consumers Union to the effect that "CU's 1996 statement that the 1988 Samurai 'easily rolls over in turns' was limited to the severe turns in CU's short course avoidance maneuver. Consumers Union never intended to state or imply that the Samurai rolls over easily in routine driving conditions." The clarification was part of a joint announcement that stated the obvious: "CU and Suzuki disagree with the validity of CU's short course avoidance maneuver in tests of the Samurai in 1988."

So, the long and hard-fought battle was over at last. By that time in 2004 Suzuki had weathered the storm. The Samurai rollover cases had all been settled for amounts that the company could live with, and for a time Suzuki was selling a whole new generation of SUVs. However, following a plummeting drop in auto sales after the 2008 financial crisis, the company's American automobile arm filed for bankruptcy in 2012 and announced it was withdrawing from the U.S. auto market.

CHAPTER 54

Pete Nicholas and Boston Scientific

AS I HAD LEARNED years earlier in the Richardson-Merrell thalidomide case, commercial needs and medical prudence often are at war with one another when it comes to putting, or keeping, products or devices on the market. Such a case came my way again in the late 1990's, and threatened to embroil an entrepreneur and a major philanthropist.

Peter Nicholas was the son of a navy submarine captain who served with distinction in World War II. Pete graduated from Duke University after which he also joined the U.S. Navy. From there he graduated from the Wharton Business School at the University of Pennsylvania and in 1979 co-founded the Boston Scientific Corporation (BSC), a manufacturer of medical devices. Under his leadership BSC grew from a small start-up company to a global corporation with over 16,000 employees. He also became one of the country's top twenty-five philanthropists as listed by *Fortune Magazine*. He joined Duke's Board of Trustees in 1993, and later became its Chairman. He endowed the university's Multi-Disciplinary School of Environmental Studies and became one of Duke's largest financial contributors.

In August 1998 BSC brought onto the market a stent designed to prop open clogged coronary arteries and prevent heart attacks. The stent, called "NIR ON Ranger with Sox," was deployed by a balloon catheter delivery device onto which the stent was "crimped." The balloon was inflated, causing the stent to be expanded and implanted in the artery wall, after which the balloon was deflated and withdrawn, leaving behind the implanted stent to hold open the artery. The stent was designed and manufactured by a German company, Medinol. BSC was responsible for its distribution and sale.

In late August 1998 BSC received some reports from the field of "pinholes" that caused the balloon to leak during the stent implantation. The company investigated and concluded from doctor reports that it was not a safety problem. The overwhelming majority told BSC that the pinhole problem was minor and manageable, and that the stent was vastly superior to other stents available. Nonetheless, in mid-September, the BSC internal Field Action Committee (FAC) that had conducted the investigation recommended to Nicholas, then the CEO, that BSC withdraw the product temporarily until a definitive solution to the pinhole problem could be found. Nicholas immediately accepted the recommendation.

BSC informed its partner Medinol of its decision. Medinol's owners, Kobi Richter and his wife, "opposed fiercely" the BSC decision, and a long and extremely contentious conference call between them and several BSC executives, including Nicholas, resulted. The Richters emphasized the superior safety record of the Ranger with Sox over all other stents on the market and argued that BSC would be doing a disservice to its patients by withdrawing it. Dr. Martin Leon, Medinol's medical consultant and one of the most prominent international cardiologists in the country, agreed with them. As the conference call went on and became more heated, to break the impasse, Nicholas suggested they take the issue to the FDA. As he put it they faced an "enormous dilemma"—a "super-safe, super-effective device" with a problem in the manufacturing. He proposed that they tell the FDA, "We want to fix it, we want to do the right thing . . . Help us think it through." He did not know at the time that the Richters had taped the conversation.[169]

Everyone agreed that was the right course: to seek the FDA's advice while leaving the product on the market. Boston Scientific contacted the FDA, set up a conference call for September 21 and explained the issue on that call. But while the FDA was still pondering the matter, Nicholas became concerned that more negative reports were coming in. Some doctors were switching to other stents, and the manufacturing problems continued. So, on October 3, in a conference call with the members of the FAC, he told them he'd decided to withdraw the product. BSC did so promptly and issued a recall notice for all the stents that were out in the field.

The United States Attorney in Boston subsequently opened a criminal investigation. Michael Loucks and Jim Arnold in the office's Health Care Fraud Unit clearly had both the company and Pete Nicholas in their sights. They took the position that the continued shipments of the stent after the pinhole issue surfaced violated Section 301(a) of the Food Drug & Cosmetic Act, which prohibits the shipment of an "adulterated" product.

Bob Keefe, Karen Green and Steve Jonas of Hale & Dorr were representing BSC and they asked me to come in and represent Nicholas. Jack Cooney and Brian Weinstein, then a rising star associate at Davis Polk, worked on it with me.

We knew it would be difficult to persuade the U.S. Attorney's Office that the product was not, in fact, adulterated. During the call with the Richters, BSC's Vice-President for Regulatory Affairs had written that word on a blackboard as a message to Pete Nicholas and Nicholas had said, ". . . we're agonizing over this because we . . . find ourselves in a situation where we're in violation of the code and we're in fact shipping adulterated product and we cannot do that."

But we had what we believed was an overpowering argument that prosecuting Nicholas would be a gross miscarriage of justice.

Top officials in the Boston U.S. Attorney's Office were reviewing the matter. We pointed out to them that Nicholas's actions were those of a responsible executive acting in good faith. He commissioned an internal investigation as soon as he learned of the pinhole problem. And when the FAC came to him in September with the recommendation that the stents be withdrawn—in what we called "the defining moment in the case," he did not try to buy more time but immediately and unhesitatingly said yes. He only proposed that they go to the FDA after the Richters went ballistic in insisting that the product not be withdrawn. During that same phone call Boston Scientific's outside counsel Larry Pilot had advised that seeking the FDA's advice "will satisfy our regulatory interest." And finally, Nicholas had initiated the withdrawal on his own after receiving additional adverse information while the FDA was still considering the matter.

Nicholas was clearly trying to "do the right thing." But we had an additional and equally powerful argument as well. In order to obtain the Richters's testimony against Nicholas, AUSAs Loucks and Arnold had granted them immunity from prosecution. We told the officials reviewing the case that targeting Nicholas, who wanted to withdraw the stents, while immunizing the Richters, who insisted that they not be withdrawn, "would stand this case on its head."

These arguments carried the day and what would have been a grossly unfair indictment of a very fine man was avoided.

The case against BSC was resolved civilly with BSC paying $74 million to the government.

CHAPTER 55

Burlington Resources

RUSTY HARDIN OF HOUSTON had lived up to his considerable reputation when he made David Hale's lawyer blink after I brought him into Whitewater. We had kept in touch and in October 1998 he called to describe a Wyoming case with which he thought his client might need some help.

Rusty represented a Houston oil and gas company called Burlington Resources. The U.S. Attorney in Wyoming had launched a grand jury investigation into its payment of extraction royalties owed the government. The Denver office of the SEC was also looking at the matter. Rusty said that because of the breadth and complexity of the issues the company felt it needed additional resources and wanted to bring in a large firm with expertise in criminal investigations to work with him. He had recommended us, but said Burlington was also considering other firms and its general counsel, Rick Plaeger, would be coming to New York with him to interview the candidates. He asked if I was interested. I said yes.

Cindy O'Hagan, one of our best associates,[170] put together the background information that enabled me to talk effectively about the issues. With that—and I suspect some back-channel support from Rusty—Burlington chose us. I enlisted Raul Yanes, a senior associate later to become a partner, and two junior associates, Scott Klugman and Mark Mermelstein, and we started dealing with the government offices involved.

Earlier, before we or Rusty had become involved, the AUSA heading up the investigation had told the outside counsel then representing Burlington that he believed the company had defrauded the government. He said it had intentionally and systematically underpaid the royalties it owed on oil and gas taken from government land it leased in Wyoming. Indeed, in the fall of 1998, he had sent the company an agreement calling for a guilty plea and a fine of $35 million to $50 million. It was at that point that the general counsel met with the President and CEO of Burlington, Bobby Shackouls, and they decided that they needed to change their approach to the federal investigation and change their external legal representation. Plaeger recommended that they assemble a team of experienced counsel with the ability to effectively communicate with the

289

government—and, if necessary, with a jury—concerning complex mineral law issues, and with the experience to handle a complex federal criminal law investigation. Burlington brought in Rusty and us and recruited a veteran litigator, Reagan Kott, to join their in-house legal team. It also retained Barry Mabry and Butch Kirby of Ernst & Young as experts in federal mineral royalty accounting.

As we dug into it we learned the story went back years, to 1951 and the discovery by the Burlington Northern Railway of oil on its land.

After the discovery Burlington Northern established a subsidiary, Milestone Petroleum Inc. (Milestone), to manage and develop its oil and gas properties. In 1985 Milestone's name was changed to Meridian Oil Inc. (MOI). MOI served as the management entity for all the properties in which Milestone had an interest. At the same time Meridian Oil Trading Inc. (MOTI) was formed as a subsidiary to market what came out of Burlington Northern's producing affiliates. MOTI would purchase MOI's gas production at the wellhead and market it for resale.

The AUSA handling the matter early on was named Lee Pico. He claimed that in calculating royalties to be paid to the government Burlington would use the price paid by MOTI to MOI at the wellhead, even though MOTI was reselling the oil and gas at a higher price. He said that MOTI performed no legitimate economic function and was a "sham," "paper" or "straw" company.

Shortly after we came into the case Robert Murray replaced Pico as the lead AUSA. Murray had played football for the University of Wyoming and rode Brahma bulls and horses in rodeos on weekends. This put him in Rusty's league as a colorful performer, and we all spent a lot of time rating the entertainment potential of a jury trial in Cheyenne featuring these two combatants. Of course, our clients were not interested in being the subject of an entertaining jury trial. They wanted the investigation resolved without an indictment.

Over the months that followed we dealt several times with Murray and with the two SEC lawyers from Denver who were pursuing what they felt were serious accounting issues. One of them called it "voodoo accounting."[171] They were particularly critical of Burlington's policy of paying royalties based on its estimates of production at the wellhead and then, when the actual production turned out to be higher, deferring the difference. The company fully cooperated with the investigation by voluntarily presenting dozens of its employees for FBI interviews to discuss these issues, and Rusty, his associate Andy Drumheller, Raul, Cindy, Reagan and I met with the Ernst & Young team and made numerous trips, in various combinations, to try to deal with the investigators' concerns.[172]

It all culminated in a large two-day meeting held in Cheyenne in late November 1999. The U.S. Attorney for Wyoming, David Freudenthal, attended along with Murray, Pico, the two SEC lawyers and several IRS agents. The Burlington side included Bobby Shackouls; Rick Plaeger; Reagan Kott, the outside counsel team of Rusty and Andy, Raul, Cindy and me; and the Ernst & Young team of Barry Mabry and Butch Kirby. Shackouls and Plaeger had asked me to make the presentation for the company and Rusty had concurred. I worked hard preparing and we had a run-through session the day before at the company's headquarters in Houston.

I had gone to the Yale-Harvard football game in New Haven the preceding Saturday and had watched Yale beat Harvard 24 to 21 with the Yale quarterback playing with a severe case of tonsillitis and a 103 degree fever. He passed on every play in the second half and his last connected for a winning touchdown in the last half-minute of the game. I had contracted a bad cold and I coughed and sneezed my way through the dress rehearsal for the Wyoming presentation. At one point, a concerned Bobby Shackouls asked, "Bob, are you sure you are going to be up to doing this tomorrow?"

I said, "Bobby, back East in the Ivy League, where football is really football, the Yale quarterback played a whole game with tonsillitis and a 103 degree fever to beat Harvard. If he can do that, I can handle this presentation tomorrow."

I made the presentation, with a lot of help from Rusty and Bobby, and it went well. The investigation did not end there, but we made progress. And six months later, after a series of follow-up meetings, Murray sent word that it looked good for us. Freudenthal, however, wanted to meet in person to deliver his decision. We flew back to Cheyenne in July 2000.

Freudenthal told us he had decided not to indict Burlington. He said he and Murray, who agreed, had been impressed by the changes Shackouls and Rick Plaeger had made after they took over the company. Among their moves was eliminating MOTI so the sale at the wellhead went directly to the ultimate purchaser. The case lent itself to a civil resolution at this point.

Freudenthal added that he would not honor the SEC's request for a Rule 6(e) order. This would have allowed the SEC access to the documents and other information obtained by grand jury subpoena that it felt was necessary to bring an accounting case against the company. We got the impression that Freudenthal resented Washington, D.C.

centered authority and did not want to help the SEC make a case against the company he had decided not to indict.

So, the investigation that started with a proposed plea agreement ended with a total victory. Freudenthal went on to become Governor of Wyoming, where he served two four-year terms, and Burlington continued to prosper until 2006 when it was acquired by ConocoPhillips.

Bobby Shackouls, Rick Plaeger and Reagan Kott were three of the best clients a lawyer could hope to have. They showed us their gratitude in deeds as well as words. In December 1999, shortly after the presentation in Cheyenne, they invited Raul, Cindy and me to go duck hunting with them at the Burlington Lodge in southern Louisiana. Raul couldn't go because of a pressing matter for Citibank, but Cindy and I went. They were great hosts and we had a great time—and even shot and brought home some ducks.

On the first of those early mornings in the duck blind as they were waiting for the sun, Cindy and Reagan decided to let Raul know what he was missing. They punched his number into one of their cell phones and when Raul came into the office and listened to his messages he heard a quacking duck call, then, "Hi Raul. This is Reagan and Cindy. We miss you."

Later in the spring Burlington did it again, taking Rusty and his wife, Tissy, and Janet and me on a redfish fishing expedition. This was another great time—aside from my having to live down that fact that Janet caught a lot more fish than I did.

RAUL YANES

Raul went on to become the multi-threat star at DPW that his early career promised when he came to us in 1993 out of Dartmouth, Harvard Law School and a Seventh Circuit clerkship. The highlight of our work together was the Burlington Wyoming case. Another episode we shared demonstrated his resilience.

That was the day we—Raul and I along with Mike Carroll and Denis McInerney—were headed to Washington for a meeting with Michael Chertoff, then the head of the Criminal Division of the DOJ. We were representing Arthur Andersen. The Enron task force had recommended an indictment of Andersen for destroying documents and we were appealing that decision.

The four of us got on the 8 a.m. Acela at Penn Station and settled into one of those four-seaters with a table in the middle. We spread out all our papers and were just about to start working when the conductor came through saying, "All tickets to Boston, please." We were on the wrong train—first stop New Haven.

Fortunately the Washington train was just on the other side of the platform, and we snatched up our papers in a mad scramble and made it just before the doors closed. Raul decided to relax at that point and get something to eat. He went to the café car and came back with a bowl of fruit and a glass of orange juice. When he spooned a blackberry out of his fruit bowl and bit into it, it exploded and sent dark juice all over his white shirt. In the ensuing commotion someone knocked over the glass of orange juice and spilled orange juice all over his lap. So, we had a feeling from the outset this wasn't going to be a great day.

Raul was unflappable, however. He went through the meeting with his coat buttoned and no one was the wiser. But we failed to persuade the DOJ. It was indeed a bad day—for us, for Arthur Andersen, for the accounting profession and for the DOJ in making the decision that—true to our prediction—put Arthur Andersen out of business, all essentially for the allegedly criminal actions of a few people in one office. Later the Supreme Court reversed its conviction and Arthur Andersen ended up not being convicted of anything.

Raul followed a path that I believe characterizes the most dedicated lawyers in the finest DPW tradition. He left Davis Polk in 2003 and embarked on a remarkable six years of public service. He started in the White House, working for White House counsel Alberto Gonzales. When Gonzales became Attorney General he took Raul with him to the DOJ. After serving for several months as counselor to the Attorney General Raul was recruited away by Joshua Bolten, then the head of the Office of Management and Budget, to succeed another Davis Polk alum, Jennifer Newstead, as his general counsel. And when Bolten became President Bush's Chief of Staff he recommended Raul for the vitally important position of Assistant to the President and Staff Secretary in which he served for two-and-a-half years before returning to Davis Polk.

CHAPTER 56

Bicycling

ABOUT THIS TIME, with years of involvement with the Suzuki Samurai and then Burlington Industries, I found myself taking a personal break from fossil fuels in my recreational life. My years of bicycling thus far had featured many enjoyable short hauls. My favorites were along the water in Connecticut and along the White River in Vermont a few miles from our house in Barnard. Janet rode with me in both places, and we had also done bicycling trips in Puglia, Italy; Burgundy, France; and on Canada's Prince Edward Island. But even longer rides awaited.

The first of these had its genesis in the winter of 2000 when I was with my two brothers at our annual Martin Luther King weekend family skiing get-together in Steamboat Springs. One of my brother Mac's good friends was a Denver judge named Ray Satter. He came up to Steamboat from Denver every year for one night, cooked us a spectacular pancake breakfast and then drove back to Denver. After several years of this, my curiosity finally got the best of me.

"Ray," I said, "you come up every year and brighten our weekend, cook us this great breakfast, but you never ski. If you don't like skiing, what do you like?"

He answered that he loved to bicycle. He rode to work in Denver almost every day of the year, including in the winter. But he especially liked long rides of hundreds of miles extending over several days. "This year," he said happily, "I'm going to do RAGBRAI."

RAGBRAI was the name of a ride sponsored by the *Des Moines Register*—the Register's Annual Great Bike Ride Across Iowa. Ray said he and two couples from Denver were doing the ride. I recalled that a good friend of mine from Darien, Don Tredwell, had done this ride several years earlier. Don lived in Racine, Wisconsin now, I figured he'd want to do it again, and I volunteered the two of us without hesitation, "I'll get my friend Don and we'll come with you."

The ride takes a week, the last week in July, going west to east to take advantage of the supposedly prevailing wind. Riders traditionally dip their rear wheels in the Missouri River at the start and the front wheels in the Mississippi at the finish. The route varies from year to year, and contrary to what many people think Iowa is not all

flat—there are many significant hills along the way.
Different small towns serve as overnight hosts; local
high school football fields are set up as campsites,
with riders' tents transported by truck from town
to town, and local churches put on pasta dinners.

With Don Tredwell and Ray Satter

There was also ample food along the way. Every day, about ten miles from the start, riders could
stop for the Pancake Man. He had a long griddle
with a batter-filled pan above it running its full
length. He pressed a button and fifty pre-formed
pancakes would drop down and start cooking.
There was never a shortage of pancakes as the riders passed, since they were spread out having started
early or late depending on what they'd done the
night before.

An hour after we passed the Pancake Man a
roadside sign announced, "Only 5 miles to Mr. Pork
Chop." And five miles later there he was, grilling
pork chops alongside a small pink van with a pork chop painted on the side. We had
one and moved on only to find—two hours later—the same sign and five miles farther
the same pink van. By the end of the week it would be a long time before I was ready
for another pork chop.

RAGBRAI was by no means a race. The average ride per day was about sixty-five
miles, but we had all day to get there. And the other riders were entertaining.

One family of six rode a bicycle built for five—five sets of pedals and handlebars
in tandem—towing a wagon with family member No. 6, a baby. "Team Bad Boy" was
a rider with two wagons, one carrying a boom box blaring out rock music and the
other with a blender for making daiquiris and other frozen drinks. On the last day, as we
neared the finish where we'd dip our front wheels in the Mississippi, a banner displayed
on a parked school bus made everybody smile. It read, "If you're not having fun, lower
your standards."

I had fun doing RAGBRAI but, like the marathon, it was a one-time event.

Not so the Pan Mass Challenge, a ride that raises money for the Dana-Farber Cancer
Institute in Boston through its Jimmy Fund. This extraordinary event, held on the first
weekend in August, raises more money for charity than any other fundraising athletic

With Sue at the Provincetown finish

event in the country. I rode it for the first time in 2003, when I was among 3,500 riders who raised $16 million. I rode it five more times, and on my last ride in 2011 the numbers had swelled to over 5,000 riders and $33 million. Because virtually everything needed to support the event is donated, 99 percent of the money raised goes to Dana-Farber.

My daughter, Sue, was my riding companion on these rides, so I became part of a group from her town, Wayland, called "Team Jean," which trained and rode together in honor of one of their members who had terminal cancer. The Boston Red Sox were among the corporate sponsors; the players were playing ball in August but front office officials and players' wives rode as "Team 9"—Ted Williams's number. Senator John Kerry was a regular, choosing the longer of two first-day routes and in 2011 pacing the field with Lance Armstrong riding alongside.

Team Jean started in Wellesley on the first day—the shorter route to Kerry's Sturbridge start—and rode eighty-two miles to Bourne and the Massachusetts Marine Academy, the overnight stop. The routes favor back roads and small towns and cheering spectators offering water, encouragement and thanks. Many riders carried photos of family members or friends lost to cancer. After a night of barbeque and rock music, we set out at 5 a.m. the next day for Provincetown, another eighty-mile ride this time on Cape Cod. At the finish there was another barbeque and then a ferry ride back to Boston, where we were met by a fireboat spouting streams of water in the harbor and family members on the dock carrying signs of welcome and congratulations. It made riders forget their tired legs and plan to come back the next year.

I don't know if I was the oldest rider in my last year in the PMC, but I was the next year, at 81, in a shorter cancer fund-raising ride, the Connecticut Challenge in Westport. It was a modest twenty-five miles, with a nice ride along the water near the finish.

In all the riding I've done over the years, in local and farflung locales, on charity challenge races and just for fun, I don't think there's a better way to see the world than from a bicycle. Unless it's from a sailboat.

CHAPTER 57

Alfred Taubman

ONE OF THE THINGS about a white collar defense practice is the doors it opens into all walks of life. Rarely will you gain insights into the art world and high-end retailing, for example, as I did when defending Alfred Taubman. You will, of course, see witnesses scrambling to save their own skin in all types of cases, and that was true in Taubman's case as well.

Taubman was born in 1924 in Pontiac, Michigan, the youngest of four children of first generation German-Jewish immigrants. His father's construction business suffered during the Depression, and Alfred was nine when he had to go to work to help support the family. He was dyslexic and struggled in school, but graduated from high school and enrolled at the University of Michigan. He left during his freshman year to serve in the Army Air Corps during World War II, returning after the war to study architecture. However, he dropped out after his junior year to start his family and career.

His first full-time job was as a field engineer with a construction company. But he decided he wanted to open his own business. He got his chance when a woman he knew wanted the bridal salon she'd commissioned redesigned. Having worked for an architect part-time, Alfred persuaded her to give him a chance. He borrowed $5,000 and started the Taubman Company. The bridal salon was a huge success. From there he started building small stores and eventually strip malls in the suburbs of Detroit.

Taubman soon proved to be an innovator and visionary in the retail construction market. His greatest strength was an ability to visualize the way people move through spaces. Using these innate skills he conceived and created the "destination" shopping centers that became the company's hallmark. He noted that suburban populations were increasing and that federal and state highway systems were expanding and improving. In the early 1960's Taubman began planning large regional shopping centers in California and throughout the Midwest that would typically contain from 150 to 200 stores, two to three times as many as their counterparts. These large shopping centers embodied Taubman's groundbreaking theories about optimal design, population flows, marketing and human nature.

Author Malcolm Gladwell, writing about the history of the modern American mall in the *New Yorker*, concluded that Taubman may not have invented the mall, but he certainly "perfected it."

As a result of his shopping mall success, Taubman made a fortune that *Forbes* estimated at $3 billion. He was on the list of *Forbes* 400 Richest Americans for two decades.

In 1983—the same year his Michigan Panthers won the United States Football League championship (and lost $6 million) in the league's inaugural season—Taubman was approached by David Westmoreland of Sotheby's. The renowned art auctioneer had been facing hostile takeover advances and Westmoreland wanted Taubman to bid on the company as a "white knight." Taubman organized a group of investors and Sotheby's accepted their bid. That December Taubman became Chairman of Sotheby's.

He determined in his new role to make some fundamental changes in the way Sotheby's did business. As he wrote in his book, *Threshold Resistance: The Extraordinary Career of a Luxury Retailing Pioneer,* Taubman wanted to "introduce the auction experience to a broader audience of consumers around the world and encourage the development of new collectors and connoisseurs." By bringing more transparency to a "closed and unnecessarily intimidating business" he was going to "break down the threshold resistance that had been holding us back and stifling the art market for as long as I could remember."

And that's what he did, having "great fun breaking down barriers, winning new customers, and selling some of the most interesting art, antiques, and collectibles ever offered at auction."

Taubman chaired the Board for seventeen years, working with President and CEO Michael Ainslee and then Diana D. "Dede" Brooks, who succeeded Ainslee. Under his leadership and with his innovations Sotheby's auction sales increased from $573 million in 1979-80 to $3.2 billion ten years later. But there were storm clouds on the horizon.

In 1997 the Antitrust Division of the Justice Department started an investigation into alleged price-fixing between Sotheby's and its arch-rival Christie's. Its focus was the setting of commission rates paid by sellers of paintings sold at auction by the two houses. The investigation dragged on and Sotheby's lawyers, led by Steve Reiss of Weil Gotshal & Manges, thought it was going nowhere. Then out of the blue, on January 29, 2000, a headline on the front page of the *Financial Times* broke the news that Christie's, in order to obtain amnesty from criminal prosecution, had admitted to the Justice Department that it conspired with Sotheby's to fix sellers' commission rates.

This came as a total shock to Sotheby's lawyers. An even greater shock came a few months later with the news that Dede Brooks, after assuring the lawyers that she had done nothing wrong and there was nothing to worry about, was saying that she had agreed to fix prices with Christopher Davidge—her counterpart at Christie's—and that she had done so on instructions from Taubman.

At that point, on the recommendation of Don Pillsbury, a former Davis Polk partner who was Sotheby's general counsel, and Taubman's personal lawyer, Jeffrey Miro from Detroit, Taubman retained Davis Polk to represent him. I was the lead lawyer, working closely with Scott Muller and Jim Rouhandeh. They were also handling civil litigation brought by disgruntled sellers seeking treble damages from both Sotheby's and Christie's for the higher commission rates resulting from the conspiracy, which representatives of both auction houses had admitted.[173]

In March 2001 the Justice Department filed an indictment in the Southern District of New York against Taubman and his counterpart at Christie's, Sir Anthony Tennant. The indictment charged that they were the architects of the conspiracy and that Brooks and Davidge had entered into a price-fixing agreement on their instructions. Taubman vehemently maintained his innocence. He agreed to take a lie detector test administered by the former head of the FBI's polygraph division, and passed with flying colors. We presented the results to the Justice Department and to Sotheby's Board of Directors, but unfortunately this was not admissible in court.

The trial was set for September 2001, then postponed to November after the New York offices of the DOJ's Antitrust Division were damaged in the 9/11 attacks. When the trial started before Judge George Daniels, Taubman was the only defendant in the courtroom. Tennant was in England, secure in the knowledge that price-fixing was not an extraditable offense.

Although Tennant was absent he played a large role in the outcome of the trial. Dede Brooks was the only direct witness against Taubman. But Tennant had written a memorandum describing a 1993 meeting with Taubman that proved to be the most damaging piece of evidence. It was admissible because Tennant had sent the memo to Davidge "in furtherance of the conspiracy," and there was no way to cross examine it.

I opened by telling the jury this was a "one-witness case." We had not decided at that point whether Taubman—who was in poor health—would take the stand, so I was careful not to say, "This all comes down to whom you believe, Alfred Taubman or Dede Brooks." Instead I said, to the same effect, "This all comes down to whether you believe Dede Brooks." Our defense was simple. We did not dispute that Davidge and Brooks had engaged in a price-fixing conspiracy. The key issue was whether Taubman was a part of it, or whether Brooks was falsely implicating him to save herself.

Brooks had a Plan A and a Plan B, I told the jury. Plan A was denying the conspiracy altogether. Indeed according to testimony from the inside and outside Sotheby's lawyers, who had investigated the original price-fixing charges, she had used personal persuasion to convince them that she had done absolutely nothing wrong. But once Christie's and Davidge made their deal with the government and "I did nothing wrong" was no longer viable, Brooks moved to Plan B: yes, there was a conspiracy, but Alfred Taubman was a part of it. In fact, she had acted on his instructions.

"He is her 'get out of jail free' card," I said to the jury. "And as you listen to her describe Plan B, if it sounds convincing, well, just remember she is a very good liar. She convinced the Sotheby's lawyers in Plan A that there was no conspiracy at all."

The government started its case with the testimony of Melinda Marcuse, Taubman's personal assistant who kept his diaries. Through her, they established that Taubman and Tennant had met twelve times between February 3, 1993 and October 31, 1996. The third meeting took place on April 30, 1993. Tennant met with Davidge later that day and according to Davidge described the earlier meeting as a "very good" one. Tennant's written memo contained, Davidge said, what Tennant described as "a full and frank summary of his meeting" with Taubman. He had put quotation marks around certain statements in the memo, he told Davidge, to indicate that those statements were made by Taubman.

A portion of the memo read, "A schedule exists. We should get back to it. 15% downward on a sliding scale." Davidge testified that that referred to the companies' published scale of fees for the seller's commission. Another statement read, "They are considering publishing a scale as with the buyer's premium." Davidge said that meant that Tennant and Taubman had "discussed the possibility of producing a scale which would be the same as the buyer's premium which would be not negotiable." Tennant's summary continued, "If anyone wants to bargain on their new scale they will tell them to go elsewhere." Davidge testified that he understood that this sentence "was emphasizing the point that if people didn't accept the fixed nature of the commission rates, that they wouldn't be willing to bargain and that their reply to their clients of Christie's and Sotheby's should be 'I'm sorry, that is our rates and you have to accept it. If you don't like it, then find another auction house.'"

The April 30th summary ended with, "He and I should now withdraw but stay in touch with a view to seeing how things go and intervening from on high if need be." Davidge said he understood this to mean that the "platform for these agreements had been laid by Mr. Tennant and Mr. Taubman," and that he and Brooks would be responsible for implementing them.[174]

Both Davidge and Brooks testified that, beginning a few weeks after the April 30 Tennant and Taubman meeting, they had a series of meetings extending over the next two years. These culminated in an agreement in early 1995 on a non-negotiable seller's commission schedule, which was formally announced by Christie's in a press release in March 1995. Sotheby's followed shortly thereafter with a similar announcement.

Scott Muller challenged Davidge's credibility in an extensive cross examination. It focused on his repeated lies to his superiors about his involvement in any conspiracy. "You lied through your teeth!" Scott charged, and Davidge reluctantly agreed. Scott also brought out that in return for his cooperation, which was essential to Christie's obtaining amnesty from prosecution, Christie's allowed Davidge to keep an $8 million severance package despite his criminal conduct. That enabled me to argue in my summation that the government had essentially bought Davidge's testimony for $8 million.

My cross examination of Dede Brooks focused heavily on the Plan A/Plan B scenario. This required her to admit that she had lied in Plan A while claiming to tell the truth in Plan B. I also focused on her direct testimony that Taubman had told her in April 1993 that Christie's and Sotheby's "were both killing each other on the bottom line and that it was time to do something about it" with a move to "increase pricing given the level of the market." Yet at board meeting after board meeting for over eighteen months, according to board minutes, nothing was ever said about the need to raise commission rates.

We argued that Brooks had done this on her own starting in late 1994 when, after she became CEO, Sotheby's stock price declined dramatically—in large part because commission revenues were down—and she needed to boost the stock price to save her reputation and her own finances since her stock options were under water.

Much of effective cross examination comes down to research, and our hardworking and thorough team of associates[175] found something that allowed me to close my cross examination of Brooks with the trial's most dramatic moment. Brooks had appeared on the PBS television show "Wall Street Week with Louis Rukeyser." He had asked her, "How honest is the art game?" She looked at him and said with great sincerity, "I am confident that we are really setting a new level of standards in the business because, after all, our integrity is all we have." Our team had come up with a copy of the video.

I played the excerpt for the jury and then asked Brooks, "At the time you said that, you were in the middle of a price-fixing conspiracy?"

She paused and then admitted, "Yes."

We called two powerful character witnesses in Taubman's defense. One testified to his impeccable reputation for honesty and integrity within the business community. The other was Damon Keith, a judge on the United States Court of Appeals for the Sixth Circuit who had been Taubman's friend for many years. His testimony gave us an opportunity to bring out the extent of Taubman's philanthropy. He had given prodigiously to a number of charitable institutions, and at $150 million—most of it to the Taubman School of Architecture and the University Medical School—was at that time the largest single donor to the University of Michigan. But his contributions went beyond merely writing a check.

Judge Keith described how a sales anomaly in one of Taubman's businesses had led to a plan to improve the quality of education in Detroit's inner-city schools. Taubman owned A&W Root Beer, and he was curious why the one-third pound hamburger he had introduced to the A&W menu was not selling. He learned that when his customers looked at the menu offerings—$1/4$ pound versus $1/3$ pound—they ordered the quarter-pound hamburger because 4 was bigger than 3. Taubman concluded that the quality of teaching in the public schools was unacceptably low and asked Keith to join him in leading a program he would finance. The Michigan Partnership for New Education would have on its board the CEOs of General Motors, Ford and Chrysler, other business leaders, and the Presidents of the University of Michigan, Michigan State and Wayne State. They recruited the Dean of the Michigan State School of Education to be its Executive Director. And Taubman himself, with Keith, visited numerous elementary schools to talk directly with students and teachers in order to be able to make meaningful recommendations for improvement.

Judge Keith was an impressive witness. He was the first African-American appointed to the United States District Court in Detroit, had served with distinction for many years on the Sixth Circuit Court of Appeals and was selected by President George H. W. Bush in 1991 to head the Presidential Commission on the Bi-Centennial of the United States Constitution. One result of the Constitution celebration is that every federal courthouse in the country now displays a plaque featuring the Bill of Rights, with an introductory message from Judge Keith. The Code of Judicial Ethics frowns upon—but does not forbid—judges serving as character witnesses, but Judge Keith did not hesitate in coming to his friend's defense. The last question to him was, "Judge Keith, how did you come to be a character witness for Mr. Taubman?"

He said, "As soon as I heard he was in trouble, I called him and said, 'Alfred, what can I do to help?'"

The biggest decision was whether Taubman would testify. It was a classic "he said, she said" situation and logic dictated that the jury would want to hear from him. Taubman's health, however, made this a very difficult call. He was seventy-seven years old, had had several strokes and three heart attacks, suffered from diabetes and sleep apnea and was taking twenty-six separate medications every day—closely monitored and adjusted daily. He had difficulty concentrating and had almost no recollection of what had occurred at the meetings with Tennant, other than a very positive recollection that he had not agreed with Tennant or asked Dede Brooks to fix prices. In addition both his personal physicians, one from Michigan and the other from New York, said they were concerned about his ability to physically survive a lengthy and grueling cross examination. Based on all of those factors we concluded that it was just too much of a risk to have him testify. We made that recommendation to him and he accepted it.

The issue for the jury remained the same throughout the trial. Had Brooks and Davidge entered into the price-fixing conspiracy for reasons of their own, which we argued, or had they had been instructed to do so by Taubman and Tennant? I summed up by saying, "You cannot convict Alfred Taubman unless you believe Dede Brooks beyond a reasonable doubt and I tell you, Dede Brooks is a walking reasonable doubt."

The government relied on the meetings between Tennant and Taubman and Tennant's memorandum to Davidge to defend her credibility.

The jury was out for two days and then returned a guilty verdict against Taubman, a huge disappointment for us and for him. The government asked Judge Daniels to impose the maximum sentence of three years, which was called for under the relevant sentencing guidelines. We asked for probation and no jail given Taubman's "legendary" philanthropic activities[176] and his poor health which, we argued, required constant personal attention that the Bureau of Prisons was not in a position to provide. The Probation Department agreed with us and recommended a sentence of no jail.

In the end, Judge Daniels took a middle course. On April 22, 2002 he sentenced Taubman to a year and a day at the Bureau of Prisons medical facility in Rochester, Minnesota—right next to the Mayo Clinic. The extra day came at our request, to make him eligible for a 15 percent reduction in his term, or about two months.

While disappointed that he had received a prison sentence, we were gratified that it was far less than what the government, supported by the sentencing guidelines, had asked for. We were equally gratified by the reaction of his friends. Unlike so many situations where a person in trouble watches his erstwhile friends disappear, Taubman's gave him an outpouring of support. And in testimony to the way he had lived his life, no institution to which he had contributed—not Michigan, not Harvard, not Brown—removed his name from any of the buildings or the programs he had endowed.

What was more, there was a waiting list to visit him in prison. Visitors were limited to three a day for no more than four hours, and when Angela Burgess—who had written the sentencing memorandum (Judge Daniels later told me it was the best he'd ever seen)—and I wanted to visit him the line ahead of us was two months long.

The wait was worth it. When we finally went to Rochester we were totally surprised at what we found. Alfred, now seventy-eight, had lost thirty-five pounds. He was in great physical condition from daily workouts and a steady diet of healthy foods. His sleep apnea was gone and he was sleeping through the night. He had regained his mental sharpness and engaged us in stimulating and provocative discussions on a number of topics.

Taubman left prison in May 2002 after serving ten months. He was in far better health than when he went in, and immediately resumed his enormously productive philanthropic activities. Most impressive, to me, was his defense of stem cell research in the State of Michigan. The issue was a referendum that would have banned research on embryonic stem cells, a ban opponents believed would drain research funds and talent from the State as researchers went elsewhere to pursue their work. Alfred contributed $5 million and led the campaign against the ban. The opposition won and significant stem cell research has continued in Michigan.

As this is written Alfred is still going strong and I enjoyed seeing him last fall, as I do every year while watching Michigan football at Michigan Stadium.

CHAPTER 58

Michigan Law School Fellowships

I SHARE WITH Alfred Taubman and Fred Wilpon (Chapter 59) a great fondness for the University of Michigan, where I got the legal education that was the foundation for my career. My connections there are long and deep, and in 1997 I was privileged to receive from President Lee Bollinger an honorary degree, conferred at Michigan Stadium in a pouring rain that did nothing to dampen my enthusiasm for the honor.

More recently, for the last eight years, I have enjoyed serving on President Mary Sue Coleman's Advisory Group, a body composed of twenty-five or so alumni from all parts of the University that meets twice a year to discuss important University issues. In this time I've also served on two committees appointed by Law School Dean Evan Caminker and his 2013 successor Mark West to help them with issues affecting the Law School and to assist with alumni relations and development. In October 2013 President Coleman gave me the opportunity to embrace both my college and grad school institutions by asking me to represent the University of Michigan, as her delegate, at the inauguration of Yale's 23rd President, Peter Salovey.

But I was able to make my most meaningful contribution to Michigan as the result of talks I launched with Jeffrey Lehman, then the Dean of the Law School, in 1999. I told him of my deep commitment to the University and the Law School and said I wanted to do something to show my gratitude. As we talked through it we focused on the concept of loan repayments for graduates going into government service. I had gotten the idea from Samuel J. Heyman, the founder and Chairman of the Washington-based Partnership for Public Service, who had established such a program at Harvard.

My talks with Dean Lehman extended into 2001. The terrorist attacks of 9/11 increased my sense of urgency, and we announced the program in early October of that year. Dean Lehman said at the time that it "speaks to our nation's confidence in its democratically elected government. And like our response in the days and weeks after September 11, it affirms the University of Michigan Law School's continuing responsibility to provide leadership in our world."

My remarks were more personal. I said that the fellowships were intended to benefit what had proved to be two of the most vital elements of my career—Michigan Law

Receiving an honorary degree

School and government service. They would ease the path to public service for law students for whom loan debt and other financial considerations were an obstacle. It also sent the message that a period of early government service is a valuable and worthwhile career path.

"This benefits both the Law School and the government," I said. "It will give Michigan Law School graduates the opportunity to have a public service experience that otherwise they might not have been able to afford. It also will give the government a continuing flow of these talented and highly motivated young lawyers."

The fellowships are for graduates who are entering government service, either immediately after graduation or after a clerkship. I endowed a fund sufficient to give each of three recipients a $5,000 cash stipend and cover payments for both college and law school loans for a period of three years. I established general criteria that emphasize a demonstrated commitment to public service values, academic achievement and the nature of the government position. The Fiske Fellows are chosen by a faculty committee using those criteria. In 2012 gifts to the program from two grateful clients enabled the law school to raise the number of recipients a year to four.

Of the thirty-seven fellows selected since 2001, eighteen have gone to the Department of Justice. The others have gone to the State, Energy, and Education departments, the House of Representatives, the CIA, the EEOC, the FDA, the EPA, district attorneys' offices in New York, Buffalo and Philadelphia, the New York City Corporation Counsel's office, and the Navy Judge Advocate General's office. Almost all of them have stayed in government service.

I am very proud of these results. I've met the recipients at dinners in Ann Arbor each spring with the Dean and members of the faculty and staff. We've also had two reunion dinners, after the fifth and tenth years of the program, in Washington, and I've been gratified by the remarks many of them made for inclusion in the dinner programs.

An appellate litigator in the Justice Department's Tax Division wrote that she had argued a dozen cases and briefed many more in three-and-a-half years, several of them concerning issues of first impression or requiring novel arguments. She wrote, "I can't imagine I would have had the opportunity to do this work in private practice." But, she pointed out, her paycheck as a starting lawyer at a private firm would have been almost three times higher. "The Fiske Fellowship . . . made it possible for me to take a public service job directly out of law school."

A litigation attorney in the New York City Law Department wrote, "The Fiske

A Fiske Fellows Reunion

Fellowship made it possible for me to live in New York City and begin the career that I really wanted without feeling like I had to choose between my goals and my finances."

And, a trial attorney in the DOJ's Civil Division thanked me for "making government service more accessible and encouraging more graduates to consider this worthwhile path."

I really appreciated those comments, which were typical of many others, for they confirmed that the objectives I had in setting up the program have been fulfilled with great success.

CHAPTER 59

Fred Wilpon, Saul Katz and
the New York Mets

AS YOU'VE GATHERED BY NOW, if you didn't know it already, sports has been a recurring theme in my personal and professional life. The wide range of sports I've enjoyed as a participant, coach and spectator has been part of a lifelong education. Play is more than just play; how you play reveals your character.

And of course play at the professional level is big business, too, business that grows increasingly complex. My first glimpse of the complexity of the sports business came back when I helped defend the U.S. Football League's antitrust suit against the National Football League. The years since had made it more complex still, as I learned from representing Fred Wilpon and Saul Katz at various stages of their ownership of the New York Mets and their near-loss of the team in the wake of the Bernie Madoff scandal. It seemed fitting that Fred, like Alfred Taubman, was another connection to the University of Michigan and that they both figured among my final cases.

Fred Wilpon grew up in Bensonhurst, Brooklyn where he was a star pitcher for the Lafayette High School baseball team. At the time he was considered a more promising prospect than his teammate, Sandy Koufax. Fred went on to Michigan where he pitched for the Wolverines baseball team until an arm injury in his sophomore year cut his career short. After graduation he returned to New York where he teamed up with his brother-in-law Saul Katz in a real estate business, Sterling Equities, that became highly successful. But he remained interested in baseball and in January 1980 he and Saul joined with Nelson Doubleday to buy the New York Mets from the Payson family.[177]

By 1986 they and Doubleday each had a 50 percent interest under a contract that allowed either one to "put" his interest to the other at a price to be determined by an independent appraiser. If the put's recipient chose not to buy the interest, the person making the put could purchase the other's interest at the appraised price. Doubleday decided in 2002 that Wilpon was financially weakened and put his 50 percent interest to Wilpon, expecting him to decline allowing Doubleday to acquire total ownership. But to his surprise, Wilpon accepted the put and agreed to purchase Doubleday's interest, which would make Wilpon and his Sterling Equities partners the 100 percent owners of the Mets at the appraised value of $391 million.

Doubleday refused to go forward with the sale. He claimed that the appraised price was unfairly low as the result of a "sham process" by Major League Baseball to depress team value. Wilpon retained us to enforce the agreement. The Mets play in Queens, and so we brought suit in the Eastern District of New York. Shortly after we filed the suit Doubleday capitulated and the sale went forward to Wilpon and his partners in the corporate persona of Sterling Equities.

On April 1, 1982 the Mets signed a contract to televise their games for thirty years over SportsChannel, the regional sports network operated by Cablevision. The contract would expire after the 2011 season and had no early termination clause. Such a clause was added in 1996 in the form of a new Section 7.4 of the agreement. It provided that "either party will have the right to terminate this Agreement by delivering written notice to the other during the 150-day period ending April 1, 2004, such termination to be effective on November 1, 2005."

Section 7.4 also required that when the notice was given the terminating party had to pay 115 percent of the annual rights fees that would otherwise have been payable in 2006, or $54 million. So, while the notice would be given and the payment made at the beginning of the 2004 season, the contract would remain in effect through the close of the 2005 season.

In 2004 the Mets' owners decided they wanted to form their own sports network, comparable to the Boston Red Sox' NESN and the New York Yankees' YES. So, they gave SportsChannel the required notice and made the $54 million rights fee payment. They then launched negotiations with Time Warner Cable and Comcast to form a new network—Sports New York or SNY—that would be owned by the Sterling partners, Time Warner and Comcast. The new network was to televise Mets games as well as other sporting events.

The parties reached an agreement and on October 11, 2004 the Mets announced the formation of the network and its plans to start televising the Mets games beginning with the 2006 season. But on October 27 SportsChannel filed a lawsuit in New York State Court in Manhattan. It sought a declaratory judgment invalidating the termination notice and enjoining the Mets from moving ahead with its new broadcast venture.

SportsChannel based its argument primarily on Section 2.4 of the contract, which provided that:

"During the term [of the contract] [Sterling] shall not . . . grant, transfer, license, sell, produce, distribute or otherwise exploit or use . . . any Pay TV rights to any Mets games. . . ."

Their lawyers argued that the phrase "Mets games" was not limited in time and, therefore, clearly included Mets games played in 2006.[178] They moved for summary judgment, claiming that the "plain language" of Section 2.4 prohibited the Mets from negotiating for the televising of future games, even though notice of termination had been given, while the Cablevision contract was still in effect as it was until November 1, 2005. This would mean that the Mets couldn't make plans for the 2006 season until a few months before it began, potentially leaving them at the mercy of SportsChannel to televise their 2006 games on less favorable terms.

The case was assigned to Justice Helen Freedman. The "plain language" argument impressed her, and she indicated during a conference in her robing room that she was inclined to accept it. Sensing disaster, I pressed hard to be able to submit an affidavit from David Howard, the Mets business manager—and former Davis Polk associate—on the negotiations for the 1996 amendment. This, I said, would support the Mets' position that the term "Mets games" was intended to apply only to games played while the contract was in effect. Cablevision's lawyers, sensing victory, argued that the language was clear on its face and that parol, or extrinsic, evidence was unnecessary and unjustified. It was a very intense argument—the ultimate outcome of the case hung in the balance—but in the end she allowed the affidavit.

Howard made two key points in his affidavit and in the deposition that followed. He described Section 2.4, which was part of the 1982 original contract, as what was known in the business as an "exclusivity" provision. Its purpose and meaning were solely to give SportsChannel the exclusive rights to televise Mets games during the life of the contract.

He also said that during the negotiations leading up to the amended agreement he made it clear to SportsChannel that if the Mets were going to pay $54 million for the right to terminate the agreement they had to be free and clear to negotiate a new contract once notice was given and the payment was made. This final point, he said, "became a mantra that we repeated on numerous occasions during the course of the negotiations."

Howard pointed out that during the negotiations SportsChannel had never said anything to the contrary. No one from the network ever claimed at that time that Section 2.4 prevented the Mets from negotiating for a new contract once the notice was given and the money was paid.

SportsChannel did not put in any affidavit in opposition.

Our summary judgment brief, written primarily by Eric Grossman,[179] with help from Brian Weinstein and Ross Galin,[180] placed heavy reliance on several cases, as well as the Restatement of Contracts, which held that "a party who willingly and without protest enters into a contract with knowledge of the other's interpretation is bound by such interpretation.[181] In addition, Brian came up with the idea of going through the entire contract, finding other times the phrase "Mets games" was used, and pointing out that in context the term referred to games played when Cablevision had the Mets' television rights, not when it did not. We found a number of such examples. One was typical. It required the Mets to notify SportsChannel of any change in the schedule that would affect the status of "Mets games," a notification that would be pointless for games occurring when the channel had no TV rights. Brian listed these examples in a supporting affidavit.

Justice Freedman, on August 17, 2005, granted our motion and dismissed the case. Her opinion relied heavily on Brian's analysis, noting that "in many instances the parties plainly use 'Mets games' to refer only to games that will be played while the contract is in effect." She went on to conclude, that, as a matter of law, the term "Mets games" must be construed to refer only to games played through November 1, 2005:

> Sports Channel's interpretation of the Contract would lead to an anomalous result that is both commercially unreasonable and contrary to Sterling's reasonable expectations. It defies common sense that Sterling agreed to pay SportsChannel $54 million to curtail its license term . . . , but also agreed to refrain from making binding arrangements with new broadcasters for Mets games until just before the beginning of the next baseball season. . . ."[182]

In January 2006 the Appellate Division affirmed her decision, and SportsChannel took the case no further.[183] We had won. The Mets went forward with the SNY network with Time Warner and Comcast and it has been a huge financial success.

So, by these two legal victories we had enabled Fred Wilpon, Saul Katz and their partners at Sterling Equities to do two things they badly wanted: obtain full ownership of a baseball team, and build a successful sports network that would provide financial security for the Mets.

But the fruits of these victories were put in peril just a few years later by the damage inflicted by the largest Ponzi scheme in history.

CHAPTER 60

The Mets and Bernie Madoff

DURING THE 1970's Fred Wilpon's son, Jeff, became friends with one of his school-mates, Mark Madoff. Through that friendship Wilpon came to know Mark's father, Bernard Madoff, who was in the investment banking business through his firm Bernard L. Madoff Investment Securities LLC (BLMIS). The Madoff firm was a registered broker-dealer, operating a market making business, doing proprietary trading and acting as an investment advisor.

By the mid-1980's Madoff had become a respected member of the investment community. He served as a member of the NASDAQ Board of Governors, as Vice-Chairman of the National Association of Securities Dealers and as a Vice-Chairman of the Securities Industry Association. Fred Wilpon and Saul Katz heard of Madoff's good reputation and strong investment performance from friends they knew and trusted, including Arthur Levitt—later to become chair of the SEC—and Howard Squadron, President of the American Jewish Congress and senior partner in the law firm Squadron, Ellenoff, Plesent & Sheinfeld. In 1985 they began to invest through BLMIS.

Wilpon and Katz recognized that BLMIS operated like any other registered broker-dealer. They gave Madoff trading authorization and received monthly statements. These indicated transactions in blue chip securities like Exxon-Mobil and Coca-Cola when Madoff was "in the market" and U.S. Treasuries when he was not. They understood his strategy to be conservative, intended to limit the effects of market volatility by using a "split-strike" strategy to collar the trading range of blue chip securities with puts and calls and, to use an analogy the Mets' owners would have been familiar with, to "hit singles and doubles" in the market rather than home runs.

In the early years, one of the Sterling partners tracked transaction prices shown on the BLMIS statements against publicly available information to see if they were within the reported price range. They were. He also looked to see if the prices were high, low or in the middle of the range—was there any abnormal position? There was not. He tried to replicate Madoff's strategy on paper to see if he could generate a profit. He did. It was less than Madoff was reporting, but he decided that was because Madoff was better at it than he was.

As the years went by Wilpon & Katz increased the investments with Madoff for themselves, their families and their favorite charities. As their businesses grew and generated more cash the businesses, too, opened BLMIS accounts. They used them to manage liquidity in much the same manner as traditional bank accounts. They deposited cash when it came in—as when the Mets sold tickets in the fall and winter—and withdrew it when it was needed—such as to pay Mets' operating expenses including player salaries in the spring and summer. They came to trust Madoff implicitly and their investments continued to increase.

On December 11, 2008—a Thursday—the news that Madoff had been arrested sent shock waves through the investment community. A federal indictment charged that the BLMIS brokerage operation had been nothing but a Ponzi scheme for many years. In a deposition later Fred Wilpon said the news of Madoff's fraud had struck him "like a dagger in the heart." Wilpon, Katz, their Sterling Equities partners, children and grandchildren, family trusts, charitable foundations and businesses—including the Mets—lost in the aggregate of over $500 million that day.[184]

BLMIS filed for bankruptcy in the Southern District of New York, and the case was assigned to Bankruptcy Judge Burton R. Lifland. He appointed Irving Picard, an attorney at the New York law firm of Baker Hostetler, as trustee of the bankrupt estate under SIPA, the Securities Investor Protection Act. Picard's job, for which he retained Baker Hostetler as counsel, was to investigate and bring appropriate claims on behalf of the estate for the benefit of the Madoff's victims. This involved calculating which of his clients had profited from Madoff's scheme and which were left with nothing.

Pursuant to provisions of the bankruptcy code that allowed pre-complaint discovery, the trustee subpoenaed documents from the Sterling Equities partners and took depositions of several of them, including Wilpon and Katz. We were retained to represent them and litigation partner Karen Wagner and Dana Seshens—another rising star associate later to become a partner—handled the depositions.

The discovery revealed that the partners, families and businesses had over 400 separate accounts. Those that had made money—that is, had taken out more than they put in—had gained $300 million. Those that had lost money had lost $178 million.

The trustee had two years to file complaints intended to "claw back" money from the winners to the losers. In October 2010 a few weeks before the two years would elapse, Picard advised Karen and Dana that they intended to file a complaint against our clients on two separate theories:

Picard was applying the first theory to all of Madoff's so-called "net winners." In Wilpon's and Katz's case this meant recovering the $300 million in profits on the ground that this was never the result of legitimate securities trading, but money that belonged to other people whom Madoff had lured into his Ponzi scheme. That money, he claimed, should be used to repay the "net losers." The net winners opposed this because, they said, they were entitled to rely on the statements they'd received in conducting their affairs. Many of them, for example, had bought homes that now—with the recovery process underway—they would have to sell.

Picard's second, much harsher, theory came as a total shock.

The trustee said that he intended to recover from Wilpon and Katz and their partners not only their profits, but also the principal they had invested to obtain those profits. They had put in $700 million and taken out $1 billion. The trustee claimed that because the Sterling partners, particularly Saul Katz, were on "inquiry notice" that Madoff might be a fraud, they had to pay back the $700 million of principal as well as the $300 million in profits. And because of this Wilpon and Katz would also not be able to recover the $178 million they had lost in the other accounts.

At that point I became actively involved in the settlement negotiations that had begun with Picard. They continued through October and November and I argued that the trustee's position was completely baseless. That December, as I approached my eightieth birthday, I decided I would step down as an active partner at Davis Polk to take a role as senior counsel. But I told Fred and Saul that I would stay with them on this case, right through to the end.

The settlement talks continued, and went nowhere, into February 2011. That month a complaint that Picard had filed in December was unsealed. It made a number of allegations, but the principal charge—the one that grabbed the headlines—was based upon the Sterling partners' relationship with Peter Stamos, an investment banker.

Wilpon and Katz, who had virtually all their investments with Madoff, decided in 2002 that they should diversify. Katz had come to know and respect Stamos through his deep involvement with the Long Island Jewish Hospital, a Stamos client. So, he and Wilpon agreed with Stamos to form an investment company. They would call it Sterling Stamos, Stamos would manage it and Wilpon and Katz would invest some of their money.

The complaint charged that Sterling Stamos personnel repeatedly warned the Sterling partners that Madoff was "too good to be true." They had "openly questioned his legitimacy for years" and had "fingered Madoff as a fraud for years." The complaint said that Stamos and others had "recommended to the Sterling partners that they should redeem their BLMIS investment." It charged that they had "warned Saul Katz and Fred Wilpon not to invest," but that the Sterling partners had become dependent upon "the "staggering profits" they were making. This was the "inquiry notice" that should have told Katz and Wilpon that Madoff might be a fraud. With that the complaint demanded principal and profits totaling $1 billion.

The lawyer leading Picard's trustee team told the press he wanted a cash payment, regardless of source. "Whether they utilize the Mets, SNY, Sterling properties or any other resource is of no moment to us," said David Sheehan. "What we're looking for is a billion dollars."

The complaint produced a feeding frenzy in the media. Article after article questioned Fred's and Saul's financial condition, their ability to keep the Mets and, indeed, whether they could survive at all in the face of the trustee's "explosive" charges. Their reputations also took a hit. Typical was a *New York Post* story describing the complaint as "claiming they happily lined their pockets with hundreds of millions of sleazy profits while ignoring clear signs that Madoff was a lying, cheating scam artist."

The *Post* said that "the bombshell legal action brought by court-appointed Trustee Irving Picard . . . could ultimately force them to sell off the Mets to satisfy legal debts" and quoted "a source who knows Wilpon" as predicting the team's sale.

We determined to fight these charges tooth and nail. Together with Karen Wagner and David Caplan—the corporate partner for all the Wilpon and Katz matters—I issued a strong press release. We said, "Anyone who knows Fred Wilpon and Saul Katz knows that they would not have dealt for one minute with someone they thought might be engaged in fraud."

We concluded the release, "The Sterling Partners lost more than money in the Madoff fraud—they lost faith in someone they thought was a trusted friend. But their faith in the legal system remains strong, and we are confident they will prevail."

Our first move was to ask the trustee for copies of the depositions and documents that he had obtained from third parties, including Peter Stamos and others at Sterling Stamos. He refused, saying the request was "premature" and could not be taken up until the Bankruptcy Court held a discovery conference pursuant to Bankruptcy Rule 7026. We told him that rule applies to new discovery, going forward, and has nothing to do with him giving us the discovery he had already taken.

But the trustee persisted, even after the Bankruptcy Court appointed former Governor Mario Cuomo as a mediator to try to reach a settlement and we told the trustee we needed what he had so as to be on an equal footing before the mediator. When we filed a motion in the Bankruptcy Court seeking the discovery, he opposed it still saying it was "premature."

While all this was going on the lawyers who had represented Peter Stamos and the other Sterling Stamos witnesses at their depositions, called Karen Wagner. They told her that the depositions were in fact helpful to Wilpon and Katz. So, we got the depositions from them, and this is what they revealed.

Far from warning Saul Katz that Madoff was a fraud, Peter Stamos had testified that:

"I'm embarrassed to say that I said to Mr. Katz on a number of occasions that my assumption is that Mr. Madoff is . . . among the most honest and honorable men that we will ever meet. Number one. And, number two, that he is perhaps one of the—my assumption is he's perhaps one of the best hedge fund managers in modern times . . .

[The first assumption was] based on his reputation, based upon his long track record, based upon having seen him receive these awards and the positions that he held as chairman of the NASDAQ, having built this great company. He was, quite frankly, legendary, to all of us. And I stood in awe of that with Mr. Katz."

The deposition transcripts showed that no one at Sterling Stamos ever told the Sterling partners not to invest in Madoff or to withdraw their investments. What Stamos testified he told Katz was that, for diversification reasons, he should not have more than 10 percent of his investments with any manager, including Madoff:

Q: "Did you recommend to Saul Katz not to invest in Madoff?
A: No, I never told him not to invest in Madoff, to my recollection. What I recall telling him was don't put more than 10 percent of your assets in any one manager. Put the other 90 percent with us."

The depositions also showed that the "too good to be true" allegation came from a double hearsay internal email at Sterling Stamos written the day after Madoff was exposed. It quoted the chief investment officer of Sterling Stamos as having repeatedly said that Madoff was a "scam and too good to be true." It did not say he had ever told that to Katz or Wilpon. Moreover, when the CIO was deposed he testified he "had no reason to think there was anything wrong at BLMIS" and that he viewed Madoff as "very talented" and regarded his investment strategy as "amazing." He was not asked about the email on that first day of the deposition, after which it was adjourned and never resumed. The complaint was filed two months later.

We filed a motion for summary judgment, attacking the key allegations of the complaint.[185]

We took the basic legal position that under Uniform Commercial Code Article 8 and the federal securities laws, the amounts shown on the monthly statements received from BLMIS constituted "antecedent debt" from BLMIS to the Sterling partners. Thus the payments made by BLMIS to our clients could not be fraudulent conveyances, as alleged by the trustee, because they were payments to discharge that debt. We claimed that the trustee could not invalidate those transfers unless he could show that the Sterling partners were knowing participants in Madoff's fraud or, at the very least, "willfully blind to it."

We also asked for a ruling that even if the "antecedent debt" position did not stand up, under Section 546(e) of the Bankruptcy Code, the trustee could only recover "profits" or principal going back two years.

In March 2010 United States District Judge Jed Rakoff ruled, in a suit by the trustee against HSBC Bank, that if the issue for determination in any case in the Bankruptcy Court involves an interpretation of the federal securities laws, or a conflict between the bankruptcy law and the federal securities law, the case has to be withdrawn from the Bankruptcy Court to the United States District Court. He held that SIPA, the statute under which the bankruptcy judge had appointed the trustee, was part of the federal securities laws and that because there were questions regarding its interpretation the HSBC case had to be withdrawn to his court.[186]

So, after Picard filed his opposition to our summary judgment motion, we filed a motion before Judge Rakoff seeking the withdrawal of our case to him. We argued that the trustee's theory for invalidating BLMIS payments to the Sterling partners depended on an interpretation of SIPA that gave him greater powers than existed under the Bankruptcy Code, and that this presented both an interpretation of SIPA issue and a SIPA conflict with the Bankruptcy Code issue. Karen Wagner argued the motion for removal over the opposition of the trustee and SIPA, and Judge Rakoff granted the motion.

He then ruled on our summary judgment motion. He held that our "antecedent debt" argument did not stand up, but agreed with us that under 546(e) the trustee could only get profits and principal going back two years. He also agreed that the test to recover principal was "willful blindness," not inquiry notice.[187] Finally, he ruled that while he was skeptical that the trustee could prove willful blindness, there was enough of an issue of fact to deny summary judgment.[188]

He set the case down for a jury trial. But we had already dramatically changed the landscape. Because of the two-year limitation, the $1 billion potential liability had been reduced to a maximum of $386 million of which approximately $86 million was profit and approximately $300 million was principal. And the trustee's burden of proof for recovering the $300 million was set at a very high bar. The business press largely agreed that the trustee would have a very hard time meeting it.

As the March 2012 trial date approached we had a number of meetings to discuss what witnesses would best drive home our point that Wilpon and Katz had not been willfully blind to the Madoff fraud. We came up with two blockbusters:

Bob McGuire sat in on our strategy meetings. He was a former AUSA under Bob Morgenthau and had served as New York City's Police Commissioner. He and Fred Wilpon had been close friends for many years. McGuire reminded us that in 2006 Wilpon had contributed $500,000 in McGuire's honor to the Police Athletic League, Morgenthau's favorite charity, to establish baseball programs for inner-city kids. When the three of them met to discuss where to invest the money, Fred had said to Morgenthau, "You can give it to my broker, Bernie Madoff, if you wish. It will be safe."

The trustee objected when we designated Morgenthau as a trial witness. He said he was just a character witness, a role not allowed in civil cases. We told Judge Rakoff, "We are entitled to argue to the jury that no one who felt there was a strong probability that Madoff was running a Ponzi scheme would tell the sitting Manhattan District Attorney that his favorite charity's money—invested in the name of the former Police Commissioner—would be safe."

Morgenthau was a legend in the New York legal world. Another witness was a bigger legend still. Fred had been friends throughout his life with his former Lafayette High School baseball teammate, Sandy Koufax. They were best friends. When Koufax consulted him about his investments Fred had given the Hall of Fame pitcher the same advice he'd given Morgenthau.

Again, the trustee objected to Koufax as a witness, and we made the same argument: "Why would someone who thought there was a high probability that Madoff was running a Ponzi scheme advise one of his best friends to invest with him when he had nothing to gain from it?"

A few days before the trial was due to start the trustee approached us with a settlement proposal. Negotiations ensued with ours conducted by Bob Wise, the DPW litigation partner who was going to try the case. When it was approved in May it brought the case to a resolution that the Sterling partners regarded as very favorable.

We agreed that the trustee could collect profits going back six years totaling $162 million. That preserved his appellate position on the 546 (e) two-year ruling.

The trustee agreed to drop all claims that the Sterling partners had not acted in good faith and to say he had done so "after a review of all the evidence." That meant Wilpon and Katz were being treated not as complicit—as having looked the other way, or as being on inquiry notice—but like all the other innocent victims. It meant that the trustee's claim for returning any amount of principal was gone. In addition, it meant the partners could now recover the $178 million on the accounts where they'd lost money.

Moreover, the settlement allowed Wilpon and Katz to pay the $162 million over five years, with payments for the first four years limited to the amounts they received from the trustee for the $178 million in losses.

The press—including *The Wall Street Journal*, *The New York Times*, the *Daily News*, and the *New York Post*—recognized that the settlement was a very attractive resolution for the Sterling partners.

Judge Rakoff said that his only regret in the case not going to trial was that he wouldn't have Sandy Koufax as a witness in his courtroom.

In June the Sterling partners hosted a thank-you dinner at the Four Seasons for everyone at DPW who had worked on the case. I made the closing remarks and recalled those "dark days in early 2011 when the bankruptcy court unsealed the complaint." I recounted the media frenzy it produced and the questions cast on the partners' reputations. In the end, however:

> "Our clients' faith in the legal system turned out to be justified . . . And most important was the public recognition in the media that their reputations had been vindicated. As *The Wall Street Journal* put it 'The Wilpon-Katzes have been exonerated.' The *Daily News* put it even more simply—'they got their good names back.'
>
> All of this was the result of a team effort at Davis Polk that I was very proud to be part of. And we were extraordinarily grateful to have such loyal clients who, from day one, put their faith in us and continued it in unwavering fashion right to the very end. We could not have represented a finer group of people, and that is what makes this result we achieved so especially gratifying for all of us at Davis Polk."

I was feeling quite nostalgic at that point. The case, for me, had the sense of an ending. It wasn't quite the capstone to a long career, but I was surrounded by battle-tested friends who knew, from both sides of the bar, the extraordinary effort and sacrifice that good lawyering requires, and the incredible rewards it can bring. This was just one more example, the result of a team effort at Davis Polk that I had been very proud to be part of. Our clients had been loyal, they had put their faith in us and we were grateful at that dinner to be able to celebrate together.

A LAST WORD

THOSE THINGS I'VE just described have come together remarkably often during my career. I've been lucky in my clients, of course, but luckier still in my affiliation throughout my career with Davis Polk. I've had fine colleagues who have exemplified what the law is all about. We've worked together in the trenches and more often than not produced results that served our clients well.

The firm itself has been a lighthouse and a refuge. When I stepped down as an active partner after a fifty-five year career, I had spent forty-six of those years at Davis Polk. I had had handsome offers to move to other firms. But I was never really tempted.

One reason was the collegiality I'd come to expect. It was always for me the hallmark of the firm, and the years did nothing to change that despite the firm's enormous growth over that time. I think that's remarkable. The partnership is another source of the firm's strength. I cannot think of a group of better lawyers and finer people than my litigation partners. And every time the litigation I was involved in brought me together with a partner from another department, corporate, for example, or tax, I found myself working with someone at the very top of his or her profession. As I told my partners in my farewell speech, "Truly, in the words of Rudyard Kipling, at Davis Polk 'The strength of the pack is the wolf and the strength of the wolf is the pack.'"

There is also the overall vision of what the firm means in the firmament of the law. It provided mentors whose example I relied upon—like the indispensable Hazard Gillespie—and mentorship of younger lawyers remains a commitment of the firm. It has understood and supported the call of public service even when it might not have been convenient, and the lawyers returning to the firm brought with them experience they could not have gotten any other way that benefitted the firm's clients. Its contributions to *pro bono* work and to local and national bar association entities have also been exemplary.

Those were some of the things I thought about that day at the Four Seasons with my colleagues and old friends, and I think some version of those thoughts almost every day. It's been a magnificent time, and it still is.

AUTHOR'S NOTE

AN IMPORTANT ASPECT of my white collar crime practice was trying to avoid an indictment or regulatory proceeding against a client that was under investigation by the government. Those in which I was successful that never became public are not mentioned in this book. The ones that are discussed in this book all became public through corporate public filings with the SEC, newspaper articles or court decisions.

APPENDIX

HONORS AND AWARDS

1987   Federal Bar Council Emory Buckner Medal for Outstanding Public Service

1997   University of Michigan HLLD

1997   Federal Bar Council Whitney North Seymour Award for Public Service while in Private Practice

1998   New York Lawyers for the Public Interest—Law & Society Award

2000   Jewish Theological Seminary—Simon H. Rifkind Award for Public Service

2001   Legal Aid Society—Servant of Justice Award

2005   Vermont Law School HLLD

2007   New York City Bar Association Medal

2007   American College of Trial Lawyers Leon Silverman Award for Advancing the Administration of Justice

2007   Fordham Stein Prize

2008   American Lawyer Lifetime Achievement Award

2011   Michigan Law School Inaugural Distinguished Alumni Award

2013   New York Law Journal Lifetime Achievement Award

NOTES

1. The autobiography was entitled *Somethin' Might Be Gainin'—Recollections and Ruminations*. The quote appears at page 38.

2. *Id.* at 39.

3. My son Bob is an assistant attorney general in the Connecticut Attorney General's Office; John's daughter Addie is an environmental lawyer with the Justice Department; his son Hal is a Senior Counsel International at Conoco Phillips; and Mac's daughter Julia, with her law degree and Masters Degree in Law and Politics, has taught pre-law courses for 25 years."

4. Joni Mitchell—"Big Yellow Taxi."

5. One of my good friends at Davis Polk had been Peter Fleming. As I was leaving the Southern District to come back to the firm, Peter—a staunch Democrat—was leaving Davis Polk to join Bob Morgenthau, the newly-appointed U.S. Attorney in the Southern District. In June 1961, the firm had its annual office outing at the Rockaway Hunt Club in Cedarhurst, Long Island and Peter was invited back. He was an excellent golfer, and at the dinner that night was called up to receive the award for the lowest net score—a miniature golf club. In his response, Peter said—"So the Democrats won the election, and you lost me to the U.S. Attorney's Office. But look what you got in return—Gillespie, Walsh and Fiske—(waving the golf club) vote Democrat!"

6. One of the other problems for GE and Westinghouse was that the two experts for the defense did not agree with each other on certain important points, although both reached the same ultimate conclusion. GE and Westinghouse each strongly believed their witness was the best, and when they could not agree on one of them, called both. Kohn did a lot of damage to both witnesses—and their ultimate conclusions—by stressing the areas of conflict.

7. One of the reasons the litigation could be settled at levels which would not put some of the defendants out of business, and seriously cripple others financially, was that the plaintiff utilities were all customers of the defendants, who would be continuing to do business with them in years to come. They had a fiduciary duty to pursue the claims, but also an economic incentive to keep the settlements at a reasonable level that would allow the companies to stay in business and provide competition.

8. The Hornets also had an annual post-season dinner, where a player would be awarded a trophy in the form of a plaque on which was mounted an important piece of hockey equipment with the inscription "The most on the ball cup."

9. Our team at one time had a Yale captain and the all-time high scorer from Harvard.

10. In addition to the Darien Hornets games, while I was in college we used to have a Darien versus New Canaan pick-up game every morning at 8:00 a.m. during Christmas vacation. No matter what parties we had been to—or how late we'd come home—everyone always showed up for those games.

11. We produced a map of the United States with a red flag pin indicating each city where *The Northern Miner* was on a newsstand. When we offered the map with the flags in evidence, the SEC objected, citing lack of foundation. So, Gillespie spontaneously called Dan Kolb, a first-year associate (later to become a prominent senior partner at Davis Polk) to the stand. Dan had prepared the exhibit and Gillespie took him through it flag by flag, to document the factual basis for each, while his eight-month pregnant wife—who had just happened to come down to watch the trial that day—watched nervously from the back of the courtroom.

12. *Sec. & Exch. Comm'n v. Texas Gulf Sulphur Co.*, 258 F.Supp. 262, 296 (S.D.N.Y.) aff'd in part, rev'd in part, 401 F.2d 833 (2d Cir. 1968).

13. *Sec. & Exch. Comm'n v. Texas Gulf Sulphur Co.*, 401 F.2d 833 (2d Cir. 1968).

14. *Id.* at 854. The court said in a footnote: "The record reveals that news usually appears on the Dow Jones broad tape 2–3 minutes after the reporter completes dictation. Here, assuming that the Dow Jones reporter left the press conference as early as possible, 10:10 a.m., the 10–15 minute release (which took at least that long to dictate) could not have appeared on the wire before 10:22 a.m., and for other reasons unknown to us did not appear until 10:54 a.m." *Id.*

15. *Henry v. Richardson-Merrell Inc.*, 366 F. Supp. 1192 (D.N.J. 1973).

16. *Henry v. Richardson-Merrell Inc.*, 508 F.2d 28 (3d Cir. 1975).

17. One of the most important pieces of evidence came from a warehouseman in the southern part of the state. He was interviewed by Betty Jo ("B.J.") Pearce, a Davis Polk associate from Greensboro, North Carolina who—in 1974–1975—was the only woman working on the case from any one of the 22 law firms. I told her to take a para-legal with her to take notes; she replied, "Bob, I know this is unusual, but would it be all right if I took my mother instead—she can take good notes?" I agreed it was unusual, to say the least, but eventually said okay. When they walked into the warehouseman's office, where he had a set of books spread out on the table, his eyes lit up; he ran across the room and gave B.J.'s mother a big hug—it turned out they had been high school classmates. He then excused himself, went into the back of the building and came back with another set of books, saying, "I think this is what you really want."

18. *Windham v. American Brands*, 68 F.R.D. 641 (D.S.C. 1975).

19. *Windham v. American Brands*, 539 F.2d 1016 (4th Cir. 1976).

20. *Windham v. American Brands*, 565 F.2d 59 (4th Cir. 1977).

21. *Shultate v. National Association of Securities Dealers*, 509 F.2d 147 (5th Cir. 1975).

22. He later became a judge on the Connecticut Supreme Court.

23. She later became a united states magistrate judge and then a U.S. district judge in the Southern District.

24. Bill liked to tell the story that one day, while he was waiting for his FBI clearance, he walked by a small novelty store on 116th Street and the owner came out, pulled him aside and said, in a hushed voice, "The FBI was here asking questions. Don't worry, Mr. Tendy . . . I tell them nothing."

25. He was succeeded as Executive Assistant by Barry Kingham, one of the most respected prosecutors in the office.

26. In the fall of 1986, Attorney General Edwin Meese made a special trip to New York to present a plaque commemorating Bill's public service life, coupled with a tribute from President Reagan. The

plaque bore the following inscription: "Presented to William M. Tendy upon entering his thirtieth year of public service to express the gratitude of the United States of America, its government and its people, for his extraordinary contributions and spirit."

In 1992 the Fiske Association, comprised of all AUSAs who served with me from 1976–1980, created in Bill's memory the William M. Tendy Award, presented at the Association's annual dinner every year to one of our group who has performed exceptional public service since leaving the office.

27. This was perfectly appropriate under the existing asset forfeiture regulations.

28. *Fullilove v. Kreps*, 584 F.2d 600 (2d Cir. 1978).

29. *United States v. Werker*, 535 F.2d 198 (2d Cir. 1976).

30. *United States v. Amrep Corp.*, 545 F.2d 797 (2d Cir. 1976).

31. Later to become a United States district judge.

32. The concern about the defendants' willingness to do anything to avoid conviction was starkly revealed in a later trial of one of them, Guy Fisher. Evidence established that he had plotted to murder the two principal witnesses in the Barnes case and also AUSA Sear.

33. We, indeed, did that—after the trial and the resulting publicity, Geronimo appeared before the grand jury, represented by an experienced defense lawyer assigned by Judge Werker, and after hearing his testimony, the grand jury declined to indict.

34. Those incidents were described by Diaz in graphic detail—not only on the witness stand, but later in his book entitled: *Dancing with the Devil—Confessions of an Undercover Agent*, which he co-authored with Neal Hirschfeld and which was published by Simon & Schuster in 2010. On the fly-leaf under the heading—"Advance Praise for Louis Diaz and *Dancing with the Devil*," I gave the book, and Louis Diaz, a well-deserved accolade:

> "Louie Diaz put his life on the line, going undercover to develop evidence that was crucial in the conviction of the theretofore 'untouchable' narcotics kingpin Nicky Barnes. *Dancing with the Devil* recounts this story and many others in a graphic, colorful, and explosive first-person account of an extraordinary law enforcement career."

35. *United States v. Barnes*, 604 F.2d 121 (2d Cir. 1979).

36. Later he become an AUSA, a federal judge, and director of the FBI.

37. In one conversation at his union offices, Scotto was overheard saying the government must not be close to making a case because, if it were, President Carter would have been told about it and Scotto would not have been invited to the lunch.

38. Later to become a judge in the Southern District of New York.

39. *Socialist Workers Party v. Attorney Gen. of U.S.*, 458 F.Supp. 895, 918 (S.D.N.Y. 1978) (quoting Judge Griesa's May 31, 1977 opinion).

40. *In re Attorney Gen. of U.S.*, 565 F.2d 19, 23 (2d Cir. 1977).

41. *Id*. at 23–24.

42. *The New York Times* weighed in with an editorial captioned "Fencing With the Rule of Law." The editorial said: "This is not a criminal case in which the government would be forced to choose between

exposing an informant as a witness and abandoning prosecution. It is a civil case in which the plaintiffs risk being deprived of the right to prove the damages they claim. . . . We hope Mr. Bell reviews the matter with care and gets a grip on policy. He should ponder the spectacle of federal officials in contempt of court. [His] most important work is to uphold the law, not to fence with it."

43. *Bell v. Socialist Workers Party*, 436 U.S. 962 (1978).

44. *Socialist Workers Party v. Attorney General of U.S.*, 458 F.Supp. 895, 900 (S.D.N.Y. 1978).

45. *Id.* at 901.

46. *Id.* at 903.

47. *In re Attorney Gen. of U.S.*, 596 F.2d 58 (2d Cir. 1979).

48. *Id.* at 64.

49. *Id.* at 65.

50. *Id.* at 67.

51. *Socialist Workers Party v. Attorney General of U.S.*, 642 F.Supp. 1357 (S.D.N.Y. 1986).

52. In the late 1960's Organized Crime Strike Force Units were established by the Justice Department in a number of cities around the country, including New York. Reporting directly to the Justice Department's Organized Crime and Racketeering section, the concept was to have specialized units of prosecutors and FBI and IRS agents working together concentrating entirely on Organized Crime investigations and prosecutions. This produced an often uneasy relationship with the United States Attorneys, many of whom felt they should have responsibility for every investigation and prosecution within their district. One of those who felt that way was Dick Thornburgh, United States Attorney in Pittsburgh. When he became Assistant Attorney General in charge of the Criminal Division he decided to merge the strike forces into the U.S. Attorneys' Offices and with my enthusiastic concurrence started with New York. The merger was completed in the summer of 1976. That was the only such merger effected before the Carter administration took over. Beginning in 1988, when Thornburgh became Attorney General, he merged the rest into the U.S. Attorneys' Offices in their respective jurisdictions.

53. We obtained a conviction but it was reversed by the United States Supreme Court. *Chiarella v. United States*, 445 U.S. 222 (1980).

54. Karen Wagner, Bill Wurtz and Linda Thomsen became partners at DPW. (Linda also served as an AUSA in the District of Maryland and later as the Director of Enforcement of the SEC.) Rod Benedict became Deputy General Counsel of PricewaterhouseCoopers; Ann McDonald started her own firm with Jayne Robinson, another DPW associate; and Susan Johnston became a director at Weinstein, Pinson and Riley, P.S.

55. One of the specific suggestions was "give them Buffalo v. Cincinnati"—those being two of the worst teams at the time. When the schedule came out one of the games was, in fact, Buffalo v. Cincinnati. The NFL proof showed it was just a coincidence: the schedule had been made up by a person without knowledge of the presentation.

56. The documents relevant to the "force a merger" strategy had not been produced in response to our document requests to Myerson's team at Finley Kumble, but had been in response to our subpoenas to former USFL owners.

57. *United States Football League v. National Football League*, 842 F.2d 1335, 1370 (2d Cir. 1988).

58. She had no good answer as to whether the facts that produced a 188 percent increase in New York existed in the other eleven USFL cities.

59. *United States Football League v. National Football League*, 842 F. 2d 1335, 1342 (2d Cir. 1988).

60. *United States Football League v. National Football League*, 887 F. 2d 408, 411 (2d Cir. 1989).

61. John Elam (Columbus, OH); Frank Jones (Atlanta, GA); Gene Lafitte (New Orleans, LA) and Ralph Lancaster (Portland, ME).

62. Considering the storm that was created by the disapproval of certain of these candidates, it was perhaps fitting that the conference call that produced the negative vote on one of them took place on September 27, 1985 just as Hurricane Gloria, a category 1 hurricane with winds of 100 miles an hour, was hitting the Connecticut coast. We had been told to evacuate our house on the water—the police actually carried my 83 year old mother-in-law out of the house and up the hill to a neighbor's. The power and the telephones were out, so I took the call at the local police headquarters, where I was then serving on the three-member Police Commission.

63. Actually, Steve Markman and I were good friends. He was a strong ally in the fight over my proposed nomination for Deputy Attorney General (Chapter 29, *infra*) and he consulted me for advice when he was selected as the United States Attorney for the Eastern District of Michigan.

64. Later that year it came out in the *Legal Times* that Boyden Gray, then White House counsel to President Bush, had made numerous contributions to Democratic candidates.

65. *Mercury Bay Boating Club Inc. v. San Diego Yacht Club*, 150 A.D.2d 82, 88 (N.Y. App. Div. 1st Dep't. 1989) (quoting Judge Ciparick).

66. *Mercury Bay Boating Club Inc. v. San Diego Yacht Club*, 1989 N.Y. Misc. LEXIS 927 (N.Y. Sup. Ct. Mar. 28, 1989). Featured prominently in this analysis was a quotation that had appeared in the *San Diego Tribune* before the race:

> "The San Diego Yacht Club said it would meet New Zealand on the water in a three-race series for the America's Cup. *But, San Diego officials also said they believe they have the right to set up conditions they think will make it virtually impossible for New Zealand to win.*" (*San Diego Tribune*, Dec. 3, 1987, emphasis added.)

67. *Mercury Bay Boating Club Inc. v. San Diego Yacht Club*, 150 A.D.2d 82, 90 (N.Y. App. Div. 1st Dep't. 1989).

68. *Id*. at 91.

69. He had been a litigation partner in the New Zealand firm of Russell McVeigh, situated in Auckland and was then a prominent barrister specializing in international litigation. He later went on to become a Justice on the New Zealand High Court.

70. He has designed over 60 boats, including an International 14, the 12 meters *Canada I* and *Canada II* that were America's Cup challengers in 1983 and 1987, the *Sonar*, the *Ideal 18* and one of the most popular boats of all time —the *Laser* (currently there are more than 180,000 around the world).

71. *Mercury Bay Boating Club Inc. v. San Diego Yacht Club*, 76 N.Y.2d 256 (1990).

72. *Id*. at 272.

73. *Id*. at 273.

74. *Id.* at 274–75.

75. Arthur Liman had represented several criminal defendants during my term as United States Attorney, following in the footsteps of Judge Rifkind, who had from time to time represented criminal defendants as far back as the late 1950's when I was an AUSA. He had won a major acquittal of J. Truman Bidwell, the Chairman of the New York Stock Exchange, in a tax-evasion case during the Morgenthau years.

76. In August 2013 the *American Lawyer* published a list of what it called "The Top 50 Big Law Innovators of the last 50 Years." I was listed as one of ten who had created a practice specialty at their firms—in my case, white collar defense.

77. A story circulated that on one occasion, Thayer, who was an avid and very proficient golfer, lost $500 in a golf match at Washington's Burning Tree Country Club because, on the last hole, while he had a par, his partner had shot a 10. After ranting about the 10 through several scotches in the locker room, Thayer finally proclaimed, "I can't believe it—a bleeping 10. I could shoot a 10 blindfolded." The others took him up on it—there was a double or nothing bet for the whole $500. They took him back to the 18th hole. They put him in the right place over the ball, and with the right club for the distance—he was on the green in 3, but then had to putt, which was decidedly more problematic. He had 7 putts—shot a 10—and won the $500 back.

78. Arthur Golden, then a rising star associate, worked with me on this and several other cases, including the tobacco auction case. He went on to become one of the firm's most important partners and served on the Management Committee.

79. The F-15, F-16, F-18 and F-20 fighter planes, and the B-1B bomber.

80. Gary went on to become the Director of Enforcement, where he compiled a very impressive record, with a number of very successful high-profile cases. In 1989 he joined Davis Polk and was one of the firm's most productive partners until he left in 2001 to go to Credit Suisse, and later to Morgan Stanley—in each case as general counsel. In 2012 he left Morgan Stanley to become Global Chief of Legal Compliance and Regulatory Relations at Bank of America.

81. Harris also received a four year sentence. He, too, had a number of supportive letters, including one very controversial one from the same United States Attorney in Dallas who had written the SEC endorsing the administrator of the lie detector test. Written on his official Department of Justice stationery, it drew harsh criticism from top Department of Justice officials and Judge Richey.

82. Garey went on to become a partner at Davis Polk, a member of its Management Committee and a President of the New York City Bar Association.

83. Pat later became a part of the Whitewater team, an AUSA in the Southern District of New York and a partner at DLA Piper.

84. Sheila's participation in the case is a great story. She had worked on the case pre-indictment, and then had left on maternity leave. She returned in the middle of trial preparation. She wanted to stay with the case and her husband, Doug, was extremely supportive. He agreed to delay his entrance into medical school for a year so he could come down to Miami with Sheila and take care of the baby while she worked on the trial. After the trial she became an AUSA in Boston, a partner in the Boston firm of Foley, Hoag & Eliot and after Doug took a job in a Nashville teaching hospital she became a partner at Waller Landsen Dortch & Davis.

85. *Nat'l Union Fire Ins. Co. of Pittsburgh v. Brown*, 787 F. Supp. 1424 (S.D. Fla. 1991).

86. During our nine months in Florida, our team took advantage of the surroundings to enjoy the times when we were not working. We chartered a sailboat; we flew over to Bimini to go bone fishing; and a few times we played golf. One Saturday three of us (Carey Dunne, Pat Smith and I) went out to play at the Miami Beach public golf course. When we arrived we were asked by the starter whether we minded having a fourth player, a local golfer, join us. We said no and all four of us went out to the first tee. As golfers are prone to do, we asked him, "So Ed, what do you shoot?" He said "86." When we said, "Well that's better than any of us do," he replied, "Well what I mean by that is I play until I hit the ball 86 times—then I go home. Some days it's on the 10th hole; some days it's on the 11th or 12th—and one time I got all the way to the 13th." The day he played with us it was on the 11th or 12th: he hit his drive and said, "That's number 86," picked up his ball and went home.

87. This argument so enraged Tom Barr, the head of Cravath's litigation department, that he wrote a letter to then Attorney General William Barr demanding that Norman Moscowitz be censured by the Department of Justice. (To my knowledge, he never received a response.)

88. *United States v. Brown,* 79 F.3d 1550, 1562 (11th Cir. 1996).

89. *Id.*

90. According to Clifford, Marshall and other military figures believed that recognizing Israel as a State would antagonize the Arabs and threaten national security by cutting off the flow of Mideast oil and driving the Arab countries into the Soviet camp. Marshall bitterly opposed Clifford even being present at the critical meeting where this issue was discussed, believing that Clifford was there only to advance political arguments. After the decision was made Marshall never spoke to Clifford again. Clifford: *Counsel to the President: A Memoir* (1991).

91. His clients included General Electric, AT&T, ITT, RCA, DuPont, Howard Hughes and Hughes Tool, Time Inc., Standard Oil, Phillips Petroleum, El Paso Corporation and Knight Ridder. (He served on the Board of Directors of Knight Ridder and Phillips Petroleum.)

92. In the middle of all this—on June 3, 1991—my wife Janet had her sixtieth birthday. It was impractical for me to try to get home, so she flew down to Washington and stayed with me at the Watergate. That night, with leave from Clifford to take an evening off, on Bob Bennett's recommendation and with the use of his driver we had dinner at the Inn at Little Washington, aptly described as a "romantic fantasy world far removed from the harsh realities of modern day life"—about 70 miles west of Washington, D.C.

93. Clifford was also an excellent tennis player. Walking up the stairs in the Federal Reserve building on our way to the room where the questioning was going to take place, he stopped and pointed to a portrait on the wall: "He was my tennis partner"—referring to former Federal Reserve Chairman William McChesney Martin with whom he had won the Missouri State Championship.

94. The same—equally unavailing—arguments against an indictment had been made to Robert Mueller, then head of the Criminal Division of the Justice Department and later to become Director of the FBI.

95. See the full discussion of this at page 157 *supra.*

96. Later to become a judge on the Court of Appeals for the District of Columbia.

97. SBA regulations prohibited CMS from making loans to fund the purchase of land or to pay off other loans. The loan application, made on behalf of Susan McDougal d/b/a Master Marketing, stated that Master Marketing was an advertising consulting firm and the loan proceeds would be used for operating capital for the business. Title 18 U.S.C. § 1014 and 18 U.S.C. § 2 provide that the making of a false statement ". . . for the purpose of influencing . . . the action of a small business investment company . . . upon any . . . loan " is a criminal act by the person making it or anyone aiding and abetting it.

98. There was ice everywhere. Nina Totenberg missed the press conference because her husband had a serious fall on the ice and was taken to the hospital. When I arrived home that night the driver could not get up the hill at the beginning of the street where I lived, so I got out and walked the one-third mile to our house.

99. After Whitewater, Denis returned to Davis Polk, became a partner, left in 2010 to serve for four years as Chief of the Fraud Section of the DOJ, and returned to Davis Polk in September 2014. Julie became a tenured Professor at Georgetown Law School, where, in addition to serving as Associate Dean for the J.D. Program she wrote the definitive treatise on White Collar Crime. Mark is now a partner at Simpson, Thacher and Bartlett.

100. After Whitewater, Bill went back to King & Spalding—became the United States Attorney for the Northern District of Georgia (Atlanta) and is now a United States District Judge.

101. After Whitewater she went back to Hale & Dorr. In February 2008 she was appointed by Governor Duval Patrick to the Massachusetts Appeals Court.

102. Now a judge on the Court of Common Pleas (Hamilton County) in Ohio.

103. Both Joyce and Michele were from Brooklyn—and that produced some interesting culture clashes. When Joyce arrived in Little Rock, I picked her up at the airport and took her to the office. Denis was meeting with Gretchen Hall, a Little Rock FBI financial analyst. The three of them talked for a few minutes and Joyce left. Gretchen turned to Denis, and said, in a thick Arkansas drawl, "That Joyce—she sure has some accent."

104. After Whitewater they both went to law school; Frances became an Assistant District Attorney in the Queens County District Attorney's Office and John joined the legal department at Comcast in Philadelphia.

105. The RTC was an independent federal agency in charge of disposing of failed savings and loans and pursuing civil and criminal cases against those with responsibility for the failures. It was headed by a political appointee named by the President and confirmed by the Senate. Because President Clinton had not yet nominated a head of the RTC, Altman had been serving in that position and top Treasury officials—including Josh Steiner, Chief of Staff to Treasury Secretary Lloyd Bentsen and Jean Hanson, general counsel of the Treasury, had been assisting him (the position of general counsel at the RTC was also unfilled at that time).

106. Despite our strong differences of opinion, Congressman Leach and I got along well. On August 16, 1994, after I was replaced by the Independent Counsel Court, he delivered a statement on the floor of Congress entitled "A few good men who happen to be lawyers." It was about me, Ken Starr, Lloyd Cutler (who had stepped down as White House Counsel) and Abner Mikva (who had replaced him). Congressman Leach had good things to say about all four of us. After saying, "In my floor statement on passage of the independent counsel statute, I indicated my high regard for Mr. Fiske and my

assumption that most in the legislative branch presumed his reappointment," he complimented "the group of exceptional attorneys assembled by Mr. Fiske" and went on to say that "in his tenure in office, Mr. Fiske met his constitutional obligations well and faithfully."

After making equally positive statements about the others, he concluded by saying, "These four attorneys—Robert Fiske, Kenneth Starr, Lloyd Cutler and Abner Mikva—bring great credit to their profession. They ennoble public service."

107. A January 21, 1994 editorial captioned "Too Much Baggage" commented that while I was "an upstanding member of the New York bar," and "for most posts . . . would be an outstanding choice"—referencing their support for my nomination as Deputy Attorney General—("Why Justice Needs Fiske," June 22, 1989) this appointment needed someone "not in the least connected to the scandals circling the globe" and that "given the extreme sensitivity of the special counsel post, surely it would have been possible to find someone other than a prominent member of Mr. Clifford's defense team. Yes, Mr. Fiske is widely seen as upstanding; his list of character witnesses would be almost as long as his client's. But such a list is cool comfort to the growing number of Americans who think that something is wrong in high places." It ended by saying: "We wish Mr. Fiske the best of luck with his investigation, but his curriculum vitae makes a Congressional probe of Whitewater all the more necessary."

108. Hearings Relating to Madison Guaranty S&L and the Whitewater Development Corporation, July 27, 1994, p. 63.

109. Foster had had an "anxiety attack" earlier over the failed nomination of Zoe Baird for Attorney General. He told his sister everyone was criticizing him and he blamed himself for letting down the President.

110. The same statute that was at issue in connection with the ABA Judiciary Committee meetings.

111. In 1995 the Senate Judiciary Committee, which was holding hearings on Whitewater, released excerpts from notes written by Foster in March 1993 which related to the work he was then doing on the Clintons' 1992 tax returns. The issue was how to treat the $1,000 the Clintons had received from the sale of their interest in Whitewater to Jim McDougal. Foster's notes reflected a concern that the issue might lead to an audit which would "open up a can of worms" about the amount of their prior investment. Foster dealt with that concern by treating the $1,000 as fully taxable and claiming no deduction for any prior investment—a result that, as reflected in his contemporaneous notes, he felt "avoids any audit of issue."

112. That investigation was completed by Ken Starr and Robert Ray. Their final report concluded that there was insufficient evidence to support a prosecution for obstruction of justice or any other criminal conduct.

113. Rusty Hardin was unavailable for this trial, so I recruited Jim Ed, an experienced trial lawyer—member of the American College of Trial Lawyers and former United States Attorney for the Eastern District of Missouri (St. Louis). He lived on a farm and had a small two-man law office in Caruthersville, Missouri, part of the "boot" that adjoins northeast Arkansas. He was folksy, charming, spoke with a thick drawl and wore boots—riding in the back seat of his car meant you were going to spend a lot of time brushing hunting dog hairs off your suit. He was a perfect choice: Matthews' lawyer, Bill Bristow from Little Rock, complained to Judge Reasoner during the trial that he was being "out country-lawyered."

114. Section 592(a)(2), dealing with preliminary investigations to determine whether an application for the appointment of an Independent Counsel should be made to the Independent Counsel Court, states that:

> "In conducting a preliminary investigation under this chapter, the Attorney General shall have no authority to convene a grand jury plea bargain, grant immunity or issue subpoenas."

115. Tim was then a third year associate at Davis Polk who I had worked with on several matters and in whom I had a lot of confidence. He joined the team after Hale started cooperating and the investigations expanded. Since Whitewater Tim has been a private investor.

116. In early July I interviewed a very promising candidate, Bradley Lerman, who was a partner in a Chicago law firm and a former Assistant United States Attorney under Dan Webb, who had highly recommended him. We hit it off—and everyone in Little Rock really liked him. I remember telling him, "I would like to bring you on right now, but as a matter of prudence I think I should wait until I am reappointed. So, as soon as that happens, you can count on joining us." (He was later hired by Ken Starr.)

117. Now Head of Risk Planning for Consumer and Community Banking at JPMorgan Chase.

118. He quotes an internal memo written to Sentelle and Sneed: "I have serious doubts that we should replace Mr. Fiske unless we can find someone who is well known and who will have the full confidence of the public as well as the President's supporters, and the President's critics. I realize this is a pretty stringent requirement but unless we meet it we will have no principled reason to appoint a substitute for Mr. Fiske." Gormley wrote that Butzner did not believe that Ken Starr met those requirements because he believed he was a Washington insider and was active in partisan politics.

119. I learned later that after Mark received a phone call from Jo Ann Harris giving him the news of my replacement, he called Little Rock and there were animated discussions between the lawyers in Washington and the lawyers in Little Rock while I was still on the plane on the way to Orlando. Everyone was furious at what had happened and no one wanted to stay on.

120. Volume I, p. iii.

From Volume I, Appendix 5:

- "During the course of his investigation Independent Counsel Fiske discovered that Christopher Wade had purchased Lot 7 at Whitewater Development in the name of an acquaintance, who thereafter applied for a bank loan, pledging this property as security, without disclosing that Wade was the real owner;" (p. v)
- "Regulatory Independent Counsel Robert B. Fiske Jr. extensively investigated a series of related transactions involving fraudulent loans from Madison Guaranty and David Hale's CMS." (the $825,000 loan); (p. viii)
- "Prior to Independent Counsel Starr's appointment, Independent Counsel Fiske had substantially completed his investigation of three real estate appraisers, including Robert Palmer, who had done work for Madison Guaranty;" (p. xxxv) and
- "During regulatory Independent Counsel Fiske's review of information relative to whether Madison Guaranty's funds were directed to Whitewater Development or to campaigns for public office by President Clinton, evidence was developed of possible crimes relating to transactions involving the 1990 Clinton gubernatorial campaign account at the Perry County Bank in Perryville, Arkansas." (p. lxx)

121. I had two good friends in Little Rock: Alston Jennings and Mose Smith. I knew Alston through the ACTL—he had been President in 1983. Two days after my appointment was announced, I received a letter from him congratulating me, and saying "my house is your house." Regretfully, I had to tell him that for appearance reasons I could not associate with him at all since President Clinton had been a partner in his firm, Wright, Lindsey & Jennings. Mose Smith, a Little Rock doctor, had been a Yale classmate and a member of my 1952 Wolf's Head Senior Society delegation. We had stayed close over the years. He told me he wanted to have a dinner for me to meet his Little Rock friends. After reviewing the guest list—and eliminating almost half who were in some way connected to our investigation—I went ahead with it. After an article appeared in the *Arkansas Democrat Gazette* a few days later—"Independent Counsel hits the social circuit"—we did not do that again, but we did play squash and go fishing on the Little Red River.

122. Since 1994 we have had regular reunions of the entire team.

123. I made friends there; when I left they had a farewell ceremony and gave me a "Little Rock Athletic Club Staff" sweatshirt. I also was given a "Milford Track" tee shirt by the people at one of our favorite lunch places.

124. In Professor Gormley's book—*The Death of American Virtue*—he states that "Starr's Report confirmed point by point Robert Fiske's conclusions that Foster had committed suicide in Ft. Marcy Park, reaffirming the original report filed by Fiske in 1994." It did and came up with a few additional points. It described an oven mitt which was found in Foster's car that had fibers, a portion of a sunflower seed husk, and some lead which were also found in the pocket of Foster's pants, supporting the conclusion that the materials had been transferred from the mitt to his pocket by the gun—consistent with a scenario in which Foster transported the gun from his home in the oven mitt and then transferred it to his pocket as he walked into Ft. Marcy Park. The Starr Report also dealt with two issues that we had not: it contained an analysis of the carpet fibers on his clothing which it concluded came from a carpet in his home and it also determined that the only persons whose hairs could have been on his clothing and who could have been asked to give samples were persons already known to him (stating that the relevance of hairs in a murder investigation is only when there is a known suspect who is a stranger to the victim). Finally, Starr's investigators conducted a search for the bullet in a much larger area of the Park: they concluded that the fact that they did not find it did not preclude a finding of suicide in the Park for the same reasons we did. His report did not express any conclusion as to what had, or had not, motivated Foster's suicide. It said "Rather, the issue is *whether* Mr. Foster committed suicide and . . . compelling evidence exists that Mr. Foster was distressed and depressed in a manner consistent with suicide."

125. One year the Liskow partner who was with Chief Judge Politz made a too-sudden move and the pirogue capsized, dumping the Chief Judge—and the guide and the dog—into three feet of cold water. Fortunately, the Judge had a good sense of humor.

126. A lot depended on the weather up north. Cold weather would drive the ducks down south; if it was warm in the north, there would be a lot fewer ducks.

127. Judge Politz grew up in Napoleonville, Louisiana and after graduating from LSU Law School in 1959 became a very successful trial lawyer with a firm in Shreveport. He was appointed to the Fifth Circuit by President Carter in 1979 and he became Chief Judge in 1992. He was widely acclaimed for his work ethic, his energy, his charisma and his attention to detail in his effort to see that justice was done in every case. He was also widely acclaimed for his collegiality with his fellow judges and his deep commitment to delivery of legal services to the poor. Finally, a line in his obituary said "Any account of the life of Henry A. Politz would be incomplete without mention of his remarkable sense of humor."

128. A few years later when Judge Davis was Chairman of the Judicial Conference Committee on the Federal Rules of Criminal Procedure, he persuaded Chief Justice Rehnquist to appoint me to the Committee where I spent a very interesting six years with judges, Department of Justice representatives, other private lawyers and law professors working on proposed amendments to the Rules.

129. See *In re McBryde*, 117 F.3d 208 (5th Cir. 1997).

130. Later to become Attorney General and then Governor of Arizona, Secretary of Homeland Security in the Obama administration and President of the University of California.

131. See *In re McBryde*, 117 F.3d 208, 216 (5th Cir. 1997).

132. 28 U.S.C. § 137 provides that:

> "The chief judge of the district court . . . shall divide the business and assign the cases so far as [the] rules and orders [of the court] do not otherwise prescribe."

133. See *In re McBryde*, 117 F.3d 208, 216 (5th Cir. 1997).

134. The award honors a judge who has made a significant contribution to the improvement of the litigation process. He is one of twelve judges who have received the award since it was established in 1980.

135. See *In re McBryde*, 117 F.3d 208 (5th Cir. 1997).

136. This is a very important concept. Section 372, which establishes an administrative procedure, is not designed to circumvent or substitute for Article III appellate review on the merits.

137. He later became the CEO of Columbia-Presbyterian.

138. This was the first time either Michael or Art, third and fourth year associates respectively, had examined a witness in any type of proceeding. It had to be a daunting experience, bringing out evidence of abusive conduct by a district judge who was sitting there watching them, in front of five other federal judges, including the Chief Judge of the circuit, but they both carried it out with great skill and aplomb.

139. "The Judicial Council's investigation and subsequent discipline of Judge McBryde represents the most significant application of the Judicial Conduct and Disability Act, 28 U.S.C. § 372 since its enactment in 1980." *McBryde v. Committee to Review Circuit Council and Disability Orders of Judicial Conference of United States*, 83 F. Supp.2d 130, 140 (D.D.C. 1999).

140. Consisting of three circuit judges and two district judges from around the country with Chief Justice William J. Bauer from the Court of Appeals for the Seventh Circuit presiding.

141. With respect to the "merits argument" the Review Committee held:

> "Although a judge indeed may not be sanctioned out of disagreement with the merits of rulings, a judge certainly may be sanctioned for a consistent pattern of abuse of lawyers appearing before him. The fact that that abuse is largely evidenced by the judge's rulings, statements, and conduct on the bench does not shield the abuse from investigation under the Act." (Review Committee Report, p. 15).

With respect to the sufficiency argument, the Review Committee held:

> "The evidence adduced regarding Judge McBryde's patterns of conduct is more than sufficient to support the Judicial Council's findings. Even if [the testimony of witnesses favorable to Judge McBryde] is believed . . . there is nothing in it that undercuts the impressive mound

of evidence that Judge McBryde has frightened and intimidated a significant portion of the local bar." (Review Committee Report, pp. 19–20).

142. *McBryde v. Committee to Review Circuit Council and Disability Orders of Judicial Conference of United States*, 83 F. Supp.2d 135 (D.D.C. 1999). McBryde was represented in the Article III litigation by Arnon D. Siegel of Washington, D.C. (a former DPW associate) and David Broiles of Fort Worth (who had been with Judge McBryde during the administrative proceedings).

143. The vote was 2–1 (Williams and Silberman) with a concurring and dissenting opinion by Judge Tatel who agreed with the constitutional analysis, but questioned whether all of the individual actions by Judge McBryde warranted sanctions. *McBryde v. Committee to Review Circuit Council and Disability Orders of Judicial Conference of United States*, 264 F.3d 52 (D.C. Cir. 2001).

144. The trial, which resulted in the largest verdict in Georgia history at that time, was the subject of a book—*Side Impact, How a Georgia Jury Slammed General Motors for $105 Million*. The book featured Butler's cross examination of General Motors' then President Robert C. Stempel.

145. On remittitur the Trial Court reduced the damages to $20 million compensatory and $20 million punitive.

146. One of the Judges on the Court was Stephen N. Limbaugh Jr., a first cousin of Rush Limbaugh. Their mutual grandfather was Rush H. Limbaugh Sr., a prominent lawyer in Cape Girardeau, Missouri who had argued more than 60 cases before the Missouri Supreme Court, had been President of the Missouri Bar and when he died, at age 104—as the nation's oldest practicing lawyer—was heralded as "a lawyer's lawyer" who had been a mentor and role model for many Missouri lawyers. When, as President of the American College of Trial Lawyers in 1992, I attended the annual dinner of the Missouri Fellows, it turned out to be his 101st birthday. Everyone sang "Happy Birthday" to him, and when he was introduced we were advised that he was the largest producer of business for his firm that year (he had settled a very sizable personal injury case).

147. On one of our trips to the Clerk's Office Frank Gundlach told us about Harry Truman's application to the Missouri Bar. There was a framed copy of his handwritten application on the wall, submitted in 1947 when he was still President. According to the application he had attended the Kansas City School of Law for two and a half years, although he had never gone to college. While acknowledging that he had received no scholastic degrees, he said that he had received "a great many honorary ones." Under the employment section, Truman said he had "served for eight years as Presiding Judge of the Jackson County Court, ten years as a U.S. Senator, three years as Vice President, and two years as President of the United States." As character references he listed "all U.S. Senators from 1935 to date, Vice Presidents from 1932 to 1940" and "all Cabinet members USA at present." His application was not granted because he had not graduated from law school. Later that year, well after we had argued the case, the Supreme Court of Missouri granted him an honorary membership in the Missouri Bar.

148. *Rodriguez v. Suzuki Motor Corp.*, 936 S.W.2d 104 (Mo. 1996).

149. On remittitur, the Court again reduced the compensatory damages to $20 million.

150. Jennifer left DPW after this case to become Deputy Assistant Attorney General at the DOJ, then an assistant counsel in the White House Counsel's office and finally general counsel of the Office of Management and Budget before returning to DPW where she became a partner.

151. Now a special counsel at Covington & Burling in London.

152. He argued the second appeal himself.

153. *Rodriguez v. Suzuki Motor Corp.*, 996 S.W.2d 47 (Mo. 1999).

154. In 1998 Judge White was nominated by President Clinton for the United States District Court in the Eastern District of Missouri. But in 1999, led by opposition from then Senator (former Governor) John Ashcroft, the Republicans blocked his nomination in a vote on the Senate floor—the first time that had happened since Judge Bork's failed nomination for the United States Supreme Court. Ashcroft's opposition was based principally on the ground that White was soft on criminals, as evidenced by his rulings in death penalty cases. In 2013, he was nominated again by President Obama, and was confirmed by the Senate in 2014.

155. We also argued that Consumers Union had deliberately excised footage of the Isuzu Trooper's runs from the video tape shown at the press conference announcing the test results to downplay the fact that the Trooper also had trouble making it through the course. In addition we charged Consumers Union with submitting a false affidavit in which Sheehan, Wood, Nappi and Knoll stated it was Denison, not Nappi, who said "All right, Ricky baby!" after Small tipped up the Samurai. Nappi later admitted that he, in fact made the statement.

156. The same findings, the exclusion of which led to the second reversal in the Rodriguez case.

157. There had been news stories highlighting the Samurai's instability and propensity to roll over. In addition, during the evaluation and break-in process, the Facilities Manager of ATD had rolled the Samurai on a snow-covered gravel road at 15 MPH.

158. *Suzuki Motor Corp. v. Consumers Union of United States, Inc.*, 2000 U.S. Dist. LEXIS 19608 (C.D. Cal. May 24, 2000).

159. *Suzuki Motor Corp. v. Consumers Union of United States, Inc.*, 292 F.3d 1192 (9th Cir. 2002) withdrawn and superseded on denial of reh'g en banc, 330 F.3d 1110 (9th Cir. 2003).

160. *Suzuki Motor Corp. v. Consumers Union of United States, Inc.*, 330 F.3d 1110, 1133 (9th Cir. 2003).

161. The majority had said "Although Consumers Union had its own interpretation of why it modified the long course and retested the Samurai, we, of course, cannot credit that interpretation over Suzuki's at the summary judgment stage." *Id.* at 1115.

162. *Id.* at 1144.

163. *Id.*

164. *Suzuki Motor Corp. v. Consumers Union of United States, Inc.*, 292 F.3d 1192 (9th Cir. 2002), aff'd on reh'g, 330 F.3d 1110 (9th Cir. 2003) (en banc) (Judge Kozinzki dissenting).

165. *Id.*

166. *Id.* at 1116.

167. *Id.* at 1119.

168. *Consumers Union of United States, Inc. v. Suzuki Motor Corp.*, 540 U.S. 983 (2003). While I came close in my career, I never had an argument in the United States Supreme Court. I appeared there once—but it was not for a client. It was in 2006, as part of a Supreme Court Historical Society program to reproduce famous arguments in the court's history. I was asked to play the role of Aaron Burr's defense counsel in a reprise of his 1807 trial for treason before Chief Justice Marshall. Justice Antonin Scalia played the part of Marshall and his son Eugene played the part of the prosecutor. We argued it in the Supreme Court—in front of a large crowd—and Justice Scalia ruled, as had Justice Marshall, that the prosecution had not proved its case.

169. The tape was later produced in discovery during a very contentious civil suit which Medinol had brought against BSC.

170. She went on to become chief litigation counsel at Time Warner.

171. It was not unusual to have the SEC involved in a U.S. Attorney driven Grand Jury investigation when there were accounting issues involved that might implicate the accuracy of the financial statements.

172. At one of those meetings I met the United States Attorney, David Freudenthal. The first thing he said to me, with a smile was "we know all about you—you are from 'the Sovereign District of New York.'"

173. Although Christie's and its President and CEO, Christopher Davidge—who was admitting to price fixing with Dede Brooks—were given amnesty from criminal prosecution, they had no immunity from civil suits. Eventually, a class action suit brought on behalf of sellers was settled for $512,000,000 with Christie's and Sotheby's each paying $256,000,000. Taubman paid $186 million of the Sotheby portion. He explained the rationale for making this contribution, while still maintaining his innocence, as follows in his book:

> "Christie's owner, Francois Pinault, paid all $256 million of his company's portion, and I agreed to contribute $186 million of Sotheby's civil settlements personally. My level of participation was consistent with my majority ownership position. I also was fully aware that without my assistance, the company faced the very real prospect of bankruptcy. These were decisions made out of enlightened self-interest, not charity. Sotheby's represented one of my most significant investments. Abandoning the company and fending for myself would have destroyed a personal asset that, even in the midst of scandal, was worth hundreds of millions of dollars. Besides, all this had happened on my watch. I was committed to the survival of this extraordinary franchise and the preservation of its employees' livelihoods."

174. Interestingly, author Christopher Mason in *The Art of the Steal*, released in 2004, tells us what Tennant's testimony would have been. Mason, who interviewed Tennant for the book, writes: "Tennant firmly denied that he told Davidge to fix prices with Dede Brooks . . . A crime had clearly been committed by Davidge and Brooks, but he and Taubman had nothing to do with it." As for the incriminating memo, Tennant told Mason that there never was a memo: "Instead, the 'memo' was merely three pieces of paper on which Tennant had jotted down a series of notes over several days, weeks or months—an assertion that appeared to square with the discovery by Taubman's lawyers that two different kinds of paper had been used: one sheet had faint blue lines and the other two, faint gray lines. The various unrelated paragraphs, Tennant said, 'were all written at different times.'" Tennant told Mason that much of the material in the memo actually reflected information given to him by Christopher Davidge, not Alfred Taubman.

175. Neil Potischman, now a Davis Polk partner; Bill Komaroff, now a partner at Proskauer Rose; Jacob Buchdahl, now a partner at Susman Godfrey; Ed Boyle, now a partner at Venable; and Stephanie Gold, who is no longer practicing law. Both Bill and Jacob served as AUSAs in the Southern District after leaving Davis Polk and before joining their present firms.

176. Those fell into a number of different categories:

Education
In addition to the Michigan Partnership for New Education, these included the development of programs for charter schools; support of the Eton School for children with learning disabilities

(including dyslexia); creation of the American Institutions Program at Michigan, Brown and Harvard in the aftermath of Watergate to ensure that students would have a solid understanding of the country's social, economic and political institutions; and scholarships at Michigan and Michigan State Universities for highly-qualified students from Jordan on the condition that they return to Jordan and "give back" to Jordan's government and society.

University Building and Programming

These included the endowment of the School of Architecture at Michigan; the Harvard Center for State and Local Government at the Kennedy Center at Harvard; the Wharton School of Real Estate; and the Center for Creative Studies, a vocational design college in Detroit.

City of Detroit and Michigan

These included the Detroit Renaissance, established in the wake of the 1960 riots in an effort to revitalize downtown Detroit; the Detroit Institute of Arts; and the Taubman Fellowship program, which funds scholarships to local Michigan governmental officials to attend a three-week continuing education program at the Harvard Center for State and Local Government.

Health Care

Utilizing his skills as an architect and builder, he conceived the idea of a Health Care Center at Michigan (featuring private rooms instead of shared quarters which he felt contributed to disease spreading), which received national attention for its innovative design. He also designed and funded a new Medical Library at the University of Michigan and also at the Lauder Breast Cancer Center at Sloan Kettering.

177. He also retained his interest in, and support for, Michigan and Michigan baseball, endowing the Irene and Morris B. Kessler Presidential Scholarships (named after his wife's parents) and donating the money for what is now the Wilpon Baseball and Softball Complex at Michigan.

178. They asked every Mets witness, including Fred Wilpon, "Is a game played by the Mets in 2006 a Mets game?" and, of course, the answer had to be yes.

179. Now chief legal officer of Morgan Stanley.

180. Now a partner at O'Melveny & Myers.

181. Restatement (Second) of Contracts § 201(2).

182. *Sports Channel Assocs. v. Sterling Mets, L.P.*, 8 Misc. 3d 1027(A), (N.Y. App. Term 2005).

183. *Sports Channel Assocs. v. Sterling Mets, L.P.*, 25 A.D. 3d 314 (N.Y. App. Div. 1st Dep't 2006).

184. They had continued to invest right up to the end. Indeed, Saul Katz unknowingly deposited $1 million with Madoff on behalf of a foundation an hour after he was arrested.

185. The motion was filed on Sunday, March 27, two days after the trustee had filed an amended complaint reiterating those allegations. I was in Florida with my grandson, Sam, at a Red Sox spring training game. We had a conference call to discuss the press release we were going to issue. It was scheduled for 1 p.m.—the same time as the start of the game. I was on a cell phone at the ball park; it was the only conference call I have been on that started with the National Anthem.

186. *Picard v. HSBC Bank PLC*, 450 B.R. 406, 410 (S.D.N.Y. 2011).

187. Inquiry notice is essentially a negligence standard—the trustee would have to prove the Sterling partners (1) were on notice of facts that would indicate to a reasonable person (objectively) that Madoff

might be engaged in fraudulent activities and (2) did not do anything to look into it—a failure to act. Willful blindness, on the other hand, required the trustee to prove that the Sterling partners subjectively believed there was a high probability that Madoff was engaged in fraudulent activity (we said "a Ponzi scheme") and took deliberate affirmative steps to avoid confirming that belief.

188. *Picard v. Katz*, 462 B.R. 447, 453, 455 (S.D.N.Y. 2011).

CREDITS

p. 33 From *The New York Times*, June, 25, 1959 © 1959 *The New York Times*. All rights reserved. Used by permission and protected by the copyright laws of the United States. The printing, copying, redistribution of the Content without the express written permission is prohibited.

p. 37 *Life Magazine* 1957.

p. 42 From *The New York Times*, July 20, 1960 © 1960 *The New York Times*. All rights reserved. Used by permission and protected by the copyright laws of the United States. The printing, copying, redistribution of the Content without the express written permission is prohibited.

p. 57 From *The New York Times*, April 20, 1965 © 1965 *The New York Times*. All rights reserved. Used by permission and protected by the copyright laws of the United States. The printing, copying, redistribution of the Content without the express written permission is prohibited.

p. 85 From *The New York Times*, January 19, 1977 © 1977 *The New York Times*. All rights reserved. Used by permission and protected by the copyright laws of the United States. The printing, copying, redistribution of the Content without the express written permission is prohibited.

p. 90 From *The New York Times*, June 5, 1977 © *The New York Times*. All rights reserved. Used by permission and protected by the copyright laws of the United States. The printing, copying, redistribution of the Content without the express written permission is prohibited.

p. 93 Photograph by Alex Webb, Magnum Photos, used under license.

p. 106 From *The New York Times*, November 16, 1979 © 1978 *The New York Times*. All rights reserved. Used by permission and protected by the copyright laws of the United

States. The printing, copying, redistribution of the Content without the express written permission is prohibited.

p. 112 From *The New York Times*, March 20, 1979 © 1979 *The New York Times*. All rights reserved. Used by permission and protected by the copyright laws of the United States. The printing, copying, redistribution of the Content without the express written permission is prohibited.

p. 135 From *The New York Times*, November 24, 1982 © 1982 *The New York Times*. All rights reserved. Used by permission and protected by the copyright laws of the United States. The printing, copying, redistribution of the Content without the express written permission is prohibited.

p. 207 © *The Miami Herald*, April 17, 1996.

p. 225 From *The New York Times*, January 21, 1994 © 1994 *The New York Times*. All rights reserved. Used by permission and protected by the copyright laws of the United States. The printing, copying, redistribution of the Content without the express written permission is prohibited.

p. 238 From *Time Magazine*, April 4, 1994. Time Inc. Used under license.

p. 274 © *Consumers Union*, July 1998.

p. 323 Photograph courtesy Russell Williams.

INDEX

A

Abedi, Agha Hasan, 212, 213, 216, 217
Abramowitz, Elkan, 73, 81
Adams, Faneuil, 24
Adams, Nelson, 18
Adams, Taggart, 73, 82
Adham, Kamal, 213
AG Edwards Co., 193–197
Aibel, Howard, 49
Ainslee, Michael, 298
Albano, Vincent, 71
Alexander, Clifford 270
Alliance for Justice, 155–156
Allis-Chalmers Manufacturing Company,
    46–50
al-Nahyan, Zayad , 213
Altman, Robert, 211–219
Altman, Roger, 232, 233, 238, 248
American Bar Association Committee on
    Federal Judiciary, 152–160
American College of Trial Lawyers,
    146–149, 203
American Cyanamid Company, 1, 3, 4
American Stock Exchange, 67–68
America's Cup, 169–180
AMREP Corporation, 87
Anastasia, Albert, 103
Anastasio, Anthony, 99–106, 218
Anheuser-Busch, 193–197
antitrust cases, 67–68, 119, 138–145,
    297–301
Arcara, Richard, 85

Arkansas Democrat Gazette, 256–257
Armstrong, Mike, 270–271
Arnold, Jim, 287, 288
Arnold, Robert, 131, 133, 137
Aron, Nan, 155–156
Arthur Andersen, 292–293
Ashcroft, John, 270, 339
Attorney General's Advisory Committee
    of United States Attorneys, 117–118
Awan, Amjad, 214

B

Babcock and Wilcox, 124–137
Baker, Howard, 161
Baer, Harold, 102, 328
Ball, George F., 277, 279, 281, 284
Ball, George L., 188–190
Balsam Lake Club, 5, 181–182
Bando, Nick, 37–39
Bank of Credit & Commerce Interna-
    tional, 212–219
Barbour, William, 265
Barnes, Leroy "Nicky," 89–98, 118
Barr, Tom, 332
Barr, William, 332
Battaglia, Giuseppe, 34–35
Bauer, William, 337
Bavier, Bob, 171–172
Bell, Griffin, 85, 91, 110–112, 113, 117,
    147, 190, 228, 270
Bendix, 193–197
Benedict, Rod, 124, 128

Bennett, Bob, 214, 217, 218–219, 250, 332
Bentsen, Lloyd, 236, 333
Berger v. United States, 187
Bicks, Bob, 67–68
bicycling, 294–296
Biden, Joseph, 159–160
Biller, Morris, 103
Bishop, Jerry, 57, 59
Bivens, Frances, 276
Bjork, Bob, 29
Black, Robert P., 216–217
Black, Roy, 202
Blumenfeld, Joseph, 83
Bolich, Daniel, 30–31
Bollinger, Lee, 305
Bolten, Joshua, 293
Bonsal, Dudley, 57–59
Bork, Robert, 69, 154–161
Boston Scientific Corporation, 286–288
Boudin, Leonard, 108, 112
Boyle, Ed, 340
Bradley, John, 218, 219
Brady, Nick, 163
Bregman, Leon, 38–39
Breitbart, David, 92, 94–95
Breitel, Charles, 114
Breslin, Jimmy, 105–106
Bring, Murray, 65–66
Bristow, Bill, 334
Broiles, David, 338
Bromley, Bruce, 25, 70–71
Brooks, Diana D., 298, 299–302, 303, 340
Brown, David F., 198–209
Brown, Peter, 150
Brownell, George, 22
Brownell, Herbert, 15, 82, 152
Bruce, Promise, 95
Bryck, John, 229
Buchdahl, Jacob, 340
Buchmeyer, Jerry, 262–263, 264
Buchwald, Naomi Reice, 73, 88

Bufalino, Russell, 118
Burgess, Angela, 269, 303
Burke, Arthur, 264, 266
Burlington Northern Railway, 290
Burlington Resources, 289–293
Burns, Arnold, 161
Burton, Dan, 249
Bush, George Herbert Walker, 162, 164–165, 166, 228, 253, 302
Bush, George W., 293
Butler, Jim, 274, 275–276, 278, 279
Butzner, John, 253

C
Cahill, John, 41
Cahill, Tom, 72
Caminker, Evan, 305
Campbell Taggart Company, 193–197
Capital Management Systems. *See* Whitewater investigation
Caplan, David, 316
Cappuccio, Paul, 275
Carey, Hugh, 102, 103, 104, 106
Carlino, Charles, 37–39
Carroll, Michael, 276, 281–282, 292
Carson, Ralph, 20, 24, 25
Carter, Jimmy, 83, 84, 91, 97, 101, 104, 109, 112, 182, 211–212, 221, 246–247
Cerow, Darcy, 261, 265
Chance Vought, 191
Chapman, Robert, 65–66
check kiting cases, 188–190
Chemie Grunenthal, 60, 61
Cherkasky, Michael, 217
Cherrick, Jordan, 275
Chertoff, Michael, 292
cholesterol drug cases, 66–67
Christie's, 297–304
Christy, Arthur H., 31, 32, 115–116
Church Committee, 108
Ciparick, Carmen, 173, 175, 330

City Investing, 198

Civiletti, Benjamin, 115–116, 117

civil rights cases, 119

Clark, Merrell "Ted," 195–196

Cleary, Les, 146

Clifford, Clark, 210–219, 236–237, 250

Clinton, Bill, 148, 207, 335. *See also*
　　Whitewater investigation

Clinton, Hillary Rodham. *See* Whitewater
　　investigation

Coates, Francis G., 57–59

Cohen, William, 234–235, 236, 270

Cohn, Roy, 139

Coleman, Leighton, 23

Coleman, Mary Sue, 305

Coleman, Randy, 230

Coleman, William, 157–158, 159

Colonial Sand & Stone, 40–43

Commission for the Review of FBI Secu-
　　rity Programs, 270

Commission on Judicial Compensation,
　　271–272

Commuter League, 52

Conner, Dennis, 172–173

Connolly, Albert, 57–58

Consumers Union, 273–285

Cooney, Jack, 184, 189, 193, 195, 214, 218

Cooper, Grant and Phyllis, 146

Coordinating Committee for Multiple
　　Litigation of the United States Dis-
　　trict Courts, 47–48

Corelli, Michele, 229, 252, 333

Cornell, Irene, 106

Cornell, Nina, 142–143

Correa, Matthew, 41

Costle, Douglas, 182

Cote, Denise, 89, 92

Cotton, Rick, 271–272

Counsel to the President (Clifford), 215–216

Courtney, Elizabeth, 183

Courtroom (Reynolds), 10

Cox, Archibald, 7, 69, 116, 157, 221

Cox, Bill, 171–172

Craib, Ann, 20–21

Crovitz, Gordon, 162–163

Cuniffe, Ed, 27

Cuomo, Andrew, 270–271

Cuomo, Mario, 102, 104, 316–317

Curnin, Tom, 189

Curran, Paul, 70, 87, 120, 246–247

Cutler, Lloyd, 201, 333, 334

D

D'Amato, Alphonse, 141, 164, 165,
　　234–235, 236

Danforth, John, 164–165

Daniels, George, 299, 303–304

Danis, Benjamin, 34–35

Darien Hornets, 52

Darien Land Trust, 272

Darien Police Commission, 272, 330

Davidge, Christopher, 298–301, 303, 340

Davis, Al, 141

Davis, Edward, 202

Davis, Eugene, 259, 261, 265, 268, 337

Davis, John W., xiv, 19

Davis Polk, 43–68, 168, 259–322

Davis Polk & Wardwell, 122–145

Davis Polk Wardwell Sunderland &
　　Kiendl, 18–26

Days, Drew, 83

Dean, Arthur, 24

Dean, John W., 107

DeAngelo, Tony, 16–17

*Death of American Virtue, The: Clinton vs.
　　Starr* (Gormley), 253, 336

DeBella, Tore, 202, 205, 206

Denison, Ronald, 281

Dennis, James, 264

Deputy Attorney General, 162–167

Devine, Jack, 233

Dewey, Thomas E., 15

Diaz, Louis, 96, 328

Dimock, Edward, 31

Dioguardi, John, 36–39

DiPalermo, Joey, 74–75

Divorce Mediation Training Associates, 7

Dodyk, Paul, 200, 201, 204–205

Doherty, Nancy, 261–263

Doisy v. Edwards, 275, 276

Dole, Bob, 236

Donaldson, William H., 21–22

Donlan, Jack, 141

Doubleday, Nelson, 308–309

Dow Jones Instant News Service, 57, 59

Doyle, John, 73, 88

Dreeben, Michael, 208

Drumheller, Andy, 290, 291

Dubis, Deborah, 274, 275, 277

duck hunting, 259–261

Duffey, Bill, 228, 256

Duffy, Kevin, 87

Dugan, Tom, 16

Dunn, Bert, 127–128, 130, 136

Dunne, Carey, 202, 269, 332

Durant, William D., 1–2

E

Eastman, Elizabeth, 246–247

Edelstein, David, 71, 74

Edmondson, James, 207

Edwards, Steve, 202

Edwards, Tom, 81

E. F. Hutton, 188–190

Ehrling, Robert F., 198, 200, 201–202, 205, 206

Einhorn, Eddie, 142

Eisele, G. Thomas, 207

Eisenhower, Dwight D., 15, 17, 152

Elam, John, 330

Ellison, Larry, 179–180

Enron, 292–293

Erny, S.S., 2–3

Esso, 24

Ettinger, Mitchell, 218

F

Faircloth, Lauch, 250

Fallon, John, 77

Farr, Bruce, 173

Fay, Michael, 172–179, 180

Federal Advisory Committee Act, 156

Federal Bar Council, 150–151

Federal Bureau of Investigation, 107–114, 243–244, 270

Federal Tort Claims Act, 107

Federal Trade Commission, 119

Ferguson, Warren, 282-283

First American, 212–219

Fisher, Guy, 94, 95–96, 97, 98, 137, 328

Fisher, Wally, 94–95, 96

fishing, 5, 181

Fiske, Addie (niece), 222, 326

Fiske Association, 328

Fiske, Bob (son), 41, 42, 70, 162, 181, 183, 326

Fiske, Hal, 326

Fiske, Janet (wife), 13–14, 18–19, 26, 39, 41–42, 64, 162, 169, 171, 181, 203, 222, 246–247, 252, 255, 257, 294, 332

Fiske, John Adams, 4, 7, 128

Fiske, Jonathan Parker Bishop, 1

Fiske, Julia, 326

Fiske, Lenore (mother), 4–5, 6, 35, 180

Fiske, Linda (daughter), 27, 42, 70, 162, 183

Fiske, McNeil Seymour, 4, 7–8, 294

Fiske, Robert Bishop (father), 1–6, 10, 35, 180, 181

Fiske, Robert B. Jr.
  background/childhood of, 1–9
  children of, 27, 41–42, 59, 88, 180, 199, 296
  Darien home, 41–42, 51–55, 203
  law school years, 10–14

marriage, 13–14
New York apartment, 77–78
Fiske, Sue (daughter), 70, 162, 222, 296
Fiske Brick Company, 1
Fitzhugh, William, 230, 251
Fleming, Peter, 184, 326
Floyd, James, 132, 137
Flynn, Michael, 264, 266
Foley, Tom, 235, 270
Ford, Gerald, 69, 71, 84, 196
Foster, Lisa, 243
Foster, Vincent, 220, 224, 240–245, 248,
    249–250, 257
Fowler, Cody, 146–147
Fox, Don, 45
Freedman, Helen, 310, 311
Freeh, Louis, 101, 226, 244, 250, 258, 270
Freudenthal, David, 291–292, 340
Frigidaire Corporation, 1–2
Fuller, Vincent, 201, 202

G
Galin, Ross, 311, 341
Ganey, James Cullen, 47
Garland, Merrick, 222
Garment, Leonard, 85
Garza, Emilio, 264
Gearan, Mark, 233
General Development Corporation,
    198–209
General Electric, 46, 49
General Motors (GM), 1–2, 274–275
General Public Utilities, 124, 127–137
Gephardt, Richard, 235
Geronimo, Robert, 92–95, 96
Gershman, Debbie, 252
Gerth, Jeff, 223
Gillespie, Hazard, xii–xiii, 24, 25, 26,
    32–33, 38, 40–42, 44, 46–50, 56–57,
    70, 115, 120, 322, 327
Gingrich, Newt, 235

Giuliani, Rudolph, 75, 120, 162, 186–187
Gladwell, Malcolm, 297
Glanzer, Seymour, 185
Goldberger, Paul, 96
Golden, Arthur, 331
Golden, Beth, 252
Goldwater, Barry, 196
Golliver, Joyce, 229, 333
Gonzales, Alberto, 293
Gormley, Ken, 253, 335–336
Gotbaum, Victor, 103
Gotham Beef Co., 30–31
Graber, Susan, 282
Graham, Maurice, 276
Grand, Paul, 185
Grassley, Charles, 164
Gray, Boyden, 330
Gray, William, 164
Green, Karen, 287
Greenberg, Daniel, 39
Griesa, Thomas P., 108–114
Griswold, A. Whitney, 155
Grossman, Eric, 311
Grossman, Marshall, 284
Grumman Aircraft, 196
Grunewald, Henry, 30–31
Guarna, Domenico, 34–35
Gumpert, Emil, 146, 147–148
Gundlach, Frank, 275, 338
Gurfein, Murray, 112

H
Haden, Charles H. II, 186
Hafetz, Fred, x, 73, 88
Hale, David, 224, 230–231, 234, 251–252
Hall, Gretchen, 333
Hall, Paul, 103
Halperin, Max, 30–31
Hamill, Pete, 106
Hancock, Stewart, 176, 178–179
Hanson, Jean, 232, 233, 333

Hanssen, Robert, 270
Hardin, Russell "Rusty," 228–229, 230,
    289–293, 334
Harrell, Morris, 68
Harris, Billy Bob, 193–197, 331
Harris, Jo Ann, 222, 225, 228, 335
Harriss, Gordon, 264, 268
Hatch, Orrin, 159, 160, 164
Herblein, James, 132
Herlands, William, 37–38
Hess, Leon, 141
Heyman, Sam, 305
Heymann, Phil, 117, 221–222
Higginbotham, Patrick, 264
Hill, Robert M., 67–68
Hills, Carla, 270
Hincks, John, 44
Hinton, Longstreet, 56–57
Hirsch, Charles, 242, 249–250
Hirschhorn, Joel, 202, 205, 217
hockey, 51–55, 256
Hoffa, Jimmy, 36, 118
Holder, Eric, 233
Howard, David, 310–311
Hubbell, Webster, 231–232, 244, 251
Humphrey, Gordon, 164
Hynes, Patricia, 87

I

Ickes, Harold, 233
Impellizzeri, Frances, 229
Independent Counsel Act, 221–227, 250
International Ladies' Garment Workers'
    Union, 39
International Longshoremen's Association,
    100–106, 118
Iran/Contra affair, 158, 221, 233–234

J

Jackson, Bill, 67, 68
Jackson Engineering, 104–105

Jacobs, Ed, 21
Jaffe, Joe, 73
Javits, Jacob, 23, 33, 70–71
Jaworski, Leon, 116, 147, 157
Jeffress, Bill, 264, 265–266
Jennings, Alston, 148, 336
Jenrette, John, 65–66
Johns, Andrew, 181
Johnson, Lyndon, 84, 210–211
Johnson, Sterling, 76–77
Johnston, Susan, 124, 128
Jonas, Steve, 287
Jones, Frank, 228, 330
Jordan, Barbara, 159
Jordan, Hamilton, 115–116
Judicial Panel on Multi-District Litigation,
    49–50

K

Kamenar, Paul, 163
Kathryn Rodriguez v. Suzuki, 273–279
Katz, Saul, 308–321, 341
Katz, Sharon, 276
Katzenbach, Nicholas, 159
Kaufman, Alan, 87
Kavaler, Tom, 189
Kaye, Judith, 269–270
Kean, Thomas, 64
Keating, Ken, 33
Keefe, Bob, 287
Keenan, John, 227
Keeney, Jack, 201
Keith, Damon, 301–302
Kelsey, Frances O., 60–61, 64
Kelvinator Company, 2
Kendall, David, 246
Kennedy, John F., 20, 41, 63, 84, 210
Kennedy, Robert F., 36, 42
Kennedy, Ted, 156–157, 159
Kennedy, William, 243–244
Kenney, John, 73

Kerry, John, 296
Kiendl, Theodore, 21, 29
King, Carolyn Dineen, 268
King, Henry, 195
Kingham, Barry, 327
Kipling, Rudyard, 322
Kirby, Bruce, 176–177
Kirby, Butch, 291
Kirkland, Lane, 103
Kirtland, Robert, 31
Kleindienst, Richard, 69
Kleinman, William "Colonel," 38
Klingsberg, David, 130
Klugman, Scott, 289
Knoll, Robert, 280–281, 339
Kohn, Harold, 49, 326
Kolb, Dan, 327
Kollar-Kotelly, Colleen, 268
Komaroff, Bill, 340
Kookaburra III, 172
Kott, Reagan, 290–292
Koufax, Sandy, 319–320
Kozinski, Alex, 283
Kravitch, Phyllis, 207

L

Lafitte, Gene, 159, 259–261, 330
Lake Agomac, S.S., 2
Lamont, Thomas S., 56–57, 59
LaMothe, Louise, 281
Lancaster, Ralph, 330
Lance, Bert, 211–212
Landau, Irwin, 280
Lankler, Rod, 227, 235, 241, 246, 250
Laqua, Joey, 104
LaRossa, Jimmy, 99–102, 103
Lawton, Bettina, 193, 194
Leach, Jim, 233, 234, 235, 333
Lee, Burt, 163
Lee, Rex, 82
Lehman, Jeffrey, 305–306

Lehtinen, Dexter, 201
Leisure, George, 15
Leisure, Michael, 229
Leisure, Peter K., 139, 140, 143–145
Lenz, Widukind, 61, 63
Leon, Martin, 287
Lerman, Bradley, 335
Lev, William, 34–35
Levi, Edward H., 69, 108, 117, 159
Levine, Alan, 100
Levitt, Arthur, 313
Lewinsky, Monica, 257
Lifland, Burton, 314
Liman, Arthur, 139, 331
Limbaugh, Rush, 338
Limbaugh, Stephen, 338
Lindsay, John, 103, 104
Lindsey, Bruce, 233
Ling, James, 191–192
Ling-Temco-Vought, Inc., 191
Lippman, Jonathan, 271–272
Lipton, Marty, 16, 214
Loucks, Michael, 287, 288
Louis Vuitton Cup, 172, 179
LTV Aerospace Corporation, 191
Lumbard, J. Edward, xii–xiii, 15–17, 24–25, 27, 82, 86, 112, 115, 120
Lynch, Gary, 194

M

Mabry, Barry, 291
MacCourt Products, 8
MacMahon, Lloyd, 192
Madison Guaranty Savings & Loan Association. *See* Whitewater investigation
Madoff, Bernard, 308, 313–321
Mansfield, Walter, 150–151
Mara, John, 144
Marcuse, Melinda, 300
Markman, Steve, 155, 156, 163, 330

Marks, William, 251

Marshal, Burke, 159

Marshall, George, 210, 332

Martin, John, 75, 120

Mason, Christopher, 340

Massey, David, 269

Matthews, Charles, 230, 251

Mazur, Bob, 89, 92

McBryde, John H., 259–269

McCall, Carl, 103

McCarrick, Shirley, 62–63

McCarthy, Sharon, 270

McClellan, John L., 36

McDermott, J. Ray, 124, 130

McDonald, Ann, 124, 128, 135

McDougal, James, 222, 223–224, 225,
     234, 252, 334. *See also* Whitewater
     investigation

McDougal, Susan, 224, 230, 252

McGrath Services, 101, 103

McGuire, Robert, 217, 319

McInerney, Denis J., 227, 228, 229, 230,
     251, 252, 292

McKay, James, 161

McKean, Quincy Adams Shaw, 24

McMullen, John, 48

McNeill, Laura, 277

Medinol, 286–288

Meese, Edwin, 161, 327

Mehrtens, William, 83

MER/29, 66–67

*Mercury Bay Boating Club vs. San Diego
     Yacht Club,* 173–180

Meridian Oil Trading Inc., 290–291

Mermelstein, Mark, 289

Mervis, Clark, 202

Mescon, Richard, 74–75

Meserve, Robert, 154

Metzenbaum, Howard, 159

Metzner, Charles, 87

Mihaly, Marc, 182

Mikva, Abner, 333, 334

Milford Track, 181

Miller, Jack, 201

Millstein, Ira, 145

Miro, Jeffrey, 299

Mishkin, Suzanne, 193

Mitchell, John, 69, 107

Moe, Dick, 163

Monsanto, "Fat Stevie," 96

Monsky, Mark, 102

Montella, William "Sonny," 100–106

Morgan, J.P., 23, 173

Morgenthau, Robert, 73, 74, 120, 184,
     217, 214, 216–219, 227, 319, 326

Morrissey, Francis X., 154

Mortenson, Stan, 202

Morvillo, Bob, 184–185

Moscow, John, 216–217, 218

Moscowitz, Norman, 201, 205, 207, 332

Moseley, Tom, 108

Moyer, Jay, 139, 140

Moynihan, Daniel Patrick, 84–85, 221

Mueller, Bob, 228, 332

Mulholland, Mark, 271–272

Muller, Scott, 100, 185, 186, 252, 299, 301

Murdock, Dan, 73, 75, 109

Mulrow, William, 271

Murray, Albert, 188, 189

Murray, Robert, 290–291

Myerson, Harvey, 139–140, 144, 145

N

Nalecz, Andrzej G., 275, 277–278, 279

Namorato, Cono, 184–185

Napolitano, Janet, 261, 337

Nappi, Joseph, 282, 339

Naqvi, Swaleh, 213, 216–217

NASDAQ, 67–68

Nathan, Fred, 16–17, 25, 150

National Association of Securities Dealers, 67–68

National Environmental Policy Act, 119

National Football League, 138–145

National Union, 202–203

Neal, Jim, 185, 186

Nesbitt, Lenore, 201–202, 204, 205–206, 208

Newman, Gus, 99–100, 218–219

Newstead, Jennifer, 277, 293

Newsweek, 194

New York Mirror, 36, 37, 39

New York Daily News, 37, 44, 76, 97, 105, 226

New York Law Journal, 76

New York Marathon, 123, 128–129

New York Mets, 308–312

New York Post, 84, 92, 316, 320

New York State Commission on Drugs and the Courts, 269–270

New York Stock Exchange, 67–68

New Zealand, 181

New Zealand (boat), 173–179

Nicholas, Pete, 286–288

Nixon, Richard M., 69, 84, 107, 157, 221

Nolan, Dick, 66–67

Noriega, Manuel, 213

North, Oliver, 158, 233–234

North Atlantic Treaty Organization (NATO), 1, 6, 35

Nuclear Regulatory Commission, 128

Nunnally, Lisa, 274

Nussbaum, Bernard, 224, 233, 245, 250

O

Oakes, James, 83, 112

Obermaier, Otto, 120

O'Hagan, Cindy, 289, 290–292

O'Hearn, Walter, 101, 102–103, 106

Oracle, 179–180

Osofsky, Norman, 266–267

O'Sullivan, Julie, 214–215, 227–228, 251, 256

Owen, Richard, 127, 133, 136

P

Palin, Sarah, 54

Palmer, Robert, 335

Pan Mass Challenge, 295

Pardes, Herbert, 265

Parker, Robert, 265

Parker, Stuart, 108

Pattullo Modes, 30–31

Pearce, B.J., 327

Pepper, Claude, 74

Perotta, Fiovorante, 16

Perretti, Pete, 63, 64

Philip Morris, 65–66

Phillips, Carter, 275

Picard, Irving, 314–315, 316, 318–319

Pico, Lee, 290

Pillsbury, Don, 299

Pilot, Larry, 288

Pinter, Leib, 118–119

Pittle, R. David, 280, 281–282

Plaeger, Rick, 289, 291, 292

Poindexter, John, 233–234

Politz, Henry, 259, 261–268, 269, 336

Pollack, Irving, 40

Pollack, Milton, 74–75

Pope, Anthony and Fortune, 40–43

Porter, Michael, 140–141

Posner, Richard, 154

Postmaster General, 76

Potischman, Neil, 340

Powell, Louis, 147, 156

Prado, Edward, 265

Pretzel Bell, 13

price-fixing cases, 46–50, 297–304

Provenzano, Tony, 118

Prudential Bache Securities, 189
Pryor, Sam, 18
Public Works Employment Act, 83

Q
Quinn, Jim, 145
Quinn Marine Service, 100–106
Quinn, Mike, 276

R
Racketeer Influenced Corrupt Organiza-
    tion (RICO) act, 99
racketeering cases, 36–39, 99–106, 118
RAGBRAI, 294–296
Rakoff, Jed, x, 318–319, 320
Rauh, Carl, 214, 218
Ray, Robert, 255, 334
Reagan, Ronald, 154, 156–160, 161–162,
    192, 195, 201, 327
Reasoner, Stephen M., 230, 251
Reay, Donald, 241
Rech, Ola, 269
Reconstruction Finance Corporation, 1, 4
Redfearn, Timothy, 108
Reeves, Jim Ed, 251, 334
Rehnquist, William, 148, 159, 253, 268,
    337
Reiss, Steve, 298
Reizen, Richard, 202, 204, 206,
Reno, Janet, 207, 221, 222, 224, 225–226,
    250, 252, 253
Resolution Trust Corporation, 231–232.
    See also Whitewater investigation
Reynolds, Quentin, 10
Richard, Maurice, 63–64
Richardson, Elliot, 69, 117, 157, 221
Richardson-Merrell, Inc., 60–64, 66–67
Richey, Charles, 196–197
Richter, Kobi, 287
Riesel, Victor, 36–37
Rifkind, Simon, xi–xii

Rij, Theodore, 37–39
R.J. Reynolds, 65–66
Roberts, John, 148
Robinson, Jayne, 329
Robson, John, 163
Rodriguez, Grace, 214–215
Rodriguez, Kathryn, 273–279
Rodriguez, Manuel Alfonso, 87
Rogers, William, 159
Rogovin, Mitchell, 115
Roistacher, Charles, 196
Rollock, Leonard, 96
Romano, Benito, 162–163
Rooker, Julia, 193–194, 196
Root, Clark, Buckner & Howland, 1, 4
Rosenblatt, Paul, 261
Ross, Robin, 163
Rothman, Frank, 140, 141
Rouhandeh, Jim, 299
Rozelle, Pete, 140, 144
Rubell, Steve, 115–116, 118
running, 78, 123, 128–129
Ruth, Henry, 116
Ryan, Sylvester J., 49
Ryno, Sandra, 193–196

S
Sabshin, Melvin, 265
Safire, William, 190, 224
sailing, 169–180
Salovey, Peter, 305
Salerno, Anthony "Fat Tony," 118
Santos-Figueroa, Harry, 86–87, 91
Satter, Ray, 294–296
"Saturday Night Massacre," 69, 157, 161,
    221
Savage, Arthur, 27
Sawyer, Sheila, 202
Saxbe, William, 69
Scalia, Antonin, 154, 159, 339
Scalia, Eugene, 339

Schaerr, Gene, 275
Schechter, Loren, 189
Scheinkman, Michael, 271–272
Schrager, Ian, 115–116, 118
Schwarz, Fritz, 19
Scotto, Anthony, 99–106, 118, 328
Sear, Tom, 89, 92, 95, 100, 328
Securities and Exchange Commission (SEC), 40–43, 56–59, 81–82, 193–197, 289–293
Securities Investor Protection Act, 314–315
Segal, Bernard, 154
Sentelle, David, 253, 335
Seregos, Nicholas, 104–105
Seshens, Dana, 314
Sessions, William, 244
Seymour, Lenore. *See* Fiske, Lenore (mother)
Seymour, McNeil V., 6
Seymour, McNeil V. Jr., 6
Seymour, Mike, 120, 150–151
Seymour, Whitney North, xiii, 147
Shackouls, Bobby, 289, 291, 292
Sharpe, Doyle, 193–194, 196
Sharpstein, Richard, 202
Sheehan, David, 316
Sheehan, Kevin, 280–281, 339
Sherman Act, 67–68
Shields, Geoffrey, 182
Shields, William, 218
Shumate, Gaston, 67–68
Siegel, Arnon, 338
Silberman, Lawrence, 338
Silver, Sheldon, 271
Simpson, Alan, 164
Skelos, Dean, 271
Skidd, Leo, 53–54
Skinner, Sam, 163
Small, Rick, 282
Smart, Inez, 94

Smith, Allan, 11–12
Smith, Mose, 336
Smith, Pat, 202, 227, 252, 332
Smith, William French, 159
Sneed, Joseph, 253, 335
Socialist Workers Party v. Attorney General of the United States, 107–114, 119
Sotheby's, 297–304
Spector, Arlen, 164
Speedy Trial Act, 86
Sporkin, Stanley, 82
sports, 51–55, 78–79, 123, 128–129, 169–183, 256, 259–261, 294–296, 308
SportsChannel, 309–312
Sports New York (SNY), 309–312
Squadron, Howard, 313
Stahl, Charles, 241
Stamos, Peter, 315–316, 317–318
Stanton, Louis, 29
Starr, Ken, 252–255, 257, 275, 333, 334–336
Stars & Stripes, 172–179
Stein, Mark, 227, 229, 241, 252
Steiner, Josh, 233, 333
Stephanopoulos, George, 238–239, 257
Stephens, Jay, 238–239
Sterling Equities, 308–321
Stevens, John Cox, 169–170
Stewart, Charles "Pete," 99–100, 102–103, 106
Stich, Carl, 229, 241
Stillman, Charlie, 184, 218
Stimson, Henry L., 72
Stotler, Alice Marie, 281–285
Struve, Guy, 142
Studio 54, 115–116, 118
Sturges, Wesley, 10
Suhre, Walter, 195, 196
Sullivan, Thomas, 62–63
Sununu, John, 163, 165, 166, 167

Suzuki Samurai cases, 273–285
Suzuki v. Consumers Union, 280–285

T
Taft-Hartley Act, 99, 102, 104
Tallon, James, 271–272
Tannenbaum, Myles, 142
Tashima, A. Wallace, 282
Tatel, David S., 338
Taube, Tad, 142
Taubman, Alfred, 138, 141, 297–304, 305,
    340–341
Telvi, Abraham, 36–37
Tendy, Bill, 73–75, 98, 327–328
Tennant, Anthony, 299, 300, 303, 340
Tennessee Valley Authority, 46
tennis, 78–79
Tese, Vincent, 141
Texas Gulf Sulphur, 56–59
Texas Instruments, 45
thalidomide, 60–64
Thayer, Brynn (daughter), 193, 197
Thayer, Margery (wife), 197
Thayer, Paul, 191–197, 331
The New York Times, 32, 42, 44, 56, 85, 89,
    97, 106, 112, 115, 135, 165, 194, 223,
    224, 225, 247, 270, 320
The Wall Street Journal, 162, 163, 165, 194,
    224, 236-337, 244, 320
The Washington Post, 194, 233, 247, 323
Thompson, William C., 103
Thompson, William C. Jr., 271–272
Thomsen, Linda, 124, 128, 329
Thornburgh, Dick, 70, 161–167, 329
Three Mile Island, 124–137
*Threshold Resistance: The Extraordinary
    Career of a Luxury Retailing Pioneer*
    (Taubman), 298
Thurmond, Strom, 159, 164
Time, 194, 238, 239
Tinsley, Janet. *See* Fiske, Janet (wife)
Titone, Vito, 178

Tompkins, George, 173, 175
Totenberg, Nina, 222, 333
Trager, David, 85
Tredwell, Don, 294-295
Trubin, John, 85
Truman, Harry, 210, 338
Trump, Donald, 138–139, 141, 143, 144
Tucker, Jim Guy, 230, 231, 251, 255
Tuso, Charles, 37–39
Tyler, Harold R. Jr., 68, 69–71, 82, 117,
    157–160, 162, 164, 175, 177, 179

U
Ulrich, Jack, 38–39
United States Football League, 138–145
University of Michigan Law School,
    10–14, 52, 305–307
U.S. Attorney's Office, 15–17, 24–43,
    69–122. *See also specific case names*
    assessments of, 117–122
    Gillespie in, 32–33
    move to, 24–26
    office and team in, 72–75
    review process, 80–82
U.S. Customs Service, 34–35
USFL v. NFL, 138–145
U.S. Food and Drug Administration,
    60–64, 287–288

V
Valentino, Louis, 104
Vermont, 181–183
Vermont Land Trust, 181
Vermont Law School, 182–183
Vermont Natural Resources Council, 183
Vessey, John, 196
Vietnam War, 211

W
Wachtell, Herbert, 16
Wachtler, Sol, 27–28, 176–177, 178–179
Wade, Christopher, 335

Wagner, Karen, 124, 128, 131, 314, 316, 317, 318
Wagner, Robert, 103, 104
Walker, G. Herbert, 21–22
Wallace, Mike, 98
Wallach, E.R., 161
Walsh, Lawrence E., xii–xiii, 44, 61, 66–67, 221, 233–234, 250, 326
Washington Legal Foundation, 156, 163
Watergate, 69, 85, 157, 221
Waxman, Seth, 202
Webb, Dan, 222, 335
Webster, William, 109, 270
Weinfeld, Edward, 28–29, 38, 39, 41, 43, 74–75
Weinstein, Brian, 269, 287, 311
Weld, William, 161
Weldon, James, 191–192
Wells Notice, 59
Werker, Henry, 86–87, 91–92, 97, 328
West, Mark, 305
Westinghouse, 46
Westmoreland, David, 297
Where the Evidence Leads (Thornburgh), 165–167
Whipple, Taggart, 24, 45, 175
White, Mary Jo, 227
White, Ronnie, 279, 339
White, Tim, 252, 335
white collar crime cases, 118–119, 184–219
Whitewater Development Corporation. *See* Whitewater investigation
Whitewater investigation, 207, 220–258, 269
    assessment of, 256–258
    Clintons questioned in, 246–247
    criticism of, 236–237
    early breakthrough in, 230–232

Foster's death in, 220, 224, 240–245, 249–250
    obstruction of, 238–239
    results of and outcry over, 248–252
    Starr in, 252–255
    subpoenas in, 233–235
    team in, 227–229
Williams, David, 175, 181, 330
Williams, Julie, 193–194, 196
Williams, Margaret, 233
Williams, Paul, 27, 41, 115, 120
Williams, Stephen, 338
Wilpon, Fred, 305, 308–321, 341
Winter, Ralph, 142, 145, 154
Winter Bench & Bar Conference, 150–151
Winters, Rebecca, 270–272
Wise, Bob, 124, 320
Wise, Scott, 193
Witness Protection Program, 39, 98, 102
Wohl, Frank, 73, 88, 108
Wolff, Paul, 195
Wolohojian, Gabrielle, 228, 251, 256
World War I, 2–3
World War II, 4, 6, 171
Wurtz, Bill, 124, 128, 264, 266, 329
Wylde, Kathryn, 271–272
Wyzanski, Charles, 66

Y
Yale University, 2, 51–52, 291
Yanes, Raul, 289, 290–291, 292–293
Yoon, Jane, 270
Young, Andrew, 159

Z
Zechman, Richard, 131–132, 137
Zewe, William, 135, 137
zone defense, 128